The More-Than-Just-Surviving Handbook

ELL FOR EVERY CLASSROOM TEACHER

THIRD EDITION

The More-Than-Just-Surviving Handbook

PORTAGE & MAIN PRESS

BARBARA LAW   MARY ECKES

Portage & Main Press gratefully acknowledges the financial support of the Province of Manitoba through the Department of Culture, Heritage and Tourism and the Manitoba Book Publishing Tax Credit and the Government of Canada through the Canada Book Fund for our publishing activities.

Printed and bound in Canada by Friesens
Cover and interior design by Relish Design Studio Ltd.
Cover image: *Holding Hands*, Rhian Brynjolson, acrylic latex on canvas, 72" x 36", collection of the Richardson Group

Library and Archives Canada Cataloguing in Publication

Law, Barbara, 1950-
        The more-than-just-surviving handbook: ELL for every classroom teacher / Barbara Law, Mary Eckes – 3rd ed.

Includes bibliographical references and index.
Also available in electronic format.
ISBN 978-1-55379-232-1

        1. English language—Study and teaching as a second language.
I. Eckes, Mary, 1954- II. Title.

PE1128.A2L38 2010   428.007   C2010-901666-1

PORTAGE & MAIN PRESS
100–318 McDermot Ave.
Winnipeg, MB Canada R3A 0A2
Email: books@pandmpress.com
Tel: 204-987-3500
Toll-free: 1-800-667-9673
Fax-free: 1-866-734-8477

FSC
Mixed Sources
Cert no. SW-COC-001271
© 1996 FSC

Dedication

We would like to dedicate this edition of *The More Than Just Surviving Handbook* to two of our biggest supporters: Dorothy Eckes and Dolores Mullane. Thank you for believing in our efforts over the years and helping to promote (relentlessly) each edition of our books. And, as always, thank you, John; your consistent insight and support has been invaluable. And to our children, our passion and our fulfillment: you've made us laugh and provided wonderful examples of kid stuff to look at and consider, and we know we gave you lots to complain about!

Contents

Preface

Third Edition

When Sevdet was five, all the people in his village were rounded up and herded to a meadow. They were told they were going to be relocated. Sevdet's mother knew better. They were going to be murdered. When the guards who patrolled the meadow weren't looking, she and her mother, carrying Sevdet and his younger sister, slipped into the woods and escaped. Although they tried to convince others to leave with them, those they talked to believed that everything would be all right. It wasn't. Eleven thousand people were massacred in four days.

People arrive on our shores for many different reasons: to escape religious or ethnic persecution, to escape war, to find economic opportunities. They all have dreams. Our job is simple: to help those dreams come true. And we, as ELL teachers, are one of the main instruments in making that happen.

So much has changed since *The More Than Just Surviving Handbook* was first published. Our children, babies when we first held this new book in our hands, now are grown, in college, and on their own. We are older, wiser (?), and still racing to keep up with the evolution that has occurred in education and filtered down to our schools. Technology has altered our classrooms, our vocabulary, and our ability to communicate and study. Academic research has developed better methods to provide our language learners with the skills they will need to advance and succeed. Our students are challenged to think critically as they never have been before, because of the expanded reaches of information provided by the Internet, online periodicals, and the multiple means of research available these days.

We have extended this edition of our book to include all these changes, so you will have the tools you need to succeed in your classroom. We discuss the new options technology leaps offer teachers, and how to help students acquire the academic English they need to succeed in the classroom. You will also learn how to encourage students to think critically and manage their resources effectively. Each chapter has a reflection section and a series of case studies to help you personalize the material with the resources available to you. There are no right or wrong answers to issues raised in these sections, just the opportunity for you to examine your priorities and best prepare for your students.

As always, we have filled the book with the most wonderful examples and compelling stories we could find, so that it isn't just theory and practice, but fun to read. We believe this is the best edition yet, and we are very excited to share it with you. We hope you will find this new edition thought provoking; but more importantly, we hope it is a resource that validates your good instincts and suggests directions you may not have thought of. Most of all, we hope we have encouraged you to more than just survive the challenges that arise in your classroom, and instead you are able find solutions to each hurdle with resourcefulness and success.

We have many people to thank for their help with this third edition. We thank all the teachers who willingly and generously shared their expertise, their ideas, their students' work, and their stories: Maddy Hutter and Janet Mason, Nanci Smith, Meredith Fox, Carol Haddaway, Edith Chen, our dedicated Syrian colleagues Srour Shalash, Nibal Hanna and Hala Halak. We thank all the students who have passed through our lives, who made us laugh, who were honest, forthright, funny and hardworking, who make it all worth the effort, and make going to work a pleasure. We thank our editors at Portage & Main Press, Catherine Gerbasi, Annalee Greenberg, Marcela Mangarelli, and Leslie Malkin for their faith in us and their careful attention to detail. And, as always, we thank our loving families for their patience, their tolerance, and their continued support.

About Our Chapter Titles

In keeping with our companion book, *Assessment and ESL*, our chapter titles are named for the wonderful language errors we have collected during our careers, while also conveying the theme of the chapter. Although most of these are self-explanatory, such as "After Sawing the Doctor," some titles take some thought to understand the meaning that the writer or speaker intended to convey. Others need explanation. When Mary's kids went out on a Saturday night, she habitually said, "Don't be wild." Ta, her beloved exchange student, would turn with a grin and say, "I'm gonna wild, Mom."

Introduction

We're Gonna Wild: A Consequence of Rabid Growth

Each day during the first few weeks of school, several new students show up—Hmong, Lao, Hispanic. Two of them are also special ed. There are no translators available, and students have to be called out of other classes to translate. The influx continues through the month of October.

It can be a daunting prospect to be faced with one or more students who can speak no English. It might make you feel helpless, maybe even resentful. When a new English language learner (ELL) enters the classroom, you ask yourself: What can I do with this student? How can I teach him anything if he is not able to understand even the simplest words in English? How can I, who can't speak a word of his language, communicate with him? What can I best do to help him become a member of this class? Many times our first impulse is to panic and say, "Send him to someone else—anyone!—who knows what to do."

But resources are not always available. There may not be anyone in your district who can speak your student's language. There might not be an ELL specialist available. You might be miles and miles from the nearest library or university, or even from a sympathetic colleague. You may have so few ELL students that your school district isn't eligible for funding to buy the most fundamental of necessities. You might have one PC in your classroom, or a whole row of them in the library, which haven't been upgraded in years. Even if your school or district has an ELL teacher, she[1] may only be able to spare two half-hour sessions a week for your student. Or, your student may be getting ELL help, but may already have been mainstreamed into your science, math, or social studies class. Ready or not, he is there.

Many books have been written for ELL teachers, but these almost always presuppose a working knowledge of second-language theory, methods, and techniques—and that the teacher is working solely with ELL students. For regular classroom teachers these books are not helpful. You may have 25 students,

---

1 To retain writing clarity while ensuring gender balance, plural pronouns have been used whenever possible. When unable to avoid a specific singular pronoun, we have chosen to use masculine pronouns in reference to students and feminine pronouns in reference to teachers.

15 native-English speakers, and the rest non-English speakers. This means that you must meet the needs of many types and levels of students—your regular students, who can understand the language and keep up with the mandated curriculum, and your ELL students, who may or may not have any English at all, who may or may not know how to read. Being successful with this range of students requires a totally different set of strategies.

Chapter Overview

Chapter 1, First Days—Using Chapsticks to Have a Snake, introduces you to a hypothetical classroom made up of a range of students (both native-English-speaking and ELL students) we have known over the years. We discuss strategies for coping and for helping your ELL students get acquainted with school and classmates. We make suggestions regarding immediate activities to occupy these students until they can pick up enough English to function as regular students. And, we discuss priorities—things they must know first—as well as how to set short- and long-term goals.

Chapter 2, Testing and Placement—After Sawing the Doctor, is of special interest to principals and counselors, as well as classroom teachers. We address the issues of placing the student in the most appropriate grade; measuring reading, writing, speaking, and listening fluency; and strategies for grading.

Chapter 3, Language Learning for Students *and* Teachers—The Faucets of Language, discusses the principles of second-language learning; the factors that affect the success of the learner; what the teacher can do to promote success; and behavior—how to understand and assist your student when his behavior is inappropriate.

Chapter 4, Literacy and the Four Skills of Language Acquisition—Gun the Accelerograph Immediate, deals with basic literacy and promoting learning in every class from English to math.

Chapters 5, 6, and 7, Reading—First Meaning is Lost Cautious; Writing—A Pig Broplem; and **Speaking and Listening—Winning the Rottery,** discuss, in detail, these four skills. We answer frequently asked questions, give suggestions for teaching, and show when and how to correct errors.

Chapter 8, Content-Area Instruction—The Impotance of Science, is written specifically for content teachers. We show how to modify lessons so that students who are not fully fluent in English can succeed in content-area classes.

Chapter 9, Resources—Earnestly Extract the Lesson, discusses the most effective use of other school personnel, such as the ELL teacher, aides, and interpreters, and how to tap the resources of your school and community.

A Word About Labels

There are many different labels given to non-English-speaking students: ESL, LEP, LES, NES, FEP. None of these are very satisfactory. ESL, English as a Second

Language, is somewhat misleading, because many of our students arrive with English as their third, fourth, or even fifth language. In addition, not all ELL students have poor skills in English or require the services of a trained professional. Their reading is often on par with our English-speaking students, and their knowledge of grammar is sometimes even better, although their spoken English may be a little difficult to understand. LEP, Limited English Proficiency, LES, Limited English Speaking, and NES, Non-English Speaking, and even FEP (fully English proficient) all carry negative connotations, as if the students arrive with a deficit, needing instruction to fill the gap. In truth, they arrive with a perfectly good language of their own in which they are fluent, able to think and speak their needs with ease. They have simply been placed in a situation where the language they have is not the language they need to function in school and in the larger society. Although ESL is one of the most common terms, it is being supplanted by ELL, English Language Learners, so we have chosen to use it in this book.

Recurrent Themes, Critical for Maximizing Learning

There are several recurrent themes that we believe are critical for maximizing learning:

The Classroom Environment Is Critical

Language is learned best when the learner feels safe in his environment. The kind of atmosphere that pervades your classroom can make the difference between silent non-learners and eager learners. All students need

- A classroom where all students are wanted and respected for themselves and for the contributions they can make

- A classroom that is as stress-free as possible, where students can feel free to attempt to use their new language without fear of correction, ridicule, or punishment

- A classroom that validates the students' experiences and uses them for learning purposes

Using an Integrated Approach to Language Learning

Language is learned best when it is learned in context. In an integrated approach, the focuses are on meaning in language and on using language to communicate. The four skills—reading, writing, speaking, and listening—are parts of a whole, and all four skills are essential components of each activity. Reading does not occur in isolation, but is extended to include discussion and writing; composing does not take place without a great deal of prior discussion and reading. And opportunities to learn the language arts are not limited to language arts classes, but are integrated across the curriculum to include content classes too.

An integrated approach also means that, instead of concentrating on component parts—the alphabet and phonics before learning to read; vocabulary, then sentences, then paragraphs before learning to write; grammar and the correct pronunciation of English words before being allowed to engage in conversation—students learn to read and write by reading and writing whole stories and texts, and they learn to speak by jumping into conversations regardless of whether or not their English is correct and complete.

An integrated approach means that all teaching and learning activities have meaning and purpose. This means finding things out because the answers have real, practical value, or writing well because the work is going to be shared with others.

It means the teacher has faith in the learners and sets high expectations for them, whatever their literacy level or competence in English.

Teachers recognize that there is no "right" age or sequence of learning the strands of language, but that there is "a continuum of learning" on which students learn according to their own individual stage of development.

The Importance of Models

Language is learned best when the student is surrounded by real language used for real purposes by real people. Being exposed to the language and having good models are both essential to becoming competent readers, writers, and speakers in that language. The classroom should be set up so that communication in the new language is essential to your ELL students, and so that they are not ignored and forgotten because they have not yet mastered the intricacies of the English language.

Errors Are Just a Part of Learning

Language is learned best when errors are viewed in their proper perspective, as just a normal—and integral—part of learning (Samway and McKeon 2007). Any attempt to master a skill, whether skiing, skateboarding, writing, or learning another language, involves trial and error during the course of practice. Many of us who studied a foreign language in high school or college learned the hard way that errors were viewed as faults, as graphic demonstrations that something was not learned. Errors were punished and eradicated. The current focus on testing and accountability, as well as the trends in reading instruction (for example, a resurgent focus on phonics), perpetuate this viewpoint. Perfection is the goal, whether in grammar, pronunciation, reading aloud, or writing.

Research has shown that errors should be viewed as stages in the learner's progression toward competent reading, writing, or speaking in the new language (Corder 1967). Learners start with the big issues, such as getting their thoughts articulated and their needs met. Gradually they sort out the details—the correct tenses, the word order, the right words—refining and honing their knowledge of the language. This doesn't happen overnight; it is a long, slow process. Recognizing learning as a process and errors as a natural phenomenon involves an entirely different attitude toward errors. They are not signs of incompetence or faulty learning, only that something has not yet been learned; therefore, they are not to be pounced on and "fixed" immediately, but considered as indicators of progress, to be noted and tolerated.

Change

Many things have changed in the two decades since we first conceived of and wrote the first edition of this book. Things we never even dreamed of—the Internet, cell phones, podcasts, YouTube, Facebook, video consoles for online gaming—are now such an integral part of our everyday lives we barely consider them and we can't imagine living without them.

We've watched kids change. Kids today are technologically wired, savvy, and linked to each other in multiple ways. The environment outside of school throbs with information. They know more than we did, and they know how to find out what they want to know. So many students are plugged in so deeply we can't get them to unplug, and they can't leave their phones alone for a second! They exercise various ways to access each other, wider audiences, and information. However, they are not so good at the practical issues like finding authoritative sources, locating the right online materials, or discerning the hidden agendas behind what they do find online. They know how to use social networking and can inform (or bully) each other well on it. This group is both lucky and cursed. They are more distracted than any other age group we have ever seen. But if they can focus on the good things available to them, they have the world at their fingertips.

In *The Trophy Kids Grow Up* (2008), Ron Alsop notes that kids "possess significant strengths in teamwork, technology skills, social networking and multitasking." They want attention and guidance, as well as constant positive reinforcement. They also want structure and to have step-by step-instruction, with explicitly spelled out guidelines. Within those guidelines, they want flexibility.

Alsop is, of course, talking about middle- and upper-class kids. Although even inner city kids have cell phones, their access to the kind of technology the rest of us take for granted is often limited to time in the library or the computer lab at school. This is having the effect of widening the gulf between the two groups, making our jobs even crazier, and the stakes higher.

We've watched demographics change. "In 1990," writes Goldenberg (2008), "one in 20 public school students in grades K–12 was an English language learner (ELL), that is, a student who speaks English either not at all or with enough limitations that he or she cannot fully participate in mainstream English instruction. Today the figure is 1 in 9. Demographers estimate that in 20 years it might be 1 in 4."

Most of the immigrants and non-English-speaking students are concentrated in high poverty areas, with few resources and overtaxed teachers. Contrary to the popular image of the disappearing rural life, it is rural areas that are experiencing the most growth. In states such as South Carolina and Kentucky, the growth has been 250 percent (Johnson and Strange 2007). Many of the areas' newcomers are beset by poverty. Schools are small and remote, and they often have few resources, not to mention teachers with experience and expertise in delivering adequate services and coping with the challenges of working with ELLs. Or, students are bused long distances to schools consolidated by bureaucratic decisions that had little to do with the quality of learning and much to do with administrative efficiency. Worse yet, "the states where the educational outcomes in rural schools require the most urgent attention are the states with the most impoverished, minority, and ELL rural students [but] they are also the states where schools receive the fewest resources (Johnson and Strange). In addition, teachers are often far from universities where they could get adequate training and support. So, while we've been making gains in terms of solid programs in urban areas, problems in the biggest areas of concern have become more acute.

We've witnessed growth in the number of ELL students in our classes who are native born citizens. Three-quarters of children of immigrants are born in the United States and are therefore U.S. citizens (Capps 2001). Theoretically, these students should come to school with enough English to function well in the regular classroom, but this isn't necessarily the case. They may have grown up in homes where none of their family members speak English and have little exposure to English beyond what they see on television or hear when they go to the store. They may have limited interaction with English speakers.

We've watched the field of ELL change. From the days when Barb first started teaching ELL—when there was next to nothing in the literature about elementary language learners, when she had just inherited nine schools, eight grades, and a box full of books 20 years out of print, and when she literally had to make it up, flying by the seat of her pants—we have arrived at a point today where there is a mind-boggling number of websites, books, and journals devoted to the practice. Somehow, this doesn't seem to make the life for the average teacher any easier. How to choose? What to read? What's a priority? When can I find time? How do I translate what I've read into what I do in my classroom? We have tried to do this for you. We've waded into the flood, fished out what makes sense, and tried to do some of the translating so that you can make your own decisions based on who's sitting in those seats expecting and needing your best.

We've watched how our understanding of learning has grown—in particular, the realization of the importance of academic English. We will discuss this issue throughout the chapters, because it is important to focus on the impact and the necessity of academic language for success in school.

Gee (2007) puts it this way: Three things are involved in active learning: "experiencing the world in new ways, forming new affiliations, and preparation for future learning." When we enter a new domain, such as science, or history, or even cooking, we learn new ways of seeing and operating. When we take a cooking class, we learn to distinguish between oregano and basil, what happens when we combine certain ingredients. We also join a group of people who function in specific ways. For instance, people who enter the domain of chemistry learn the vocabulary of chemistry, the methods of conducting experiments, and the discipline it takes to successfully complete an experiment without burning down the lab. In music, they learn the vocabulary of flats and sharps, major and minor, as well as how to read music and how to put their fingers in the right place in the correct sequence so that the sounds they make are pleasant and don't scorch the ears of the listener. The last thing that happens, according to Gee, is they gain resources that "prepare [them] for future learning and problem solving in the domain."

By placing the necessary importance on academic learning and vocabulary, we open the doors for our students to enter their chosen domains—doors that would otherwise be closed to them. The seriousness of this matter cannot be overstated.

We've watched the field of education change. We've watched all that technology enter the classroom. We've witnessed the world shrink dramatically under globalization. We've observed how George W. Bush's No Child Left Behind policy brought ELL out of the broom closet and into the spotlight under the banner of "high expectations for all," "accountability," and "higher standards," but also how the policy led to untold grief for schools and teachers alike in the punitive, combative struggle for compliance. We've also watched what Paul Houston, executive director of the American Association of School Administrators, called the "era of amateur school reform, where we have non-professionals making the decisions about the directions we should go." (Sturgeon 2006). We're not just thinking of Bill Gates and his forays into building the "schools of the future." We're thinking of the legislative entities that have bought into the notions that higher standards, basing teachers' salaries on student performance, and a gigantic influx of technology into classrooms will "fix" what ails our schools.

They won't. What makes a difference is you. You, working long nights, weekends, thinking, planning, agonizing over what will interest, fascinate, draw out kids, and invite them into the learning community. Howard Gardner, in *Five Minds for the Future*, (2007) writes, "Education is inherently and inevitably an issue of human goals and human values...Science can never tell you what to do in class or at work. Why? What you do as a teacher or manager has to be determined by your own value system—and neither science nor technology has a built-in value system." But you do. And as a teacher, you know your kids. You know what they need, where they are on the continuum of learning, and what is the best way to get them where they need to go. So, while we talk about the trappings and accoutrements of technology, everything still comes down to you and those faces on the other side of the desk.

In a 1998 position paper, CATESOL (California Association of Teachers of English to Speakers of Other Languages) defined important factors we need to consider in educating English language learners. We address the following factors in this book:

- **Differences.** Students are not all alike. Our students come with differing levels of literacy and language proficiency, from different schooling systems and different experiences in school, from vastly divergent languages. We need to be prepared to teach them all.

- **Standards.** All students deserve to be held to the same standards as their English-speaking peers.

- **Language of instruction.** While research shows that learning to read in the home language is the ideal (August and Shanahan 2006), it is not always feasible or possible. What is possible, however, is providing students with "language-rich, developmentally appropriate programs of English language development which include exposure to print." (CATESOL)

- **Initial and ongoing assessment.** We need to be prepared to determine levels of proficiency and literacy when students arrive on the doorstep. We also need to be equipped with appropriate measures to assess their learning in school.

- **Methodology.** We need to be prepared to address the variety of educational, social and linguistic needs of students in the most grounded, meaningful ways available.

- **Materials.** In an ideal world, English language learners would have access to the same rich resources available to English speakers. This does not always happen for a variety of reasons (such as numbers, funding, size of school and program, variety of languages), which have nothing to do with the good will or intentions of the district, the school, or the teacher. Knowing how to make the best of limited resources is better than being caught relying on funding and technology that may disappear.

We've also watched the serious nature of fun and gaming take hold among researchers and gain ground swiftly. Computer and video games are the biggest industry in entertainment today—$11.7 billion is spent annually on computer and video game software in the U.S., and this figure is getting higher (Entertainment Software Association). This is important for educators, because good video games can offer insight into learning. Good games involve what gamers call "pleasant frustration," where the player operates at the outer edge of his capabilities, and is motivated to achieve higher and higher levels of competence as he adapts to changing conditions and challenges. Good games are never boring. Good games "encourage and facilitate active and critical learning and thinking" (Gee, 2007) and, "failing to engage learners is not an option." Kids will play well-designed games for days on end, throwing down their books as they come in the door to get to the console. They try and fail and try again, spending hundreds of hours learning. The games push kids beyond their boundaries and force them to think and adapt. But if the game is too hard, or too easy, or there's nothing more to learn, they'll abandon it.

We, as teachers, need to pay attention to this phenomenon. We're not advocating putting a game console in the corner of the classroom, but we need to analyze what it is in video games that keep kids engaged and coming back, and work to implement that in our classrooms, and replicate the feeling of "flow" (Csíkszentmihályi 1996), or total engagement, that is so prevalent in the excitement of playing and winning.

Another change to education that we have witnessed is the newer focus on critical thinking. Critical thinking goes beyond the usual abilities to reason; it involves thinking about thinking, in other words, analyzing the thoughts and beliefs that guide your behavior. It requires monitoring, in a systematic way, what your assumptions are, what inferences you make based on those assumptions, and the implications of those inferences in your thinking and your teaching (The Critical Thinking Community). It means thinking critically about your own teaching questions, what you do in the classroom, the choices you make, and the value system that is the foundation of those choices and actions.

To this end, we have included case studies of challenging situations and students, as well as questions that encourage you to reflect on the contents of each chapter, activities to extend and personalize the content, and ideas for looking ahead to what you may need to do or have on hand in the future. Just as we did in the previous two editions, we give lots of examples. What matters is how you take those ideas and examples and incorporate them into your own teaching styles, value systems, and situation.

What Today's Young People Need

One of the primary questions we need to ask is, what do young people need in order to "live, learn, and work successfully in an increasingly complex and information-rich society, [and to become] informed, responsible, and contributing citizens?" (International Society for Technology in Education 2000).

We believe young people need to:

- **Be multi-literate.** These days, literacy doesn't simply mean being able to read and write on two-dimensional planes. It also means competency in audiovisual and spatial realms.

- **Be able to work collaboratively with others.** Businesses and education are moving away, sometimes reluctantly, from the old, centrally planned, top-down management framework to one that operates on a level playing field, where people work on collaborative teams.

- **Master problem-solving skills.** They need to be able to identify problems that crop up, analyze them, and produce feasible solutions.

- **Possess communication skills.** These skills need to extend beyond their future workplace. Young people must be flexible enough to communicate with people from other cultures, using different conversational styles, and applying different rules of behavior depending on the part of the world they are in. Today's technological possibilities mean we must be able to operate across limitless horizons, unbounded by political borders and ethnic lines.

- **Be able to access data, and decide how to use it.** This includes knowing how to navigate in the modern library to locate books or online resources. For wealthier schools, technology becomes every educator's dream. When limited to the books on hand, particularly in the poorer schools, the access to data is seriously limited, and the digital divide grows wider.

- **Be able to sort the junk from the important data.** Anyone can post on the web these days. Much of it is sheer hogwash and, more dangerously, driven by agendas that students have neither the experience nor the skills to interpret and see through. They need to be able to judge whether posted data has an ulterior, and possibly sinister, motive, or whether it is legitimate, well-reasoned, and accurate. Contemporary books are generally subjected to intensive review processes, and as teachers, you are the gatekeepers to what comes into the classroom and your students' hands. But given the easy access that many students have to all facets of the outside world, this control has slipped from our fingers. It's doubly important now that we use whatever means we have available to teach them the skills of judgment and thoughtful selection of what to read and believe.

As the world continues to change, we in the field of second-language acquisition are struggling to change with it. The questions change. And sometimes, even when the questions remain the same, the answers seem to be different. But one fact remains: students are arriving in schools with little or no proficiency in English. And whether we teach them in their first language, put them in special programs, or mainstream them immediately, they will, like students everywhere, march through our school systems and either graduate or drop out. Thus, the clarion call for us remains the same: try to better their lives and their chances for success by always looking for ways to improve our teaching. Our goal is to approach the task with an open mind—to do more than just "survive" the experience. We hope this book can help you to do that.

Case Studies: How to Best Use the Real-Life Narratives Included in this Edition

We decided to include case studies at the end of each chapter of this edition of *The More Than Just Surviving Handbook* to confront you with real-life kids, situations, challenges, and dilemmas and to help you think critically about what you might do should you be confronted with similar issues. The stories are of real kids, wrestling with real challenges, and they bring to life the issues we as teachers of English language learners grapple with daily. By using narrative to illuminate abstract theories of language learning, we are attempting to translate complex issues, goals, and ideas into vibrant reality.

These case studies, and the questions that follow each one, are meant to move you from the theoretical information we provide in the chapters to your own personal insight, and ultimately, to informed decisions that you can put into action. There are no right answers—you will not find quick yes-or-no solutions to the questions we raise or answers in the back of the book. These sections are meant to help you think through the education of your students and search for better ways to serve them.

Using case studies effectively takes practice and experience. Learning how to analyze them and formulate thoughtful and intelligent solutions doesn't happen automatically. Allow yourself time to get past the uncertainty and the fumbling. These case studies are deliberately thought provoking, controversial, and designed with the notion that disagreement is good. They can be used to open discussion with colleagues and for other professional development initiatives. You can also discuss these issues with a larger community of ELL educators on the publisher's blog (go to <www.pandmpress.com/blog>, and click on *The More-Than-Just-Surviving* button). They present urgent and serious dilemmas that need to be solved. Most importantly, they are generalizable: if you can think through the ideas you have to consider to reach your conclusions, then you can use those same thought processes when considering your own students.

There are clear steps that you can take to work through what's important and what you should do when you are confronted with a challenging situation or student. It's easy to get bogged down and overwhelmed, but working through the problem step-by-step makes it easier and clearer. The following framework[1] will help you to work through any of the case studies we present in *The More Than Just Surviving Handbook* and, ultimately, any real-life challenges that you face with your English language learners.

1. **Review the case, and identify the relevant facts.** When you are trying to find a solution to a situation or to answer a question, the first step is to identify the key facts so that you can figure out what is going on before deciding what to do. Read the case carefully. Identify what facts are relevant. Push yourself to find as many facts as you can. Try for 10.

2. **Determine the root problem.** Decide what in the case is contributing to the problem and/or is symptomatic of the issue. Ranking each fact or item of evidence will help you to decide how important it is and the order in which it should be addressed.

3. **Generate questions about the case.** Questions require you to express an opinion, make a decision about a future course of action, or propose a solution. Questions also call for you to explain your reasons. Ask yourself questions such as the following:

- How could I approach this issue?

- What would happen if…?

- Would it help if…?

- What else could I do?

---

[1] Adapted from: Armstrong, Sally. *Using the 8 Step American Management Association (AMA) Problem Solving and Case Analysis Process.* Grand Rapids, MI: Davenport University, 2005.

4. **Generate alternatives.** If the case requires a solution, a decision, or an opinion then you need to consider *all* the options. Brainstorming will help you to generate a list of possible alternatives. In this step, you do not need to be judgmental. Virtually any idea goes; if you do not list it, you cannot then choose it as the best option.

5. **Evaluate alternatives.** Once you have listed all your alternatives, the next step is to narrow them down to those that seem most attractive. After you've screened your list, take the relevant facts that you gathered in step 1, and apply them to each of the remaining alternatives. This provides you with the necessary supporting evidence to reject most of the remaining alternatives and decide on the best one.

6. **Choose an alternative.** After evaluating all your options, choosing the best alternative is usually a straightforward next step, but it is also one that is often skipped. State your preferred solution simply and clearly. Then, justify your solution. Why is it more appropriate than the others? What reasons do you have for ruling out the other courses of action?

7. **Plan to take action.** This may not work for all cases, but in many you need to define how you will turn your solution or decision into action, how, when, and what you will monitor to ensure things are working out as planned, and what you will do if they are not.

8. **Implement your plan.** If the case requires a solution or a course of action, it is important to describe how you will execute or implement it. The following chart will help you to do that:

Action Required	Action By	Time or Date Required/Deadline

9. **Have a back-up plan.** It can be a good idea to have a contingency plan in case things do not go as expected. Kids, parents, other faculty may not react the way you hope. What then? Will you make modifications to your existing plan? Will you start the process over? Will you choose some other alternative that you've already identified? What would that be?

For All the Yodits...

The first edition of *The More-Than-Just-Surviving Handbook* was meant to be modest, forthright, and easy to access, crammed with as many funny, wonderful examples of student work as we could find. That has become our hallmark over the years. We have strived to maintain that accessibility in this third edition, which has been adapted and updated to help you better serve your students, to give you ideas, strategies, and examples with what Gardner calls a "generous dollop of creativity" thrown in (2007).

We want to state emphatically up front—lest it be suggested that we think ELL is nothing but problems, and that students are prone to flounder and fail—that the majority of our students are optimistic, remarkably resilient in spite of many hardships, hard-working, and, of course, a true joy to work with. Yodit, from Ethiopia, is a classic example. She sat with a grin on her face every class period, enjoying the constant bickering between Kee, from Myanmar, and Lucia, from the Dominican Republic, and keeping Kee and his equally naughty friend Duong, from Vietnam, on task during group work. She threw herself into every activity and went the extra mile to complete each task, determined to be proficient in English so she could fulfill her dream of becoming a nurse.

Here is Yodit's own writing about her future and her friends. Her words reflect not just her own personality, but also that of many of our students;

My future
My long term goal are to become a success full women. I would like to be a good nurse. And I would like to have a great marriage and great family. And I have plan to invite my parents and I have plan to bake home to visit my all family. I wish to help people with God.

My friends
When I in Ethiopia I had one girl best friend and I had a lot school friends. I had good time with them. And hear I have two best friends. I mat my boy friend. I am so happy to mitting hem. He give me strength and hope full.

This book is for all the Yodits in our lives and the happiness they bring us.

Chapter 1

First Days—Using Chapsticks to Have a Snake

This chapter deals with the arrival of the new ELL student and provides strategies to help the teacher cope. We focus on

- Preparing for the arrival of the new student
- Familiarizing the new student with school and classroom routines
- Utilizing school and community resources for support in working with the new student
- Teaching strategies for the first days
- Planning for the year—setting up short- and long-range goals

It's the 24th of January. The school year is almost half over. "Thank goodness," thinks Mrs. Ramsay. As she walks by the front desk on her way to pick up her mail, Mary Lou, the school secretary, says, "We've got another one for you. His name is Bounkham. Doesn't speak a word of English. He starts this morning."

The Main Characters—Our Hypothetical Classroom

We have created a hypothetical classroom made up of real students we have known over the years as well as our own (perfect!?) children. These students represent a range of personalities, abilities, reading levels, and spoken and written English proficiency (please refer to Chapter 2 for explanation of levels of proficiency). We have chosen to do this because we feel that it makes the issues we are presenting more real and allows us to highlight and illustrate certain points within the book. We do not use all the students equally or all the time—you might find them in an elementary classroom or in a grade 10 science class. Don't look for them in every chapter. (Please note as well that, for expository purposes, we may sometimes present a student who is not part of the following list in order to demonstrate a specific issue.)

It is unlikely, but not impossible, that you will have a class that displays this range. Unless you teach in a college town, as Barb did at the beginning of her career, you probably won't have the diversity of cultures in your classroom. The decisions you make, however, will be very similar to the decisions made by the teachers we present during the course of the book.

Good luck!

The English Language Learners

Bao: Hmong. Preliterate, no English skills. Arrived in the United States, and went to school for a few months in Fresno with the expectation of going on to where the rest of her family is located. Bao is quiet but can be very naughty when she feels like it (Level 1).

Fernando: A recent immigrant from a small town in Mexico. Nonliterate in either English or Spanish. He cannot write his own name. He tries his heart out (Level 1).

Salvador: Mexico. Semiliterate. Came from a small village where he did not go to school. He has been in a bilingual program and does not have skills to function in a school where there's absolutely no bilingual support. Nice kid, who struggles, barely keeping his head above water (Level 2).

Beverly: Taiwan. Attained a very high level of literacy in her first language. Very feminine. Wears a carefully combed ponytail and glasses. Does everything neatly and with care. Says very little in class. Speaks in her native tongue to her best friend, Angel (Level 2).

Angel: Taiwan. Tiny, shy, does not attempt to speak English at all. Uses her friend, Beverly, as the buffer between her and the rest of the world. She does good work, but it's hard to tell what is her own doing and what was done in conjunction with Beverly (Level 3).

Franco: China. Father owns a restaurant in town. Very sociable. Very good in math. His test scores classified him as non-English speaking, but his understanding of English is much higher. He pretends to know less than he really does. He's squirrelly and hard to keep on task. Was not held accountable for any of his work during his first year in this country (Level 3).

Yoshi: Japan. Has professional parents. Resentful of being here. Sullen and unresponsive. Refuses to participate in class. Sits by himself with his chin resting on his fists. Will do work alone, but no amount of coercion or persuasion will get him to be a participant in class or in a group (Level unknown).

Newton: Vietnam. Was born in this country. Should be much more proficient, but has not seemed to learn English very well. He is the class geek. The other kids won't sit next to him and fight for other seats. He is very artistic and draws careful pictures that are remarkably accurate. He is a loner and an outsider, but it's difficult to tell if that's his choice (Level 2).

Abir: Egypt. Very shy, never talks above a whisper. Absent much of the time. Does not turn in any homework. Conferences with her father reveal that she is needed at home to baby-sit younger siblings. Her parents believe that the year they are spending in this country is a year lost academically for Abir, and they put more emphasis on her studying her subjects in Arabic. If the truant officer were breathing down their necks, they probably wouldn't send Abir to school at all (Level 2).

Andre: Eastern Europe. A refugee. His schooling was disrupted for several years in his home country. He spent time in a western state in an ELL program taught largely by teachers of his own language group, who, for whatever reason, did not teach much at all. His progress in his native language plateaued long ago, but he has not made progress in English either. He knows neither how to read nor write in English (Level 3).

Florien: Italy. Only needs fine-tuning on the writing. Because he learned British English, his spoken English is so correct he comes out sounding like a native-English speaker. He's so charming and charismatic, the girls, as well as the teachers, just love him. He gets away with murder (Level 5).

Boris: Russian. Son of professional parents. Speaks Russian exclusively at home, and has a large chip on his shoulder. Talks out of turn constantly. Fights with others in the class. Used to the imposed discipline of his native school system, he cannot cope with what to him appears to be total lack of structure in the classroom (Level 5).

The Native-English Speakers

Kate: Bright and perceptive, not excellent academically, but well-organized, persistent, and dedicated. Her strength is her wisdom that is far beyond her years. Extremely kind, willing to try anything, a born leader.

Ellie: Exceptionally articulate for her age. If acting as a buddy for another student, she can explain the subject in a variety of ways. Very sensitive, interested in other cultures, and will go out of her way to make friends with newcomers. Has no organizational skills.

Austin: Very smart; has a huge vocabulary and prefaces every sentence with "although." If he doesn't see the point of what you're doing, he'll argue. Good-natured, but everything has to be on his terms. Does not like to be touched or even have people close. Does not work well in groups.

David: Musical and very bright, but don't ask him to draw anything. Ambidextrous, but not comfortable using either hand in writing or drawing. Good at reading and math, not interested in sports. Easygoing, good-natured, and very steady. He can be an anchor.

Rory: A handful, the class clown who wants to fool around. Hard to keep on task. Knows more about computers than the computer teacher and can hack his way into programs.

Ashley: Demonstrates that she can be smart, but is disorganized. Homework is often late and often not done correctly. Distractible, volatile, can be sweet, but very explosive. Can divide the group; very smart at knowing how to create dissension and hurt people's feelings. Will try to talk her way out of any trouble she gets herself into.

Jeremy: An average student, but really motivated; game for anything, the goofier the better. Any teacher is lucky to have him, because if she can't think of someone to start something, he'll start it. Gets overwhelmed if an assignment has too many steps. Needs specific instructions broken into parts. Succeeds if he has a check-off list of steps to follow.

Nick: Physically very coordinated and athletic, with exceptional large-motor skills. Small-motor skills are limited, as is his patience for activities that require their use. Will not attempt anything if he can't see the point, or if he knows up front he won't succeed. Does poorly on standardized tests, even when he knows the material. Very much like Jeremy in his inability to follow through on assignments that require several steps.

Robbie: A quiet, nice kid who is average in most things, but above average in math. Hard to engage sometimes. Tends to be overlooked in class, because he's not high profile—he's not naughty, articulate, or sparkling, but he's good at approaching problem solving from a variety of different angles. Tends to bail out on standardized tests because they're boring, and he knows he can do it, so his real talent isn't recognized.

Molly: Comes from an unstable home. Comes to school unprepared, with many things undone. She's Kate's best friend. Acts silly a great deal of the time and doesn't stay on task, often leading the other girls astray. Can bring out the worst in good kids. Very creative and funny, should be in a gifted and talented program, but struggles academically and socially. Refuses to relate to adults.

Destiny: Very verbal and charming. Has lots of street smarts and is able to use the skills she has and the environment surrounding her to cope with challenging tasks in the classroom. Quick to catch on when given individual attention or paired with a strong student.

Spencer: One of seven brothers. Did not know, upon being asked, how many boys there actually were in his family, or how to spell his last name. His mother has moved to this town to get away from the gangs of the big cities. Very low reading skills, but a bright, funny, affectionate kid who's very willing to try, eager to learn. Looks out for his younger brothers.

Preparing for the Student

Unless you've been in Mrs. Ramsay's situation before, the first day an ELL student arrives can be distressing for the new student, for you, the teacher, and for the rest of the class. For the student, the day can be as traumatic as the one described in figure 1.1. At best, he might feel awkward and apprehensive;

at worst, terrified and helpless. As teachers, we're used to having some degree of control, but nothing erodes that confidence faster than an inability to communicate with someone. Mrs. Ramsay was not an old hand at this, but in her second year in a low-income, inner-city school, she was getting used to it.

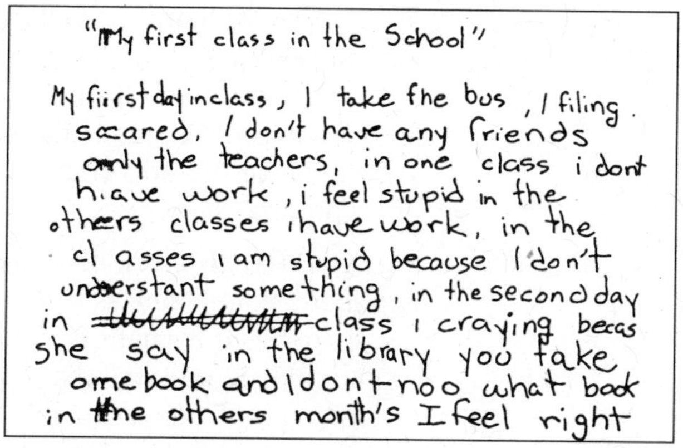

Feelings of apprehension and nervousness are natural. Even if you've been at it for years, it can be a truly intimidating prospect to be faced with the responsibility of teaching a student—or a group of students—with whom you are unable to communicate. It's only human to feel a wave of panic when that non-English-speaking student is first brought to your classroom. However, when you realize that this apprehension is only a fraction of what the new student is experiencing, it becomes a little easier to get past that first gut-level reaction of "Oh no, why my class?" You can begin to come up with strategies to turn the situation into a positive one—for you, the new student, and the rest of your class.

"My first class in the School"

My fiirst day in class, I take the bus, I filing scared, I don't have any friends only the teachers, in one class i dont hiave work, i feel stupid in the others classes i have work, in the classes i am stupid because I don't underrstant something, in the second day in ~~the~~ class i craying becas she say in the library you take omebook and i dont noo what book in the others month's I feel right

Figure 1.1 A student's reflection of her first day at school.

What to Do First—Establishing a Relationship

In an ideal situation, students will come to school with their parents to register and then return the following day, or after they have taken care of such necessities as immunizations and validation of immigration papers. This gives you some preparation time. In reality, students like Bounkham frequently arrive one morning with no notice (and often after the school year has begun), leaving the two of you to make the best of things. With or without lead time, some very important first steps must be taken to establish a relationship with the student.

- **Be prepared.** We cannot overstate the magnitude of preparation, one of the most important aspects of welcoming strangers. A study of refugee resettlement in England noted that "creating efficient infrastructure is critical for welcoming a young refugee to the school. This includes an excellent induction program, streamlined and easy-to-read materials to give to parents, accessible information for teachers about the child, and delegation of welcoming and monitoring tasks to appropriate staff members" (Kaye 2006).

- **Have both materials and ideas on hand, "just in case."** This does wonders for morale (both yours and the new student's). Being prepared means being mentally ready for the task of helping the new student become part of the class, as well as having the classroom and the individuals in it primed for the potential arrival of a newcomer.

- **Have a welcoming classroom.** Mrs. Ramsay comments, "The physical appearance of the classroom needs to be inviting. It should say, 'Come in, sit down, you'll like it here!'" Decorations should reflect not only the activities of the students, but their tastes as well. ELL students have special needs to find a home in the classroom, and efforts should be made to represent all cultures.

- **Sensitize the class.** If you've been alerted beforehand, try to learn as much about Bounkham as you can before he comes to class so that you can share this information with the other students. This will help them accept Bounkham and make him part of the class. Mrs. Ramsay didn't have any lead time for Bounkham's arrival, but she knew that it was likely, given the nature of the school. To prepare for that day, she had the class brainstorm and discuss how it might feel to be immersed in a new country or, in the case of Native Americans, a new environment, where they don't speak, read, write, or understand the language. She read the books *Crow Boy* by Taro Yashima and *I Hate English!* by Ellen Levine to get them thinking along those lines.

- **Make the student feel welcome.** Even if you don't know a single word of Bounkham's language, you can show encouragement, sincerity, and empathy through gestures and body language. Smiling is universal.

- **Make sure you know how to pronounce and spell the student's name.** If you can't figure out the pronunciation of Bounkham's name from the intake form, ask him. Don't try to anglicize his name unless his parents have expressed this wish or he has changed it himself. Calling Bounkham "Bob" could make him feel even more alienated, as if his given name was not good enough. Identity is intricately tied to one's name, and to change it, either in the mistaken belief that the change will make him feel more part of the group or because his name is difficult to pronounce, can damage his integrity and feelings of self-worth. If he changes it, as Angel, Beverly, and Franco did, accept that too.

- **Introduce the student to the class.** Use a map to show the class where Bounkham is from. He may be able to point out his country and tell the class a little about it.

- **If possible, learn a few words and phrases in the student's native language**, such basics as "Hello," "How are you?" and, "Do you understand?" Even a simple thing such as "Hello" (in his language) will make him prick up his ears and brighten up, as well as convey that you are sincere and caring.

- **Be a model of respect for the other students in the class.** People of all ages can be cruel, especially when they don't understand another person's culture or dress. Showing respect for one's right to wear a turban, braids, or clothes we consider garish sets the parameters for appropriate behavior toward the new student no matter how different he may be.

At the Elementary Level

- Give your new student a name tag, but make sure all the other children in the class have name tags too. Wearing the only name tag in the room can make a child feel alienated and singled out. Making name tags is a perfect classroom activity to get the newcomer and the rest of the class involved in learning each other's names. You might consider including Bounkham's parents' names, address, and phone number on the reverse side—information that would be invaluable should Bounkham become lost on the way to or from school. But use your own discretion in providing name tags that include students' addresses and phone numbers. Mrs. Ramsay's school was in a dangerous part of town; having such a label on a small person could lead to trouble. However, she decided that a name tag with information was preferable to a child wandering aimlessly about unfamiliar streets, unable to ask for help.

- Take digital photographs of each student in your class, then use these to make a wall chart according to the seating arrangement of the classroom. This will reinforce the matching of names with faces.

At the Secondary Level

- Always introduce your new student to the class using the correct pronunciation of his name. High-schoolers, in particular, can wreak havoc with an unfamiliar name. If you can, supplement this introduction with some discussion of the geography and culture of his country.

- For the first days, ask for a class volunteer willing to help the new student with classroom procedures. In this classroom, Jeremy volunteered. He agreed to help Bounkham with such basics as the routine for starting class, providing him with paper and a pencil, sharpening the pencil, finding and using classroom resource materials, and so on.

Sometimes a group of students will pitch in and help out. So much of what happens depends on the class makeup and the ELL student's personality. Robbie and Nick took charge of demonstrating the special equipment they had in the classroom including the computer and DVDs. If Bounkham is outgoing and has some English, chances are that other students will help him get acquainted with no prompting from you.

At lunch break on the first day, the boys found out that Bounkham was interested in soccer. This made him an instant hit on the playing field—it didn't matter if he didn't know any English at all, as long as he could kick the ball to them. By the end of break time, he already knew the names of his fellow classmates and was trying out a few words. He was friendly and willing to try to say anything, not caring if he said it wrong. The other boys really liked him and were willing to help out with anything he needed. Thus, there was a group of boys, including Salvador, Franco, and Florien, who got along well with Bounkham both inside and outside of class.

Newton, on the other hand, had arrived in October. He was shy and awkward. He wasn't into sports. He didn't seem interested in making friends. After a couple of days, the boys gave up trying. Mrs. Ramsay worked hard to make Newton part of the group, but it was tough going. She had to accept that it would take time for him to join in actively. She paired him with Ellie and Kate as often as their tolerance would allow. Their effortless kindness encircled him too, so that although he rarely spoke, he was implicitly included.

As Mrs. Ramsay saw Bounkham relax, she included him in small group activities, ones that included the volunteers who helped him. Her objective was for both Bounkham and Newton to move from interacting only with individuals, to interacting with a small group, and finally with the whole class.

- Conduct an introductory, small-group activity for junior-high or high-school students; for example, create a bulletin board of favorite pictures or photos that your students bring in and label. Then, in small groups, have the students share why they chose to bring in the picture they did. Bounkham will be exposed to different hobbies, pastimes, and so on, and will be able to associate the new faces he sees with activities that may interest him. This can be especially helpful when the new student is trying to get to know classmates who don't sit in the same seats every day.

Learning the School and Its Routines

As quickly as possible, acquaint Bounkham with his new school and community. He needs to know the layout of the school, the daily routines, and some basic survival phrases. Because many students have never been in a school before, or because their country's school system is radically different from ours, assume they know nothing. It is also important that parents are given some basic information about the school. In Appendix A, we provide a sample information letter to parents. If parents are not sufficiently literate in English, this may need to be translated.

The average school day, with the routines and transitions we take for granted, can be overwhelming for a non-English speaker. For example, Mary's high school has a regular Monday/Wednesday/Friday schedule. On Tuesdays and Thursdays a block schedule is used. In a short week, Tuesday has Friday's schedule. Fernando, bewildered by the changes, came down nearly every day to ask what schedule it was and where he was supposed to be.

One can only guess how many times a student has come to school in the morning only to find the schoolyard deserted and the doors locked, because neither the student nor his parents understood it was to be a holiday. Or, they could not read the bulletins and had no one to translate. In a harsh climate such as where Barb lives, where the winter temperatures can plummet far below zero and schools only close when the temperature hits about −35°F, being locked out of the school, especially if parents have gone to work, is a frightening and dangerous situation.

High-school ELL students are at a further disadvantage, because many announcements about the school's frequently changing routine (for example, assembly schedule, half-day teacher meetings, and so on) are made over a public address system often garbled by the noise of an inattentive homeroom. The English-language learner must struggle to understand the content of these messages; with no visual cues, he often fails to understand. An alert homeroom teacher would write important announcements on the board so that literate ELL students could read the messages as well as hear them. When notices are sent home, schools with available resources might consider having school communications translated into the ELL students' native tongues or enlisting community interpreters to ensure the messages are received. In addition, most schools these days have web pages. If Bounkham has access to a computer, have another student show him how to find the school site and where to find any important announcements posted on it.

You can help ease the adjustment period by providing some sort of orientation for the student. Many schools have "Welcome to our School" DVDs, which can be translated with voiceovers for the different languages present in your school. Even if your student and his family do not own a computer, they can watch it in the school computer room, at the home of a neighbor, even at the local library. Also try to have the video posted on the school's website. Students are then able to learn the routines and regulations on their own time and discuss among themselves those things that need clarification.

Helping to create a welcome DVD or podcast is an ideal project for enterprising and technology-savvy students. It can be narrated by students proficient in the languages of your community (subject, of course, to careful analysis and editing by an adult proficient in that language).

Things Your Students Need to Know

Getting Around at School

- How to find the washrooms (and how to tell which ones are for which gender)

- How to find their way around the school: the location of the playground, the cafeteria, the gym, and their classes. For example, if Bounkham is in junior high or high school, he will need to find his way from one class to another in the allotted time. He will also need to know the amount of time given for morning break and lunch.

- How to find the main office, the nurse's office, the counselor's office, and so on. Bounkham needs to know where to bring late slips, where to go if he doesn't feel well, and so on.

- How to find the way back to the proper classroom from any of the above places (It might help to write your room number on a card for Bounkham to carry if he leaves your room for anything; in a new place, all doors and even all teachers can look alike. You might also consider making a simple picture map of the school for Bounkham, to help him find his way around.)

- The names of a few key people, especially yours. In many cultures it is a sign of respect to call a teacher "Teacher," but time and time again, teachers have been dismayed that a student still does not know their name, even after months of being in school.

- How to open and close a locker, particularly if it has a lock with a combination

- The mechanics of the school day

  - When must a student arrive?

  - When are recess periods or breaks?

  - When is lunch period?

  - When is the school day over?

  - What are the dates of holidays and school closures?

The School Routine, Rules, and Expectations of Behavior

- School rules

  - What if a student is going to be absent or late? Do his parents need to let the school know ahead of time?

  - Does he need to bring in a written explanation for an absence?

  - In secondary schools, are there absent slips that all the teachers must sign and then turn in at the end of the day? Where do these slips need to be returned (handed in)?

- Procedures

  - Are there one-way hallways, or is traffic designated to move in one direction on one side and another on the opposite side?

  - What do students do when they enter class? In elementary school, do the students line up in a single line, or in separate lines for boys and girls? Do they stand outside the classroom door or in another designated spot on the playground?

  - When and where does a student hand in his homework?

  - What does a student do

    - In an emergency?

    - If he's tardy?

  - How does he answer questions?

  - How does a student signal whether or not he understands?

- Expectations of behavior at school

  - How should students address you?

  - Does a student need to raise his hand to be acknowledged?

- Does he need to stand by his seat, as many cultures demand, when it is his turn to speak?

- Is talking allowed when working in small groups?

- Is cooperative work allowed, or is a student expected to work on his own? (Mary had a student who was constantly admonished for cheating in his content classes. When a meeting was held with Ming and his teachers, they discovered he had no idea that working on a paper with another student was wrong. At the school he had attended in his homeland, students always worked on the answers together.)

- What is the school's policy and procedure for detention?

- If a student has a detention after school for misbehavior, where is he to go and for how long?

- What is he expected to do during detention? (With regard to detention, or in emergency situations when the parents need to be contacted, have a list of volunteer interpreters handy for translating the message.)

- Lunch
  - Where do students go to eat?
  - Does Bounkham need to bring a lunch, or can he buy it at school?
  - What is the procedure in the cafeteria?
  - Is he aware that the food and how to eat it (for example, picking up a hamburger with his hands, instead of using a fork and knife) may be unfamiliar?
  - If he buys milk for lunch, is it a cash sale, or is all the money collected on a specific day?
  - Does he display a card? What if he runs up a negative balance?
  - What do students do when they finish eating?

- Breaks
  - Where are students allowed to go during breaks? (In elementary schools, are there particular play areas for specific age groups?)
  - Are there any places they may not go? (In many high schools one area is designated for seniors only. If Bounkham is not a senior, he needs to know that area is off limits.)
  - How do the students know when it is time to go back to class?
  - When is a student allowed to go to his locker?

- Getting home
  - If a student is being picked up by a family member, where does he wait for them?

- What should he do if they don't come?

- Where is a phone if he needs to call his parents or other family members? Is money required to make a phone call?

- What route does he take to get home if he must walk?

- Are parents made aware of any child welfare legislation that governs the minimum age at which a child may be at home without adult supervision?

- If a student rides the bus to and from school, where does he wait for it?

- How does he tell which bus is his?

- How does he tell the driver where he needs to be let off?

One tense afternoon, at a junior high school where Barb worked, a new student boarded the first bus that passed after school. She ended up going downtown instead of to her housing project. For two hours, her parents and teachers waited anxiously until she was located.

Use Resources Within the School and the Community

As a teacher with 20 or more students (or, at the secondary level, 120 or more students), you may not have time to give one new student a comprehensive orientation. Fortunately, even the smallest school can draw on a number of resources to help ease the ELL student's first day. If you are unable to give your new student an orientation during the morning break or at lunch (and face it, how many teachers really have an entire break period free?) consider these alternatives:

Use Student Help

- Find another student who speaks the same language. Many immigrants are classified as speaking one language, but because they've spent time in refugee camps or other countries they often know multiple languages that you can tap. A student who is already familiar with the school and its routines and requirements can explain to the new student, in his own language, what is expected of him and help him adjust to his new surroundings. At the high school, Mrs. Ramsay found another student who was released for the day to help Bounkham get from class to class. The first day of school is bewildering enough for incoming freshmen and must be many times more frightening to one who hasn't experienced North American schools before. Bao spoke only Hmong, but her older brother also knew some Lao. Mrs. Ramsay allowed him to sit in the class for a day or two to help ease the transition.

- Assign a buddy. Put an English-speaking student in charge of showing the new student around, making sure he gets from one place to the other without getting lost. Mrs. Ramsay looked at the personalities in the class. Although Kate and Ellie were responsible girls, she decided that pairing Bounkham with a boy would be a better idea. Most of the non-native-English-speaking boys, who would understand what Bounkham was going through, did not have strong enough proficiency—except Boris and Andre. But Boris was not a good role model, nor was Andre, who had plenty of troubles of his own. She decided not to place the entire burden on one person. She selected Robbie, because he needed to take on more responsibility, David, because he was steady and patient, and Jeremy and Nick, because they were sociable and friendly.

Use Adult Help

- If your school or district has an ELL teacher, she may be able to help guide the student through this first day (or days) at school.

- A bilingual teacher or aide may be able to give the student his first-day orientation to the school.

- In the event that you have neither an ELL nor a bilingual teacher available, any sympathetic and patient adult—a librarian, a parent volunteer, a resource teacher, a counselor, or a principal—might be entreated to adjust his or her schedule to make time for your student on that all-important first day.

- Consider finding a mentor for the student. Many schools have found adult volunteers who agree to devote weekly or monthly time to students to help them succeed. It can be very beneficial to a new student from another country to have an adult's consistent support as he adjusts.

Use Cultural Resources

If Bounkham is one of the first students from Laos placed in your school and you have no idea where to find cultural support for him, check the following resources in your community:

- Cultural support groups already working within the community (for example, Cultural Family Community Services, or International Students' Organizations on college campuses)

- The ELL department at the local college or adult basic education programs

- The Internet and the White Pages. For instance, Google "resources for the Hispanic community," or "Catholic Community Services," "Lutheran Social Services," or other church-related organizations. In the telephone book, look in the "Easy Reference List of Government and Public Services" or similar listing.

- The Mayor's office, which often has an immigrant and refugee services center ("Consumer Information," "Constituent Service," "Ombudsman," and so on)

- Lawyers, especially those associated with civil rights groups, pro-bono committees of bar associations, the Legal Services Corporation (LSC), The

United Methodist Committee on Relief (UMCOR), or Farmworker Legal Services (FLS)

- Voluntary agencies that work in refugee resettlement, such as international institutes/centers; national religious service groups (for example, Catholic charities, world church services, world relief refugee services, Mennonite Central Committee)

- Churches, temples, the public library, and other agencies, such as the Salvation Army

- For emergency interpreters/translations, AT&T offers Language Line Services, an over-the-phone translation service in 140 languages (see <www.usa.att.com/traveler/access_numbers/view.jsp?group=language>). Other translation services can be found online, including Babel Fish (<babelfish.com>) and Freetranslation.com.

First-Day Teaching

Once a new student is placed in an appropriate grade, assigned to a class (or set of classes), and given an orientation to the school, you can get down to business. Bounkham has settled into his desk, and has taken inventory of his books, pencils, and pens. It's a fairly safe bet that he's not going to bolt for the neighbor's yard. It's social studies time. The other students are getting their books out; he sits, hands folded, quietly watching you. He's ready to learn. But he doesn't speak English, and you don't speak Lao. How will you teach?

If Bounkham speaks no English, it may take a while for him to start to participate. However, this does not mean putting him "on hold" until he talks. As time goes on, you can use different alternatives for individualizing instruction so that your student will be learning at least some basic subjects. But for now, you can help him adjust to the classroom and begin to learn English.

Things to Do to Help the Student Adjust and Begin to Learn

- **Give him a place of his own.** For younger children, this may be a cubby to keep things in. For older students, it may be a desk or an assigned seat. If the students select their own seats each day, you may have an area where students keep supplies. Show Bounkham where to keep his materials for use in your class. This sense of a personal space will make him feel included, which will help prevent him from hovering in the doorway until everyone else is seated and ready for class, and allow him to slip to his desk without feeling self-conscious.

- **Give him something definite to do.** This activity does not have to be elaborate, just something to occupy him so that he doesn't have to sit doing nothing while the rest of the class works. Make it a simple task that he can enjoy and achieve some success at.

Many elementary schools that frequently have ELL students drop in during the school year keep an "emergency kit" of things for a newcomer to do when he first arrives. This kit is filled with magazines, pictures to cut out and color, and items to sort and identify. Many of the manipulatives we discuss on page 173 are appropriate for this kit, and may be used by the student whenever he cannot participate in a particular classroom activity.

For older students, books or magazines with interesting pictures, such as *Time*, *National Geographic*, *Sports Illustrated*, *Ranger Rick*, or even old calendars, are useful. The students can copy or create labels of item categories, or practice writing their names, family members' names, addresses, and so on. They can also label different items found in a classroom. In content-area classrooms, students can label such things as equipment or materials.

We advocate supplying students with picture dictionaries, such as *The Oxford Picture Dictionary*, so that they can begin learning new vocabulary immediately. The realistic pictures depict everyday life in and out of school. Note that while this dictionary is acceptable for older children, the number of items on a page might be overwhelming for younger elementary students.

- **Allow him time.** Don't be dismayed if Bounkham only sits and watches for the first few days or so, or if he doesn't speak at all. It is important that he be able to choose whether or not to become involved. The main thing is to be prepared. Have a kit of worthwhile activities planned and ready, as discussed earlier, so that he doesn't have to sit doing nothing, only to get bored, frustrated, or disruptive. It doesn't take long to put an "emergency kit" together, and it will save you a great deal of anxiety and guilt when your new student does show up.

- **Establish a routine.** We cannot overemphasize how critical this is to a student. Knowing exactly what he's to do first, and where he's going to go next, makes life simpler for students like Bounkham. For a non-English speaker, everything has to be learned by observing, so routine is essential. Bounkham will feel less self-conscious if he can anticipate what is going to happen in class. And, as the process becomes familiar, he will become more inclined to risk error by speaking. It also makes your planning easier, because you will follow the same steps with each new student.

- **Compile a list of phrases or questions that you might say to or ask of the student as well as some of the phrases or questions he might need to say to or ask of you.** Record these on a sheet of paper that your student can carry around. If possible, have someone translate and explain them to the student. For example:

Things your teacher might say to you

- Please open your book to page ____.
- Answer the questions
- Write the answers
- Work by yourself/in pairs/in groups

- Listen to...
- Do you understand?

Things you might say to your teacher

- I'm sorry, I don't understand.
- Would you repeat that?
- What does _____ mean?
- How do you say _____ in English?

(Adapted from Churchill House School of English worksheet: "Classroom Language")

- **Include the student in class activities.** The first few days and weeks of school are lonely times, and ELL students may feel alienated and alone. Being part of a group will help Bounkham overcome those feelings. Even if he cannot participate fully—or at all—he will benefit from the exposure. A buddy system may decrease the possibility of anxiety and alienation.

- **Seat the ELL students with care.** This is another instance where Mrs. Ramsay had to think strategically. Seating had to be judicious as well as flexible. Hers is a lively class with many strong personalities. Frankly, we struggled with this part as all teachers do. It's not enough, with ELL students in your classroom, to arrange them in alphabetical order. They need access to you, and to each other, as well as to students who can and are willing to help them.

  To help us think this through, we gave the list of students' personalities to pre-service teachers (who are planning to teach all different grade levels and classes) and asked them what they would do if they had this class. The results surprised us, and they also helped us see the possibilities. Some teachers were willing to gamble. One group put Boris and Ashley together because they "deserved" each other. Another group put Boris in a corner by the door so he could leave whenever necessary, without disrupting the class. They all worried about Angel and Beverly as well as Boris and Ashley.

  The personalities of the different students, the personalities of the teachers, and their teaching philosophies all had to be taken into account. The layout of the room and the purposes of the class also figured into the seating arrangements.

  We discovered there is no one right way to seat ELL students. Still, we found it exciting and fun to watch the thought processes of the pre-service teachers and the care they took in thinking the problem through. We have replicated some of their suggestions, as well as their rationales, so you have a model upon which to base your own decision making (figures 1.2–1.4). Where would you seat Bounkham?

- **Find social avenues and ways for him to become a part of your class.** Kaye (2006) says that "integrating young refugees into...social groups

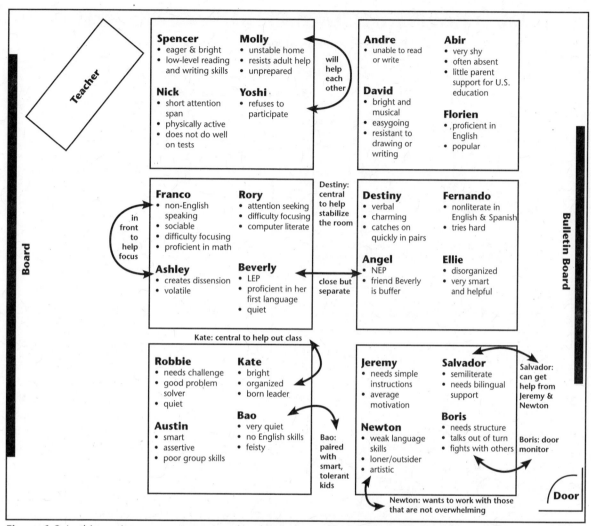

Figure 1.2 In this seating arrangement Angel and Beverly are close, but not together. Two anchors are at every table, along with second-language learners and/or students with behavioral issues. Boris is by the door. He was given the job of door monitor, with the idea that if he had a specific job he would attend to it with diligence, and it would make him more responsible.

requires 'finding common activities that they can share' rather than telling [other students] to be nice to their new classmates. These friendships with [other] children not only increase a young person's confidence speaking English but give refugees more confidence overall."

- **Allow him to use his native language.** This is a tricky suggestion. We are often stressed by the idea that if we allow the native language we are delaying acquisition of English, and letting the student "get away with" something, or that if two students are talking together and we can't understand, they're goofing off. However, we've found, over the years, that many students do much better if they're allowed to discuss ideas and content together in their own language. If one of them "gets it," he can

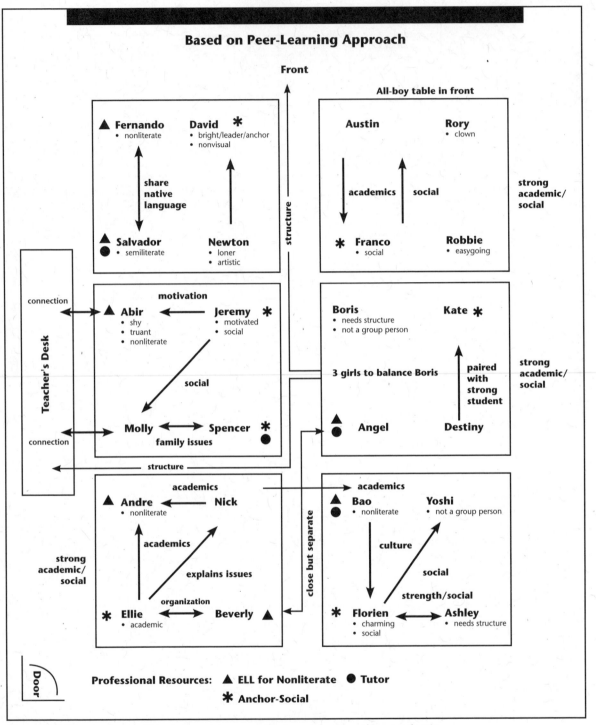

Figure 1.3 The anchors in this seating arrangement are social, rather than academic.

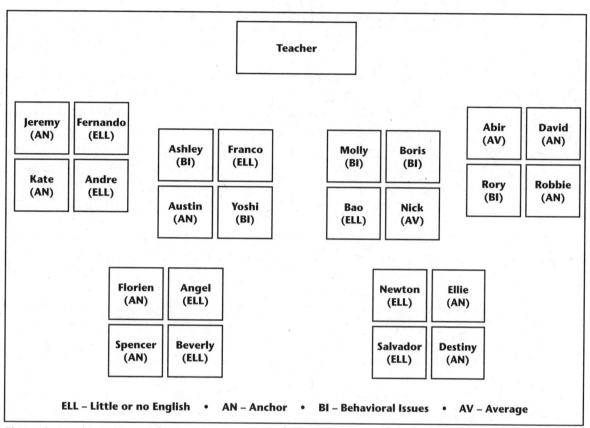

Figure 1.4 In this seating arrangement, one well-behaved or average student was put into each group. Beverly and Angel are seated together, but not next to each other, to give stability.

explain to another, and they all benefit. This is tricky of course, and you have to watch carefully. But, if you've ever been to a foreign country you know that you can hear an English-speaking person across a crowded stadium, and it's an intense relief to be able to communicate with someone.

Planning for the Year

Setting short- and long-term goals is a good remedy for curing the panic you may feel when a non-English-speaking student is assigned to your class. Mapping out your objectives helps you see that you can achieve realistic goals with this new student; making sure your goals fall into short- and long-term categories keeps you from overwhelming yourself or him! But don't make any long-term goals for the first few weeks. Bounkham will be adjusting to all the people and things he encounters at the school and may seem to know less English than he actually does. Only when you know you have a good sense of your student and his learning style should you make long-range plans for his curriculum. The following steps will help you to manage.

Prepare Coping Strategies

- **Have a game plan.** It is not enough to assume that the student will "pick up" English on his own. We've seen, all too often, students sitting in the back of the class, doing nothing, not being included until they've somehow learned enough to function. Bounkham needs you to help him make sense of the new language so that he is able to catch up and work at grade level with his peers.

- **Have expectations—*high* ones.** Expect your student to learn. Learning does not stop because he is grappling with a new language. Although he may not speak a word of English, Bounkham is capable of sophisticated and penetrating thoughts in his own language. We need to guard against underestimating his potential for making serious contributions to classroom discussions. Bounkham can learn new words, and he can learn concepts from the activities he participates in. Your expectations of him are positive encouragement that you believe in his potential.

  A study in Britain found that many teachers, especially those who are inexperienced in working with English-language learners, believe young refugees are experiencing upheaval and distress. "The idea that young refugees are traumatized and troubled can cause teachers to lower their expectations of the student or excuse poor schoolwork or attendance for reasons of being compassionate...Well-intentioned teachers may avoid putting new arrivals 'on the spot' by asking them questions in class, or treat them differently from other students in an attempt to make them feel less intimidated" (Kaye 2006). But low expectations do your students no favors. If your expectations are low, it can lead you to set the bar for learning and the kinds of activities you plan at a level that is too elementary and therefore won't challenge your student and help him move ahead (Schinke-Llano 1983).

  High expectations are manifested in the kinds of learning opportunities you engage him in. They're reflected in the kinds of questions you ask. For instance, if you're looking at a picture of a person introducing a new puppy to the family, are you asking simple recall questions—the "Are there two dogs in the picture?" kinds of questions—or are you engaging the student with questions like, "How do you think the old dog is going to react?" and "What can you do to help the two dogs be happy together?" Monitor yourself about your perceptions of your students and their proficiency levels and abilities. Make sure you're not dumbing down.

  Accept the fact that the ELL student will be behind. If you feel anxiety because you believe Bounkham has to be caught up with the rest of the class in four weeks, you are setting yourself up for some real misery. Understanding that he will be filtering content through limited-language proficiency allows you to focus on the bigger picture and helps you to appreciate his little successes.

Establish Short-Term Goals

- **Record what the new student can and cannot do.** Mrs. Ramsay discovered that Bounkham did not have strong reading skills. Over the next few days, she watched, in a variety of situations, how much he was able to communicate. He could write full sentences. He was able and willing to interact with the other students. When partnered with another, stronger student, he could handle the assignments; he watched to get a feel for things, then took off on his own. She watched to see if he was able to demonstrate any prior knowledge in the content areas. He knew math. He didn't have formal background in science or the social studies units they were working on. It was her task to figure out whether this was due to lack of vocabulary or to concepts that he had not encountered during his previous schooling. She also needed to figure out if he needed to adjust to a new learning style.

  He did. Bounkham did not know that if he did not understand a concept, it was appropriate to ask for help. Mrs. Ramsay found that he simply pretended to do work, wrong or right, rather than ask for clarification. Having Bao explain, as best she could, helped him realize what he could do and what he needed to do. Keep records of Bounkham's starting points and progress. That way, you will know what he needs and how well he is doing.

- **As you are getting acquainted, set some short-term goals for your student based on your observations.** For the first week or so of class, Mrs. Ramsay focused on getting Bounkham to participate in the classroom routine and to begin to use English. This included anything from acknowledging instructions to turning in a written assignment. She tailored the goals she had set to her perception of his abilities.

- **When teaching the new student to communicate, give him vocabulary that will be useful.** Teach him words and popular idiomatic expressions that he will hear and be able to use immediately. Don't teach vocabulary that has little to do with this student's everyday life. These are meaningless memory-eaters, and time could be spent more fruitfully on vocabulary that will give him instant feedback. Mrs. Ramsay taught Bounkham important phrases such as "I don't understand" and "Where is the (bathroom, library)?" and other survival words to get him through the day. The boys taught him how to say, "Whatever." She also gave him small assignments, such as mapping the school. This was an activity that he could work on while others were engaged in tasks beyond his language abilities.

- **Teach essential content-vocabulary.** For example, Mrs. Ramsay was teaching a unit on matter. The words *matter, air, solid, liquid, gas, weight,* and *space* were fundamental vocabulary to this unit. This was vocabulary that could not be simplified. Even if Bounkahm could not read the text, he needed to know these words to participate in the experiments and understand even the rudiments of the lessons.

35

It is becoming clearer and clearer just how important it is to teach academic language right from the beginning. In the United States, we tend to teach informal, "survival" English first, and then academic language. However, according to Dr. Robin Scarcella (2009), it is possible—and imperative—"to lay the foundation for academic language" from the beginning, even when teaching conversation skills.

- **Use audio-visual materials,** which are wonderful tools for language learning. Films, recordings of popular songs, video of educational TV shows, YouTube videos, photos, slide shows, and comic strips can all help to develop communication skills. All kids think movies are a treat, a break from the daily routine, and they pay attention. It especially helps Bounkham and the other less proficient students.

- **Find out the new student's favorite activities and interests,** and develop related assignments that will encourage and advance his attempts at learning the English language. English is most effectively learned when generated from attempts to communicate, not from a focus on perfect grammar and syntax. Mrs. Ramsay found that Bounkham was a sunny, friendly, likable child who took everything in stride and liked video games, soccer, and music. He was willing to attempt anything.

   He was particularly adept at using his hands. He liked working on the computer and could often fix problems that arose, simply because he had a knack for knowing how things worked, even though he didn't have the language for it. Like many of the other boys in the class, he was not good at doing seat work; he was continually up and around. Rather than have him plod through workbooks, Mrs. Ramsay planned activities for Bounkham that were short in duration or required an active role, making the most of his strengths.

- **Encourage extracurricular activities as springboards for English acquisition.** Many school clubs and after-school activities can provide firsthand exposure to all kinds of vocabulary in a variety of contexts.

   If your student wants to play on the school's soccer team, he will be exposed to English vocabulary used for a game he probably already knows how to play. Whatever club or activity the student joins, the motivation to learn English will arise from the need to contribute to his chosen interest and communicate with others involved.

Establish Long-Term Goals

- **Develop an overall plan.** Now that you know something about your ELL students, develop strategies for the long run. This step might seem self-evident, but it is a critical one. Rather than have "getting through the book" as your objective, envision the course as a whole. What do you want them to learn? (We discuss this further in chapter 8, "Content-Area Instruction.")

- **Select themes for teaching/learning units.** For instance, in junior-high or high-school history, you can use themes such as *expansion*, *waves of immigration*, the *Colonial era*, the *Civil War*, and so on. (Be sensitive to certain topics/themes that might evoke traumatic and negative emotions for some students.) For science, Mrs. Ramsay decided to examine a nearby plot of land as the seasons changed. She planned for students to gather data at specified times each month, keeping careful records of plant and animal life, the effects of various types of weather, as well as other activity on the land. They would classify species and varieties of life, speculate on changes that might take place, and revise their predictions based upon new data gathered. Each successive observation would improve everybody's skills, and they would all benefit from the repetition involved in the study.

  Repetition gives the course a coherent structure and makes each segment successively easier to understand—benefiting not only the ELL students, but other students as well. Repetition also gives a course shape and symmetry. Often, history or science courses seem little more than a jumble of unrelated facts and dates that are memorized for a test, only to be forgotten immediately afterward. In an integrated, thematic approach to instruction, students can see the course as a comprehensive whole, related to the world outside and to the people who live in it. This isn't always feasible, but offers a lot of fun possibilities if it can be accomplished.

- **Establish minimum competencies.** When you know what you want to cover by the end of the semester, decide on a "bottom line" set of concepts your students must learn in order to pass. You can then use this list to evaluate your ELL students. Note that it is easy to assess ELL students in terms of how much they are missing the mark, how much they don't know, when compared to your English-speaking students. In establishing basic goals, you can measure, instead, how much they *can do*.

  Mrs. Ramsay was teaching the unit on matter, mentioned earlier. This concept is one that is studied in several grades in school (including second grade and, in greater depth, in junior high). If Bounkham is in second grade, you can be sure that he will get this again later. If he's in eighth grade, and missed it the first time, you can look at some of the activities at the lower levels and adapt.

  For this unit, Mrs. Ramsay wanted all students, including Bao, Bounkham, Angel, Beverly, Fernando, and Salvador, to understand

  - Basic vocabulary

  - What matter is

  - That matter has weight and takes up space

  - That matter exists in different states

  - Steps for conducting experiments

  - How to predict and write up findings

- **Prioritize your list.** Mrs. Ramsay decided that understanding the vocabulary was important. She also wanted all students to be able to understand that gas changes from liquid to solid and back again. Conducting the experiments and writing up the findings in articulate ways was beyond Bounkham and Salvador, but the others could try.

- **Adapt your lessons to the levels of the students.** Mrs. Ramsay had tried this unit the previous year and was not particularly happy with how it had turned out. It seemed that whatever she did, many of the students didn't "get it." She needed to gear the lessons more closely to the literacy abilities of Salvador, Fernando, Bao, and Angel, as well as Destiny and Spencer. She also had to make it challenging enough for Katie, Ellie, David, and Ashley.

This year, she decided that a lead-in was important, both to grab students' attention and to get them thinking about the subject. The first thing she did was show a clip of the movie *Terminator 2: Judgment Day*. In the clip, after a grenade explodes against the front of a tanker truck carrying liquid nitrogen, the T-1000, coming into contact with the liquid nitrogen, freezes into a solid statue. A single shot from Terminator's gun blows the T-1000 into a million shards. But intense heat causes the T-1000 shards to liquefy again, fusing together first into larger blobs, then into a central mass until T-1000 reforms itself.

The students watched the film clip three times: the first for fun and the second to observe the changes. They wrote down how they saw the T-1000 change form (see figure 1.5a–b).

During the third viewing, the students assessed their writing for accuracy and detail. Those students who were satisfied with their writing were given the option to read it aloud for the group, giving the struggling

> Frist it was a human but really was made out of, a liquid. Then later it fezzas in to ice and when the gaund was hot it metal and became a liquid and formed so he looked like a human

> The Bad guy turn to ice then the hot lava melt the ice then he turn liquid nitrogen then he turn a policeman.

Figure 1.5a–b Students' descriptions of what they observed.

Figure 1.6 Students identify the various states of matter.

students the opportunity to hear a model of good observation, and a chance to reevaluate what they had seen and written.

Then, while her English-speaking students were reading the science textbook and answering questions, Bao, Salvador, and Fernando were making posters. Mrs. Ramsay gave them magazines and specific instructions for finding 20 pictures of solids, 10 of liquids, and 5 of gases. They were asked to make a collage and identify the various states of matter (figure 1.6). The more proficient ELL students (Abir, Newton, Angel, and Beverly) labelled the different items. This allowed the limited-English speaking students to participate, to demonstrate their understanding, and to continue along with the unit at their own level.

When students made charts of the properties of the various states of matter, the less-proficient students listened and copied (figure 1.7).

In many of the experiments Mrs. Ramsay did with her students, she included the less-proficient students. By pairing or putting them in groups with more proficient students, they could watch, take part, draw their understanding, and, if possible, write up their findings.

Solid	liquid	Gas
• you can feel it	• moves easily	Can not se easily
you can broch it	• It's wet	you can feel it whe
The shape can not be changed easily	• Stays together	it moves
We use solids for a lot of things	• It can make other things wet	Some gas smalls
you can see Solid easily	• can change temperatures	chang it's shape
can change temperatures	• When you add color to a liqud the whole liquid changes	you use air in tires
	• liquid take the shape of the contain- er you put it in	
	liquids can changes in to solids	

Figure 1.7 A student's chart showing the properties of states of matter.

Requirements for ELL Students

- During the first nine weeks, literate ELL students are accountable for
  - All math
  - All work done in ELL assignments or with their tutor
  - Tasks modified for the ELL student, such as book reports that require the student to take the book a chapter at a time and do a simple retelling of the story
  - Contributions to group work
- During the second nine weeks, literate ELL students must
  - Take all work sheets
  - Put their names on them
  - Do as much as they can
  - Hand them in—you can grade the more advanced students after the second nine weeks.
- During the third nine weeks, the students must
  - Be able to do almost all the work
  - Be graded with others, with some allowances (for instance, if they didn't finish a test because they needed to make constant references to a dictionary, they can finish later in study hall or after school)

Figure 1.8 An example of a grading structure for literate ELL students.

- **Develop a grading structure for literate ELL students.** Mrs. Ramsay designed an evaluation system to mark the progress made by Bounkham, which reduced the gray areas during grading time.

    As an example, we have included the format one junior high school has adopted for grading within specific marking periods (figure 1.8). This format is ambitious, but if the ELL students are aware that they will be accountable for certain things, they have certain goals to shoot for, rather than a vague "when they learn English."

Conclusion

The first days with a limited-English speaker in the classroom are the hardest for everyone concerned. At times you may feel that the going is slow, and results are few and far between. Chances are your student feels the same way. Nurture attitudes of patience, compassion, and a sense of humor to encourage the student's process of assimilation. Celebrate the successes no matter how small they may seem. In spite of the frustrations, this can be a rich opportunity for all of you.

Reflections, Projects, and Projections for Discussion

- Review Figure 1.1, which shows an ELL student's reflections of her first day. Think about a time you found yourself in a new or strange situation. What or who in particular helped you, and how? What did you do to cope?

- Analyze the layout and the physical appearance of your classroom, or a classroom you have access to. Think about specific ways you can make your class and your classroom more welcoming.

- Look at the cast of characters and the seating charts we've developed (figures 1.2–1.4). How would you seat these students, and why? (Or, how would you seat some of the ELL students in classes you have already?)

- Analyze your own school, or one nearby. What procedures and plans are in place for incoming language learners? What more does this school need to do to be ready? Brainstorm ways to make your own school more "newcomer friendly," then implement them.

- Produce a "Welcome to Our School" DVD.

- Make a checklist of resources, books, DVDs, translators, and so on that you have available.

- Think about what you can do to clarify your classroom routines. Make sure important information (names, assignments, rules) is always available in written form.

- Find out what policies (for language learners or newcomers) you need to be aware of in your school district, state, or country. What is mandated?

- Decide what resources and materials you will need in order to be prepared for newcomers. Also, decide what direction you will take, and whether or not you will need translators or materials in a different language.

- Assemble a set of guidelines that you can have on-hand in case a new student enrolls in your class. What rules should he know? What are your priorities? What are your pet peeves?

- Make a collection of activities to have on hand should a newcomer arrive. What tasks can you immerse him in while you get your bearings and until you can fully assimilate him into the class?

- Bao, Newton, Salvador, and Abir (see pages 16 and 17) are placed in the same class. Choose a level or a content area. Establish minimum competencies for each of them. Would the competencies be the same for each student? If so, what is your rationale? If not, how would they differ? What would you reasonably be able to expect of each of them after three months? Six months? Nine?

- Gloria has been assigned to a school that is unprepared for the recent influx of limited-English and non-English-speaking students. She is fluent in Spanish, but none of the new students understand that language either. The school has no procedures, no plan for placement, nothing to welcome the newcomers. Teachers are afraid and resentful. Gloria is the only one who has any experience working with non-native speakers. Where should she start? What are her first priorities? What steps can she take to welcome these new students and help them to function? What specific things can she do to give the teachers confidence and a place to start?

Case Study: Abir

Abir is enrolled in your school part way through the year. She tests at a level 2 (see pages 60–62). She is very shy at first and never talks above a whisper.

As time goes by, that changes. She begins to reveal the most contrary personality the school has ever seen. She is very vocal about things she does not like. She has a difficult time writing assignments but does not take suggestions for improvement well. She always has a reason she can't follow the suggestions you give her. She leaves classes in a huff or gets angry and cries, complaining how mean you are. She is argumentative with you and other students in the class, proclaiming things are much better at her school in her home country. Although secretly you feel relieved when she's absent, these absences are much too frequent to allow for any continuity of schooling. When she is in school, she does not turn in any homework.

Conferences with her father reveal that she is needed at home to babysit younger siblings. Abir's parents believe that, although the situation in their country is dire and that they may not return at all, the time spent in this country is time lost academically, and they put more emphasis on the study of her subjects in Arabic. If the truant officer weren't breathing down their necks, they probably wouldn't send Abir to school at all. She is getting so far behind that she may not be allowed to matriculate to the next level.

A meeting is called with her counselor, her parents, teachers with whom she has the biggest problems, and you. You are primarily responsible for Abir. The main academic outcome of the meeting is that either she must get her work in, or she will not move on.

- How can you help Abir adjust to school?
- What rules and procedures must you enforce to limit her behavior?
- How would you go about it?
- What are the most important issues concerning this student?
- What positive steps can you take to accomplish the goals you need to meet?
- What are your short-term goals?
- Long-term goals?
- Can you think of a method of working with this student to minimize the battles?
- What procedures do you put into place to monitor her progress and document the measures you have taken?

Chapter 2

Testing and Placement—After Sawing the Doctor

In this chapter, we provide practical guidelines about

- Placement of ELL students

- Testing issues, including how to test ELL students

- How to make use of the test scores

Tomás arrived at school in the middle of May from a small town in Mexico. He was nine, but was placed in a third-grade classroom. He was a darling boy, with smiling eyes and a front tooth that was chipped twice. He spoke not a word of English. Barb, who had been testing all incoming children in that school for the past year and a half, came with her usual materials for testing reading and writing—graded reading passages in English and a writing prompt. Barb's Spanish comprehension is fair at best; she can follow along when she knows the topic of conversation, but when faced with the need to communicate, the Spanish gets mixed in with French and finally dribbles away altogether.

With a lot of goodwill and a few false starts, they established that Tomás was nine, he was born in September, and he had three brothers in town with him and two more in Mexico. He would not attempt to read in English, but willingly wrote what he had already communicated in a manner that revealed that he was literate in Spanish (see figure 2.1). But that was all they accomplished, so they gave up and went back to the classroom.

It was, altogether, an uncomfortable and less-than-revealing encounter that took Tomás away from the classroom and probably left him wondering what the heck all that was about. And Barb was frustrated, because had she had the right materials (a selection of reading passages in Spanish and an appropriate writing prompt he could read and respond to), she could have found out more information that was useful to Tomás's classroom teacher.

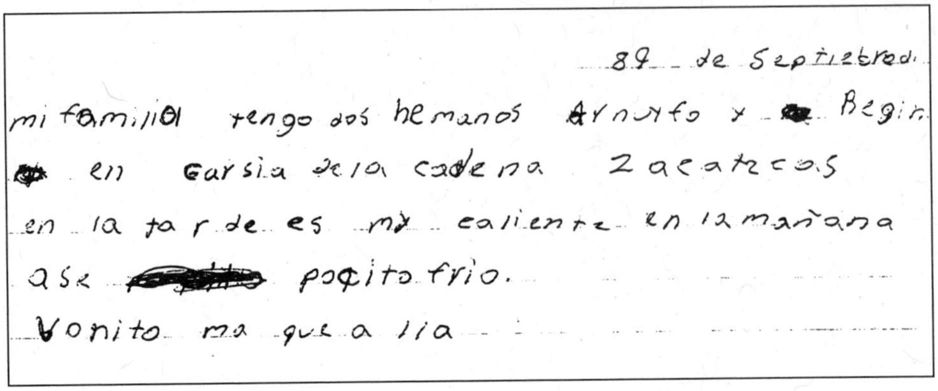

Figure 2.1 Tomás's writing sample.

The questions that arise from such an encounter are

- What do we want to know?

- How do we find out what we want to know efficiently and accurately?

- What do we do with that information once we've obtained it?

Testing

In the United States, federal law requires that all students coming from a non-English-speaking background

- Be surveyed within 30 days of school enrollment to determine if they speak a language other than English

- Be tested in their native language within 90 days of enrollment if they are not sufficiently fluent in English

In Canada, schools are required to determine eligibility for funding in special programs, like ELL, and to submit yearly information concerning assessment of students by a certified teacher.

There are many tests available. Even in those cases when no standardized tests have been translated into the languages your students speak, it is possible to learn much about your students and their proficiency levels. You can then make competent decisions about which programs, classes, and grade levels to place them in.

Initial Decisions

Ideally, your school will have been given prior warning that a new ELL student is coming, and whoever is responsible for that student can make unhurried decisions about his placement. Unfortunately, this is often not the case. Parents or guardians will bring the student to the school, medical papers in hand, and leave him there, forcing placement in a classroom without any type of assessment.

The person(s) responsible for the initial testing and placement of ELL students varies remarkably from school to school. Ideally, testing and placement will be the responsibility of an ELL specialist, or, in cases where no specialist is available, a counselor, a special education teacher, or a principal. The reality is that these people are often overextended, so the job of testing and placement is handed over to someone else—a teacher, an aide, or a parent volunteer. This is regrettable, as these people are often not provided with the necessary training and sometimes lack the sensitivity for this task.

Before the new student comes to school, or as soon as possible after his arrival, a home-language survey should be administered to determine whether he speaks a language other than English at home. In Appendix B, we illustrate a sample survey. An older student can fill this out at school with an adult's help. Younger students are often unreliable about the languages spoken in their homes, so the parents or legal guardians can be asked to fill out the survey. The help of an interpreter/translator is often required.

Placement

To illustrate the issues involved in placement and evaluation of students, we will track the progress of five students.

Bao is brought to school by a church sponsor. Her father was killed, and her mother had died in childbirth. She is here with her uncle. The scanty records that arrived from Fresno seem to be for another child named Bao. Her uncle says she is nine.

Boris, 13, is a confident boy with a swaggering manner and a loud voice. His parents are college educated, and he has studied English in school.

Newton, whose parents were refugees, is 16. He has lived all his life in this country, but speaks little or no English.

Spencer is five and has just moved here from a large, inner city. His mother has moved to this town to escape the ghetto after his older brother was killed in a drive-by shooting. He speaks a non-standard variety of English.

Charlie is a six-year-old from a reservation. His parents have moved temporarily to this district to seek medical help for a younger sister. He is fluent in his native language and has learned some English, but is not proficient.

The Grade-Level Issue

The school's first job is to place each student in the proper grade with the right teacher. Bao is tiny and appears much younger than her nine years. She smiles shyly, but will not speak. The principal is tempted to place her in the first or second grade. Boris has had some English but does not speak it fluently. The counselor argues that he should be placed in the sixth grade rather than the eighth grade, because the content is less demanding, and he will have an easier time learning the language without the pressure of studying new subjects he has not encountered before. Newton's parents think that he would do well in the 10th grade. Spencer and Charlie have not had any preschool experience at all. Their placement is relatively simple: because of their age they can be put into kindergarten with their peers. Charlie's main limitations are his lack of fluency in English and the challenges associated with adjustment to a new culture and environment.

Boris and Bao's lack of content knowledge and required skills are not reason enough to warrant placement in lower grades. These students should be placed with classmates of their age group for several very important reasons:

- Their emotional and social needs can be met only by being with their age-mates. "Educators must always remember that the first rule for placing ELL students in a language instruction educational program is that they should be placed at the chronologically age-appropriate grade level. The most important reason for age-appropriate placement is socio-cultural. Students progress faster and work harder when they are with their peers" (Moe 2006). In some cases, Moe asserts, with agreement from parents, a year below, or maybe, in special cases, above can be considered, but "more than a two year grade level difference is not acceptable." Handscombe (1989) says that social integration is much more important than language needs. It may be devastating to Boris's ego to place him with younger students, severely affecting both his motivation and his self-esteem. Separating Boris or Newton from students their own age due to proficiency or prior schooling, no matter how well intentioned, can backfire badly. At best it may hinder their development, linguistically, academically, as well as socially, because being integrated into a group gives them access to and experience with language, as well as providing a sense of place. Denying them this access can "sometimes lead to other problems such as disruptive behavior or lack of interest. Inevitably, the student will sense alienation, failure, or punishment, be poorly motivated to communicate in English, and have a lack of socialization opportunities with peers" (Wausau School District).

- Lack of fluency in English does not indicate limited intelligence. Even though a student's lack of English makes him unable to cope with grade-level work at first, he is not necessarily behind in cognitive development. What is more, the English spoken in the eighth grade is not appreciably different from that spoken in the sixth grade. Many students experience boredom and frustration when required to repeat content they have gained in their first language. It may well be that Bao, Boris, and Newton are perfectly capable of doing work at grade level. But you need to find out.

- Students beyond the primary grades can often learn to read faster than younger children, simply because they are more mature.

- More than any other factor, success with ELL students depends upon a commitment by teachers and administrators to acknowledge and meet the students' special needs. Academic achievement is directly linked to the quality of instruction, not just the placement of the student.

At the Elementary Level

As noted, Charlie can be placed in kindergarten with his peers. Most kindergarten curricula blend the development of prereading and prewriting skills with an exploration of the child's world. Activities at this level are predominately hands-on and rich in language-learning opportunities. The teacher will need to allow Charlie more time to demonstrate his mastery of lesson concepts, because he is juggling language learning at the same time as he is adapting to a new culture. For example, Charlie and Spencer do not have much experience and may take longer to learn how to read. First, they will need to connect print with meaning. Charlie must learn words for concepts and his alphabet. The teacher must be sensitive to Charlie's and Spencer's unique learning curves and assess their progress appropriately.

With Bao there is some flexibility. Under certain circumstances and with careful consideration, it might be permissible to place a child such as Bao one grade lower than her age-mates (but not more than one). If the school has split or multi-age classes, this would be the best option, as both her affective and cognitive growth would be ensured. Placing Bao in a class made up of third- and fourth-grade students would allow her to work with the younger children *and* socialize with her age-mates in the fourth grade.

What if subsequent testing reveals that Bao has no age-appropriate academic skills at all? With no prior schooling, she will be starting at square one. It is very difficult to teach a child who is at the pre-kindergarten level when there are 25 other students in the class. The experience would be frustrating, not only for her (because she can't do the work), but for the teacher (who won't have the time to help her).

One solution would be to place Bao in a first-grade classroom where the teacher would be better equipped to handle her needs until she learns her basic skills. However, this choice is not best for the student. For a child like Bao, being with her age-mates is the most important consideration. She will be able to participate with them in physical education, art, and music, and join them during recess and at lunchtime; this will allow Bao to make the friends that are so critical for second-language learning (not to mention, for happiness).

But she will need to work with her reading and math peers in those skill areas. This might necessitate going to the first-grade classroom or to the school's learning or resource center (if the school has one) for math and reading, or working one-on-one with a tutor, with resource assistance, or with part-time ELL support. Pulling her out of class or separating her for special help is, admittedly, not the ideal situation, but does offer a balance that responds to her varied needs. Some elementary schools coordinate their "centers," having reading and math at the same time throughout the school. In this way, students can move from center to center according to their needs without missing out on other classroom activities.

At the Secondary Level

The placements of Boris and Newton involve other considerations. For the same reasons outlined previously, both students would benefit from placement in the grades appropriate to their ages, with careful selection of the classes they take. There is some leeway in placement depending on (1) the existence and complexity of programs available in your district, (2) whether or not there is an ELL teacher, and (3) what tests reveal about Boris's and Newton's skills, particularly if the needs of your students surpass the instructional design of regular ELL programs in the community school.

If your school has a significant number of non-English and limited-English speakers, as more and more schools do, you may already have a program in place. The most proactive schools with large ELL populations have built programs based on the five WIDA (World Class Instructional Design and Assessment) levels of proficiency,[1] with modified instruction (often called sheltered instruction, or SDAIE [Specially Designed Academic Instruction in English]). It is beyond the bounds of this book to describe programs, because each one must be formatted to fit the needs of the population and shifts and refocuses itself depending on the vagaries of immigration and the ebb and flow of newcomers.

If your school has an ELL teacher, Boris and Newton could be placed in an ELL classroom or with the ELL teacher for one or two hours a day. If there is no ELL specialist, then other arrangements—aides, peer tutors, and/or volunteers—will have to be made.

If Boris and Newton can understand, read, and write English, consider placing them in regular classes all day with some support from tutors during study periods or after school. Here are some course options:

- Math, a course where ELL students tend to do well, because it is, in many ways, language- and culture-free. Until they attain a level of English that allows them to understand word problems, however, they will need individual help in this area.

- Science, a hands-on course with many opportunities for ELL students to watch and participate with their classmates

- Art, which allows non-English speakers to express themselves in ways other than verbally

- Music, particularly choir, which relies on a great deal of repetition and provides an emotional outlet

- Physical education, which is, in many ways, language-free (In games such as football or basketball, verbal instructions are "context embedded," that is, the activities are rich in visual cues, and the language the student hears or the instructions given are accompanied by gestures and demonstration.)

English is the most important class for instruction in reading and writing. Although we insist elsewhere that reading and writing should take place in all classes, English class is the one in which ELL students will receive the most direction in the acquisition of English language skills. In language arts, students must be involved in more than simply learning language; they must

---

1 The WIDA levels of proficiency can be found near the end of this chapter, on page 60.

learn how to use language to learn. According to Chamot and O'Malley (1986), ELL students need to learn study skills that help them succeed in content areas in which course concepts—not the language—are the focus.

For Boris and Newton, courses such as history and social sciences should be added later. These courses are "context reduced"—students cannot rely as much on visual cues to determine the meaning of the content matter. What is more, these subjects require a great deal of reading. When Newton and Boris have gained more English proficiency, these courses can be added.

If ELL students' academic skills are poor, or if they come to school illiterate, then remedial help in some form is the only alternative. In Newton's situation, extra help is probably required. He will need time to adjust, gain fluency, and complete his required course work. He can take grade 9 and/or grade 10 courses without shame, and catch up as his proficiency grows. Some school districts have implemented five-year programs for their ELL students. As some students need a year or more before they begin to function well in class, a five-year plan allows them the time they need.

Be sure to consult parents about placement. Many feel strongly that their child should be placed with their age-mates; others will go along with whatever recommendations you make, as long as they are based on sound assessments. Some parents may even want their child placed a grade ahead, believing that the schools in their country of origin are academically ahead of the new school. That's what Boris's family thought. They argued that the schooling in his country was of such rigor that he would be bored and, should they go back, he would be a year behind in his studies.

Placement, then, is a tricky business. Each placement should be dealt with on an individual basis, taking into consideration the student, his schooling history, his parents' wishes, and what administered tests reveal about his skills.

Assessment Through Testing

Testing is a complex and difficult issue. At the risk of oversimplifying matters, we have established some basic guidelines to help you through the maze of testing procedures and jargon.

Many commercially produced tests are on the market. Some common ones are the LAS (Language Assessment Scale); the BINL (Basic Inventory of Natural Language); the BSM (Bilingual Syntax Measure); and the IPT (Idea Proficiency Test). Others are also available.

Deciding Which Test to Use

Language competency is a very murky area—it is difficult to measure scientifically. Whether or not standardized tests are valid is a matter of controversy. Reliable tests should

- Demonstrate who should be labelled ELL, that is, who is in need of language services because his English proficiency is low

- Be consistent. If one test shows Boris needs ELL services, it should be possible to corroborate this by conducting other tests.

- Highlight skills a student has mastered, thereby predicting the student's ability to succeed in regular academic programs

- Identify a student's specific linguistic and academic needs. Does he speak well but need help in writing? Does he write well but speak haltingly?

- Tell you the student's proficiency level with the various skills: what grade level he reads at, how much he can write, what vocabulary he knows, and how much he understands

- Have "high content validity": does the test measure what it claims to measure? Often, the validity of a test is confounded by the language proficiency of the test-taker.

You may have heard complaints about commercially produced assessment tests: that they are useless—or worse. We feel it is important for you to understand why these complaints are often based on reality. Frequently, the test results are ambiguous or incorrect; they do not accurately reflect students' English language abilities. These tests fail for one or more of the following reasons:

Why Tests Fail

- **Many of the tests are culturally biased.** One test asks students to identify pictures of an elephant, a dinosaur, a submarine, and a watermelon. Bao might not know the English word for *house* or *table*, but at least she has the words in her own language and understands them because of her own life experience. Unless she has seen a watermelon or a submarine (even in pictures), she does not have the equivalent word in her own language. Asking her to identify something she has never seen or experienced is not a fair measure of her English vocabulary.

- **Many tests are linguistically biased—the instructions are not translated into the appropriate language.** For example, when instructions like "Tell me if the two words on the recording sound the same or different" are not translated into Amharic, or Hungarian, or Urdu, you have no way of knowing whether your ELL student actually understood what he was supposed to do—if his answer accurately reflects what he knows, or if it is a response to his inaccurate perception of the instructions.

- **Some tests are too ambiguous; you cannot determine exactly what they are telling you about your students' competence.** For example, if Newton leaves blanks on a cloze test, is it because (1) he did not know the appropriate vocabulary word in English, (2) he did not know the grammatical structure of the word he wanted to use, or (3) he did not understand the context of the sentences he was to complete?

- **Other tests include assessment on very minor, isolated points, giving equal scoring weight to each point.** This does not give the speaker from another culture a chance to show what he can do in English. For instance, one point might test the student's ability to distinguish between minimal pairs and phonemes—the discrimination between the smallest units of sound in English—such as /v/ and /b/ or /sh/ and /ch/. This will only tell you which sounds a student does or does not hear. Knowing that Charlie cannot distinguish between *very* and *berry* is of little use to you and of negligible importance in the overall task of learning the language.

- **Many tests have arbitrary cut-off scores, so they don't necessarily measure a student's competency.** For example, a test might specify that a score below 80 percent indicates that the student functions at the "limited proficiency" level. The companies that design these tests use nice, round figures, because they are easy to work with. However, there is no direct relationship between the score and the student's actual ability level. Newton may score 81 percent on the test, above the test's stated limited proficiency level, but in actuality may function on a limited basis in English. In a similar vein, Boris may achieve a grade of 100 percent on a test and still not be able to compete with his English-speaking classmates. The test may measure Boris's skill "at a fourth-grade level," but it does not measure Boris's ability to cope in the classroom.

- **Many tests provide incomplete information.** Commercial tests should be used only to provide guidelines for placement and to determine if an incoming student will require ELL or bilingual services. These tests are designed to differentiate between those who have enough English to function in the classroom and those who are truly limited in their English. Not all foreign students are ELL students, nor are all Native Americans. (Boris might actually know enough English to keep up with his English-speaking classmates.) Use these tests to help with placement, and go elsewhere to find more specific answers to your questions on how well a student reads or writes.

- **These tests do not help you make instructional decisions.** It might tell you what level your student is functioning at, but *not* how that translates into what you need to do tomorrow in the classroom.

Supplemental Tests

Although you are required to use at least one standardized test in the U.S., supplemental tests can be developed to find out other information that teachers really need to know. These supplemental tests should be given by the classroom teacher, as this is the person who requires the information.

Individual students' proficiency levels in listening, speaking, reading, and writing vary depending upon their experiences in North America and their own countries. Some might have advanced speaking and listening skills, but poor reading and writing skills. Others might be proficient in reading and writing, but will be able to understand little spoken English or not speak well enough to be understood by others. Therefore, you need to test all skills to determine how much your student knows.

For example,

> Can Charlie speak any English? How much does he understand?
>
> If it is established that Boris has some literacy in English, can he handle the classroom assignments?
>
> Can Bao read and write?
>
> What specific areas does Newton need help with?

Once you have this information, you can decide the course of your instruction and monitor your students' progress. All four language skill areas—listening, speaking, reading, and writing—must be tested.

Testing Hints

Before testing, you must have a list of things your students need to know. In the Student Vocabulary Test (Appendix C), we list some survival words and concepts that are important; you can start with these. But vocabulary is just the beginning; you also want to discover whether students can understand and produce extended discourse—speech beyond the word and sentence level. Students' proficiency refers both to their knowledge of the language and their ability to use it. Here are some testing tips to keep in mind:

- Try to make a test situation as low-key and stress-free as possible. Put your students at ease. Take the time to explain why you are testing them and why you are taking notes; some students will be nervous anyway, but this helps to create a less threatening atmosphere.

- Don't take students away from the class for testing when their classmates are involved in more entertaining activities.

- When testing, try to include at least one thing the student can succeed at. If students can't get through the oral section of the test, don't assume they will be unable to do the written section. Many students who have studied English in school in their country of origin can read and write much better than they speak (and often put native-English speakers to shame with their knowledge of grammar).

- Stop testing when the students indicate fatigue or frustration. You can always come back to do another segment later.

Testing Listening Comprehension

Test your students' "receptive proficiency"—how much English they understand. When testing identification of vocabulary, we suggest the following:

- Use real objects as much as possible. For example, use a desk rather than a picture of a desk.

- If you cannot use the real object, use a photograph (cut out of a magazine or catalog), not a drawing or painting. Many children, even those from literate North American families, cannot make sense of little whimsical figures or line drawings. Students from nonliterate cultures often have great difficulty making a connection between what they see in real life and two-dimensional drawings or paintings.

- Using photographs, ask test questions about things that are fairly universal, such as boys, girls, children, trees, clouds, and so on, not about culturally laden objects, such as hamburgers.

- Ask only one question at a time—don't combine questions. Test for colors, then shapes, but not both at the same time. Have the student look over a page of colored squares, then ask, for instance, "Which is the red square? Which is the blue square?" Don't ask complex questions like, "Where is the red triangle?" or "Where is the black pen?"

- Use simple commands. Find out if the student can understand simple sentences and can follow classroom instructions. In Appendix C, items 11 and 16, we list a number of commands they will be expected to know.

Testing Oral Language Ability

Spontaneous speech will elicit a language sample that is most representative of your student's oral language ability. This is best accomplished through an informal interview. Many students are shy and self-conscious, so you need to think carefully about how to elicit speech. While working in several programs that needed a quick sorting mechanism to determine oral language proficiency, Barb devised a series of questions designed to elicit an increasingly sophisticated command of the language:

What is your name? Simple fact. This is an easy one and shows interest in the student. But it isn't always that easy. Several students Barb was working with had chosen their own English names from a book. Horace, who was an extremely naughty little boy, didn't pronounce his name correctly, nor did he write it in a form that enabled us to guess what name he really intended (he spelled it Hosense). He also did not recognize "Horace" when he was called upon. It was frustrating to be shouting at a child who was flailing at another boy, when he didn't even know he was the one being yelled at. But if they understand and can answer, they have at least some English.

How old are you? Another simple fact question. However, if the student answers, "I'm fine," you can tell the limitations of his English. This answer usually means the student has memorized an answer to a question he has been taught and is not listening to the sense of the question, but is picking up parts of it.

When is your birthday? This can tell you, in many cases, the level of the student's English proficiency. In other cases, the student may simply not know, which can be an indicator of gaps in education, cultural difference, problems in transition, or lack of linguistic and cognitive input. Spencer, for instance, did not know when his birthday was; he knew that his birthday came when the weather was warm. His family life had been extremely disrupted, and he had moved often. Not knowing his birth date was perhaps understandable at the age of five. But when he moved into another district at the age of 12, he still could not tell the teacher.

Tell me about your family. Again, this question demonstrates interest on your part and gives students a topic that they are familiar with and have feelings about. The complexity of a student's answer gives you an indication of his level of functioning. Angel, for instance, looked confused by the question and answered, "I am little English." This revealed that she was just a beginner, and the question was too complex for her. Florien, on the other hand, talked confidently and enthusiastically about his two older sisters and his younger brother, revealing his command of the language.

What would you do if...? This conditional and much more advanced question requires speculation on the part of the student. When Barb was in California she would ask, "What would you do if you saw a bear coming through the door?" Often she would have to mime a bear. If the question was greeted with a shrug, she knew the student didn't understand. If a smile appeared on the face of the child, she knew she had communicated. Answers that revealed understanding ranged from "run" to "I would go RARRRR! and run away." Another possible question to be used in a school is "What would you do if the school caught on fire?"

It doesn't take much more than that to get a sense of how conversant a student is in our language. In fact, it's so informal and so deceptively simple, it's possible to overlook the richness of the information you can get. If you take the attention away from yourself and the "testing" situation and put the child at ease, you can glean a great deal of information.

Testing Reading Proficiency

First, you need to find out if the student can read at all. Once you establish that the student is literate, you can determine his level of proficiency.

Although the home language survey (Appendix B) should have given you a good indication of the student's level of education, confirm this by giving him something like the written instructions for a writing sample. Place the instructions sideways on the table. If he turns the paper right side up so that the words can be read, he is probably literate. Now, ask the student to write his name, watching to see how he does it. If he holds his pen awkwardly and writes with difficulty, the student probably has little experience with reading or writing.

Give the student a brief questionnaire similar to the home language survey that asks for name, address, date of birth, and age, as well as some personal questions, such as those asked during the oral language assessment (see Appendix D for an example). The way in which the student answers the questions and fills in the blanks will enable you to make rough assessments of reading and writing skills.

The following tests (story retelling and testing writing proficiency) each focus on specific areas of language acquisition and should be given to the student by the teacher. While these tests are helpful when trying to determine an appropriate grade level, they by no means provide definitive results. They are most useful for the teacher who must plan short- and long-term learning objectives for the students. Again, observation of the student while taking the tests is invaluable.

Story Retelling

If you have been trained in miscue analysis, you can use it with your student. If not, you can have the student read a story by himself, then retell the story to you. His retelling will give you a fairly accurate picture of how much he has understood. As with the oral retelling assessment, you may have to help the student with prompts. Once again, key questions that lead, but don't give the answers away, are useful.

We don't recommend having students read the story aloud to you for several reasons:

- Reading aloud is a separate skill.

- Being required to read aloud when a student is unsure about his reading skills and may be self-conscious about his accent makes the situation uncomfortable. It can often cause the student to pay more attention to his pronunciation than to his understanding of what he is reading.

- Students' oral mistakes often don't reflect their comprehension. Many students who make errors may actually be able to understand the majority of the story.

- As the test giver, it is easy to get frustrated and be tempted to jump in and help when you listen to a student trying to read a passage aloud. It is best to avoid this situation.

Story retelling requires that students use English to repeat the story they've heard or read. As their poor speaking skills may not allow them to communicate what they actually understood, the tester must keep in mind that story retelling is not a precise measuring instrument, only a tool that will provide some insight into students' reading abilities.

The following example contains a story retelling by a high school student whose first exposure to reading was in English. Somaly read *Jacki*, by Elizabeth Rice, a story about a cat who raises a baby rabbit with her kittens. The rabbit thinks she is a kitten too until she sees another rabbit, a "stranger," hanging around the barnyard. After seeing her reflection in a water trough, the little rabbit discovers that she is like the stranger, and when she sees him again, she knows it is time to leave with him and lead a rabbit's life.

Somaly's retelling:

Story about a mother cat was one. He had her baby born—you know, coming out from her. Then about one week or two week they try to open their eye. And then a mother cat had seen rabbit—the little rabbit—and she took her home and living with her family together. You know, and then they live at—in a mother cat home together and rabbit be a cat baby too. And then one cat and one rabbit that stay on the new "starger"—it kind of thing different you know—rabbit and cat stand in the moonlight and they looking something in the moonlight and they saw it. That's it!

Somaly understood the story line about a cat adopting a little rabbit into its family of kittens. She remembered the details of the kittens opening their eyes and the mother finding the baby rabbit. However, from the point in the story where the "stranger" is introduced, Somaly lost the thread. She was not able to guess the meaning from the context, so she did not understand that the "stranger" was another rabbit. She fudges in her retelling: "starger—it kind of thing different you know" and tiptoes around the ending.

Somaly demonstrated she had understood many parts of the story. She also showed some language skills when she retold part of the plot involving the rabbit's relationship with the cats. Somaly's retelling would allow the assessor to see that she had some basic reading skills, but she would need much more reading practice and vocabulary exposure to develop those skills. This information would help her teacher find a starting point for class work.

Testing Writing Proficiency

Writing samples help determine students' ability to communicate coherently in writing.

Obtaining and assessing a spontaneous writing sample, which reflects the student's genuine response to a subject he has an interest in or experience with, is the best way to assess the writing ability of the student.

Give students several topics to choose from and a set amount of writing time (15 minutes for younger students; 30 minutes for older students). Topics might include "something you like to do," "your family," "your first day in this school," or "something frightening that happened to you." (See chapter 6, "Writing," for a more detailed discussion of writing assignments.)

Your scoring criteria for this writing sample should be prioritized beginning with the most important writing skills—those that involve communicating the message—and ending with mechanics. It is easy to be dismayed by a paper filled with grammatical or spelling errors, but these surface errors should not outweigh more critical factors.

The following writing samples are from students who came from Taiwan to take a summer school course in English (figures 2.2–2.6). They had studied English formally in an after-school program for varying lengths of time. Their work samples were chosen as examples, because the students are all roughly the same age, but they display very different skill levels in both speaking and writing. Please note that the questions we asked were specifically geared to their experiences; we had learned beforehand that they would be touring the Southwest prior to their arrival at the school, and we could gear our questions, including the writing sample, to those experiences. Also note that we changed some of the questions, partly in response to their varying skill levels, but also because we found that we were getting the exact same answers from both the less proficient students and the more proficient students. This led us to conclude that those who went before were coaching the ones who came after! Test anxiety was running high.

James

- What's your name? *My name is James.*
- How old are you? *Hello.*
- How long have you studied English? *Yes.*
- Tell me about your family. *I don't know.*
- (We skipped the last question [see figure 2.3] because it would be too confusing.)

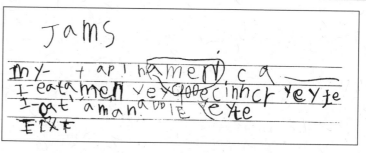

Hereafter, James was affectionately known as "Jams." It is obvious that James is a beginning writer and speaker of English. His sentences are almost unreadable (see top right). The letter formation is awkward and elementary. The letters don't always rest on the line, and words do not always have spaces between them, demonstrating that he has not had much practice yet. There is little organization and only a few recognizable English words. But he does know how to write English letters, and one sentence, which looks like "I eat many very good things," shows an understanding of English syntax.

Content
- Topic is not fully developed
- Two specific details are provided

Organization
- Opening sentence is included

Vocabulary
- James uses a few words correctly. Most others are not distinguishable.

Language Skills
- Many errors, no evidence of knowledge of past tense
- Very basic sentence structure: I + verb

Mechanics
- No punctuation

Level of Proficiency
- Ranked as a high level 1 (see pages 60–62)

Figure 2.2

Royal

- What's your name? *Royal*
- How old are you? *12*
- How long have you studied English? *2 years*
- Tell me three things you like about California? *Here is very good.*
- If you saw a bear in the window what would you do? *(Shrugged)*

Royal shows experience with English. He uses a very good strategy of writing in Chinese words he hasn't learned in English. This demonstrates mastery of his native language and is a valuable clue for testers, even if they are not fluent in the other language. His answers are relatively simple, but he pays attention to detail, lists a number of things, and shows organization.

Content
- Topic is developed
- Specific details are provided
- Description is given

Organization
- Opening sentence is included
- Very orderly, moved from one example to the next
- Transitions used
- Closing sentence is included

Vocabulary
- Effective word choices made, correct use of word forms

Language Skills
- Royal sticks to the present tense
- Grammar is simple but accurate
- Little sentence variety used

Mechanics
- No spelling errors made
- Has control of most punctuation (commas, periods)

Level of Proficiency
- Royal is a level 2. He shows more skills than James and can be asked to complete more difficult tasks.

Figure 2.3

Matty

- What's your name? *Matty*
- How old are you? *12*
- How long have you studied English? *five or six years*
- Tell me three things you like about California? (*No answer*)
- If you saw a bear in the window what would you do? (*No answer*)

Matty's oral skills are not much better than Royal's. She wrote less, but demonstrated, through her writing, a better command of English. Her sentences are more complex. She uses sophisticated connectors such as *so* and *but* correctly.

> My trip in America
>
> We go to the D , I can see Mickey and his girl friend , it is very laidy , so I like. Than I and my friend go to play , but

Content
- Topic is somewhat developed
- Specific details are provided
- No description given

Organization
- Opening sentence is included
- One transition (*than*)

Vocabulary
- Effective word choices made and correct use of word forms

Language Skills
- There is overall control of agreement
- Good sentence variety used
- Effective use of word forms, connectors

Mechanics
- No spelling errors
- Commas and periods used correctly

Level of Proficiency
- Tentatively ranked as high level 2, but further assessment needed to discern whether she can function in the classroom

Figure 2.4

Lady

- What's your name? *Lady*
- How old are you? *12 years old*
- Why do you choose the name "Lady"? *Because my teacher call me Lady all the time*
- What do you like about California? *I like Los Angeles. They have many many funny things and many people.*
- If you saw a bear in the window what would you do? *Climb up tree and loud help me*

Lady wrote much more than the others. She uses connectors such as *and* and *but*, creating complex sentences. She uses adjectives such as *many*, *funny*, and *cool*. This shows a much broader range of English experience and proficiency than the others..

> My trip in America   Lady
>
> We go to many many fun place like Disney Land , Sea World . Mid Lake and Holly wood bowl.
> In Sea World we can saw much kinds of the fish, and the fishs will do mar funny shows it's very good very funny.
> Disney Land is very big and they has much things, but the best show is the Fa mulan of afternoon they with music walk by my eyes.
> This night we saw very cool dence

Content
- Topic is well developed
- Specific details are provided
- Adequate description is given

Organization
- Opening sentence is included
- Very orderly, moved from one example to the next
- Transitions used

Vocabulary
- Effective word choices made, and correct use of word forms

Language Skills
- Sticks mostly to present tense
- One grammatical error ("can saw"), but there is overall control of agreement
- Good sentence variety used
- Effective use of word forms

Mechanics
- One spelling error made
- Has control of punctuation

Level of Proficiency
- Lady has reached a level of proficiency at which she can be expected to do grade-level work, with assistance.

Figure 2.5

Alice

- What's your name? *Alice*
- How old are you? *12 years old*
- Are you glad to be back? *Yes*
- What do you like about California? *Traffic is very good in California, the air is good. Here is so cold.*
- If you got lost, what would you do? *To go ask a policeman*

One can tell by the length of her essay that Alice has a good deal of proficiency. Compared to James's paper, for instance, it is obvious how much more practice Alice has had in forming her letters and writing in this language. She does not need to insert Chinese characters where she doesn't know the English word. She exhibits voice in her writing when she talks about seeing Mickey Mouse and compares America to Taiwan.

My trip in America is very funny. we go to very good place, last week, we go to seaworld, in there, have many fish and fish show. we play very happy. I want to go there again. And we go to disniland. we saw mickey. oh! god! is so so funny. And we go to hollewood. in there has E.T. ...... many many. last day. We go to shopping. we cost many money to buy something. toys. is so quit. And I like here, here is very good. Los Angeles is a good city. The trfic is so good. The air is trible. but is better than Twain. Twain's trfic and air is very bad. Yestoday, we go to shopping more. there is so big. and some body is get lost. There sails many things. And afternoon we go to this summer camp

Content
- Topic is developed
- Specific details are provided
- Adequate description is given

Organization
- Opening sentence is included
- Very orderly, moves from one example to the next
- Transitions used
- Closing sentence is included

Vocabulary
- Effective word choices are made, and correct use of word forms

Language Skills
- One grammatical error made, but overall control of agreement
- Good sentence variety used
- Effective use of word forms
- Her own voice shows through in writing

Mechanics
- A few minor spelling errors made (*trfc, trible, sails*)
- Good control of most punctuation
- Very good description given

Level of Proficiency
- Alice is capable of much more difficult and challenging tasks than James and Royal. She needs less ELL intervention from the teacher and less accommodation of language. Alice has begun to approximate what we might expect from a native-English seventh grader (in fact, she has done better than many).

Figure 2.6

Making Use of Test Scores

The standardized assessment tests, in addition to your school's own supplemental tests, can provide information about what your students are capable of understanding and producing. However, it is unrealistic to think that scores from these tests will tell you everything you need to know about the new students. The main purpose of the test is to give the teacher a sense of how to begin to plan for the newcomers in the classroom.

Categorizing Students

English proficiency is now being defined in terms of both oral and reading proficiency. We believe this is of singular importance. We have seen, too many times, students exited from programs solely on the basis of their oral proficiency. They enter regular classrooms, flounder, and often fail because they have not achieved academic language proficiency. As we stated in the introduction, the labels students are given (LES, LEP, FEP) are frequently inaccurate and do not take into account each student as an individual. We believe the following levels of proficiency are more useful. They allow you to prescribe goals and objectives for your students based upon their English competency. If you feel overwhelmed by all the data that the test scores generate but need somewhere to start your planning, you can begin with these definitions, adapted from WIDA (World Class Instructional Design and Assessment):

Level 1: Beginning/Preproduction (WIDA Level: Entering)

These students do not understand, speak, read, or write in English with the exception of a few isolated words or expressions.

Strategy: These students need a great deal of support. They need to learn survival English to

- Function in the school environment
- Understand routines and rules
- Function in everyday situations (outside school)
- Adapt to climate
- Adapt to a new culture
- Understand holidays

Oral skills

- Begin conversations
- Communicate needs
- Follow directions
- Reading skills
- Recognize the alphabet
- Begin literacy activities

Assimilate level 1 students into the school routine. Coordinate with the ELL support teacher (if you have one), and work on beginning reading skills, background and concept building, and vocabulary. Use one-on-one tutoring, "buddies," and concrete vocabulary. In chapter 5, "Reading," we list many strategies for students such as Bao and James; although James is very low, he is much higher than Bao. Level 1 strategies would work for both of them.

Note: See Appendix E for an example of a checklist designed specifically to assess emerging readers.

At the high-school level, level 1 students derive little benefit from being in mainstream classrooms such as social studies, science, and so on. At this level, oral and reading skills are too low to understand the language of the classroom. Students would benefit from intensive work with an ELL teacher and classes that build basic, core vocabulary.

Level 2: Beginning/Production (WIDA Level: Beginning)

- Students at this level understand simple sentences in English but speak only isolated words and expressions. They understand and speak conversational and academic English with hesitancy and difficulty.

- Students understand parts of lessons and simple directions.

- Students are at a pre-emergent or emergent level of reading and writing in English, significantly below grade level.

Strategy: These students need less intensive support than students at level 1. They have more of the fundamental knowledge that we take for granted, and they usually have basic interpersonal communication skills (BICS). Students at level 2 benefit only minimally from regular classroom instruction without a great deal of support. If you have bilingual support, they can continue working in the first language, building concepts and vocabulary as well as skills in the second language. Students can be mainstreamed for art, math, phys ed, and music. They need to learn content and reading for all subjects. At the secondary level, students would benefit from learning the same content material at a pace geared to their language skills.

Level 3: Intermediate (WIDA Level: Developing)

- These students understand and speak conversational and academic English with decreasing hesitancy and difficulty.

- With effort and assistance, students can carry on conversations in English, understand at least parts of lessons, and follow simple directions, but make noticeable errors in grammar.

- These students have developing comprehension and writing skills in English. Their English literacy skills allow them to demonstrate academic knowledge in content areas, with assistance.

Strategy: Students at this level are usually able to function in the classroom, but need considerable assistance, especially in the content areas. Students need a wide variety of learning experiences that stimulate and encourage language use. The emphasis of your instruction should be on moving students closer to grade level. They need reading/writing assistance in content areas to achieve at an appropriate level for their age and grade. Your academic expectations of level 3 students should be higher than those placed on level 1 and level 2 students.

Level 4: Advanced Intermediate (WIDA Level: Expanding)

- These students understand and speak conversational English without apparent difficulty, but they understand and speak academic English with some hesitancy.

- With assistance, these students continue to acquire reading and writing skills in content areas needed to achieve grade-level expectations.

Strategy: Cognitive academic language development is essential for success in content areas. Oral language proficiency, by itself, is not an accurate measure of holistic language proficiency nor is it a predictor of academic success. In high school, these students can be mainstreamed for classes such as science and held accountable for schoolwork in art, math, and science. However, these students still need help and support.

Level 5: Advanced (WIDA Level: Bridging)

- These students understand and speak conversational and academic English well.

- They are near proficient in reading, writing, and content area skills needed to meet grade-level expectations.

- These students require occasional support.

Strategy: Fully mainstream these students, but continue to give them reading and writing assistance in content areas to achieve at a level appropriate for their age or grade. Even at this level, students are not free from error and may still exhibit lack of background knowledge and/or gaps in reading skills.

Level 6: Full English Proficiency (WIDA Level: Reaching)

- Students understand, speak, read, and write in English, and they possess thinking and reasoning skills needed to succeed in academic classes at or above their age or grade level.

- These students have mastered the specialized language in the subject areas at grade level.

- Students are capable of fluency, accuracy, complexity, and sophistication in their use of English.

Complete proficiency in English can take a long time—Collier (1989) speculates that it can take as long as seven years. Staying on top of what your students know, and balancing their needs with your high expectations, can move them forward to success.

Note: See Appendix F for a detailed form to use when rating writing samples. A student whose writing sample receives the "beginner" rating in any of the five categories is significantly limited in his ability to write in English.

Follow-Up

Be prepared to informally reevaluate ELL students as they become familiar with the school and class routine. Because students are often apprehensive about tests, or because they might feel inhibited in a new environment, their abilities in English may seem weaker than they actually are. They often show their true colors only after they relax and feel more secure. You may find you have to adjust your materials up a level or two as your students adjust to the daily routine.

Note: To demonstrate how to plan a course of instruction, we have included sample IEP (Individualized Educational Plan) forms for the students we have used as examples. (See Appendix G.)

Conclusion

Testing and placement are issues with many gray areas—there are no clear-cut, foolproof answers. Remember that evaluation of test results must be based on the particular student being assessed. Be prepared to be flexible. We have attempted to provide some guidelines, but most decisions must be made on a case-by-case basis, depending on what you and your administrators, the students, and their parents feel are best.

Reflections, Projects, and Projections for Discussion

- Recall a time when an assessment truly measured what you were able to do. What about the assessment or test made this so?

- Recall a time when an evaluation or assessment did not measure your abilities or skills. Why didn't it? How did it make you feel, and what could have been done instead to accurately measure your abilities or skills?

- Once a student is placed, do you have a system for assessing his progress? What methods of assessment will you use to document his progress, and who will this information be for—you, the administration, the parents?

- Assemble a package of materials with which to assess a new ELL student. What do you want to know that will give you enough information to place him in a reading group, give him writing tasks he can succeed at, and so on? Keep several copies of the materials in an easily accessible place so that you don't have to scramble when a new student arrives, and you or a helper can administer this assessment quickly and easily.

- What is a student expected to know at the beginning of grade 1 (for instance, or grade 5, or grade 8, or first semester American History)? What about in January of that grade? By May of that grade? How does having these expectations impact your individualized educational plan for the student?

- In the case studies section (please see below) are writing samples for five students (Vianney, Richard, Yoshuane, Liz, and Tommy). What do these artifacts tell you about their language proficiency? At what level is each student functioning? How do you know? At what grade level would you place each student? What else might be pertinent to know about each student in order to make an appropriate placement into classes, and provide him with appropriate texts and materials? How would you find out more about each student?

- Choose either one of the five students whose writing samples are shown over the next several pages (see case studies), or one of the students whose work we have presented earlier in the book. Think about the class/grade you teach. What assignments could you reasonably expect this student to do?

   What phases does this student need to go through in order to reach the goal? (If this student can write a sentence, what steps does he need to accomplish in order to write an essay?)

Case Studies: Bao, Vianney, Richard, Yoshuane, Liz, and Tommy

Bao

Bao is enrolled in your school. The person who brought her to school said that she knew a little English and had been in school in Fresno before she moved here. When asked her name, she did not answer, but took out a pencil and wrote a lot of random letters (see figure 4.3, page 113). Then, she was asked:

How old are you?
No answer

Tell me about your family.
No answer.

What are you going to do after school today?
Play.

The person assessing her did not ask any more questions, as it seemed obvious that she either could not or was not willing to answer.

Bao could not recognize her name from a field of a series of names. When given a sheet on which the letters of the English alphabet had been printed, she read them as random letters, but mostly called them *G*. When shown a series of numbers, she read "*E, A, I, J, M, J, M, G, BO, B, J.*" When shown the colors, she appeared to be guessing randomly. She did not attempt to identify shapes; in fact, she did not seem to understand the concept of shapes.

- Where do you start with a student like Bao?

- What are your priorities?

- What do you know about Bao based on the information given?

- If Bao were seven years old, where would you place her?

- What if she were 9, 12, or 17?

Vianney

Here is Vianney's placement interview:

> What's your name?
> *Vianney.*
>
> Can you spell it?
> *B a q.*
>
> How old are you?
> *Seven. Two and a five.*
>
> Tell me about your family.
> *My family is a sister and a little one is three.*
>
> What are you going to do after school today?
> *Play with my sister. I with my little one baby.*
>
> Tell me how to get home from here.
> *Over there's my house.*
>
> What would you do if the school caught on fire?
> *(Did not understand the question.)*

Vianney read all her upper and lowercase letters correctly. She also read a series of first grade words—*I, see, yes, can, will, to*—correctly from the list.

Together with an adult she read the pre-kindergarten book *The Ghost*. She read "I see" correctly, and when the adult pointed to the pictures she could "read" *door, window, table, cat,* and *Mom.* She read for meaning, and demonstrated that she was beginning to use sound/letter correspondence.

Vianney wrote the following:

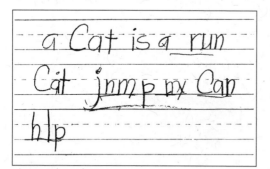

Figure 2.7 Vianney's writing

She read these sentences aloud as: "A cat can run. A cat can jump. A cat can play."

- What do you know about Vianney based on the information given?

- Is she operating at grade level?

- Vianney is seven. Would she succeed in a second-grade class, or would it be preferable to place her in first grade?

- What if she were 17 instead of seven? What placement would be appropriate then?

- What are your priorities for Vianney?

Richard

Richard came to America to experience summer camp. He seemed to be a nice enough boy, but the other kids didn't like him. It became quickly apparent that he still wore diapers, and his parents had sent along Tommy (see page 69) to tend to him and change his diaper when he made a mess.

Here is Richard's placement interview:

What's your name?
My name is Richard.

How old are you?
Eight.

How long have you studied English?
One year.

Name three things about California.
(No answer.)

What would you do if you saw a bear?
(No answer.)

And here is what Richard wrote:

Figure 2.8 Richard's writing

- What do you know about Richard based on the information given?

- If Richard were enrolled in your school what placement decisions would you make?

- Is he operating at grade level for his age?

- What assumptions can you make about Richard's ability to catch on to English and grade-level curriculum, based on his experiences with literacy, which you can't make with Bao or Vianney?

- How does the information about Richard (he still wore diapers and needed a baby sitter along to change them) impact your decisions, or is it even relevant?

Yoshuane

Yoshuane was in fifth grade when he was tested using the Language Assessment Scale (LAS). He had a very easy time with the oral portion of the test. Here is his retelling of a story he listened to:

> *Uh, uh, the girl the girl is I forget what's that uncle called um she didn't see him she since she was six the last time she ever saw him. One night there was a guy that came and started knowcking on the door and it was her uncle and and he said if she could hold this guitar for me to eat and they placed the music and ah the girl's dad was dancing and then she went she went um she was um went to sleep.*

Here are Yoshuane's answers to one page of the LAS.

Figure 2.9 Yoshuane's answers

- What do his answers tell you about his skill level?

- Does this give you any usable information about what to do in the classroom?

- What other information would you want, and where could you find it?

- Based on what you know about him, what grade would you place Yoshuane in, and what kind of support does he need?

- What are your priorities with Yoshuane?

Liz

Here is Liz's placement interview:

What's your name?
Liz.

How old are you?
Fifteen.

How long have you studied English?
One year.

Name three things in California that are different from Taiwan.
(No answer.)

At this point the assessor tried to draw her out using other questions:

Do you like America?
A little.

Is Taiwan better?
Yeah.

What do you like to do?
I like eating.

What kind of food?
Rice.

Do you like basketball?
No.

Do you like music?
No.

Here is Liz's writing:

My first day in America is very bad. because by very long
Tomther I am in Los Angeles.
Is very happy and very fun because we are first play
We can see shop because we are want shopping
I get 3 close I am very very happy
We go to play again Disneyland is very good play
We can see mosths ribbits bird and dogs
Go to this I have more friend I and they is very happy

- What do you know about Liz based on the information given?

- What does the relative sophistication of her writing reveal about her proficiency that her speaking does not?

- How can you account for the difference?

- What features of her writing give you clues about the level she is operating at?

- If she enrolled in your school what placement and programmatic decisions would you make?

- Is Liz operating at grade level for her age?

- What assumptions can you make about her ability to succeed at the grade-level curriculum based on this sample (her writing and the placement interview)?

- What kinds of assistance will Liz require?

Tommy

Here is Tommy's placement interview:

> What's your name?
> *Tommy.*

> How old are you?
> *Seventeen.*

> How long have you studied English?
> *Since I was 13.*

> Tell me about Taiwan.
> *It's dirtier than America. The air is very polluted. And I think the schools are better. I want to go to the university here in California. Then, I'll join the army back home. I can get a better career in Taiwan if I get a degree from America.*

Here is Tommy's writing (see right):

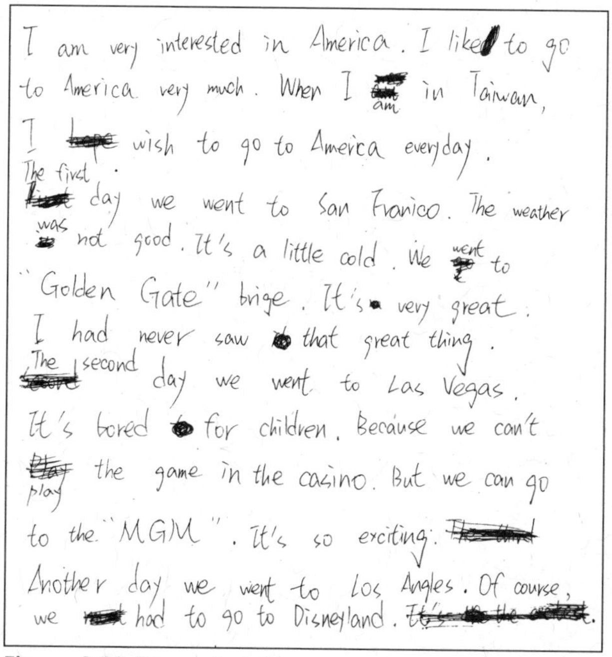

- What do you know about Tommy based on the information given?

Figure 2.10 Tommy's writing

- If Tommy were enrolled in your school what placement decisions would you make?

- Is he operating at grade level for his age?

- What assumptions can you make about his ability to succeed with the grade-level curriculum based on his fluency?

- Can you assume that he will be able to function without any assistance at all? If not, what sort of help might he need and should you give?

Chapter 3

Language Learning for Students *and* Teachers—The Faucets of Language

In this chapter, we discuss principles of second-language learning. We focus on

- What we know about language learning

- A quality program—the factors that influence how fast and how well a newcomer learns English

- Behavior, and what affects it

- Facilitating cultural adjustment in the classroom

- Teaching strategies that help to maximize learning

A Comparison of Two Language Programs

We wanted this chapter to be more than a simple presentation of facts and theories, so we decided to illustrate the principles of second-language learning in the form of an anecdotal history of Barb's experience as an elementary- and secondary-level ELL teacher.

For three years Barb taught ELL in a small Midwestern town adjacent to a large university. The foreign population in the university's married housing complex was so large that each "village" had its own elementary school with its own resident ELL teacher. Barb was responsible for ELL in all the other schools in the district—five elementary schools and two middle schools.

With 25 to 30 students in each of eight grades in seven different schools, Barb had only limited time available to spend with each student—pulling the younger children out of their regular classes for perhaps an hour and a half each week, the middle schoolers for an hour each day.

With such limited access to an ELL specialist, all students were mainstreamed; each student was integrated within the classroom working alongside his classmates and taking part in regular classroom activities as best he could. When the newcomer could not keep up with his English-speaking peers, Barb would supply the teacher with supplemental activities to keep him busy.

Although the pull-out program had its drawbacks—particularly as the students had limited time with a trained ELL teacher and were mainstreamed immediately without any survival English—the students, by and large, did very well. The teachers worked hard to provide them with the best opportunities for learning English.

During her third year, Barb was transferred to a position as full-time ELL teacher at one of the university housing-village schools. Instead of using the same kind of pull-out ELL program found in the other district schools, this school had implemented a self-contained ELL classroom. All ELL students needing assistance spent half the day there, returning to their classrooms in the afternoon for math, physical education, music, and art.

On the surface, this program looked ideal, with several positive features:

- All ELL students were given half a day in the self-contained classroom to work specifically on their English.

- Class size was considerably reduced for regular teachers by having the ELL students spend the morning with another teacher. Thus, classroom teachers could concentrate on their English-speaking students without being held back by those who did not have the understanding to keep up with the mandated curriculum. They were not burdened by the extra preparation and explanation time required when working with ELL students.

- The ELL students were able to work with a teacher who was specially trained in teaching ELL. This appeared to be preferable to remaining in a class for most of the day with a teacher untrained in ELL methodology.

- The ELL classroom provided a safe haven for the students, with a teacher who could give attention to their needs. It was a place just for them, where they could feel secure, valued, and appreciated, rather than being lost in the crowd competing against children who could speak the language of instruction.

This school's program is similar to many others, and many schools searching for ways to meet the needs of ELL students find it an appealing option. A teacher with a third or more of her students unable to speak English is faced with a double load: trying to meet the needs of both groups, but at the same time being required to finish the mandated curriculum by June. The self-contained ELL program lightens her load enormously.

Although there were many positive features to this program, there were also many negative effects due to the reality of the classroom situation. Barb was responsible for more than 30 children, from grades one through five, representing nine different language groups: Spanish, French, Portuguese, Chinese, Japanese, Korean, Hindi, Farsi, and Indonesian. Some, like first-grader Guillermo, had been in the country for over a year, having come to school as a kindergarten student. Others, like fifth-grader Chatphet, arrived in the middle of November, having spent five years in an Indonesian school. Six-year-old Vaji was slow to catch on to the concept of reading, though she spoke English well. Ten-year-old Helga, a smart, aggressive learner, was ready to take on content material in the new language. Third-grader Yoichiro could read well in Japanese, but resented being in America and fought against learning any English. Quiet, gentle, second-grader Laban, who could read Chinese, rarely spoke, but made the transition from Chinese to English with stunning ease.

This range in age, in needs, and in students' abilities to speak and read in English made planning extremely difficult. Thirty-three students meant thirty-three different challenges. Grouping was the obvious answer. But how? According to age? Competence in speaking? Grade-level in reading? And what would Barb teach them? How to say "hello"? What an umbrella is? Colors? Helga and Chatphet were going on to the middle school the following year. Spending time making cut-outs of umbrellas on a rainy day was a waste of their valuable time. They needed to do more than learn only grammar or vocabulary. Barb needed to fill in the academics that were being missed while they were away from their classroom, because a year spent learning only English was a year lost with content matter in subjects like science and social studies.

Barb had two bilingual aides, Spanish-speaking Emma, and Midori from Japan. Both were intelligent, dedicated women who worked hard to make the atmosphere pleasant and the learning experience a successful one for each child. Neither, however, was a native-English speaker, and neither spoke perfect English. This meant that for the majority of the day, the children listened to English spoken either by their classmates, who had not fully learned English, or by adults, two of whom had not fully mastered English either. The models to which the children were exposed were not adequate or appropriate for their needs.

The friendships that formed in the ELL class extended to the playground and after school. For example, Japanese boys played only with each other, talking in Japanese. Several of the little girls in the class made friends, but only communicated in rudimentary English sentences, which were rarely extended and enriched by exposure to the English of their peers.

The solution to meeting the needs of all students was grouping, which was a compromise between age, reading ability, and language competence. However, since each child was working at a different level, all needed constant supervision. The student-teacher ratio was about 11 to 1, larger than the optimal ratio for a situation such as this when each student is working at a different level.

Most important, these children were isolated, segregated from their peers, away from the mainstream for that portion of the day when most of the content and skill development took place, listening only to their teachers and the imperfect English of other newcomers. Lack of access to fluent, model English speakers significantly slowed both their English acquisition and their assimilation. The process of acquiring enough "survival" English took much longer.

What We Know About Language Learning

Even though the self-contained program was set up with the best of intentions, the teachers who originated and supported it were operating under certain assumptions that run counter to what we know about language acquisition. We have outlined some of these ELL-learning myths:

Incorrect Assumptions

- Language must be taught.

- Input in the new language must be sequenced and carefully controlled.

- The language teacher is in the best position to decide what vocabulary and concepts to introduce, and when to do so.

- Newcomers need to master English before they can learn any subject matter.

- Once students have learned the language of instruction—in this case, English—their problems in the classroom are largely over, and they should be able to handle their academic assignments with no difficulty.

- Regular classroom teachers are not equipped to give their ELL students the best opportunities for language learning.

Research Results

A great deal of research has been done on first-language and second-language acquisition. This research has revealed that

- **Second language learning is most effective when the setting is natural.** Communication is a two-way street; there is a speaker who has something to say and a listener who wants to hear it. Without these three components—speaker, listener, and message—there is no communication. Learning a language is much more than just learning the vocabulary or the grammatical rules; it's knowing how and when to use those rules even in ordinary conversation. This may seem self-evident, but much of the second-language teaching that takes place in schools ignores this fact and teaches only vocabulary and rules. The result is students who can conjugate verbs but cannot carry on a simple conversation.

- **Students learn from their peers.** Because the use of language is first and foremost a social activity, students learn best from those they work, live, and play with every day. They learn to make sentences and interact in order to meet their social needs: to make friends, to be included in games, to express themselves. No matter how dedicated and resourceful the teacher is, she cannot provide the kind of input that learners need to understand how to use the language in real-life situations. The language that students learn from their peers is a *living* language; they have learned it only by and through communication within situations that are important to them.

- **Although second-language learners usually learn certain forms in a set order (such as learning the *-ing* ending on verbs before they learn the articles *a, an, the*), presenting language in a sequence (such as the present tense first, then the past tense) is *not* the most effective way of teaching.** This method ignores the needs of learners by limiting their exposure to as much grammar and vocabulary as can be easily presented and practiced at one time. Students may need to say things such as, "I took my mother to the doctor yesterday, so I couldn't come to school," or, "I am going back to Mexico for a few weeks. I'll be back after Christmas." They may need to comprehend advanced language forms such as, "If you don't hand in all your assignments, you'll get an *F*." Sequencing forms rigidly, teaching structures one at a time, and proceeding only when the structure is learned (the way many of us were taught foreign languages) limits students' ability to function within all the situations they might encounter.

- **A new language is learned best when the primary focus is on the meaning, not the form.** In other words, students learn how to make friends, satisfy their own needs, and learn new things by *using* the language, not by perfecting grammatical forms (such as tenses) one at a time. Learners make mistakes; this is a natural part of learning anything. However, with practice, they gradually get better at figuring out the rules. Communication comes first, then grammatical rules are learned as a part of learning to communicate effectively, not the other way around.

- **Non-native-English speakers do not need to master English by studying it formally as an isolated activity *before* they can begin regular class work.** Language should be learned through content material as long as the material is understandable. ELL students generally have more ground to make up and less time in which to do it.

- **There is a misperception that learning to speak English well will equip ELL students to handle regular class work.** Research has shown this is not necessarily so. It often takes five to seven years to achieve sufficient fluency in academic English to compete on par with other English-speaking students. To hold students in ELL classes or special programs until they are fully proficient in all areas is unrealistic, impractical, and, in the end, impossible.

- **Although support from bilingual or ELL personnel is helpful and important, it is not enough.** You, the classroom teacher, are a key factor in the success of the ELL student, provided you employ appropriate methods for teaching non-English speakers and you supply both understandable situations and opportunities for the student to interact with classmates.

A Quality Program

The two programs Barb taught—the pull-out program and the self-contained ELL classroom—were vastly divergent solutions to the challenge of teaching ELL students. Each had positive features, but neither was ideal. The pull-out program provided small-group tutoring on gaps in learning and individual help with class work. The self-contained program attempted to deal with the linguistic needs of the students in an intensive way.

Accelerators and Roadblocks to Language Learning

Accelerators

Language learning is easier when

- The purpose of using language—reading, writing, speaking, and listening—is real and natural
- The focus is on communication
- There are lots of opportunities to talk and interact with native-English speakers
- Talk is about interesting topics
- Mistakes are part of learning
- Language is always used—or studied—within a context, not as isolated letters, words, or sentences
- Language has a purpose for the learner
- Students speak only when they're ready
- Sufficient time is provided for learning
- Students can talk to each other in their own language
- The first language is viewed as a valuable resource

Roadblocks

Language learning is harder when

- The reasons given or situations created for using language are artificial
- The focus is on the form, not the function (communication)
- ELL students are isolated
- Talk is dull and uninteresting
- Mistakes are viewed as bad, and the implication is that it's more important to get it right than to get a message communicated
- Language is studied out of context
- The particular use of language studied or assigned is irrelevant for the learner
- Students are forced to speak
- Students are pressured to complete work or make progress
- Students are not allowed to speak and converse in their native tongue
- The first language is not valued; it is denigrated or forbidden

Figure 3.1 What we know about language learning

Barb's experience may be nothing like your own. You may be teaching in a district with 1 or 12 students whose first language is not English. The school district might be ignoring the related issues. Or, you might be teaching in an area that has large numbers of ELL students, and the schools have mounted a full-scale ELL program with many bilingual or ELL teachers.

But, no matter how many ELL students you have in your class or district, the issues remain the same. Over the past several decades, and since the first edition of this book was published in 1990, the number of non-English-speaking students arriving in our schools has burgeoned and shows no sign of leveling off (Capps et al 2005).

School systems and community support systems, particularly the ones that are new to the issue of educating ELL students, are straining to meet the needs of these newcomers. We must strive to put together quality programs that will meet their needs.

How do we do this? What constitutes a quality program? How are students' needs best met? Handscombe (1989) writes:

> *A quality program for second-language learners will neither segregate all students until they are "fit" to join their peers, nor will it place them in a regular classroom with the expectation that they will learn all they need to learn on their own...The ideal is a program that supports second language students' learning for the entire day.*

In the early days of our careers, the language teacher often assumed the responsibility (and the blame) for the limited-English students. The time spent with this specialist was regarded as the "real" learning time. During the remainder of the day, the students simply marked time until they were proficient enough to participate fully in regular classroom activities. This was the situation when Barb began teaching 25 years ago, and, to our dismay, we continue to see this scenario today. Much of ELL teaching is simply Band-Aid work. We can, however, give one cheer to former President George W. Bush's odious No Child Left Behind (NCLB) Act of 2001 for at least forcing schools to take notice, take stock, and finally take action. The business of English language learning has emerged from the bogey room, and many schools are finally taking the needs of our students seriously.

Preparing Students for Real Life

The traditional roles of the classroom teacher and the language teacher—the former teaching content and the latter teaching language—are rigid, artificial, inefficient, and inexcusable. What we need today are

- A common agenda

- Partnerships between stakeholders

When we reviewed this section of the first edition of our book, our assertions seemed, at first blush, hopelessly naive. However, upon reflection, we remain committed to these two fundamental principles 20 years later. They underlie everything else. But, even though they seem simple, they are punishingly difficult to achieve. Why? Because we still see

- Endless bickering between ideological factions

- Political agendas that supersede the needs of the students

- A lack of communication between the levels within the education system (elementary, middle school, high school, and college)

- Inadequate attention and funding, which results in some students being relegated to a corner of the classroom and, at best, second-class status

- Aimless wandering (by teachers, administration, and political powers) without concrete goals or a plan for setting objectives

The ultimate goal of education today is for our students to become critical thinkers, problem solvers, collaborators, and effective communicators. But many students graduate from high school without some or all of these skills. They are unprepared for a post-secondary education—and, eventually, for the real world.

A recent study conducted by the Strong American Schools initiative and called *Diploma to Nowhere* (2008) stated baldly, "A hoax is being played on America. The public believes that a high school diploma shows that a student is ready for college-level academics. Parents believe it too. So do students." According to the study, about 34 percent of incoming college freshman find, to their shock, discouragement, and disillusionment, that even if they got A's and B's in high school, they need remedial work in either English, math, or both. The cost of this remediation to the public is about two billion dollars a year.

Whose fault is this? The easy thing to do is to blame teachers. It seems that the educators above always blame the ones below (high school teachers blame elementary teachers, college teachers blame high school teachers) for not preparing students effectively. But we work very hard to prepare our students. However, other agendas get in the way.

There are multiple factors which result in students being unprepared for post-secondary education and for the real world. Parents, administrators, and outside demands put on the school all play into a school's lack of focus on what is supposed to be the ultimate goal of education. Parents bully teachers for better grades. Administrators occasionally get into the act, sometimes focusing on students' athletic abilities rather than on academic ones, or to keep the bottom line looking good. If you are a teacher without tenure, do you back down when the principal wants you to adjust a grade or when parents are screaming at you and the vice principal is looking out the window? Most schools and teachers do their best, but other things can hinder their best efforts.

Mary's kids went to a suburban school. They went on to Berkeley, prepared for college because they had teachers who helped them get them ready, a home where school and homework were important, and friends who wanted to achieve too.

Barb's kids went to an inner-city school where the student population was 95 percent minority. Barb's daughter, Kate, graduated in a class of 114 students—of the 300 that started in 9th grade. She still had great teachers and got a solid education, not just in academics, but in life itself.

Barb recently finished teaching a community-college class of unprepared adults. Over the weeks, the class dwindled to two students. Sometimes only one student came to class. Abusive husbands, hospital visits, broken-down cars, jobs with changing hours—life gets in the way. Cobb (2005) remarked that "it is typically endurance rather than ability that is the greatest barrier to success." Many of our English language learners lack the endurance for success due to life circumstances. Many live in poverty, some are illegal immigrants, several struggle to overcome emotional baggage, and some have major responsibilities at home.

It isn't enough to teach your subject. You need to know what's coming next and how to get there. This is doubly important when every language learner who walks in the door is a wild card—a unique combination of variables, which means the status quo won't work. If Bao arrives in the seventh grade not knowing the English alphabet, how do we get her ready to graduate fully proficient and reading at grade level? What steps do we need to take? Every teacher needs to know the whole picture and how what she does fits into that picture so she can operate as effectively as possible. And regardless of the choices that a school makes about programs, courses, and curriculum, the needs of the students *must* come first.

The entire point of educating *all* children, including immigrant children, is to prepare them to function within the larger society. Lucas (1997) writes:

> [To] participate fully in...business, government, and education, all residents must have a command of English...A primary goal of everyone associated with the education of immigrants and English language learners is to help them develop English skills strong enough to move into mainstream classes, where they will be integrated with native-born students and where they can participate in the regular curriculum and instruction.

The majority of the controversy among educators and other stakeholders has been about how we achieve that goal. If we keep this primary goal firmly in mind, however, perhaps we can transcend the squabbling that has crippled programs and hindered progress. The first priority should be the child. What does he need? Where is he now, in terms of learning the curriculum, of English proficiency? Where does he need to go? One size does not fit all. This means that the program model cannot take precedence over the population at hand. Any and all programs have their merits and can be successful if they are based on the particular needs of the students within that school or district.

A Common Agenda

Language is everybody's business and everybody's responsibility. This means:

- All teachers must be prepared to accept and teach immigrant students.

- Classroom teachers must adapt their curriculum and their teaching style to include students who are less than proficient in English.

- Schools must be responsive and flexible to the needs of newcomers in terms of access to academic concepts and skills, time to learn English, trained personnel, and alternative and multiple pathways to achievement (Lucas 1997).

- There needs to be recognition that there is no one best way.

Research shows (EdSource 2007) that effective schools

- Promote collegiality, cooperation, and communication. This means supportive administrators who encourage open doors and teachers who trust each other enough to share what they're doing. It means knowing the principal is watching your back and not his, a principal who understands that a school is only as good as the morale of its teachers, who isn't punitive, who concentrates on getting you what you need to do your job well.

- Focus on all students and their achievements, not just on the under-achievers. When schools and principals have a clear picture of the present situation and a definite vision of the future, they know how to orchestrate efforts so that the school supports the weaker students without punishing the teachers who work with them.

  When Barb taught middle school in Las Vegas, she was called into a meeting concerning standardized test scores. At enormous cost in terms of time and resources, the test scores had been broken down to each minute item of the standards, and just how short of the "passing" mark students were for each item tested had been calculated. Teachers were told to focus on any items that students were within a point or two of passing. For instance, it was calculated that students scored –12 in the area of "Nouns, Pronouns, Modifiers: Irregular Plurals and Homonyms"; therefore teachers were told to focus their attention on those areas, with the rationale that extra coaching in that discrete area would bring students up in the next round of testing.

  This is the ultimate example of misuse of time and energy due to ignorance on the part of administrators. One thing had been sacrificed for another. Gone was the richness in curriculum. Gone was what benefits all students—everything but the minute points of grammar. The students who didn't need to work on commas were ignored, to focus on the needs of those few who did. If we dump our curriculum to focus on those who are failing, we forget those who sail. In the same vein, if we focus on one language group—in this case, the English speakers—and let the others—the ELLs—slide, because there are fewer numbers, we are failing that latter segment. We can't forget our ELLs any more than we can we forget our mainstream students.

- Ensure the availability of instructional resources. Resources include trained teachers, enough materials for both classroom teachers and specialists to adequately do their jobs. It means taking ELL out of the broom closet and providing professional development to keep up to date.

Partnerships Between Stakeholders

Education stakeholders include the ELL teacher, the bilingual teacher, the classroom teacher, administration, students, and parents. ELL and bilingual teachers can offer their expertise on language learning and second-language methodologies, while classroom teachers can offer their knowledge of the curricular content to be covered and skills to be learned. When these stake-holders collaborate, at the elementary level, ELL students are integrated within the classroom with their English-speaking peers (unless sheer numbers preclude it), and the ELL or bilingual teacher works within that classroom, or with small groups in another locale, on concepts that the rest of the class is learning. In some schools, the ELL teacher team teaches closely with content teachers. Regular meeting and planning are priorities to ensure that both the students' language needs and content needs are being met, and that both teachers are making maximum use of their time and energy.

High school students have needs that are different from elementary students, and they require different programs. They are making multiple transitions: from a known cultural milieu into an unfamiliar one; from childhood, through adolescence, into adulthood; from the protected, insular, one-teacher classroom of elementary school to the sometimes overwhelming array of classes at the secondary school (Lucas 1997). High school students have less time than elementary students to learn English and master the academic content required to graduate from high school (Chips 1993). Traditional high schools are often not equipped (and are resistant) to adapting their structure or programs to the needs of these students. At the high school level, bilingual support, or one or more ELL classes per day, is probably the minimum newcomers need at first. The ELL teacher can reinforce concepts taught in the content classes, or if trained teachers are available, content can be taught in the first language. Once again, the coordination of objectives is paramount.

In addition, partnership means collaboration within the school and outside the school: between students and teachers, among students, between schools and families, and with community-based organizations and institutes of higher learning (Lucas 1997).

Content teachers should identify and define the minimum amount of knowledge and competency a student needs to receive a passing grade for the class—knowledge of essential vocabulary and concepts (see chapter 8, "Content-Area Instruction"). Armed with this knowledge, the ELL teacher can review with the students, accurately diagnosing content and language deficiencies. Language structures can be taught within the framework of these lessons, making them both usable and useful: for history classes, they can work on correct use of the past tense; for science classes, they can work on cause and effect, and *what if* questions.

One method now widely practiced is the "Sheltered English" approach.[1] This instructional process teaches subject matter in an understandable way to students whose English is not sufficiently proficient to manage in regular content courses. It is not "watered down" content; it is content offered at the language level of the student. History, for instance, is taught to ELL students in high school using a lower grade-level book. The ELL students study the same content as students in regular history classes and receive credit for completing

---

1 In California: Specially Designed Academic Instruction in English (SDAIE). For more detailed discussion of this approach see Echevarria and Graves 1998, Echevarria et al 2000, Lucas 1997, and Short in Faltis and Wolfe 1999.

a requirement for their high school diploma. Modified instruction appropriate for ELL students is also effective practice for your regular content-area classes, which means you aren't sacrificing the needs of your native-English speakers while working with the language learners. (We demonstrate how to do this in chapter 8.)

Learners, Teachers and Language Learning

Language learning is a balance between the learner and the language-learning environment, between "input" and "intake." Input is the language the student hears and encounters daily. Intake is how much of this input the student actually processes and acquires. On the input side of the equation, there is the teacher, the amount and quality of her training, the materials and methods used, and the manner in which (and how often) the teacher corrects errors.

The climate within the classroom is an important factor in language learning: does the learner feel accepted and free to try out his new language without fear of ridicule and punishment? Another factor is the amount of exposure the student gets to the language: does he hear it only at school, speaking his native language at home? Does the student get input only from the teacher? Or does he have English-speaking friends who will talk to him and guide him through the linguistic maze?

You can provide an optimal environment and still have your students learn at different rates and with varying degrees of success. This is because so much learning is dependent on the students themselves. Regrettably, input does not necessarily equal intake.

Intake and the Learner

On the intake side, there are many factors that influence how much language the learner is able or willing to learn: factors within the learner himself and factors related to the learner's culture. In fact, as Samway and McKeon note (2007), second language acquisition is really "a function of variables" that come together to impact success or lack thereof.

We will discuss several of the most important variables within the learner that affect language acquisition. The psychological factors that either allow in or screen out the incoming language are called "affective filters" (Burt and Dulay 1982).

Important Factors That Affect Language Acquisition

- **The learner's personality.** Is the student outgoing and confident, or withdrawn and shy? Bounkham is very talkative and attempts to make himself understood by using gestures and examples. He is very motivated and interested in opportunities to express himself. He participates in any activity gladly, studies hard, and jumps into conversations, laughing when he stumbles or makes mistakes. By the end of his first year in his new school,

Bounkham is able to take part in all classroom work, while Newton, who is shy and quiet, is just beginning to make headway. He doesn't seem to be very active outdoors, except that he enjoys the solitary activity of riding his bike. He needs to be coaxed to talk and to become involved in activities.

- **Attitude and motivation.** A student's aspirations also play a role. Many students are driven to succeed, or are pressured by their families to earn degrees and get ahead in the world. Does the learner really want to know this new language? Andre tells his tutor time and again that he doesn't *want* to learn English. He anticipates going home very soon. His progress is very slow, and he forgets what he learned the day before. Fernando, however, wants to learn English in a hurry. As the eldest son, he must help his family adjust to life in America, interpreting at the doctor's office or with the landlord, buying groceries, and paying bills. He also wants to make friends and get into the swing of things as quickly as possible, and one way to speed up this process is to learn English.

- **Previous educational background.** If your student has been to school before, he knows at least some of the routines, the expectations, the functions of different people. If he hasn't, he may not even know how to sit in a desk. He may not be able to focus for an entire day, when he's used to being outside. He may have no experience with print, and thus have to start literacy from scratch.

  Fong, for instance, arrived in the U.S. at age seven with no previous educational experience. He was placed in kindergarten, because he had no print awareness, even though he was two years older than his classmates. His older brothers and sister were in middle school. They needed to begin with the alphabet as well, but they also needed to be taught general hygiene. They were beginning to smell! Mrs. Gilman, the ELL teacher, had to take them aside and counsel them about bathing regularly.

- **Age.** Mary knows of one family of seven that came from Laos. The children's ages ranged from 8 to 30. They had all been in the United States for the same amount of time and had all attended English classes. Within the year, the younger ones were able to speak well enough to translate for the older ones. By the second year, the younger ones had little accent and were making great strides in catching up with their peers in class. The older children did not progress nearly as well.

  Teachers intuitively sense—and they see this in their classes constantly —that younger learners learn better and faster. But some researchers claim that older learners are more successful over the long haul. Although this controversy has largely been abandoned, it lingers. According to Stephen Krashen (1982), what is at issue is the difference between acquisition and learning. Younger children simply learn differently from older ones. Little ones acquire a second language much like they do the first: by listening, understanding, and eventually speaking—largely an unconscious process. They aren't aware that they are learning the language; they are simply aware that they are communicating. While older learners do a great deal of acquiring too, they also seem to need to learn language consciously, sometimes painstakingly, by learning vocabulary and the grammatical rules.

The age factor in language learning is a murky area that has not been satisfactorily clarified by experts. Partly because they are motivated to make friends and have few inhibitions about making mistakes, young children jump right into learning the new language. Older learners, however, have many other things on their minds. They have responsibilities to school and family and cannot devote the same amount of time to focus on learning. Older learners are also less willing to experiment with new forms, and more interested in saving face, playing it safe with linguistic structures they are sure of, rather than embarrassing themselves in front of native-English speakers. Older learners also have more linguistic demands placed on them than do younger ones. Young children are usually only required to communicate orally, and their language skills can grow along with their minds as they grapple with more and more sophisticated ideas. Adolescents and adults are required to use more complex types of language to coincide with the complex reasoning processes demanded by school and society. These language skills take much longer to acquire than the interpersonal language skills needed to get by on the playground or in the street.

- **State of mind.** Mary had a student who came dutifully to class, never missing a day. However, soon after class got underway, Boua would rest his head on his hand, unwilling to participate in class activities. If asked questions, he would politely answer with a smile but still seemed to hang on the edge of things. When Mary finally found an interpreter, she discovered that Boua had suffered head injuries fighting in his country. The bullet, still lodged in his head, caused horrendous headaches. He came to class because he wanted to learn English and felt some comfort by being able to participate, if only marginally. How your student is feeling, how stable his life is, how preoccupied he is with emotions like loneliness and homesickness, with culture shock, or with outside distractions such as family responsibilities, profoundly influences his ability to absorb and use the input he is receiving.

  This last variable is extremely complex. Often the things that affect your student's state of mind are either beyond his control or operate at an unconscious level. These factors are so important that we have devoted the entire next section to them.

Behavior and What Affects It

Moving is difficult under any circumstance. For some of us, moving across town, away from familiar scenes and faces, can be a wrenching experience. How much more those feelings are magnified for students who come from halfway around the world! Barb's youngest was six when they moved to Syria. Most of the time he seemed happy and well-adjusted, but at the most inopportune times he would have tantrums that left the family totally aghast, embarrassed, and helpless. He was too young and too bewildered to be able to understand what he was experiencing much less articulate his feelings of loss and confusion, so they came out as horrendous behavior no one quite knew how to address. (Thankfully, the moment they returned to the U.S., he was back to his old happy-go-lucky self, and the tantrums never returned.)

The changes ELL students have to cope with are many and great, and they may never get to go home again. These can have a far-reaching effect on their assimilation and can also sometimes lead to behavioral issues. Understanding what's going on is part of the key to coping.

Changes ELL Students Experience

- **A change in geography and climate.** Students from tropical Southeast Asia, for example, who are relocated to places such as Minnesota, are unprepared for the severity of the winters. Barb remembers wearing mittens and a winter jacket to go trick-or-treating with her children and seeing many of the neighborhood children of newly arrived immigrants running around in sandals and t-shirts. One boy, relocated from the refugee camps in Thailand wrote:

  > *The weather was so cold and snowing. I never saw the snow before. I thought it was ice. I asked my dad how can you live here? Everything was dead. I said the big tree was dead too what else is going to be safe.*

- **A change from rural to urban settings.** Refugees from the farms of Cambodia and Laos have found themselves thrust into inner-city tenements with few trees or birds, without even a tiny plot of land to till. Native Americans from reservations find themselves having to adjust to the big city.

- **A change in size of the living environment and/or the economic situation.** Many refugees, often farmers or previously well-to-do businessmen, have lost everything and arrive in this country with only the clothes on their backs. Abir's family, who had servants back in their home country, is now crowded into a tiny apartment.

- **A change in the culture of school.** Schools are different in North America from most other parts of the world. In many other countries students wear uniforms, they sit in rows, they are not expected to render their own opinions or to talk among themselves. The student-centered learning of many classrooms today seems chaotic and ungoverned to those who come from the "transmission approach" to education. Many students are at a loss for how to function in classrooms such as these, and, like Abir, avoid school as much as possible, or, like Boris, become almost uncontrollable at times.

- **A change in social status or opportunities and goals.** A number of refugees, such as many of the Cubans and Vietnamese, were the elite, well-educated professionals in their home countries and arrived to find their licenses or degrees invalid in North America. Doctors and dentists can often find work only as gardeners or factory workers, unable to make the most of their skills. Boris's mom was a physician in their home country. In order to get a license here she would have to start over completely. She works as a cashier in a gas station. Boris finds this very demeaning and is ashamed of her.

- **The reason for the changes.** Although many new immigrants come to the United States or Canada to find a better life, others, like Andre and his family, fled their countries out of fear for their lives, not out of a desire to live elsewhere. For them, the move was a forced choice. According to one expert, an immigrant leaves his homeland because the grass is greener; a refugee leaves because the grass is burning under his feet. Thus, refugee students often have emotional ties to their homeland and continue to nurture the hope of returning there, only allowing themselves to become marginally involved with their new home. Andre's mother refuses to learn more than the rudiments of English. There's no point, she argues, when she's going home anytime.

  One student wrote:

  I do not know how well others are doing in term of trying to adapt American's culture. My family is not doing well; my parents are giving up trying to make living from scrap. They said that they are too old. Both of my parents has no education. As they begin to live a comfortable life with stable income and properties, they had to fled to a totally different country with almost everything different. Very few people who live in their country for many generations understand the pain and suffer immigrants have build up inside.

- **The change itself.** For many, the move has been traumatic, if not life threatening. Francis has missed several days in a row. When one of the other students mentions, as if it is common knowledge, that he has a bullet in his leg, the teacher asks, quite innocently, if he was a soldier. Abe, another student from a country that has seen endless warfare says, casually, "In Africa, everyone is a soldier."

  One can only guess at the experiences some of our students have been through. They won't talk about it, nor is it our place to ask. Some have seen their parents murdered or their families separated by war. Some must deal with the guilt of being the child chosen to live, while their siblings were left behind to face certain death. Many have lived through days at sea on unseaworthy boats without food or shelter; others have walked hundreds of miles to safety. Many have left loved ones behind and are faced with the anxiety of not knowing whether these people are still alive. They live in a sort of limbo, waiting for their lives to right themselves somehow.

  One boy wrote:

  When I was a small boy, my mom died. I was crying every day looking for her. Because the enemy killed her. We didn't have food. We didn't have clothes. Because the enemy came to fight at my country, I'm not happy for the one that make my country fall down to another hand. They called mine was their. Now, we are just like the chicken. I think the chicken was more important than we are. We have a language, but we don't use mine. We use another language. Its too hard, when I think about that. It makes me cry. Do you know how hard we study English?

- **A change in the language.** This element compounds the loss of a student's lifestyle and homeland for all our students. Being unable to speak English slows students' ability to adjust to North America. They can't understand the school routine. They can't make friends easily. They can't fit in. They have no one to show them the ropes and, most important, no one who is able to provide the emotional support and reassurance that they are accepted.

  One student wrote:

  I have an advantage over many other ELL students because I have had a lot of instruction in English and the textbooks that I used in the Philippines were often in English. My biggest problem is I still feel shy about using the language. I find it difficult to understand everything that is said in class, so when I get home I have to read everything in my textbook to make sure I understood. I probably won't ask questions, and you probably won't guess that I'm still struggling with the language.

- **A change in the way language is used.** Another widely researched issue is the linguistic cues and patterns of interactions used by different language and ethnic groups (see Au 1980, 1985; Heath 1983; Michaels 1981; Philips 1972; Fillmore 1986). School, particularly in the areas of reading instruction and assessment, can serve as a gate-keeping organization. Mismatches between what teachers assume is correct and the linguistic styles of the students can result in frustration and, possibly, negative attitudes toward one another. For example, students who speak loudly might be thought of as aggressive. Those who believe that interrupting is a sign of being engaged can be thought of as rude.

  Teachers who are culturally sensitive can adjust their styles of interaction to those of the students. This isn't easy, and when you have a number of different language backgrounds and styles within one classroom, you can go crazy trying to accommodate them all. At the risk of oversimplifying an enormously complex issue, we want to state that over the years we've found that an open mind and a genuine liking of the kids can go a long way to overcoming these sorts of hidden barriers.

- **A change in their relationship with their parents.** Often younger children find themselves shouldering many of the responsibilities that were traditionally designated to adults. Andre has found himself translating at the doctor's office or the license bureaus; he writes the checks; he steers his bewildered parents and grandparents through the maze of bureaucracy. This has caused an imbalance in the power structure within his family, and the roles are reversed or muddied. His father is not the head of the family anymore: in many ways, Andre is. The fallout that occurs has been acute in some families, leading to rebellion and disrespect, and, at worst, a rejection of the old culture. The North American emphasis on freedom of thought and the encouragement to discuss his point of view has led Andre to openly rebel against the very strict hierarchy of his traditional society.

Culture Shock

The following charming letters, written by students and responded to by another student, who is wise beyond her years, exemplify some of the issues that confront our newcomers.

Dear Senorita Fix It:

I have a serious problem. I am Korean and I'm living in an apartment with two Americans. We are having a desagreement about food. My roommates don't like the smell of the Korean food. They don't like the smell of Kim Chee and the sauces I use. They won't let me cook. They say; "Eat sandwiches," but I'm bored with American food. I eat it for six month and I'm loosing weight. What can I do? Please, help me. —*Getting Thin Fast*

Dear Getting Thin Fast

You must know that there is a lot of oriental people here especially form Japan. I know that Japanese food is similar to Korean food. It's a good idea join whit these people and to cook together. In this way you can make friends and resolve your problem at the same time. And you can remember to that there is no damn for 100 years and there is no body that can bear that.

Dear Senorita Fix It:

I am a exange student. My only idea when I came was to study hard and make a major, but I meet a girl here. We started being good friends, then we started going out and finaly we fall in love each other. We both know than I need to come back to my country as soon as I finish my major, but I really love that girl. What can I do? Please, help me. —*Signed: Heart Broken*

Dear Mr. Heart Broken:

Do you know What the word preocupied means? PREOCUPIED, PREOCUPIED means to be ocupied in something before it happens. Many times we do that. We are extremly worried about something that we think is going to be to hard and wasting energy thinking about that and when it comes it doesn't bring any problem. I think that you are having an extremly beautiful experience in your life. Sombody who share with is one of the best things in the word that somebody can have. How can I thing about tomorrow if I have not resolve my today's problems? Time solve everithing and luck has the last word.

Dear Senorita Fix It:

I'm a exchange student. When i knew about the program, I thought that it was a great oportunity to come tu the United States and to learn English and other classes at the same time. I worked hard and safe money to come and now I'm here. But things are not as I expected. I've got problems with the language. Is hard for me to espeak and to understand English. I've got a job, but I dont like it and I need to do that because I need the money. Dormitories are to far from bars and others fun places and you can't go if you don't have a car. More than I've got problems with my roommate. He use my food card and drink my juices!! So, now I wonder my self, what am I doing here? PLEASE HELP ME! —Signed: Loosed

Apreciated loosed:

Many, many times we blame to our family, or school, our teachers, the country, the weather, etc. about our "bad luck". Here, there and anywhere life is hard and we need to fight to be better. I just wanna ask you. Is mom here? Is somebody of your family 10 miles around or 100 miles?

While students are individuals, they are also members of the particular culture they were born into. The culture of a society embodies elements that are tangible: clothing, food, festivals, social customs, and so on. It also encompasses the intangible elements: the values of the society, its world view, its attitudes concerning life and death. Our culture helps define us mentally and spiritually. It also dictates how we interact with society.

Many students from other cultures, including Native Americans, are confronted with the awesome task of functioning in a society they don't understand. There is a mismatch between our culture and the one of their heritage. Their own culture has a different set of norms for simple things we take for granted, such as how to address the teacher, how close to stand to the person they are talking to, how loud to talk. Much of what they see and hear in North America is in direct conflict with their own set of cultural values: people sitting with their legs crossed so that the soles of their feet are showing, dating, displaying affection in public, openly questioning a teacher's point of view. They often feel confusion, conflict, and helplessness over the wide disparity between what they have hitherto believed, unquestioningly, to be right and what they experience in everyday North American life. These feelings are defined as "culture shock."

One boy from Ethiopia put it this way:

I come from a culture and a language very different from yours. In fact, our whole way of making our society is very different. The school I went to is also very different in many ways. I'm still having culture shock. Yes, my parents chose to come to canada to make a better life for us, so I really want to try hard.

Faced with the task of coming to terms with this new culture, students like Boris, Beverly, and Angel must decide for themselves how they want to fit in and what kinds of compromises they are willing to make in order to succeed.

Becoming acculturated to the conventional North American way of life can sometimes lead to conflict. Many ELL students feel that they must abandon their old ways. Children, who are often more adaptable than their parents, embrace our culture more readily, which can lead to tension between the generations. Hibe, for instance, began school at age five. She was outspoken and sociable, expressing her opinions in a forthright manner. This worried her parents, who believed women have a submissive place in society. What Hibe's North American school encouraged was in direct conflict with what her parents believed was acceptable.

Gaida, who emigrated with her parents at age 11, threw herself into the North American lifestyle, becoming a cheerleader and a star on the girl's volleyball team in high school. By the time her parents returned to their country when she was 19, Gaida could no longer fit into the traditional society she had been born into, and chose, against her parent's wishes, to stay in America.

Different Cultural Behaviors

There are many conflicts between our North American customs and those of our ELL students, and we are not always quick to notice the mismatch, because these are automatic behaviors—things we do without thinking. Cultural behaviors that differ significantly from our North American ones include

- **Avoiding eye contact.** This is considered polite and respectful behavior in cultures such as Laotian, Hmong, and Hispanic. However, a North American teacher might consider a student who looks down at the floor uncooperative or sullen. How many times do we say to students we are scolding, "Look at me when I'm talking to you!" Avoiding eye contact can have serious consequences for older students and adults. Mary had several high schoolers who were turned down for jobs they were qualified for because the employer thought they weren't listening or paying attention to what he said, although they were merely showing respect by keeping their eyes down.

- **Cooperation.** Some cultures, such as Polynesian, Native North American, and Southeast Asian, embrace the principle that people help each other in all areas of life. They are unaware that in North American schools, helping a fellow student with a problem may be construed as cheating.

- **Making mistakes.** For some students, making a mistake is a greater error than leaving a question unanswered or asking another student for help—being correct is always the primary objective. For example, Mary's beginning English class of Vietnamese students became deathly quiet when state senators came to observe the classroom. This usually rowdy class was proper and silent. They were afraid of shaming their teacher by making mistakes in front of the visitors.

- **Singling out for individual praise.** In many cultures, such as Southeast Asian and Native American, the group or the family is always seen as more important than the individual. Recognizing or congratulating an individual student might confuse him, or make him feel uncomfortable.

- **Role expectations for boys and girls.** The attitude that boys and girls have different roles is most prominent among students from Middle

Eastern countries, which also ascribe different roles to women and men. Problems can arise if a student is unused to having a teacher of the opposite sex; he may react with some awkwardness toward the teacher or, he may be openly disrespectful.

- **Gender-determined motivation (either high or low) for academic achievement.** This is related to the preceding cultural attitude about role expectations. In some cultures, only males are expected to do well; the females simply mark time. They are in school as a formality, not to achieve any real learning goals.

- **Degree of formality of classroom atmosphere.** Public behavior in certain cultures is always formal. Many European schools, such as those in Germany, or Asian schools such as those in Japan, are very strict—to us, they might seem almost militaristic. Students from these cultures often view North American schools as bordering on chaos and the informality an invitation to misbehave. Teachers who wear jeans, sit on their desks, and put their feet up are viewed as extremely impolite.

- **School-system practices.** Related to the preceding issue about formality (or lack of it) in the classroom, newcomers are often uneasy about the learner-centered, process-oriented curriculum and educational practices of North American school systems, compared to the more traditional, subject-centered learning environments found in most countries in Europe, Asia, and Africa.

- **Certain types of physical contact.** In some cultures, the area around the head and shoulders is sacred, and it is considered impolite for another person to touch these areas. Therefore, a reassuring pat on the shoulder from the teacher may be interpreted as an affront by the student.

- **Certain kinds of dress.** Some cultures have rigid customs regarding proper and improper dress, particularly for girls. As a result, for instance, the clothes students must wear for gym and the requirement to take showers may cause a great deal of distress for some ELL students. Abir objected greatly to wearing shorts and a gym uniform. She would hide in the bathroom during the entire gym period.

Stages of Acculturation

Anyone who moves to a new environment—whether within their immediate neighborhood, or to a new city or town, state or province, or country—experiences, to some degree, the same four stages of acculturation as they become adjusted to their new surroundings. There are many names for these stages, but we think the easiest to remember are the four *H*s: honeymoon, hostility, humor, and home.

- **Honeymoon.** This stage takes place when the person first arrives at the new locale. It is characterized by extreme happiness, sometimes even by euphoria. This is especially prevalent with refugees who have finally arrived safely in North America. For them, their new home is truly the land of milk and honey.

- **Hostility.** After about four to six months, reality sets in. The person knows a bit about getting around in his new environment and has begun learning the ropes. But, the new place is not like his former home: he can't get the food he is accustomed to, and things don't look the same. He misses the lifestyle in his home country, the familiar places, faces, and ways of doing things. Gradually he begins to feel that he hates North America and wants to go back to his home country, no matter how bad things were there. This stage is often characterized by complaining; wanting to be only with others who speak his language; rejecting anything associated with the new culture, such as the food, the people, even the new language; feeling depressed and irritable or even angry; having headaches or feeling tired all the time.

- **Humor.** Gradually, the newcomer works toward resolution of his feelings and his sense of being torn between the new and the old. He begins to accept his new home. He begins to find friends, to discover that there are good things about where he is living, and to adjust to his life by coming to terms with both the old and the new ways of living. This is a long process, fraught with feelings of great anxiety in some, because to many, accepting the new means rejecting the old.

- **Home.** Finally, the newcomer becomes "native" in the sense that where he lives is his home, and he accepts that he is here to stay. This last stage may be years in coming, and for some it will never take place.

Thus, what is happening in students' minds and hearts as a result of the drastic changes in their lives has a direct influence on their ability to cope with life and succeed in school.

Behavior in the Classroom

How your students cope with the emotional upheaval in their lives is often reflected in their classroom behavior. The preceding affective factors greatly influence their adjustment. Some students can make the transition from one culture to another with relative ease. Franco, for instance, is a happy, sunny-tempered boy who likes everybody. It doesn't matter to him whether he can speak good English or not; he jumps right into games, discussions, and activities, making the most of the little bit of English he has.

Salvador uses his prowess at soccer to win him friends. Because he is a good player, as well as a congenial, outgoing kid, everybody likes him, and he slipped smoothly into his new life in North America.

Other students react to the upheaval with hostility and act out their aggression, rejecting anything constructive the teachers plan. Still others react with passive-aggressive behavior and selectively decline to participate in activities. Mary taught a group of ELL students who were upset that they had been transferred to her class, having to leave their teacher of six months. These students were refugees and new to this country and had little control over many facets of their lives. They were comfortable with the teacher they had, and

> I liked John. Jill. Johanna. Mark. Rachel and Sara
>
> I felt happy.
>
> I felt so tired.
>
> I felt teachers are so kind. In here.

Figure 3.2 Nina's reflection shows the importance of teachers in her life.

when the system demanded they move up a level to a different teacher, they withdrew. No matter what Mary did for the first few weeks, no matter what adjustments she made to accommodate different levels of abilities, most of the students declined to participate. It was apparent that they were making an attempt to control something in their own lives, and only gradually did they begin to relax and take part in activities.

Some students choose to withdraw completely, effectively shutting out anyone or anything that represents the new culture. Abir withdrew into her lonely self, spending most of her time complaining how unalike North America and Egypt were. She never made friends and continued to be unhappy through all of her years at high school.

All of these factors add up to a myriad of forces at work within the learner. Upon reviewing these variables, it may seem an impossible task to help some newcomers learn our language. However, what you do as a teacher is critical to their success, and there are many positive things you can do to assist in making their adjustment to this country (or, in the case of Native Americans, to their new environment) and to the English language successful.

Teaching Strategies That Help Maximize Learning

Input—The Teacher

Although all elements of a language are not necessarily taught, it is not enough to assume that, given enough time, ELL students will just pick it up on their own. Conscious and direct input from you, their teacher. is necessary.

There are five important things you can do to maximize ELL students' learning:

1. Provide comprehensible input.

2. Make the environment as stress free as possible.

3. Provide numerous opportunities for students to hear and speak the language.

4. Provide a network of support.

5. Have clear and unmistakable guidelines.

Provide Plenty of Comprehensible Input

Comprehensible input is language students are exposed to that they can understand. Your students will only learn when the information you teach is meaningful. Ideas for communicating effectively with them include:

- **Use clear, predictable, "guessable" teacher talk.** Researchers have noted that the way many native-English speakers communicate with those who don't speak the language is very similar to the way mothers speak to their young children. When native-English speakers speak to each other, their speech can be full of stops, starts, and incomplete phrases. When mothers speak to their young children, however, they adjust their speech and talk "motherese" (also sometimes referred to as "baby talk"). Making similar adjustments in your speech to your ELL students is the most helpful way to speak to them.

- **Talk more slowly.** This means at a relaxed rate, not unnaturally slow. Don't overdo it.

- **Reduce the use of idioms.** Idioms are notoriously untranslatable, that is, if you try to explain them word for word their meaning is lost. Think of trying to explain such expressions as "off the wall," "out of the blue," "grab a seat," "keep it under your hat," or "give me a ballpark figure."

- **Use the active voice and positive sentences.** The passive voice is much more difficult to understand, because students have learned that the subject of the sentence is the actor. For example, "There will be no homework assignments accepted after January 10" is harder to understand than "You must hand in all homework by January 10."

- **Monitor your sentence length; don't make your sentences too long.** Lengthy and complex sentences are often too hard for English learners to sort through.

- **Simplify your vocabulary whenever possible.** Finding simpler synonyms for words can make your speech easier to grasp. This should not include technical vocabulary. Content areas have many technical words that are central to concepts being studied. Do not substitute these words for simpler ones; students must learn them to grasp the central meaning of the lesson.

- **Use linguistic cues, or attention getters, such as "look" or "watch," to direct ELL students' attention to important points.** These signals alert listeners to the fact that you consider those points particularly important.

- **Use key words.** Choose several words that are critical to the current lesson, write them on the board, and use them frequently during the discussion so students will get exposure in several different contexts. Use phonological cues, such as tone and stress, to emphasize these words and call students' attention to them.

- **Focus the exchange on the here and now.** Abstract concepts are very difficult to understand or express in limited English.

- **Expand the one-word or two-word sentences that students produce.** When a student says, for example, "Book home," you can respond, "Oh, your book is at home. Here, use this one."

Another way to provide comprehensible input is through nonverbal cues. You can accomplish this by doing the following:

- **Use plenty of visual cues, such as concrete objects, charts, maps, pictures, photos, and collages.**

- **Act out your material, or use gestures to help get your meaning across.**

- **Point, mime, role-play, demonstrate an action.** When you direct the learners' attention to features of the object you are talking about, you are providing them with additional clues to meaning. Students can then see what you are talking about, rather than being solely dependent upon translating everything in their heads.

- **Use contextual cues.** Words and sentences are more comprehensible when they are used in a context that is understandable. Concepts, such as *larger*, *smaller*, *fewer*, and *more*, are more easily understood when they are demonstrated with real objects (such as coins) rather than explained.

- **Use more than one method to communicate or teach something.** Give assignments and lectures orally as well as by writing them on the board. Show a movie or a filmstrip on the same material as your lecture. Have a hands-on project in addition to reading assignments.

- **Check often for understanding.** Stop to see if your ELL students comprehend the material. Watch for body language, facial expressions, or signs of frustration that will alert you to whether or not they understand. Simply asking, "Do you understand?" is not enough. Many students will not admit they don't understand, either because they are ashamed or because they have been taught that their failure will be a sign of disrespect and an affront to the teacher. They often tell you they understand even when they are completely lost. Find alternative ways to check their comprehension, such as by asking them to paraphrase a key point. Encourage them to tell you when they don't understand. Develop signals—such as a little throat clearing—so that they can alert you without overtly stating so. If you teach in chunks, plan an activity to allow them to demonstrate their understanding in nonverbal ways before you go on to the next section.

- **Allow some "wait time," time for the students to hear, understand, and formulate their responses.** Often students have to translate your thoughts into their own language, then retranslate their answer back into English. Native Americans tend to need a longer wait time in their own language; you might have to wait even longer for them to translate and retranslate.

- **Give feedback, such as a nod, a frown, or a look of bewilderment, so students know how well they are getting their attempts at communicating across.**

Set Up a Stress-Free Environment

Students who are relaxed and self-confident learn better and faster. You can help to reduce the stress your students are under and nurture their self-esteem:

- **Show genuine interest in the students, their language, and their culture.**

- **Help your students feel secure.** Even if you can't speak their language, you can reassure them and demonstrate interest and concern through gestures and tone of voice.

- **Allow them to verbalize in their own language.** Many teachers feel that allowing students to talk in their own language will slow their language growth. Some schools even go to the extent of fining or punishing students for talking in their native languages. However, trying to understand a foreign language—in this case English—for hours at a time is physically and mentally exhausting. Students will often do better if they have some "gel time"—time when they are not constantly forced to translate information in their heads. Allowing students time to discuss topics together in their own language can actually facilitate learning, because they can focus solely on the content, unimpeded by their lack of fluency in English. Somebody is bound to catch on to an idea and explain it in their own language. It takes the dual pressure of learning the concepts *and* the language off the students, making it easier to learn the concepts.

- **Avoid forcing your students to speak.** Research shows that forcing students to respond orally before they are ready is a major cause of poor articulation and grammatical control, as well as stress overload (Nord 1977). Your students will talk when they are ready.

- **Accept gestures, pantomime, or drawings whenever possible.** These can often demonstrate whether students understand the concept involved and relieves them of the stress of trying to articulate their thoughts.

- **Make your students feel that they should never be embarrassed or ashamed of their errors.** Errors are a part of learning anything. If students are given the message that errors are bad, or if they are laughed at because of their mistakes, they will clam up. They will only use forms they are perfectly sure of, thus closing the door to learning new forms through practice. Look at mistakes from an analytical perspective rather than a corrective perspective: use them to tell you what your student needs to learn in the future.

- **Don't correct grammatical or pronunciation errors.** Again, meaning is more important than form. Research has shown that correcting errors has little or no value. Corrections can actually impede progress because

  - Students are given the message that being correct is more important than what they have to say

  - Students are distracted from the task at hand—communicating. If the meaning of what a student says is unclear, ask for clarification; otherwise, accept the responses as they are given. Learners start with large issues such as the correct words. As their fluency increases, they will iron out the finer points, such as word endings and tenses. Trust learners to work these things out. You can model the correct form when you respond.

- **Continually reinforce students' progress.** Keep charts, save their early papers in cumulative folders, and show them how far they've come: "This is where you were; this is where you are now. These are the words you've learned."

- **Encourage your students to share their backgrounds and cultures.** ELL students often long to talk about their homelands and cultures and are seldom given this opportunity. For example, asking students to speak about their homelands—perhaps during geography or history lessons—not only provides them with the chance to talk about their countries, but also to use English, speaking about topics familiar to them. And other students in your class will benefit from immediate exposure to a variety of cultures. A welcome byproduct is that allowing students to ask questions about the various cultures can help prevent or reduce friction that might be building in the school, because a forum is provided for an open discussion of sensitive topics.

Maximize Students' Exposure to Natural Communication

The best language learning comes from students' genuine attempts to communicate. Encourage your students' participation in activities within and beyond the classroom.

- **Promote friendships.** Introduce students to others who share their interests; encourage the student in the class who loves to "parent" to take up the cause of the ELL student; put together two lonely, shy kids; and prevail upon all members of the class to be extra sensitive and friendly towards the ELL student. As a teacher, your time and energies are limited. You cannot possibly provide students with all the educational input they require nor can you meet their social and emotional needs. Everyone wants to have friends and be liked. By promoting friendships you are

  - Easing the transition for lonely, often heartsick, students.

  - Providing students with the kind of social relationships in which "getting along" is the most important issue, and learning the language is part and parcel of being a friend. They learn the vocabulary and grammar that is important and useful, while getting feedback that is essential for refining their new language.

  Give students "play" opportunites, whether this involves playing in the sandbox or on the playground (at the elementary level), or competing in friendly games (at any level).

- **Integrate ELL students well into the class.** Make them feel part of the group. Give them class responsibilities, perhaps with another student, such feeding the fish (at the elementary level), or turning in attendence sheets or checking equipment (in upper grades).

- **Make cooperative learning an important part of every class.** Students do not need to work alone to become independent learners. Cooperative learning is a strategy in which a small group of students is involved in an activity or project with a common purpose.

  This means much more than simply lumping students into a group to work together; often, when students are grouped without any ground rules, one or two carry the weight of the assignment. For effective learning, both groups and tasks must be carefully structured. Cooperative learning involves task specialization within teams; the task cannot be completed without important input from each team member.

  Heterogeneous grouping, in which one or more ELL student may be a part of each group, is an important part of cooperative learning. Research has shown that all students—both English speakers and non-English speakers—make substantial gains in their command of the subject. Students get feedback on their attempts to represent problems, have background knowledge supplied by native-English speakers, and profit from discussing problems and observing others' thought processes in tackling issues. Cooperative effort is particularly relevant to some cultures that stress working for the common good as opposed to striving for individual recognition.

Provide a Network of Support

- **Learn about resources within the community that can offer support to your English language learners.** Depression among refugees is very high. Knowing who to turn to when you spot danger signals or behavior problems can relieve untold stress in your students' lives, as well as make your own life easier. Recognize that you are an important member of a team, but there are also many agencies to help immigrants and refugees. Find out which ones are operating in your area, so that you can turn to them when your students need counseling, answers to questions, or help wading through the mire of bureaucracy.

- **Keep the lines of communication open; be a listening ear.** Some of our students have lived through horrors we can't begin to imagine: perhaps they saw their parents blown apart in mine fields, or family members tortured, raped, and murdered by the enemy. The burden of their memories is always with them. Don't probe or openly ask them about their past. Someday something—a smell, a word, a picture—may trigger a memory, and they may share their story. When that happens, don't try to stop them; it is important to allow your students to share this memory. (Use your discretion as to whether or not it's appropriate for the rest of the class to hear.) Your place is simply to listen and to validate the memory. Let them maintain power by authoring their own story. But then steer them to a professional who can help them in their healing process; it takes a trained professional to help them along the difficult, complicated road to wholeness.

Have Clear and Unmistakable Guidelines

Shaker was a huge guy with a huge attitude. On the first day of class, when Barb was reading aloud "notes to the student" from the front of a book, he raised his hand and said, "Teacher, we can read that for ourselves." Clearly, he was setting out, not just to undermine Barb's control, but to topple it. If she didn't react fast and with force, all was lost before the semester began.

Boris could be defiant: "No, I'm not gonna do that" was a common statement coming from him. Andre had a friend call in sick for him; he was caught in the parking lot smoking during second hour. During class he prowled the classroom, asking to go to the bathroom every 10 minutes, talking with other students, messing with their papers, copying work.

Behavior is an issue every teacher wrestles with. Problems can be compounded when there is an overlay of language barriers. Discipline can be difficult and time-consuming when your students can't understand what you are trying to say. There are established procedures for dealing with abusive, defiant, or aggressive students, and it's not our place to review those here.

Coping With Misbehavior

Ideally, you should do as much as you can to prevent misbehavior before it happens. Both students and parents from other cultures may benefit from a sensitive introduction to the learner-centered approach to discipline; that is, leaving students' integrity and self-worth intact, as opposed to the more traditional, punitive approach to discipline that they may be accustomed to. But, as in the cases of Shaker, Boris, and Andre, more often than not, the ball of dissension comes out of left field and knocks you on the head before you're ready.

Make your classroom rules very clear. Explain them well, using an interpreter if possible. So much of what we consider acceptable behavior is implicitly understood by North Americans, and yet is not necessarily clear to those from other countries. For instance, one classroom's rules were (1) Students will respect all school rules and (2) Students will use acceptable language. Those of us who have grown up in North American schools will know what these rules mean. But students coming from a different culture may not. They hear their classmates swearing all the time. How are they supposed to know that this is not acceptable within a teacher's range of hearing? Unless the rules are explained to them, how will they know what respecting the rules means?

We also have to be sure that the consequences for misbehavior are explained to the students. One teacher told us she had kept a student in the classroom during lunchtime because he had incessantly talked out loud to another student. The teacher used a method of discipline that gives the student warnings by putting checkmarks on the board. When the student accumulated five checkmarks, he was kept in the classroom during lunch break. She later found out that the student did not understand this discipline method. He did not know that his talking was disruptive to her, or that the checkmarks on the board were meant for him. Ultimately, she found out that he did not even understand why she had kept him in classroom while the other students were allowed to go to lunch.

When Things Go Wrong

If you have students who are acting up, begin by reviewing the following:

- **The physical setting.** Where are your students seated? Can they hear, see, or observe properly? Do they need support from students of the same background? (Or, do they need to be separated from these students?)

- **The amount of contact for feedback, clarification, and so on.** Are students aware of what you want them to do? Do they know how to go about doing it? Do they have opportunities to work with you one-on-one? Can they ask questions and get the answers they need to do the work?

- **Your level of expectation.** Was your assessment of your students' abilities accurate, or are they getting frustrated?

- **Problems with assignments.** Have you broken down the assignment into components, with each part containing a clearly stated objective, or are students overwhelmed because it is too complex? Part of Andre's problem was that he felt he could not do the assignments and spent much of his time avoiding them.

- **Students' emotional states.** Are you beginning to see some of the danger signals—inappropriate behavior, aggression, withdrawal, or apathy? Spencer was close to giving up, and his temper often got the better of him. Finding a counselor for him helped him work through his grief.

- **Cultural mismatch.** It may be, for instance, that some students come from cultures where classes are tightly structured. In our less formal classes, students may be unable to figure out what rules are in effect and how they should behave. They may be frustrated at the contradiction between those behaviors they believe are acceptable and your behavioral expectations. This was part of Boris's problem; when the rules were stated clearly and unequivocally, he was on the road toward learning how to cope in the classroom. He had to be told exactly how to speak with the teacher, and so on; he was unable to infer these rules.

If no problems exist in your setup, and you don't believe culture is a factor, then confront students individually with the problems you are seeing. Communication may be difficult, so try to get help from a translator. A student may be able to recognize that problems exist and may even be able to tell you what would improve the situation. For example, he might be able to say, "You talk too fast, and then I don't understand how to do the assignment. Could you write it on the board?"

More likely, however, the student will deny that any problems exist. He may even react with hostility and end up blaming you for all his problems, or he may withdraw and say very little to enlighten you.

Resolving Behavior Problems

Working through the following steps can help resolve behavior problems, because, in the end, the student will know exactly what is expected of him:

1. **Review what the correct behavior is.**

2. **State clearly what he can and cannot do, using language that he can understand.** For instance, "Stay in your seat when I am talking." "No crawling under tables," or "No sharing of answers." While we want to be positive and provide positive models of behavior, the word *no* clearly sets the parameters of what is acceptable and what isn't. It often helps to learn those commands in the students' language. The first word Barb learned in Chinese was *no!* The first phrase was *no fighting.* Horace and Rex, two great kids when they were separated, could not get along. Barb has video footage of Horace walloping a blindfolded Rex during a game. Our final shot of Rex is at graduation, glowering as he accepts his diploma, because he and Horace were fighting in the stands. Knowing phrases such as "Wakarimasu ka?" (Do you understand?) and "Que pasa?" (What's happening?) are essential to have available when needed.

We are living in an imperfect world, so there is no such thing as a paradise with no pain. As long as we are still alive and well, we should not give up trying to make world a better place to live in. As a philophy put it, "Stay hardiness is the best human can do." I am here to stay.

Figure 3.3 Chome's summation of life as an immigrant.

3. **Avoid putting yourself in a position that you can't change later, such as stating unequivocally that all plagiarism will be awarded with instant failure.** Your student may not have any idea what the word *plagiarism* means and may not understand that copying directly from a book or his classmate's essay is wrong.

4. **Tell the student how he can correct the problem.** If he is in high school and has the language capabilities, he may even be able to plan strategies for correcting the problem himself.

5. **Detail the consequences if the student does not comply with the resolutions you have established.** Be flexible. Be prepared to negotiate, but hold on to reasonable standards. Nobody in the class objected when the

Figure 3.4 This lovely drawing, made by a student as a reflection of her ELL experiences, captures the essence of what a positive and joyful experience meeting new people, sharing cultures, and becoming friends can be.

teacher negotiated with Andre that he could go to the bathroom whenever he wanted, as long as he kept it under two minutes and as long as he stayed away from the others so they could do their work.

Your Role As Teacher

We cannot overstate the importance of your role as teacher in helping to facilitate your ELL students' language acquisition and cultural adjustment. You are on the front line, helping these students make the difficult transition from one culture to another. Often you spend more time with them than their parents do and can see changes or behaviors that family members cannot (or do not) recognize.

Your most appropriate role with your ELL students is to teach them English and to give them a means to become functional members of the community. This means doing the job you are trained for: teaching. It also means, conversely, not trying to solve all their problems. You are not the counselor, the psychiatrist, or the physician. It is inappropriate to try to take on these roles. Teachers can get in over their heads, or burn out fast if they try to solve all their students' problems. This is, admittedly, a very fine line to tread. We went into teaching because we like people, and we want to help make the world a better place. But if, for instance, you urge a traumatized student to tell you things that have happened to him, thinking that simply unburdening will make him feel better, you may make things worse. You can become traumatized yourself. You can become so overwhelmed that you can't do your job. The student may feel so badly afterwards that he will shy away, and the gains you have made will be lost.

You are also a model of appropriate behavior. Many of your students have lost the leadership of their parents; immigrant or refugee parents are often confused and baffled by our culture and cannot effectively interpret society and culture for their children as most parents do. By modeling correct behavior and setting limits, you are making it possible for them to learn how to act in ways we consider acceptable.

Teachers Should

- **Adopt a policy of "a little more."** Take the initiative in trying to understand your students, to be aware of the problems they face and the adjustments they're making. A little extra time invested in finding friends for these students, observing how they act and react, and making sure they understand what is expected of them can make the difference between success and failure.

  For example, Spencer had the saddest eyes Barb had ever seen. It broke her heart to look at him. His older brother had been murdered in a drive-by shooting. The four brothers in school all had different last names. Spencer had a hair-trigger temper and was often in detention, but he responded to special attention like wildflowers to rain, and his smile could light up a room. By knowing what was going on in his life, we could be sympathetic yet firm in our guidelines.

- **Learn a little more about students' cultural backgrounds.** All Southeast Asians are not alike, just as all Native Americans, all Europeans, and all Africans are not alike. Ongoing wars and political unrest have divided regions for decades, and the memories of violence, on both sides, create tensions that transcend country boundaries. At the end of the school year, one student told Barb he had slept with a knife under his pillow for the entire year; the roommate assigned to him was from a country he considered his enemy. Some ethnic groups are very class conscious among themselves and will not associate with those they feel are inferior. Culture, religion, and family patterns all influence your students profoundly. By learning about these, you can be wary of the pitfalls, and be better prepared to understand why and how your students perceive the world. This puts you in a position to modify your classroom to meet the needs of all the students in the class.

- **Be aware of the danger signals.** ELL students fall into the category of "fragile" learners. Fragile learners aren't necessarily from low-income or single-parent families, although these circumstances can be part of newcomers' situations; the fragility refers to the many stresses, traumas, and concerns beyond the students' control, which assault their senses and drain attention and energy. Overcome with feelings of loss and emotional anguish, your students are often "in crisis." Knowing the stages of grief and loss—shock, denial, anger, depression, bargaining, and finally acceptance—as well as being aware of inappropriate behavior such as laughing at sad stories, crying at a joke, or being extremely irritable or suspicious, will help you see beyond the students' behavior and look for causes rather than focus on the effect and instantly judge or blame.

Conclusion

Dealing with students from different backgrounds entails much planning and research on your part. However, the benefits in terms of the enrichment each newcomer brings to your class far outweigh the negatives. By creating plenty of opportunities for interaction, providing appropriate feedback, and being sensitive to the types of changes your students are coping with, you can set up the optimal environment for learning. We do not want to suggest that all ELL students have bad experiences. There's hope. Sooner or later, most of them break through the struggles and make a home for themselves here.

Reflections, Projects, and Projections for Discussion

- Think about yourself as a language learner. Which of the variables that affect language acquisition (for example, personality, attitude and motivation, previous educational background) apply to you? How successful have you been, or are you as a language learner? What could you do to make yourself more proficient?

- Recall a time when things have gone wrong in the classroom, or in a class you have taken. What went wrong? How did you resolve it? How could it have been resolved more satisfactorily?

- Investigate the cultures in your area. What are their norms? What kinds of things should teachers be aware of? Are there any important factors that the ethnic community is struggling with?

- What phrases would be useful for you to learn in the languages you encounter? Use the Internet to compile a short dictionary.

- Do you and other teachers in your school get adequate support from your district and from your administration? What is it? If not, analyze what's going wrong. What can you do, diplomatically and carefully, to remedy it?

- Do you, your co-teachers, and the school's administration have a common agenda? What is it? If not, analyze what the various agendas look like. What can you do, diplomatically and carefully, to build unity of purpose?

- Make a list of the people and organizations you can turn to that can help overcome cultural or behavioral barriers.

Case Studies: Andre and Yoshi

Andre

Andre was four when war started in his country. He was playing outside one day when someone began shooting at him. If his aunt had not rushed out and dragged him inside, he might have been killed. When life became too dangerous Andre's father took the family away from the house to hide in the forest; the next day their house was burned and their neighbors murdered. They left with only what they could carry, walking in deep snow. Andre's feet froze to his boots, and he could not take them off for two days. The family of five walked over the mountains in winter, hiding from soldiers, to reach a safe place. Finally, someone hid them, but Andre's father had to pay the homeowner not to turn them in. They made their way into another country, where his father worked illegally, saving money to get a visa. Eventually they made their way into the United States, with nothing more than his father's life savings stitched into the pocket of his coat. The family settled in the mountains that reminded his father of home.

After three years of moving, the family settled in a medium-sized city, and Andre arrived at school with a very scattered and disrupted school history. He could read little in any language. His records showed that he had made very little progress since his arrival in the West and that he was getting Fs in everything. Each year he missed between 25 and 30 days of school.

The first day Andre came to class he wore clothes that were a sign of gang membership. When he was introduced to Mrs. Rodriguez, his teacher, he called her "Sir." As the weeks went by he did not assimilate into his classes; he continually came up with excuses to leave class—he needed to go to his locker, to the bathroom, and so on—in order to not be in the classroom to work.

In January, Andre was not in class for a week. Other students told Mrs. Rodriguez that Andre had to go to court for stealing. He had broken into a family's home and stolen their TV. He was not jailed because he was under 18, but he threatened to get a gun and shoot another student because he had been caught. Two days after that, Andre ran away from home, quit school, and went to Chicago.

Several weeks later he returned. He seemed happy to be back at school, but behavior-wise, it was like starting all over again. In the beginning Mrs. Rodriguez had paired Andre with Franco, whose English was quite good, but after the burglary incident, the other students did not want to work with him. He bragged in class about his confrontations with the law, and they saw him as a liability and not as a peer.

Yoshi

Yoshi has professional parents—you learn that his mother is here on an exchange program as visiting professor at the local college; Dad stayed behind in Japan. Yoshi wanted to stay in Japan with Dad, and thus is resentful of being here. He is rude and disrespectful to his mother. In class, he is sullen and unresponsive. He refuses to participate, won't join groups, and sits by himself with his chin resting on his fists. He will do work alone, but no amount of coaxing or coercion will get him to be a participant in a group. So far, he has managed to make life miserable for everyone, talking loudly in class, crawling under tables while the teacher is trying to lead a lesson, ignoring all instructions as if he doesn't understand (although it's clear from other interactions that he really does), and refusing to respond to anyone in anything but Japanese. He wants to go back home. Because he has a "transient mentality," he doesn't try to make friends or learn English. What's the point if he's going to leave soon? He's been here for four months and has not demonstrated any progress in English.

Reflections and Activities – Andre and Yoshi

- What are the language learning variables (for example, personality, attitude and motivation, previous educational background) that are functioning for each of these boys?

- How would you integrate Andre and Yoshi into the classroom and quell their poor behavior? What would be your plan for improving the situation? What steps could you take?

- What factors are prevalent in each of these boys' situations? How does knowing about each one's background help you to understand their behavior?

- Is there more you need to know so you can develop a clear plan to deal with their classroom misbehavior? What more do you need to know to work successfully with each of these boys?

- What could you do to ease the transition for each boy? How far do your responsibilities extend?

- Record your short- and long-term goals for both students, considering both academic and behavioral goals.

- Since classroom behavior is a big issue for both students, how will you deal with their misbehavior? Write a contract for each student, which details the behaviors they should exhibit and what behaviors will not be accepted. What ideas do you have to encourage them to "buy into" the contract?

- What tools do you have in place for classroom management? How can you adapt your classroom for newcomers? What adjustments could you make for students such as Andre and Yoshi?

- Do you have a list of classroom expectations available for all students? Would it be understandable for a newcomer coming from a country with very different classroom expectations?

Chapter 4

Literacy and the Four Skills of Language Acquisition— Gun the Accelerograph Immediate

In this chapter, we discuss learning language within what we call a "balanced literacy and language program" and its importance for second-language learners. We focus on

- Approaches to teaching literacy
- Different types of ELL literacy
- Our assumptions about literacy in an era of change
- Strategies for promoting literacy in the mainstream classroom

Fong was 10, but in the third grade. He had arrived in the U.S. at the age of seven with no previous educational experiences and was placed in the middle of kindergarten. By the end of the first grade he was not reading. In second grade he began to fall behind his peers. By November he had become the class clown, was significantly slower than the other students, and was lacking in maturity, a sense of responsibility, and progress. He had trouble tracking print, would read to get through the passage—not to get meaning, and could not retell a story when it was finished. By third grade he was receiving help in all areas. At the end of the year, Dad wanted him to repeat third grade, but he would be 11 by then. The teachers were stymied as to what to do next.

Authentic Approaches to Teaching/Learning

In the past several decades, teachers and researchers have learned a great deal about reading. How it should be taught is less clear though—and the source of a great deal of bitter controversy. Many states have mandated by law that all teachers should be trained in the use of phonics, or that they teach using research-based materials that emphasize phonics.

In the first edition of the book, we operated under certain assumptions about language acquisition that we still stand behind:

- **Opportunities for reading, writing, speaking, and listening—the four skills of language acquisition—must be "real."** Real situations—reading to enjoy a story or to find out how to fix a bike, writing a letter to complain about a cancelled TV show—are intrinsically motivating because they have purpose. For example, ELL students often pass driver's education with flying colors in a remarkably short time. They learn to read the driving manuals and understand the instructions so that they can pass the test and get their license. Because driving is often important, not only for them, but for their families (frequently the students are the ones who do the ferrying, the bill paying, and the grocery shopping), they are intensely motivated to learn.

  Graham, MacArthur, and Fitzgerald (2007), in studying effective programs for writing (which we can expand to practically any program) state that

  > the most salient characteristic of...settings that produce high language arts achievement is that students are very engaged...That is, 90 [percent] of the time they are doing something academic, something requiring thoughtfulness, such as drafting a well-structured story or reading an appropriately challenging book, rather than something that does not require thoughtfulness, such as doing a workbook page that can be completed in less than 30 seconds, leaving many students off-task for the remaining 9½ minutes of class...

- **The language-learning situations must be meaningful—meaning-full.** We communicate in order to accomplish something: to learn, to have our needs met, to get along with other people, or just to play. We have a purpose and an audience. Infants do not learn to talk by learning that we put the subject before the verb or add *s* to nouns to make them plural. They learn words like *bye-bye, juice,* and *milk* within contexts that have meaning to them. We must provide second-language learners with the same kinds of opportunities so that they can make sense of language by using it for purposes that have relevance to them. Often, the tasks students are given are phony exercises: tracing and copying the letters of the alphabet again and again; learning lists of words simply because they all begin with the same sound or demonstrate a phonics principle; punctuating sentences that someone else has written; listing all the nouns in a paragraph; repeating two sounds until they can hear the difference. These exercises have fractionated learning into little bits and pieces that, while important components of the reading, writing, speaking, and listening processes, of themselves make little sense to the learner. Whole texts, not just isolated words or sentences, but poems, newspaper articles, novels, textbooks, letters, comic books, grocery lists, and songs all provide meaning in meaningful contexts.

- **The learning situations must also be integrated so that all four skills are used together.** Rather than simply discussing a topic—whether it be about what they saw at the zoo yesterday or the legalization of drugs—students can write (or have you write) what they know and think, discuss what they have written, and further their understanding of the event or issue by listening to each other's thoughts and interpretations. Then, they can capitalize on what they have learned orally by using their newly learned vocabulary in their reading, writing, and sharing. This means not giving students phony tasks whose only real purpose is that the teacher wants it done or that it is included in the workbook. Figure 4.1 shows an example of such a worksheet.

With the critical rethinking and refinements of what whole language means, however, and our new knowledge about what reading entails, we have modified our assumptions and their implications for teachers.

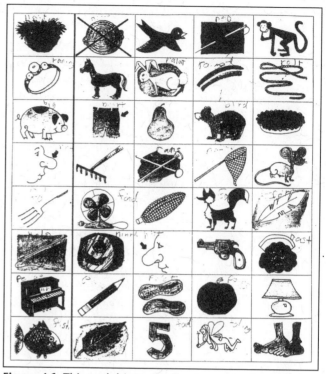

Figure 4.1 This worksheet was given to a second grader. As an exercise, it is just plain bad: it does not allow the student to grapple with sound/letter correspondences within a real context, nor does it reinforce these concepts, because in many cases he does not know the English term for the pictures. The student has attempted to write the word above some of the pictures. Unless the teacher stands over him and helps him with each picture, this student can go far astray.

Orthodoxies Versus Reasonable Choices

Nancie Atwell (1998) writes of being caught up in a set of "orthodoxies." As she gained new insights about writing, reading, and learning, she "embraced a whole new set of orthodoxies. As enlightened and child-centered as the new rules were, they had an effect similar to the old ones: they limited what [she] did as a …teacher."

We have found, too, that the continual nagging question that Atwell labored under—that very dangerous question: Am I doing it right?—limits what we and other teachers do in the classroom. This question keeps many who are successful at teaching less able and willing to be innovative. They become less willing to listen to their own experiences and trust their instincts about what the students need.

Many teachers truly committed to the philosophy of whole language felt guilty doing things that didn't seem "pure" to whole-language ideology. Teachers who taught spelling had to defend themselves. Teaching phonics was done behind closed doors. Asking students to copy the alphabet was assigned with guilt. If all activities were not integrated, we somehow felt we were selling our students short. In addition, teachers with many years of experience rebelled against whole language. They were led to believe that some of the things they were doing, simply because it wasn't "whole" or "integrated," were somehow wrong, and, therefore, they felt themselves to be less able teachers. But history has borne out that those "yeah, buts" are important; not only should teachers question the newest fad to come down the pike, but they should also pay attention to who's in the class and what each individual student needs, and respond accordingly.

Since the beginning of the 20th century, experts as well as opinionated non-experts have been fighting over the best way to teach reading: phonics, whole-word, whole language, back to basics, balanced literacy. The balanced approach, which maintains equilibrium between rich experiences and direct instruction, is a more measured and realistic approach to teaching reading. This means that we have recognized that thoughtful teachers can and should teach structures directly, incorporate phonics into their reading programs, and expect students to be responsible for skills that may require memorization.

For instance, when Barb was teaching a very large class of beginning literacy migrant workers and refugees she taught verbs and verb conjugations—but she felt guilty about it. Her reasoning was sound: students needed some structure upon which to base their writing. It wasn't feasible to expect that they would be able (within the time frame they had and their limited exposure outside the classroom) to figure out the forms for themselves; and last, but not least in importance, students wanted it. They felt secure in having these forms spelled out for them and to have concrete evidence that they were learning.

In retrospect, the decision to teach verbs explicitly was a good one. And, because it was done within the framework of meaningful discussion, it was a useful exercise that resulted in learning.

What is needed is an understanding of literacy, of reading, and of the

Verb Chart						
Verb	Translation	Past	Progressive	3rd Person Singular	Past Participle	Example in a Sentence
sleep	睡覺	slept	sleeping	sleeps	have slept	I have slept in class before.
eat	吃	ate	eating	eats	have eaten	I eat every morning.
jump	跳	jumped	jumping	jumps	have jumpes	I jumped over the wa
run	跑	ran	running	runs	have run	I run verey fast, to lunch
pat	拍	patted	patting	pats	have patted	I pat the dog.
pet	寵物	pet	petting	pets	have pet	I pet the dog.
be	是	I was we were	being	is	have been	I was little girl.
laugh	大笑	laughed	laughing	laughs	have laughed	I laugh when the wolf ate the pigs.
know	知道	knew	knowing	knows	have known	I know Chinese.

Figure 4.2 An example of a verb chart used, without guilt, with Taiwanese students.

options available for those who struggle as well as those who forge ahead against all odds.

Immersion Is Not Enough

We know that immersing students in literacy is not sufficient. Exposure is not enough. Strategies can't be left to chance. Although many children learn to read on their own, many others do not. Fountas and Pinnell (1996) write:

> *We sometimes mistakenly assume that these needs can be met just by providing good books and encouraging children to explore them. In fact, what most young readers need cannot be found in books alone…It is usually not enough simply to provide children with good reading materials. Teacher guidance is essential.*

This is especially true when students come from homes where their parents do not read at all, and their experiences with the written word are very limited.

Some students do need direct instruction in reading skills, in structuring their essays, and in learning how to locate information in texts. They may need to be told the meanings of words explicitly so that they can continue reading. Recognition of the necessity to teach skills directly was a welcome one, because, again, it opened the door for teachers to use whatever techniques are available to them to meet the needs of their individual students.

For example, students might need to be shown, many times, what their options are for figuring out an unknown word. Often, beginning or poor readers will automatically turn to the teacher for help when encountering a word they don't know by sight. They might try to sound it out. If that doesn't work, they might simply give up. If they don't learn other methods, such as looking at the context or using the pictures as cues to figure out the meaning, they don't have many options. We can't assume they'll pick up these skills on their own by watching the teacher reading strategically; teaching them explicitly is sometimes a must and is nothing less than good teaching.

Literacy Is a Social Phenomenon

Literacy is not simply the skills needed to read and write (as people assume when they believe "illiterate" people are those who cannot read). Rather, literacy is a social phenomenon that exists within a context; it is the ability to use one's reading and writing skills to participate efficiently and effectively in today's complex society.

This definition expands our view to include many of the complex tasks involved in daily living, such as reading recipes and writing grocery lists. Richie, an adult student, for example, used to boast quite proudly that he had never read an entire book. And yet, he read the paper, the TV guide, and letters from his nine children. He shared the letters with his family and discussed them in great detail. A rich web of emotions and social ties were evoked in the process.

The implication for teachers is that literacy, when viewed as a social event, becomes a setting or an environment through which many other tasks occur.

Expanding Our View of Literacy

In the past several decades we have expanded our view of literacy. Literacy is a large umbrella that includes every use of print as a creation of meaning from a text. Literacy has come to be recognized not just as a mechanical set of skills but as something that operates within a social realm. And the definition keeps expanding with our ever-growing use and reliance on technology, so that we speak of being "computer literate."

There are many types of literacies these days, but we need to concern ourselves with the bottom line. Literacy, according to Au (1993), is "the ability and the willingness to use reading and writing to construct meaning from printed text, in ways which meet the requirements of a particular social context." This definition is particularly compelling because of the notion of "willingness." We all know people who refuse to learn some type of technology, or who see no need to learn English, or the alphabet. People need to buy in to the idea of being literate in our language, in digital technology, in electronic gaming, otherwise they simply won't.

This also means reading is not an either/or phenomenon, where one either can or cannot read. There are many types of literacy events that range from reading stop signs along the way to work, to reading the back of a medicine bottle, to wading through the intricacies of a will or a lease agreement. Each task requires different types of skills and levels of attention; many tasks are group affairs—carried on with a great deal of discussion and often embedded in contexts that carry much social and emotional weight.

Second-Language Literacy

Second-language learners are not all alike. They come to us with vast differences in their background knowledge and experiences with print. Some come from countries with a high literacy rate where they learned to read in their own language; others are from cultures that have no written language and, therefore, no reading skills to transfer to the task of reading in English. It's not enough to simply label a non-reader "illiterate," because different types of illiteracy demand different strategies.

Four Types of People Who Cannot Read English

Of those who cannot read English, Haynes and Haverson (1982) distinguish four types:

- **Preliterate**. These are learners who speak a language for which there is no written form. They come from places where there are no books, signs, or magazines. They often have no idea that those squiggles on the page (which we call print) have meaning.

- **Nonliterate**. These learners speak a language for which there is a written form, but they have not learned to read. They know that reading and writing have a purpose and that those marks have meaning, but they have simply not learned the skills.

Figure 4.3 Bao's name and address. She had never held a pencil before coming to school. Her writing shows the beginnings of understanding form.

- **Semiliterate**. These students have very basic skills, such as knowing how to write their names, but not much more than that.

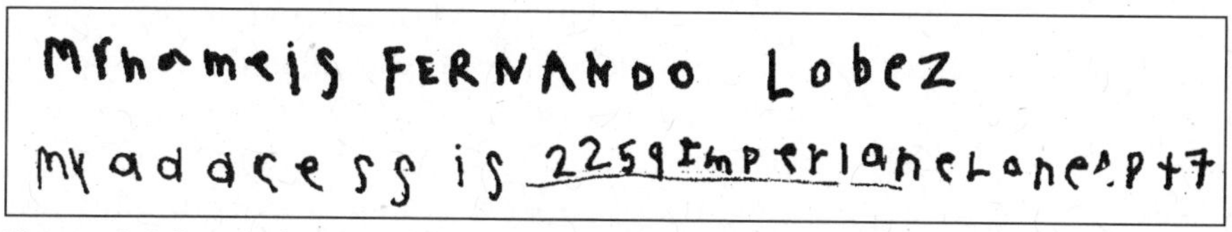

Figure 4.4 Fernando copied his name and address. Notice that he does not distinguish between *p* and *b* and does not yet know the concept of word boundaries.

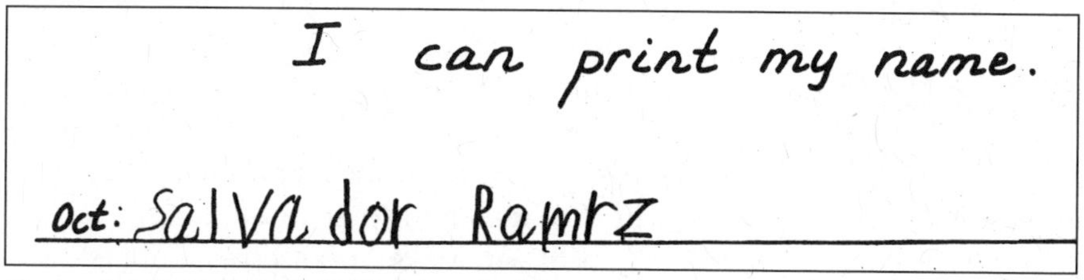

Figure 4.5 Salvador wrote his name on his own.

- **Nonalphabetic.** These are literate learners from countries whose languages do not have alphabetic writing systems. Logographic systems, such as Chinese, and syllabic systems, such as Japanese, use characters that represent complete words or syllables instead of individual letters as we have in English. These learners have learned the skills of reading and need to transfer them to the new language, but don't need to start again from the very beginning "squiggles-are words" stage.

For those ELL students who are literate in their own language, do not delay reading and writing until they have acquired advanced listening skills and oral fluency.

Figure 4.6 Here is Angel's signature in English and part of her address, which demonstrates literacy in her first language.

Second-Language Acquisition Is Different From First

Much of the research in second-language acquisition in the 1980s compared it to first-language acquisition. There are many parallels; thus many teachers, both classroom and ELL, have adhered to the old, simplified acquisition model:

LISTENING > SPEAKING > READING > WRITING

First-language learners seem to follow this pattern, spending their first year or so listening to the language around them, then speaking, and only later learning to read and write. And anyone who has tried to learn a second language knows how much easier it is to understand the language than to speak it. However, this listening-speaking-reading-writing model presents some very serious problems that need to be addressed. We know now, due to studies of young children, that this model is inaccurate. Children do not suddenly begin the road to literacy when they reach school. Most children in developed countries have a great deal of prior knowledge about reading and its purposes. During the course of a day, they encounter many types of reading. Many have a host of opportunities to use paper and pencil to communicate messages (Teale and Sulzby 1986; Schickedanz 1986; Newman 1984) long before they come to school for formal learning (figure 4.7).

Many of our ELL students, such as Andy, Glory, and Beth, studied English in schools in their native countries. They have often been taught by other non-native speakers and have spent a good deal of time learning English grammar. They may know how to read and write in our language, but cannot speak or make themselves understood. The listening-speaking-reading-writing model

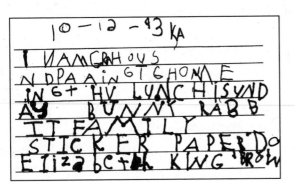

Figure 4.7 Kate's early writing: a mixture of her own composition and words copied from materials she found readily at hand.

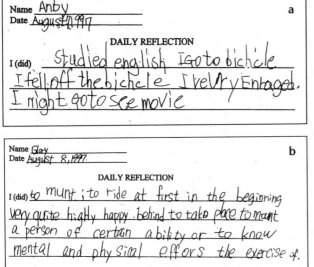

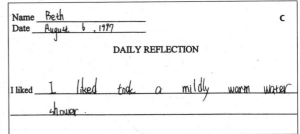

Figure 4.8a–c Andy, Glory, and Beth exhibit their very "bookish" English. They used pocket dictionaries to find words that represented their meaning. On the scale of literacy and skillful use of strategies, these three rank quite high. The word choice of such learners is often archaic and quite funny. It is sometimes difficult to guess what they are trying to say, as in Glory's case (b).

ignores their strengths by pushing them to learn to speak and listen before they are given reading and writing tasks.

Much of the literature in the 1990s in bilingual and second-language learning stated, rather dogmatically, that development in oral language should precede reading. While it is true that in order to read students need to know a certain number of words, this *does not mean that reading should be delayed.* Why not?

- **Time is passing!** If, for instance, Bao arrives in the fourth grade or the eighth grade having had no prior experience with print, spending four months, six months, or a year only on oral vocabulary is time wasted. While learners must have a core vocabulary to start reading, to delay reading and writing until they have oral fluency is to substantially delay their ability to function in the regular classroom.

- **Print can be introduced from the first.** Compelling research (Hudelson 1983; Edelsky 1986; Ammon 1985) has demonstrated that students who are limited in their speaking ability can still compose texts and learn to read. Learning to read and write should go hand in hand with learning to speak.

- **There are so many great books with few words on the market these days; teachers can find myriad resources that help students with minimal reading skills learn content and reading.**

- **Learning to read can proceed hand in hand with vocabulary development.**

This does not mean that a book is plunked in front of the student, and he is expected to read it on day one. That would be nonsensical. However, it does mean that the student can and should be a participant in reading events that take place throughout the day. Preliterate and nonliterate students often need a year or more of simple exposure to print before they can actually begin reading independently. Teachers frequently get frustrated because these students don't seem to be learning. But, if we consider that the average Western child has had five years of experience with print before formal instruction begins, there's a lot of catching up to do.

Following are places within the curriculum for you to start making the connections and building on them.

Where to Begin: Connecting the Four Skills to the Curriculum

The first step in learning to read and write in the new language is learning words that are useful to the learners—usually the first words they have learned to speak in their first language. The strategies that follow provide a bridge to the reading and writing tasks required of students, both literate and nonliterate. These strategies are examples of activities that can provide meaningful, quality instruction to groups of students working at widely varying levels of language and reading proficiency: the beauty of the following activities is that they can either be "scaffolded," in the sense that you can initiate them and take complete control of the activity, or they can be turned over to students who are gaining increasing independence.

This is not an exhaustive list, but should help you validate the fact that many of the activities you are already doing with your English-speaking students are also appropriate for your ELL students. This list should also help you develop your own methods and materials. The strategies can be used with the class as a whole or with individual students. These are rich activities, because students at different levels of ability and competence can profit from them. Many of these strategies help you create a print-rich environment. This is the first priority in any classroom, particularly one that contains ELL students. In order to establish the speech-print connection, students need to see words in action.

Figure 4.9 Elise drew this picture as an enthusiastic response to the Harry Potter books. She illustrated her own Harry Potter story called *Harry Potter and the Bird of Faith*.

Art

This is first on our list, because students do not need to know any English or be able to read a word to join in, succeed, and shine. Art is universal. It is something

Figure 4.10a–c Often, second language learners are gifted artistically. When given the chance, they can render drawings that show their understanding far more than words can or demonstrate their sense of humor. (a) Train to Nowhere: the poster for one of the Academy Award movies in the student-written drama *Sometimes Evil Has to Win*. (b) Herman shows how he felt walking on the high ropes course, and (c) Wade reflects his dismay at his sinking boat.

beginners can express themselves with and is often the one avenue they have to communicate what they know and can do. We have found many shy, otherwise unresponsive learners demonstrate creativity and mastery in drawing, weaving, or embroidery. Art is an activity that older, more proficient students can also enjoy. It can be incorporated into any activity, as we will demonstrate throughout the rest of the book. Art is a literacy activity (Dyson 1990; Schirmacher 1997). It allows students to reflect on, organize, and communicate how they represent the real world in symbolic form. Beginners to both reading and speaking English can demonstrate their understanding of stories and concepts through artistic means.

Encourage students to articulate what they have drawn: they can dictate their thoughts to the teacher or write their own words.

Figure 4.11 This wistful drawing shows a student's home in Cambodia. While the other students in the class were learning the rooms of a house, he wanted to show his teacher the home he had to leave.

Labeling

Some Strategies for Surrounding Students With Words

One of the first ways students learn a second language is by learning the English words for objects they know in their native language. Labeling embeds this task within a meaningful social context. Ventriglia (1982) notes that teachers can facilitate abstracting meaningful concepts and labeling in the second language by

- Presenting words with concrete objects or pictures
- Organizing vocabulary into units, grouping words by concept
- Expanding the vocabulary words in a meaningful concept
- Using all the senses in teaching vocabulary

Even though students may not make the connection that those squiggles are a graphic representation of the concept, seeing the squiggles every day helps reinforce the connection.

Label items in the classroom, including such things as the window, cupboard, desk, and so on. Again, put written labels on objects they already know in their first language. If they are already literate, students can also write labels for each item in their first language.

To reinforce visual discrimination and practice sight-word recognition, turn labeling into a game. Label classroom items, then make a duplicate set of labels, and ask students to match them to the labels around the room. This activity is appropriate for all age levels and classes, especially in content areas such as science and physical education, which have their own specialized vocabulary and equipment. Labeling is particularly useful when you have new students and must find worthwhile tasks to occupy them while they adjust to their new environment.

After you, an aide, or a buddy have played the labeling game with a student a number of times, remove the labels from the items, and have the student return as many labels as he knows to their proper places.

Lists

Lists are a natural development and extension of the labeling strategy. Readers and writers build vocabulary and learn to interact with the written word from seeing words in print, to watching, listening, and helping develop lists that are grouped in some logical way. Display lists of words that the class has brainstormed as a lead-in to a writing exercise, unit of study, or activity.

How do animals protect themselves?

Use teeth	Quills	Jumping
Use their horns	Some kick	Use claws
By growling	Fly	Scare enemies
Running	Camouflage	Run
Fighting	Stink	

Figure 4.12 This list was written by a first-grade teacher, made from ideas elicited from her students.

MY WISh is

presents

toYs
chris+mas

A Pis+na mn+syc isa rhois woah.

A PS+na MStcriatte DrisoYwaho na.

Figure 4.13 This is a first grader's list of what she wants for Christmas. Most of the words were copied. She composed the last two sentences herself.

Rosi BeoF

35 CuPS of SaLT
RAin Deen eyes
Buy Rost Beef
Sqash IT uP
BRown Shuger
keThuP
Buy More Rost Be
MiX It uP
Bake IT For MiNiTS
999 DiGrees

Figure 4.14 A first grader's recipe for roast beef.

Yesterday	I saw six ducks.
	I saw ~~some~~ many dragon flys.
	I saw two lizargs.
	I saw four mosguitos.
	I saw a dog.
	I saw four fishs.
	I saw a squirrel.
	I saw two ravems.
	I saw four birds.
	I saw some many ants.

Figure 4.15 This is a list of animals seen during a walk around the lake made by an older, more proficient learner.

Limei Li
Bob Ewell
1 Mayella's father
2 heavy drinker
3 liar
4 left-handed
5 hulking
6 live in the dump
7 has 8 children
8 can write his name
9 make his children go to school only the first day of the year
10 shoots animals all the season

Figure 4.16 Limei lists facts she gleaned about the character Bob Ewell from the novel *To Kill a Mockingbird*.

Figure 4.17 Lists can also be accompanied by drawing to aid in rereading.

Some examples of lists that can be used with students of all levels include

- Appropriate behavior in the classroom
- Physical education: the rules of games
- Science: important vocabulary; lab rules and procedure
- Math: technical vocabulary; words with specific math meanings, such as *product* or *square*
- Art: rules for set-up and clean-up
- Social science: vocabulary for current unit of study
- Language arts: color words; emotions; winter words; vivid verbs; story starters such as *firsts, lasts, important people, things I get mad about*

Lists can be used in many ways for many different purposes. Depending on the level of your students, either you or they can do the writing. Figures 4.12–4.17 show the many kinds of lists students can produce.

Charts

Whenever possible, combine a word with a picture by making a chart. Display charts that combine words and illustrations. Attractive, easy-to-use charts are available ready-made from most teacher supply stores, or ELL students can be given the task of making the charts, thus reinforcing the word meanings as well as allowing them to contribute in nonverbal ways to the class. Here are some suggestions for chart construction:

Elementary Level

- colors, animals, money, toys, shapes

All Levels

- Science: the human body, food chains, ecosystems
- Math:
  - symbols such as >, <, +, =, % with their verbal meanings
  - words for equivalents such as *sum = add; difference = subtract*
  - If you see *add, plus, combine, and, sum, increased by* in the problem, *add.*
  - If you see *subtract, from, less, minus, differ, less than, decreased by* in the problem, *subtract.*
- Physical education: equipment; familiar commands or techniques, such as dribbling, passing; common vocabulary
- Music: time equivalent for notes; words for symbols, such as *treble* and *bass clef*
- Social studies: maps; time lines
- Shop: safety rules; equipment and tools

Activities Using Environmental Print

Because these words are relevant to their lives, most English-speaking children know environmental print long before they come to kindergarten. Even the newest ELL students can pick out words they recognize, such as *McDonalds, K-Mart,* and *Citgo.* Goodman (in Teale and Sulzby 1986) says:

The development of print awareness in environmental contexts is the root of literacy most common to all learners...In the print-rich environment of most present cultures, young children are consciously interacting with, organizing, and analyzing the meanings of the visible language...The development of knowledge about print embedded in environmental settings is the beginning of reading development.

You can invent a host of activities that employ words seen in everyday life, such as *McDonalds*, *Safeway*, and *STOP*. Many of the words are intimately tied to a configuration or logo that gives a decoding clue. McDonalds, for instance, is written with the "golden arches" and STOP is always within the context of a red octagon. As students develop more skills, they will be able to decode the words without the use of these visual clues, but they are an important first step in equating sign-symbol correspondence.

Elementary Level

- Have children bring in clean, empty food boxes and cans, and put together a pretend class grocery store.

- Have students brainstorm all the places they see words: on labels, billboards, television, packages, traffic signs, and so on.

- With the entire class, take a tour of the school or the neighborhood to scout for environmental print.

All Levels

- Have students collect examples of environmental print and categorize them in different ways.

- Have students keep three-day journals of all the different kinds of reading they do in a day, from street signs to school assignments.

- Have a T-shirt design contest.

- Make a class yearbook.

- Make a classroom telephone directory.

I-Can-Read Books and Dictionaries

The variations on this theme are endless at all levels. This is another way to reinforce students' vocabulary and demonstrate what your regular students know; it is also an activity you can implement immediately with your new students.

- Beginning students can cut pictures from magazines or newspapers of all the words they recognize, from *house* to *lion*, then paste one picture onto each page of a blank booklet. Underneath each picture, you or an aide can print "I can read _____" (inserting the word in the blank space). Usually the students quickly remember that each page starts with "I can read" and, since they chose the pictures, they are able to "read" the book almost immediately and feel a real sense of achievement.

Figure 4.18 A third-grader's picture dictionary.

- Preliterate students can cut out pictures of things for which they know the English word, and paste the pictures into their books. In the content areas, you can implement this activity before students are able to do regular class work.

- Students can categorize words—foods, body parts, or furniture, for example—and add new words to each category as they expand their vocabulary.

- Those who are already literate and have learned more English can print the words next to their pictures (figure 4.18). Advanced students can alphabetize and write definitions for their words.

- ELL students can work with an aide or a buddy, using their dictionary for review. They can also practice the words by themselves while the rest of the class is involved in other activities. This is a terrific confidence booster; it demonstrates concretely to students how far they have advanced in their knowledge of English.

Games

Games are not simply time fillers; treat them seriously. Ventriglia (1982) notes that children acquiring a second language "appear to learn language best in conversations or in game-like situations where language is used meaningfully and is associated with some concrete reference at the beginning." Games provide this context for socializing and reinforcing language. Native English-speaking students can become the teachers and can learn valuable lessons in patience and modifying their language to provide input that's comprehensible to the language learner. Learning the rules to games requires careful listening. Games have a clear, repetitive structure, in which words are tied closely to actions. They are also strong motivators. Even the shyest, most reluctant, or nonverbal students will get involved in a game and forget their inhibitions. When the focus is on having fun, vocabulary is learned as a byproduct, and friendships are fostered. You can choose the level of sophistication of rules and vocabulary you want reinforced. The game Sorry, for instance, uses colors, counting, number recognition, and several important survival words and phrases, such as *sorry, start,* and *It's your turn.* Here are other suggestions:

- Bingo (can be modified for any type of lesson)

- Trivial Pursuit, Jeopardy (English and content teachers can make up content and adapt it to the class)

- Board games: Sorry, The Last Straw, Candyland, Operation, Hungry Hungry Hippos, Yahtzee, Clue

- For older students: Monopoly, Risk, Boggle, Scrabble

- Guessing games: Simon Says; Mother May I?; Win, Lose, or Draw

- Card games: Concentration, War, Old Maid, Go Fish, Cribbage

- Word games: Twenty Questions, Ghost

Many games can be modified, with questions tailored for any content class or lesson. Make your own version of Trivial Pursuit, Jeopardy, or Go Fish.

Games can also be tweaked to fulfill a linguistic or curricular goal. For instance, playing a version of Mother May I? while teaching prepositions is a great way to reinforce, as well as assess students' knowledge. To the right is Glory's drawing.

Those involved in adventure-based learning (Kolb 1984) have, for many years, stressed the importance of play in learning, contending that people are "happier and more productive when they have a playful attitude" (Garside 1996). We have found this is true, and the idea of challenge and fun is central to our philosophy of teaching. We insert laughter and games wherever we can.

Figure 4.19 Here's Glory's picture

Audio Recordings

Audio books can be very effective with beginning readers having trouble with phonics to older middle-school, high-school, and adult readers who have struggled with reading. There are multiple places to find audio books online, so the selection is broadening. Audio theater is another option to use as comprehension practice. You can also find good readers to do the recording, and make your own. A word of caution: working with audio recordings demands a great deal of input from and interaction with you, the teacher, and thus is not an appropriate "center" activity. If you decide to leave an ELL student to work on his own with a recorded text, be sure to check in frequently with him.

You can record almost anything—stories, songs, rhymes, or chants—and make them into digital audio files. Recordings are useful: they reinforce the speech-to-print connection as well as meaningful vocabulary and allow your ELL students to work on reading while you are engaged in another activity (but, as already mentioned, be sure to check in regularly with him). However, audio activities should not be used simply as fillers when you have nothing else for these students to do. Audio books that ELL students use should already be familiar to them, having read and discussed them with the class or another student. Don't try to break new ground with audio books; they are better used as reinforcement of previously covered material (Carbo 1992). If you are making a recording for beginning students, be sure to include a "beep" or other signal at the end of each page in the corresponding book so they know when to turn the page. Otherwise, you may, at times, discover a student "reading" three pages behind the text!

A few more things to consider about audio recordings:

- You get double benefits if you allow your native English-speaking students to do the recording for you, giving them extra practice in reading.

- Record or download songs for pleasure listening. Try to include English translations of songs from students' own cultures.

- If possible, send recordings home with students. Discussions with parents about the books in their own language will greatly benefit students.

- At the secondary level, you can record your lectures so that students can take them home and listen to them a second time for learning reinforcement. Many colleges are already using podcasts of lectures. Jump on the bandwagon. If you have the technical tools, create podcasts of key lectures for your students. You can upload them to your webpage for students who have missed class or who want to review the information.

Songs

Songs can be a delightful way to work on rhythm, pronunciation, and vocabulary. People of all ages love to learn and sing songs. You can ask your native English-speaking students to find pictures or props to teach ELL students the words of the song.

The use of songs doesn't have to be limited to the primary grades, and the songs don't have to be juvenile tunes only a kindergartner would love. Students of all ages listen to the "Top 40," whether they understand the words or not, and many second-language learners comment that they learn a great deal of their language from the radio and TV. You can capitalize on this by bringing in songs for discussion to illustrate a theme or even a grammatical point. Use recordings by such perennial favorites as Bob Dylan, The Beatles, or Peter, Paul, and Mary, social commentators like Pink Floyd, or language-development artists such as Bob Schneider of Toronto.

As mentioned, songs can be a wonderful way to teach both comprehension and grammatical points. The song "I Hope You'll Dance," by Lee Ann

Womack, for instance, is a great song to use with all students, not just ELLs.[1] Almost anything is available now on YouTube—the kids will recommend the latest songs to you. They always know. Be sure to give students copies of the lyrics to read as they follow along.

A few more things to consider about songs:

- Buy a book of camp songs or Boy Scout songs. These have been around forever, with good reason. "If You're Happy and You Know It," "The More We Get Together," and such are great for reading, pronunciation, and just plain fun. Barb made her summer students sing every day. Even though she had to put up with groans and "We no sing today, teacher," they really liked to try to outdo each other on "Valderi Valdera" and "A Hot Time in the Old Town Tonight, (FIRE! FIRE! FIRE!)." Hearing a student spontaneously start singing "Oh My Darling," during a walk or an art project can be very gratifying.

- History: Use folk songs or spirituals such as "Swing Low, Sweet Chariot" to enliven an understanding of slavery.

- Social Science: Use songs from other lands to give insight into other cultures.

- Government: Use social commentary songs such as the old stand-bys: "Eve of Destruction," by P. F. Sloan, "Rain on the Scarecrow," by John Mellencamp, or Neil Sedaka's "The Immigrant." For more current choices, try the Radiohead album *Kid A* (2000), the song "2+2=5" from Radiohead's *Hail to the Thief* (2003), or the song "Wake Up," from Rage Against the Machine's self titled first album (1992).

- English: English classes are the perfect place to study songs. You can look at poetic theme, rhyme, sense of place, as well as natural rhythm and cadence. The early Beatles' and Rolling Stones' ballads are naturals.

- It may be dangerous to allow students to choose their own songs, since many rock and particularly rap groups write a wide range of songs that sometimes includes erotic or violent material. You may want to get together with other teachers and compile a list of songs you would like to include, and let the students choose from these. Or, have students copy the lyrics and get prior approval for a song to study.

Drama

Drama is one of the most effective ways to develop language. It "can be a link between speech and writing. Through drama, children are guided to imagine, explore, enact, communicate, and reflect on ideas, concepts and feelings" (Stewig and Buege 1994).

---

1 For more ideas, go to AzarGrammar.com, <www.azargrammar.com>. The website lists all sorts of songs to teach grammar points, such as "I Still Haven't Found What I'm Looking For," by U2, and "Never Been to Spain," by Hoyt Axton, to teach present perfect in a fun and absorbing way. (Preview these. One run through of "We'll Sing in the Sunshine" is enough to make you want to slide under the desk.)

Moffett (1967) even asserted that "drama and speech are central to the language curriculum, not peripheral...I see drama as the matrix of all language activities, subsuming speech and engendering the varieties of writing and reading."

The benefits of drama for ELL students cannot be overstated. Drama brings fun and laughter to learning. Kids gain confidence in their use of English and in themselves. When students are listening and responding to stage directions and hearing others use the vocabulary, comprehensible input is built in. For instance, during a production of *Goldilocks and the Three Bears* with low-level ELL students, Mercy (playing Goldilocks) was two beds ahead of Nicola the narrator, who was just getting Goldilocks up the stairs from the living room. When Nicola read, "So she climbed into the first bed," and the chorus chimed, "This bed is too hard" Mercy leapt back onto the first bed.

Understanding dialogue and sequence comes from practice and repetition—necessary skills for language learning, but often tedious and boring. Drama builds all the skills—listening, vocabulary, reading, and writing—within a framework of fun and active participation. For instance, Barb and a group of middle- and high-school students produced their own version of *Lon Po Po* (a Chinese version of the story *Little Red Riding Hood*). As this particular group was all Taiwanese, they were familiar with the story. The students wrote their own script. In it, the wolf killed and ate the youngest child, played by Dora. The children, hiding in the dark, were alerted to imminent danger because the wolf ate very loudly, and then, when they asked him to share, threw them a bloody finger. At the end of the play, mother and father came home to find the wolf dead and the children in the tree. The narrator's final lines read: "So, the children explain what happened the night before to mother and father. After that they are very hungry so they BBQ the wolf and have a wonderful meal. The End."

The logic of the family having a wonderful meal when Dora is dead did not appeal to Barb's sensibilities, and long discussions ensued as to whether they should have the father cut Dora out of the wolf's stomach and find her alive, or whether they should mourn her loss. The group liked their ending as it was, and thus it stayed—with Dora dead. Oh well. Let's BBQ and be happy.

Everyone can participate in a dramatic presentation, even those who have little or no English. A chorus can provide safety in numbers, and the least-proficient students can be carried along with the rest of the group. For example:

Chorus: *Little pig, little pig, let me come in!*
Not by the hair of my chinny-chin-chin!

The least-proficient students do not have to have speaking parts. In many plays, parts can be built in for everyone. For example, in *Goldilocks and the Three Bears,* students portrayed a great big bowl, a middle-sized bowl, and a wee, tiny bowl, three chairs, and three beds. The children who were not actually onstage were the chorus.

Using drama doesn't have to entail elaborate plays. It can be as simple as having children enact Mother Goose rhymes such as "The Queen of Hearts" or songs like "Oh My Darling, Clementine" while the others sing the words.

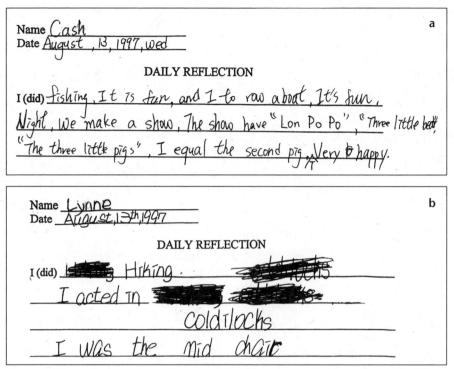

Figure 4.20a–b Here are Lynne's and Cash's reflections on their roles in (a) *The Three Little Pigs* and (b) *Goldilocks and the Three Bears*.

Secondary Level

Drama at the upper level has many other benefits. Reading a piece of literature or poetry or other genre and then returning to it to get the meat of the ideas involves multiple and complex thinking skills. Then, translating and transforming these ideas into another medium involves more thinking. There is something so magical in watching kids become characters and say or do things they would never say or do as themselves. Drama allows them that freedom.

Here are some suggestions for using drama in the classroom:

- **History:** Dramatize an important historical event.

- **Government:** Enact a pretend bill into law; poll the student body on an issue; have a pretend election; hold a dramatic trial. Trials always seem to go over big. Is Mrs. Foster, from the play, *Trifles,* guilty of murder, or is she a victim of wife abuse? Does Buddy, from Louise Erdrich's short story "American Horse," need to be taken away from his mother?

- **Social sciences:** Create socio-dramas by setting up a situation in which students have to make difficult choices and ad-lib their solutions. For example, students who participated in a simulation of arms trafficking, in which some of the players could be present at the negotiations and others could only pass notes to offer deals, learned just how difficult it is to control trafficking, how susceptible people are to corruption, and how powerless those who have nothing to negotiate (such as diamonds, guns, money) are.

- **English:** Reenact a scene from a play or a piece of literature. Doing modern-day skits of Shakespeare plays makes it accessible and fun for even the lowest reader.[2] Some examples include having students bring Mama, from Alice Walker's "Everyday Use," onto a Jerry Springer-type show, or bring Emily, from William Faulkner's "A Rose for Emily," back from the dead, and ask her what the heck she thought she was about.

Figure 4.21 Advanced ELLs, who had studied *To Kill a Mockingbird*, took on the roles of the main characters, to be interviewed by their classmates acting as journalists. This experience found its way into the drama *Sometimes Evil Has to Win* (see page 219).

Elementary Level

- Use rhymes, fairytales, and puppet shows. The latter are particularly effective with ELL students when they manipulate the puppets while you read the script. Students are responsible for understanding the material and responding on cue, but are not required to produce language themselves.

Patterned Language

Patterned language involves texts in which certain language structures are repeated again and again. It is a particularly important activity for beginning readers and beginning language users (the writers of those endless drill-and-practice foreign-language textbooks recognize the value of patterned language in language learning). Giving readers the strategy of imitating phrases helps them make the transition from labeling to sentence formation, allowing them to hear and repeat chunks of language that are meaningful. Patterned language has many positive features:

- The repetition gives students the practice they need in order to internalize a form.

- Students can use these patterns as building blocks. They make generalizations from the patterns they have learned and can then move on to create their own sentences.

- When the forms are practiced consistently, they become instinctive. Students can focus on communication and learning new structures with the security of having a few forms well learned.

Ventriglia (1982) notes that students learning a second language naturally adopt a strategy of following patterns, but they learn patterns that are meaningful and useful to them, ones that can be applied in a social context. Long, meaningless drills found in textbooks are easily forgotten. But by selecting

---

2 The Web English Teacher site, <www.webenglishteacher.com>, has many links to sites that will give you ideas.

topics that interest the learners, using phrases elicited from them, and practicing these phrases in a game-like situation, you can use patterns successfully, not only to reinforce vocabulary, but to introduce new linguistic patterns in a systematic way. Students can easily transfer the patterns they have learned and apply them to new social contexts.

Make a distinction, therefore, between these types of sentences and the traditional fill-in-the-blanks sentences found in many older texts (for instance, "This is a _____."). Barb once consulted with a tutor who had been working on such sentences with two 12-year-old English-language learners ("This is [a/an] apple. This is [a/an] dish."). They couldn't remember the difference between *a* and *an* from one day to the next, and the tutor had decided that they were learning disabled. Jumping to this conclusion based upon such insufficient data was damaging. The boys weren't learning disabled, they were simply bored struggling with a very minor grammatical point that had little relevance or significance to them in the face of the huge task of learning the English language.

With the following types of patterned language, you can avoid tedium while retaining the positive aspects of this type of continued practice of forms. For example, several students of varying levels made their own version of the story, *The Very Hungry Caterpillar,* by Eric Carle (figure 4.22). Because they knew the format, they could each reproduce, in their own words, at their own level of proficiency and skills, a book they could be proud of. *Brown Bear, Brown Bear, What Do You See?* by Bill Martin Jr. and Eric Carle is another familiar patterned language book that beginners can use to build their own sentences.

Chants

A chant is

> *a group of words that comes alive when given a rhythmical reading...Any speech exercise based on a strong rhythm contributes to the development of speech and language skills. Language learning is accelerated by having fun with and exploring the rhythm in words. An energetic approach, using oral repetition with rhythmical expression, leads to pleasant, stimulating experiences...Chanting, with its rhythmical repetition of words, transcends language differences. It is useful for children in programs of [ELL], ESD [English as a second dialect] and beginning readers* (Dunn, *Butterscotch Dreams 1987*).

You can use

- Old favorites such as "One potato, two potato, three potato, four..."

- Jump-rope songs/chants

- Commercially produced collections of chants. For example, *Jazz Chants for Children*, by Carolyn Graham (1979), features a book of childrens' chants, songs and poems as well as picture activities, a teacher's edition with instructions for classroom presentation, and an audio recording of the chants by the author with a group of children. *Big Chants: I Went Walking*, also by Graham (1994), is a short, repetitive story about a boy who goes on a walk and identifies animals of different colors.

Figure 4.22. Examples of *The Very Hungry Camper* patterned on *The Very Hungry Caterpillar* by Eric Carle. Note the freedom a basic structure gives students to express their own ideas, creativity, and humor.

Frame Sentences

What if the elementary curriculum guide mandates that you teach your students such words as *can, run, jump, I, and, the, go,* and *was* by October? Or, suppose your 10th grader says things like, "I didn't brought my homework," or "I seed that movie last week." Is there any alternative to relying solely on a basal reader or simple memorization of word lists?

One particularly effective use of patterned language involves frame sentences, developed by Marlene and Robert McCracken (1995), which allow the teacher to plug student ideas into a controlled pattern of words.

Elementary Levels

Frame sentences are structures that provide key words in a sentence, leaving space for students to fill in specific content. Use frame sentences to help students understand difficult material or to elicit what they already know about a topic. For example, ask the question, "What do you know about...?" For instance, "What do you know about mammals?"

4.23a–c In our summer program, where we taught Taiwanese kids English in an adventure setting, we included several challenge courses that necessitated students doing things they might consider frightening, such as camping under the open sky in an area known to have bears. We decided to tackle the issues head on: we talked about being scared and strategies to think through what to do when one is afraid. We developed frame sentences based on these ideas.

Setting Goals a

List things you can do.

1. I know I can ___ swim in the lake although the water in the lake is so cold.
I know I can like the food here more than the food in Taiwan.
I know I can shopping in a shipping mall if I want.

2. I think I can love to live here like my warm home in Taiwan.
I think I can eat the food here very much if I'm so hungry.

3. I'll try to study with our kind teachers here
I'll try to do myself if I can.
I'll try to like my teachers here like my friend.
I'll try to play games with my friends here.

Setting Goals b

List things you can do.

1. I know I can play BINGO.
eat chocolate.
play hulp hoop
catch a fish.
sleep
speak Chinese.
go to my haust in Taiwan.

2. I think I can see my mommy and daddy.
to go shoping
play a piano.
to go eat pizza.
to go the zoo.
play BINGO

3. I'll try play the hulp hoop. 搖 呼啦圈
to read a book in English. 在美國讀英文
jump. 跳
throw Boll 投球
catch Boll 接球
drink water 喝水

Figure 4.24a–b More proficient learners can creatively combine words and chunks of language to express their ideas.

Then, set up the frame sentence: "A mammal is an animal that has..." Any topic or issue can be introduced this way.

Frames can be derived from basal readers, from content-area units being studied, or from virtually any source. Once you get started using frame sentences, the possibilities are endless. With ELL students, this is a particularly effective way to work on a problem once you've diagnosed a need. For instance, if the student needs to work on the irregular past tense, you can begin sentences like

Yesterday I went...
Yesterday I saw...
Yesterday I ate...

Or, you can use frame sentences to teach conjunctions and transition words that ELL students often find difficult, as in the following example (note that underlined words represent filled-in blanks):

A horse can walk, and so can an elephant.
A horse can walk, but a fish cannot.
A worm cannot walk, and neither can a fish.

Beginners can simply copy examples provided.

All Levels

The McCrackens recommend using a different frame sentence every day: "Some children will grasp their first learned frame and write with it seemingly forever if we use a single frame for several days." They also stress quantity, and insist that, for proper reinforcement, the teacher elicit 30 to 40 (or more) brainstormed responses for each frame. Every day, students can chant back the previous day's frames and even brainstorm new responses.

Rhymes

Small children enjoy rhymes, often repeating them over and over again to themselves. Non-native-English speakers can pick them up very quickly and derive great pleasure and a sense of achievement from being able to recite them. Rhymes allow ELL students to practice (within the context of a whole text) the 44 sounds of English. Learners are able to model intonation, stress, and pronunciation in a fun, dynamic, and meaningful way.

Rhymes can also be incorporated into literacy activities at the elementary level. For example:

- Choose a familiar rhyme such as "Humpty Dumpty." Use one picture for each scene, and have students put the pictures in order. When they have learned the words and the sequence of the rhyme, they can begin to match pictures with words.

- Prepare a pocket chart of word cards so that students can follow the words as they chant them. Make duplicate word cards of the rhymes, and then have ELL students place them in the correct order as they recite. Beginners can start by matching word cards and placing them on top of the words of the rhyme that have been written on large paper. This not only reinforces the sound-to-print connection, but builds sight-word vocabulary.

- Say a word, and have the group find it in the pocket chart. Remove several words from the pocket chart, and have students replace them in the proper sequence, chanting the rhyme to check if the words have been replaced properly.

- Have students make their own books into which they can copy the rhymes they have learned and illustrate them. This reinforces, in an enjoyable way, not only reading, but writing and spelling, too.

- Give a rhymes "concert."

- Act out the rhymes.

- Have students record themselves reciting the rhymes. Allow ELL students to record some of the rhymes they have learned well. Have them record on several different occasions so that they can monitor their own progress when they hear their recorded rhymes played back.

Sourcebooks for rhyme-based activities are available in most teacher supply stores.

Mimicry, or Creative Copying

We skirt the chasm of plagiarism when we talk about copying another's work. But we know that good reading helps develop good writing. We know that good literature provides good models. And copying, then transforming a work can be a powerful tool to help students grow as writers. It's truly magical what students can accomplish when they are provided the structure on which to hang their ideas.

The difference between plagiarism and mimicry, as Dierking (2002) points out, is intent. With mimicking the intent isn't to claim another's writing, but to use the form and the technique as a guide, a jumping off place to build one's own work. DeCristofaro (2001) writes, "Immersion in certain kinds of reading helps all writers assimilate the tone, flavor, structure, norms, and rhetorical strategies of particular genres of writing, a prewriting that's no less effective for being osmotic and unconscious." When students copy-create, they integrate the forms, the structures, and the styles into their own writing and create something that's their own.

With this strategy, you give your students a piece of work, such as one of Aesop's fables, a poem, or a short passage, and have them mimic the structure, the style, and the diction, but replace some of the details with their own ideas.

A poem that seems, at first, inaccessible (to anyone) is Russian poet Anna Akhmatova's "Instead of a Preface" (translated into English):

Instead of a Preface
by Anna Akhmatova

In the terrible years of the Yezhov terror I spent seventeen months waiting in line outside the prison in Leningrad.

One day somebody in the crowd identified me. Standing behind me was a woman with lips blue from the cold, who had, of course, never heard me called by name before. Now she started out of the torpor common to us all and asked me in a whisper (everyone whispered there): "Can you describe this?" And I said: "I can." Then something like a smile passed fleetingly over what had once been her face.

But, in an English class where students were required to investigate corruption in countries around the world, they rewrote the poem to reflect their understanding of life in that country. The depth of their understanding and the power of their words was astounding. Here's Chan's rendition regarding her own country:

In the terrible days of Tian an men Square I spent the vast majority of my time not knowing what was going on in Beijing. In 04/22/1989 I had mad plans to go down to Tian an men that morning to watch with various poeple at various time. Everyone was running and escapting. Suddenly, one of colledge girl who wore flag shirt asked me in whisper. "Can you understand why they shot so many university students?"

And I said: "I can't."

Then something like tears full of her eyes.

Here's what Eldina wrote about the country she left as a tiny girl:

In the terrible years of the Balkan slaughter, I spent seventeen months hiding in the woods. One day seombody found me sitting on the cold ground, shivering. Standing in front of me was a man holding a rifle in his hand. He looked at me as though he did not know what to do, shoot me or walk away; pretending he never encountered me. As teers seemed to fill my eyes I whisptered to him, "Please don't hurt me." And he did not say a word. Just walked away and did not look back once.

Conclusion

With language learning, the key is authenticity rather than fractionating reading, writing, listening, and speaking into separate skills, then breaking them down even further into meaningless exercises. The activities we have included can be incorporated into the themes you are working on. They don't involve a lot of extra planning or extra work, but the benefits you reap in terms of your students' language acquisition are great.

Fortunately, most school boards and administrations recognize that helping students achieve literacy is not solely the job of the elementary teacher or the high-school English teacher. It is the job of all teachers, from the art teacher to the phys ed instructor, from the band director to the shop teacher. Reading and writing are an integral part of every course within the curriculum from math to driver education. Language instruction is everybody's business. In subsequent chapters, we will show how this can be done.

Reflections, Projects, and Projections for Discussion

- What nationalities or ethnic backgrounds do students in your class or district have? Are they literate? What types of literacy materials will you need to amass or develop to help them achieve on a par with your English speaking students?

- Choose one of the students portrayed on the next four pages or a student from the case studies in chapter 2 (Tomás, Boris, Charlie, Lady, and so on) whose skill level and hypothetical grade level fall into the range that you would teach. What content or skills are required within the core or content standards for your grade or class? How far in the curriculum have you progressed? (If you're not teaching yet, choose one standard or skill). How are you going to help this student catch up with the rest of your students and work at grade level?

- Design some development exercises for students who are developing their literacy skills (games, art, comics, and so on.) Work on exercises that address different levels of literacy.

- Map out a continuum of skills your students will need to achieve in your class over the year. How will you assess success? How will you report progress? Who will you need to collaborate with? What will you need for support?

- After a science lesson on matter, Mrs. Dickinson wrote the word *tablet* on the board. Here are different ways that students copied the word:

  Tabrt   Tablket   Tabrtin   tabkt

  Why would they do this? What should you do to correct them, or do you need to bother? Justify your position.

Case Study: Lee

Lee arrived in the spring. She had no English and had never been in school before. Because it was late in the year, the teachers gave her time to adjust to school and learn basic oral English, without really working on literacy skills. She has been at your school for a year now, and teachers are starting to worry, because her literacy skills seem to be stalled in neutral. She has difficulty copying off the board, getting each letter in the right place. Lee has trouble tracking, and she doesn't know the names of all the letters, so she can't remember more than one in her head when copying. In addition, when she has finished, (usually last in the group) she has often missed several letters (or words). Since she can't reread what she's copied on her own, she can't tell if she missed something or not. When you read it back to her, she isn't able to spot when a word is missing, she just readjusts where her finger is pointing, as if you have missed a word.

Reading Recovery proposes three main ways for students to figure out a new word or a word that is unknown: "get your mouth ready" by saying the first sound of the word; ask yourself if your "guess" make sense; and look at the picture to help you figure out the word. Lee relies heavily on the picture clues to figure out words she doesn't know. Since she isn't sure of all of the letters and the sounds they make, it is difficult for her to get her mouth ready. Also, most of this language doesn't make sense to her, so at this point she can't rely on that strategy too heavily.

- Where do you start with a student such as Lee?
- What strategies *would* work?
- What can you do to build Lee's skills in reading and writing?
- What are the priorities if she's five? eight? ten? twelve? fifteen?
- If you have limited or no ELL support, what can you expect of Lee in the classroom?
- What tasks can you give to her that she can succeed at?
- What are your short-term goals? What are your long-term goals?
- How will you find time for her to build the necessary literacy skills?
- What can you do to coordinate with the ELL teacher or other support personnel?

More Case Studies to Consider

Miguel

Here's a page from Miguel's workbook. Miguel is in third grade, born and raised in the U.S. What does his writing reveal about his literacy level? Is this the writing of a third grader? Why or why not? What features do you take into account to decide? What does he need in order to catch up to his age and grade mates? What if he's in fifth grade or seventh? Where do you go from here?

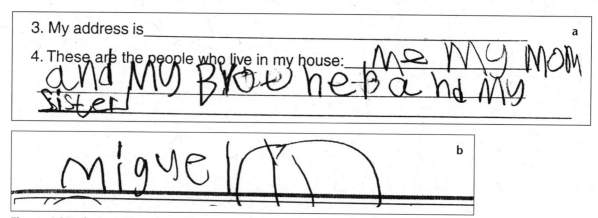

Figure 4.25a–b A portion of a page from Miguel's workbook (a), and his signature (b).

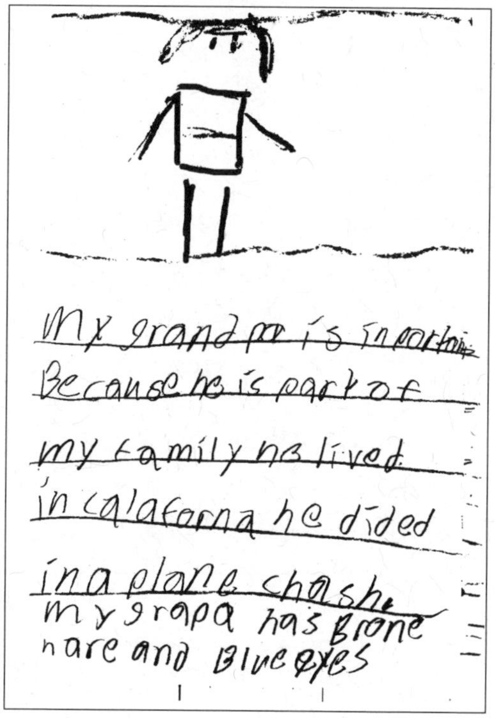

Paul

Here's a page from Paul's "Important Book," written when he was in sixth grade. What does his writing reveal? Is it at the level of an average sixth grader? What features of his writing do you take into account to decide? What are his prospects of success in middle and high school? What sorts of intervention measures can you apply to help him catch up and succeed in school?

Figure 4.26 Paul's writing about an important person in his life.

Carlos

At what level is Carlos (below) functioning? Is this acceptable work for a 6th grader? For an 8th grader or a 10th grader? What does his writing reveal about his knowledge of English and mechanics? Based on his writing what assumptions can you make about his ability to function in a grade-level class or subject? If you can't make any assumptions, what further information would you need? What assignments could you give Carlos to improve his level of functioning and move him to the next level? What specifically (reading, more writing, vocabulary, and so on) does he need to move ahead?

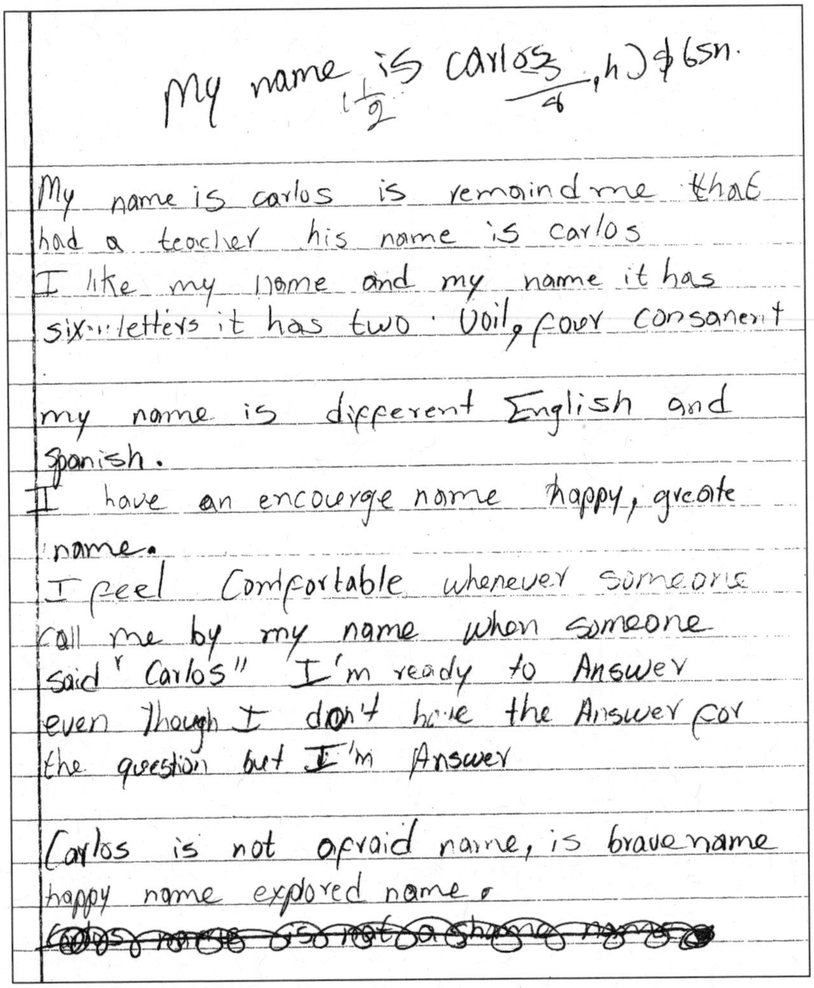
My name is carlos

My name is carlos is remaind me that
had a teacher his name is carlos
I like my name and my name it has
six letters it has two voil, four consonent

my name is dipperent English and
Spanish.
I have an encourge name happy, greate
name.
I peel Comfortable whenever someone
call me by my name when someone
said "Carlos" I'm ready to Answer
even though I don't have the Answer for
the question but I'm Answer

Carlos is not apraid name, is brave name
happy name explored name.

Figure 4.7 Carlos's writing

Josefina

Here's Josefina, responding to the same assignment:

My name is Josefina for me is been nightmare but for other is parting. My mother name me like that because her religion. She told me that she name me Josefina because I was born on March nineteen. That is the day when they celebrate Jesus' father name, that is Jose we are the Mexicans call that day San Jose day that is a very especial day for most people. We celebrate it with parties, music, food and fireworks.

That is the reason why she name me Jose and fina, the fina word it doesn't mean nothing special that I know about it. Is just make Jose word together to make it sound female.

Josefina name is being a nightmare for me, sense I was a little girl. When I was in school, kids used to make fun of my name because I had a boy's name Jose in front of Fina.

That affected me for life, very bad, so was when I stared to hate my name. My name is like a big stick tag that sticks on me every day and every where that I go, with out wanting it. Is like something contagious that I can not get rid of.

At what level is Josefina functioning? What does her writing reveal about her knowledge of English and mechanics? Based on her writing what assumptions can you make about her ability to function in a grade-level class or subject? For example, could she do grade 8 work? Or, if she were in grade 9 history, could she pass? What assignments could you give her to improve her level of functioning and move her to the next level? What specifically (reading, more writing, vocabulary, and so on) does she need to move ahead?

Eddie

Here's Eddie:

Let me ask something "if your life remains only three months and you could do three things in that time what will you do for 3 months?" I believe that most people try to their best to get money or give up on their life and stay home. As I mention about a person who gives up their life is afraid of a death. There is old Korean saying "You might as well enjoy the pain that you cannot avoid." So I enjoy my pain and make plane.

The first thing I would like do to write down my testament. I enjoy watching televisiondramas especially romantic dramas. Usually when an actor or actors it's by accident they do not write down any comment because they cannot predict on their future. So I would like to write testament for my family and my friends. For example.

Dear my family and friends.
Lovely father and mother, I am very sorry. Do not cry too much. I will not forget my family and see you in heaven and burn my dead body to ashes and when you travel to somewhere feel free to use my remaining money.

Could Eddie function in a regular classroom, without assistance, at the grade you teach? If you were teaching grade 10 history would he be able to hold his own? What types of intervention or monitoring would be appropriate for him? How long would you wait to intervene if he demonstrates he isn't keeping up?

Jihong

Here's Jihong:

The conference pointed the accident of April 28 which fully exposed some units' responsibility mistiness on management of safety in production measure incorrect and so on to teach a strict lesson completely. The State Department truly madly deeply laments disaster victim death; kindly condole the wounded and the family of casualty.

Could Jihong function in a regular classroom without assistance, at the grade you teach? What types of intervention or monitoring would be appropriate for him? How long would you wait to intervene if he demonstrates he isn't keeping up? How accommodating would regular classroom teachers be to this sort of writing? Would they even try to read it, or would they simply dismiss it as unreadable and throw it out? What can you do to make Jihong's writing clearer? And how did he manage to come up with those sentences anyway?

Chapter 5

Reading—First Meaning Is Lost Cautious

In this chapter, we discuss the basics for teaching and promoting reading with ELL students. We focus on

- The process of learning to read
- What all students need to become successful readers
- Balancing the needs of fluent and nonfluent readers
- Meeting the particular reading needs of individual students

Bao cannot read. She is classified as preliterate: she comes from a family that has no history of reading and writing and does not know that print carries meaning. When presented with a book, she cannot tell the front from the back. She was observed holding a picture book upside down, and only when she encountered a picture of a person did she turn it right side up.

If Bao arrives in kindergarten this does not present an insurmountable problem. She is immersed in print and sees the teacher modeling reading and writing behaviors daily. Bao also hears the teacher giving instruction in the many facets of reading and writing.

If Bao arrives in the second grade, she is not only three years behind in formal instruction, but about seven years behind in terms of "literate behaviors" (for example, showing understanding of concepts of print, book handling knowledge, retelling, writing). Literate behaviors attend most of our mainstream students who have handled books, seen many hours of television, and read the infinite array of signs and displays that surround people in Western countries. If Bao reaches high school without learning to make sense of print, this will present staggering obstacles to her ability to succeed in school.

In this particular case, Bao arrived at the age of 16 with no previous schooling. In two years she has learned to speak English very well and can even write a bit in English, but she still has not learned to read. She is now 18, and school officials are telling her that they have done all they can. This is her last year;

whether she graduates or not, she has to leave. Science, history, and English teachers do not consider it their job to teach reading. The ELL teacher has turned Bao over to the latest in a string of tutors and told the tutor to work on phonics. It didn't work before, but, as the teacher says, "We've tried everything else."

Fernando is a recent immigrant from a small town in Mexico. The only English he spoke during an initial session with an intake person was the word *teacher*. He has never been to school and is not literate in either English or Spanish. He cannot write his own name. If Fernando is in kindergarten, this is not too dire. If he's 16, it's a problem.

Bao and Fernando are not isolated cases. Neither are their plights. Many students come to our schools and seem to grasp the spoken language immediately but lag far behind in reading skills. When they arrive at the high school level, they have more English to learn and less time to do it (Kingwell and Clarke 2002). And the statistics are grim. Thomas and Collier (2002) baldly claim that "students with no primary language schooling (either in home country or host country) are not able to reach grade-level performance in L2 [the second language]."

Such a claim has the potential to turn into dogma. In a 1989 study called "How Long? A Synthesis of Research on Academic Achievement in a Second Language" Virginia Collier first suggested that it takes five to seven years to achieve grade level performance in the second language. This soon became an accepted fact (see Hakuta, Butler, and Witt 2000; Suárez-Orozco and Suárez-Orozco 2009). The assertion, "It takes five to seven years," soon morphed into "since it takes five to seven years…" with all its attendant implications.

This dogma not only allows us to abdicate responsibility, it sells the students short, and it lowers our expectations of them by default. We have seen students achieve success in content areas regardless of what the studies say. Students make progress and can still learn content even if they are not functioning independently. Mary's student, Hua, could read the material, participate in classroom discussions, and do well. She did have trouble getting the subtle meanings and symbols in the reading, but with some support, she could still participate in the content discussions and write convincingly about the subject matter.

These statistics, true or not, needn't lead us to throw up our hands in despair and give up or stop trying. Bao's future depends on our efforts. Some high schools allow students to stay in school much longer, even to age 25 or so in special cases. But these are few and far between. And we have to give the Fernandos in our lives as much of a running start as we can.

With the odds stacked against students like Bao and Fernando, we have to do it right. The ways we have traditionally taught North American children to read often do not work with ELL students, and, like Bao, these students struggle with the rudiments year after frustrating year. What can be done?

Defining Reading

At the height of the whole-language movement in the 1980s, everything seemed clear: many teachers believed, and proceeded, under the assumption that by simply immersing children in good literature, they would learn to read. But good teachers never abandoned teaching decoding skills as the phonics phalanx has charged. The skills were embedded within a meaningful context rather than taught as isolated entities in separate time blocks.

A groundswell of grassroots acceptance for the philosophies and practices of whole language gained momentum until it was mandated. Then, teachers who had taught successfully for many years, using methods that worked for them and their particular students, were suddenly forced, with little explanation and less training, to change—whether they believed in whole language or not. Subversion began.

In the meantime, thoughtful teachers were questioning the assumption that there was no place for direct instruction. In the last years of the 1990s, a tremendous tsunami-sized backlash ensued to the point where now, few books or studies make even passing reference to the founders and champions of whole language, Kenneth and Yetta Goodman and Frank Smith. This is supremely unfortunate, because it means that the contributions and foundations of whole language are being devalued and obscured. The Goodmans conducted straightforward research. They simply asked hundreds and hundreds of readers to read aloud. They analyzed the mistakes (miscues) the readers made, and asked them to retell what they read. Their philosophy developed out of their work with real readers, not studies made about studies.

So now what? Things have become much more complex and treacherous, especially since the pressure to improve student performance and meet all standards has reached such intensity. The tendency is to lurch in the direction of phonics and decoding, because experts say that these skills are essential in learning to read, and they are quantifiable.

One of the keys to addressing the issue is to refocus on what reading *is*, and what children need in order to learn to read. If we define reading as *getting meaning from print,* then it becomes clearer. Reading is not simply decoding written words to sound. Knowing the alphabet is not necessarily a mandatory prerequisite to learning to read. As Cooper (1997) writes, "No evidence supports the idea that students develop literacy by being taught discrete skills." If we keep this definition in mind, then we can proceed with some degree of confidence. For all learners, at every age and every level of proficiency, reading *must* be for meaning: if you're not getting meaning, you're not reading.

Figure 5.1 shows an example of a real text taken from a remote language in Asia (which uses a few English letters). It took a great deal of thought to figure out which way was right side up, which way was upside down, and which way was backward.

Can you read it? Even if you can pronounce the words (we can't!), does that constitute reading? Of course not! Just calling the words does not mean you are reading, because you are not getting *meaning*. If you do somehow manage to get the meaning of this you will be very surprised (and we're not telling).

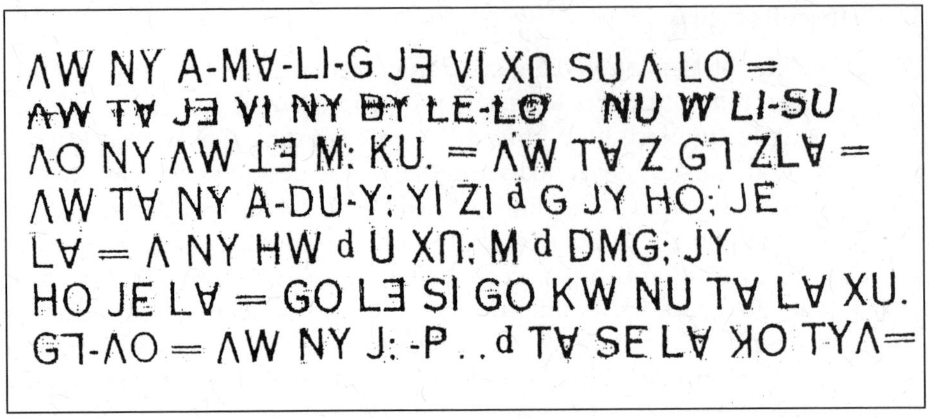

Figure 5.1 Text of an Asian Language. Can you read this?

Students calling out words correctly in English, but not being able to tell you what they understood from the text, aren't reading either. It's called "barking at print." Many teachers assume that because students *sound* as if they know what they're doing, or they're approximating what's on the page, they're readers. But unless they understand the story, they're not.

According to Frank Smith (2004), two things are necessary to learn to read:

1. The availability of interesting material that makes sense to the individual learner

2. An understanding and more experienced reader as a guide

Smith unequivocally states that what is important is knowing what reading is and knowing enough about the particular students in your class to decide how to proceed. In other words, you, the teacher, know your students best; you are the one in the best position to decide which activities will best expand their competence and proficiency.

If your entire class were filled with native English-speaking students who have had multiple experiences, have come from literacy-rich homes, and read at grade level, teaching would be relatively easy. But students such as Bao make your job more challenging and demand more flexibility. Maintaining a program that meets all of your students' needs is indeed a balancing act on its own.

What Good Readers Understand and Can Do

Good readers, according to the International Reading Association (IRA 2000) have:

- A motivation to read

- Appropriate, active strategies to construct meaning from text

- Sufficient background information and vocabulary to foster reading comprehension

- The ability to decode unfamiliar words

- The ability to read fluently

- An understanding of how speech sounds (phonemes) are connected to print

Good readers also

- Are active readers. They search for meaning.

- Make predictions, and go back to reread if their prediction doesn't match what they read

- Have goals in mind

- Read selectively. They know what to read and what not to read.

- Use their background knowledge

- Read different kinds of texts differently, depending on their goals for reading the text, the type of text, and the degree of difficulty

All of these skills and understandings have to be learned to be a good reader, not just one or two of them. Part of the confusion about the importance of phonics in a reading program is that being able to decode words is undeniably an essential skill that good readers have. Good readers *do* rely on the cueing system of sound-letter correspondence.

This issue was brought home for Barb when she was shipped off, with little advance warning, to Syria, and plunked into the Arab world with nary a word of Arabic besides *hello*. Level 1: Non-Arabic proficient. Unable to speak, read, write, or participate meaningfully in any situation. Barb and a colleague, Carol, engaged a tutor. Laboriously, they learned the alphabet one letter at a time along with some words. Barb learned the numbers by reading them on the license plates, which were written in both Roman and Arabic numerals, and by trying to read the signs on produce in the markets.

It was a great day when Barb read her first word: "باب". This translated to b + a + b = *bab*, or *door*. Certainly tedious, arduous decoding. But it was a word that meant something, and a place she recognized. She didn't decode every single word all the time, nor did she need to get through all the sounds of each word to know what it was. Once she figured out the buses (after riding long distances in the wrong direction, to her intense dismay and the amusement of the passengers) she only needed the first letter to know where to go: "ص" for Seydnaya, the bus to her friend's house, "م" for Muhajarin, the bus up the mountain to the apartment.

When their tutor did a bunk three months later, before she and Carol had learned all the letters, they were handicapped, because they couldn't read key words or make progress on their own. Barb spent a year hopelessly ignorant and frustrated, sitting in meetings where only a word or two was recognizable, getting lost, getting cheated, unable to communicate on a level she wished she could with the lovely people who surrounded her.

Her sons were studying Arabic also. They had the advantage, however. Her younger son played on the street with Arabic children. Her older son had Arabic-speaking friends; they roamed the city at will, taking taxis, shopping, smoking hookahs far into the night. Both boys learned Arabic by leaps and bounds because they were immersed in it, while Barb trundled onward.

When Barb's work with the Department of Education was finally finished, she enrolled in Arabic classes at the university, an intensive four-week course. The teacher ripped through the alphabet in three days. After that, the course was classic "whole language," the alphabet and the decoding embedded in real, communicative language. Barb learned more in a month than she had the entire eight months before that.

The point is, it *is* important to teach the letters and sounds, particularly if your students have no prior experience with the alphabet. But that's not the whole story. Barb is fair at sounding out Arabic words. And it was a total thrill when, standing in a bookstore in Cairo, she looked up a word in a dictionary and made a quick check of the Arabic spelling to see how to pronounce it—she had mastered the language well enough to be able to do that.

Arabic words have a gorgeous internal logic that English lacks, which can give you clues to meaning, and it is infinitely more reliable than English in its sound/letter correspondence (try spelling the word *of* if you can't remember, or sounding out *once*.) But even then, if you don't know what a word like "منحبك" means in the first place, what good does sounding it out do? Large quantities of vocabulary have to be introduced and learned simultaneously, or the decoding is wasted time and effort.

So the sixty-four-thousand-dollar question is: How do you balance all these myriad important skills with your English language learners?

Creating Balance in Your Reading Program

Balance, writes Cunningham (2000), "is the characteristic of a program that includes multiple methods and is sensitive to the fact that children are at different levels in each area of literacy. Only such a multifaceted program taught well can come close to teaching reading and writing well to all of today's children." As the California State Board of Education asserted in 2007, *balanced* does *not* mean "that all skills and standards receive equal emphasis at a given point in time. Rather, it implies that the overall emphasis accorded to a skill or standard is determined by its priority or importance relative to students' language and literacy levels and needs."

This caveat is noticeably missing in current language arts frameworks for many cities and states. Balance means using different methods and strategies for different kids. There is no one-size-fits-all program. Franco might need and want the old "hat, fat, cat, sat" business, because it fits his learning style. Florien is reading above grade level in his own language, but needs vocabulary in English. It would be pointless and a waste of time for him to be doing the same thing Franco is doing, or relearning the alphabet simply because Bao needs it. Balance is "decision-making by you, the teacher, in which you make thoughtful choices every day, every hour, about the best way to help every child in your classroom become a reader" (Spiegel 1998). But, to return to Frank Smith, this means that you know your class, and you know which student needs what at any particular moment.

Using rigid, single doctrinaire methods, such as focusing primarily on phonics that "center on one part of the literacy equation at the expense of others" (IRA 2000) always underemphasizes the other essential skills in gaining meaning. In addition, they limit your flexibility in adapting your program to the needs of your students.

The following list includes suggestions to help you create real balance in your reading program:

- Always keep meaning as the major focus.

- Keep a balance between teacher-directed and student-initiated reading and writing.

- Remember that skills such as phonemic awareness, letter/sound knowledge, and word knowledge develop in the process of becoming an independent reader. This means embedding the skills within meaningful activities, avoiding phonics at first and/or using it as an isolated activity removed from reading.

- Use both direct instruction and independent practice as means of furthering reading.

- Promote, right from the beginning, not just the basic skills, such as vocabulary and word recognition, but the higher-order reasoning tasks, such as synthesis and analysis, Don't limit students to questions such as:

  The names of Jacob's two children are _____ and_____.

Or

  How much of the earth's surface is covered by water?

These are simply recall questions that limit students' higher-order abilities. We must ask questions that promote critical thinking, such as:

  Why does pollution in Michigan matter to people in Georgia?

Or, for younger learners:

  What animal makes the best pet?

Or

  Should your parents limit TV time or computer games?

It goes without saying that students need more help in answering such questions, but it is important to give them the opportunity to grapple with such issues and thoughts.

Reading as a Whole Skill

Many component skills make up the act of reading: recognizing letters and words, predicting, and confirming, to name a few. The temptation for teachers of ELL students, particularly those with illiterate students like Bao, is to focus on teaching the alphabet and a large sight vocabulary before attempting whole texts. As important as these are, focusing on each skill in isolation can be counterproductive for ELL learners and can result in poor readers or even in those who are unable to read at all.

Before anyone can learn to read, the learner must understand that the language we hear and speak can be written down, and conversely, that what we see in written form can communicate something to us. Therefore, one of the fundamental things students must learn is what reading is and why we read.

In *Becoming a Nation of Readers*: *The Report of the Commission on Reading* Anderson et al stated (1985) that "the most useful form of practice is doing the whole skill of reading—that is, reading meaningful text for the purpose of understanding the message it contains." We can make the analogy to a jigsaw puzzle—no piece is useful on its own, unconnected to the rest. Only together do all the pieces make a comprehensible whole. There is only one way to learn how to read: by reading. Literacy must be introduced through the use of real and whole texts that the students find interesting or entertaining, in an environment where both reading and writing are celebrated and encouraged.

To enable your ELL students to learn to read or to make the transition to reading in English, you must make materials available and consciously direct their acquisition of reading skills: in other words, you must make time for both instruction and independent practice. All readers need

- To be immersed in real reading for real purposes

- A wealth of materials they will be capable of reading

- A helpful guide—someone to channel them in their acquisition of English-language skills and reading

- A supportive environment

- Time

Immersion—Make Reading a Daily Commitment

Any school day should include frequent opportunities to read. Being immersed in reading involves reading a variety of written materials for a variety of purposes: textbooks, magazines, newspapers, recipes, manuals, comic books, TV guides, Dear Abby, and so on. This means reading whole texts, not words in isolation. Sentences are easier to read than words, paragraphs are easier to read than sentences, and whole texts are the easiest to read of all. It seems counterintuitive, but you can get more meaning when there's less of a chance that each individual word is crucial. Both the text and the pictures (if there are any) give clues about the meanings of words and concepts that the student might miss on the first try.

Third-grader Robby, reading *George's Marvelous Medicine,* by Roald Dahl, could not decode the word *medicine* in the title. He paused and stumbled over it, then went on. Three paragraphs later, he read the word correctly, when mother said, "And don't forget to give Grandma her medicine." Within the context, and the familiar phrase, the meaning was clear.

Nowadays, many readers, including most basals, are written with the rationale that because stories are shorter and filled with simple words based on a "readability formula," they are easier. In actual fact, they often are not. This is a passage taken from an adult basic reading text:

Jim will fix the mill. Kim, his kid, is big. Kim will fix the rig. Jim will fill the bin. Jim will give Kim the pig. The pig will live in the mill. The pig will dig in the hill. The pig hid. Will the pig yip? Will Kim miss the pig? Jim hit his hip in the mill. Jim is ill. Will Kim give him the pill? The pill is in the tin. The pill is big. Jim bit it. Jim will sit in the mill with Kim. Will Jim quit the mill?

Sentences such as these, even though rigidly controlled for vocabulary, demand that readers have such words in their sight vocabulary. If pictures do not give enough reliable cues that readers can use (in this text there were none), other strategies to get meaning are not available. And besides, who wants to read such drivel?

Publishing companies responded to the need for simple materials with books that are filled with rich cues so that beginning and emergent readers can successfully make their way through a small text. The wealth of "little books" for beginning and emergent readers make finding good books a much simpler task.

For example, Destiny, in first grade, read the little book *The Ghost,* by Joy Cowley. She started out, not looking carefully at the words. By the third page, using the predictable text with the pictures as cues for meaning, she was on track. She read "BOO!" with great feeling. She chose to read it again and read it easily and accurately.

Immersion also means encountering print throughout the day, with time in each period devoted either solely to reading or to a reading-related task, such as following written instructions to make crafts, playing games with written rules, and so on.

In chapter 4, "Literacy and the Four Skills," we listed many ways to make your classroom a print-rich environment (begins on page 116). To follow are some additional ways to help your students learn to read or make the transition to reading in English.

Provide a Wealth of Materials at Your Students' Level

The concept of materials *at your student's level* is an important one. Allington (2006), in particular, focuses on how critical it is to match the texts to readers. If readers are already struggling, or reading significantly below grade level, filling their desks and lockers with books they cannot read successfully makes reading acquisition and fluency all that much harder for them. They need access to texts that provide high-success practice. Choosing books need not be a problem. There is a phenomenal array of fiction and nonfiction books available, appropriate for content areas as well as for reading pleasure. A large number of picture books on the market are beautifully illustrated with exceptional language and content. They can easily be incorporated into middle school, high school, and adult school classes, because they are not childish, simplistic, or condescending to learners.

For starters, any book on the Newbery and Caldecott awards lists or recommended by the Canadian Children's Book Centre is excellent reading. Browse through your favorite bookstore or library. Go to book fairs. Find out what kids are reading and enjoying.

How do you decide which books to choose? In *The Primary Language Record*, Barrs et al (1989) write that the books that remain perennially popular with young readers share

- A strong story
- A lively, rhythmical text
- Powerful, imaginative content
- Memorable language
- Interesting illustrations that complement the text
- Humor
- Language that is not contrived or unnatural

Books by favorite authors, such as Dr. Seuss (*The Cat in the Hat; Green Eggs and Ham*), Tomie dePaola (*Michael Bird-Boy, 26 Fairmount Avenue*), and Rosemary Wells (*Max and Ruby* series; *First Tomato: Voyage to the Bunny Planet*) are good places to start at the elementary level. And who doesn't love *Click, Clack, Moo: Cows That Type,* by Doreen Cronin or *The Napping House,* by Audrey Wood? Kids read books like these over and over and over—whether they're actually "reading" them at first or simply recalling the words from memory. And that's what cements the skill. At the upper elementary, middle-school and secondary levels, there are perennial favorites such as S.E. Hinton (*The Outsiders; That Was Then, This Is Now*), Lemony Snicket (*A Series of Unfortunate Events*), Robert Newton Peck (*Soup; A Day No Pigs Would Die*), Richard Peck (*Don't Look and It Won't Hurt; Are You in the House Alone?*), J.K. Rowling (*Harry Potter* series), Cornelia Funke (*Dragon Rider, Inkheart*), and Laura Ingalls Wilder (*Little House on the Prairie, On the Banks of Plum Creek*).

Be a Helpful Guide

A helpful guide provides materials and opportunities for students and is familiar enough about reading and the students to know what level of reading each one is at and the particular needs of each one at any moment. This is not lock-step instruction (for example, if this is Tuesday, we all should be on page 82). Allington (1998) writes, "What all children need, and some need more of, is models, explanations, and demonstrations of how reading is accomplished. What most do not need are more assignments without strategy instruction." A helpful guide is also someone who gives opportunities for thoughtful, rich conversations about reading, about texts, and about concepts that further understanding, promote deep thought, and build vocabulary and knowledge about the world.

A helpful guide is someone who

- Knows about reading
- Knows about literature
- Knows how to provide different instruction to different individuals
- Models good reading daily
- Talks to students as partners in the reading community

Good Practices for Guides to Use With All Students

A balanced reading program includes a balance of teacher-directed and student-sponsored activities. That means reading *to* and *with* students: read aloud to Bao, Salvador, and Franco, as well as to Kate, Ellie, and Rory; also allow students to read *by themselves*, whatever their level.

Reading to Students

Reading aloud to students is "the single most important activity for building the knowledge required for eventual success in reading" (Anderson et al 1985). As Carrasquillo asserts (1994), "there is no substitute for a teacher who reads good stories." Jim Trelease (1985) takes it one step further: "When teachers take time to read to their class they are not neglecting the curriculum. Reading *is* the curriculum. The principal ingredient of all learning and teaching is language."

According to Frank Smith, reading aloud, particularly to students such as Bao and Salvador (whether they be 1st graders or 12th graders), does three things:

1. It helps them understand the functions and purposes of print.
2. It helps them become familiar with written language.
3. It gives them the opportunity to learn.

There are other benefits for all students, assert Anderson et al, as well as Allen (1995). Reading aloud

- Provides a model of skillful reading
- Gets students interested in books and in reading
- Gives students a purpose for reading
- Is a key ingredient in creating the risk-free environment so essential for second-language learners and struggling readers

- Builds community, in which everyone—good readers and poor readers alike—has equal access to the text
- Builds prediction skills
- Develops a sense of story structure
- Develops vocabulary
- Promotes all four skills of language acquisition: reading, writing, listening and speaking
- Builds background knowledge about the world
- Shows students the mental operations involved in getting meaning from print, especially when you talk through what you're thinking when you're reading

It is especially important for ELL students who are either not literate or not sufficiently fluent in English to read on their own. If you have a regular reading time every day in your class, you shouldn't feel that you are wasting the ELL students' time just because they are not able to understand every word. At the very least, they see that words have meaning, that writing can be translated into oral speech, and that books are made for knowledge and enjoyment. They are listening to language and listening to others discuss and enjoy what was written. The enjoyment factor should not be dismissed lightly. School can be a stressful place for many students, increasingly so for older students, and especially for ELL students or struggling readers. Being able to sit and relax and simply listen to a story adds pleasure to their day. So don't make reading aloud to your students a reading lesson. Make it a time for enjoyment, for discussion. The learning comes as part of the package.

Besides the obvious benefits of giving students a chance to hear words in context, to develop listening skills, and to increase vocabulary, reading to students motivates them to want to read more. They become "hooked on books," which many experts contend is the key to reading success.

Don't stop with elementary-school little ones who are first learning to read or with those whose skills are low. Read to all students at all levels: middle, junior, and senior high. Just because students can read on their own is no reason to stop. Often, students' sophistication in thought and conceptual development far outstrips their reading abilities. When we were at the one-word stage of language, our parents didn't limit the books they read to us to one-word books. We listened to books far beyond our language capacity, which often included many words beyond our understanding. Third graders, for instance, are concerned with and capable of thinking and discussing ethical and moral issues they do not have the skills to read about. Even though upper-level students may gripe at first that reading aloud to them is babyish, they often get caught up in the story and enjoy listening. The same holds true for ELL students; their interests, comprehension, and sophistication may be far above what they are able to read for themselves. Reading to students continues to extend their range and exposure to different types of literature, as well as increase their vocabulary and understanding.

Don't stop with stories. Read textbooks, journal articles, magazines, and technical read-outs. Reading to students in the content areas is particularly useful. In the upper grades, reading demands are different and more difficult. Science, history, and math students in junior and senior high schools are faced with the task of extracting information from texts that presuppose a high level of reading and know-how to find the information they need. In wading through the material to find that information, they may need help. We all know that having someone read poetry to us helps us hear the rhythms and cadences in ways we can't when we approach a poem on a page. Even at the high school and college level, having someone read portions of a text aids comprehension. Barb often does this in her upper-level college classes. When approaching a difficult passage, she can explain complex concepts as she goes along and direct students' attention to what she feels is important in the text. This does not invite laziness or cheating, it simply helps. And it often has the added effect of lessening behavior problems from those who are practicing avoidance by yakking because they can't understand and don't want to admit it.

Just as importantly, reading aloud to students advances their exposure to and competence in academic language, including stress, intonation and sound patterns of words, such as *biography, biographical*. Delpit points out that not knowing these words or being able to use them makes students appear "sloppy, uneducated, or inept" (Delpit 1998, in Zamel and Spack [eds]).

Selecting Books to Read Aloud

Choose books that expose your students to different genres, both fiction and nonfiction, as well as literature of a higher quality and reading level than they can read alone. Select books that are stylistically outstanding, with pleasing words arranged in pleasing patterns. Storybooks with intense, gripping plots are excellent, as are books with vivid characters and natural dialogue. Select books that reflect a theme you are exploring or that will enrich students' understanding of themselves and others.

Reading With Students

Reading with students does several important things:

- Develops comprehension skills
- Develops and reviews use of high-frequency words and phonics skills
- Develops and cements the use of good strategies
- Cements the use of self-monitoring and self-correction
- Allows the learner to work at a personalized level with an experienced reader who takes the lead and relinquishes it at the appropriate times
- Keeps the learner from getting bogged down with more difficult text

One-on-One Reading

One of the best strategies to promote reading and further independence is to read and discuss books one-on-one with your ELL students. You can instantly gauge how much they understand, go over unclear parts, and review vocabulary in a personalized way. As you read, move your finger along under the words, synchronizing speech with print. This helps students perceive the speech-sound correspondence within a relaxed, pleasurable atmosphere. Weak readers, and ELL students in particular, can benefit from this type of reading.

One-on-one reading is especially critical for students like Bao, Fernando, and Salvador. Wells (1986) asserts that children who have not been read to, who have not had the literate home life that children like Ellie, Kate, Yoshi, and Boris (who have been read to since babyhood) have had, need more exposure to books than listening to a story read to the whole class. "They have not yet learned to attend appropriately to written language under such impersonal conditions. For them what is required is one-to-one interaction with an adult centered on a story." Turn this activity over to an older or stronger reader, an aide, a parent, or anyone with free time within the school.

Shared Reading

Shared reading—simply, reading a book together—is one of the most significant and critical strategies you can use. For the first couple of times, especially with younger or less proficient students, you will do all the reading. As students become more proficient they can join in and "share" in the reading.

At the Elementary Level

- Choose a predictable book, such as *The Great Big Enormous Turnip* or *I Went Walking*. The repeated refrains allow beginners to chime in when they begin to notice the pattern. Books such as these are important: the print tells a whole, coherent story, and the pictures represent the story told by the print. Thus, the reader can use both the language that is, or becomes, familiar on repeated readings and the pictures to supply meaning.

- Focus first on the book itself, advises Cunningham (2000). Introduce the book by reading the title and the author's name. Discuss the story with the students. This builds skill in predicting what will happen next in stories, in using the pictures as cues to meaning, and in connecting spoken language to print. Read it, reread it, talk about it, act it out. We cannot over-emphasize the importance of reading favorite books again and again.

- Read the story aloud, pointing to the words as you read. This builds familiarity with the ideas in the text, the vocabulary, and the overall format. It also allows the students to "hear" the language cadences. This is especially important for beginning language learners. With beginners such as Bao, it reinforces concepts we often assume, such as tracking, reading from left to right, and the knowledge that words have spaces between them.

- Model the thinking strategies you use for getting meaning: "I wonder what that word is? It starts with a *t*. Let's see. The [blank] has a hard shell. I'll bet that word is *turtle*. Does that make sense?" Discuss the text. Then, with the words available for everybody to see (whether from a big book, a chart, or projected) read it again, inviting all students to read with you. Encourage participation from everyone. As students become familiar with the story, even poor readers can chime in when they know a word or phrase. Within the safety of the group, they do not have to know all the words and aren't put on the spot when they don't.

- Allow students to read the story themselves. Their memory of the language of the story and the pictures in the text will guide their reading.

"I don't know what to read." "I can't find anything." "I'm bored." Sound familiar? Another important benefit of shared reading is that it gives readers a repertoire of known texts from which to choose during independent reading. Often a great deal of time gets wasted during what should be SSR (Sustained Silent Reading) by students who claim they have nothing to read, which is often a cover-up for their lack of skills, or boredom because they simply don't know what to choose. If they are familiar with certain texts, and they enjoy them, they can feel comfortable choosing them and they can experience success when reading on their own. In this way they can move toward independence and autonomy in reading.

In the latter half of third grade, Nick, for instance, read and reread *One Fish, Two Fish, Red Fish, Blue Fish* day after day, never losing enjoyment of it. He was a better reader than that and could have been pushed further. Others in his reading group were reading *Bridge to Terabithia* and *Roll of Thunder, Hear My Cry*. He didn't seem to care. It was familiar; he was consolidating his skills and developing fluency at his own pace, even though it seemed like lost time to everyone else. He stunned his teacher at the end of the year by reading *The Good, the Bad, and the Goofy* in one sitting. It appealed to his imagination and his sense of humor. His mother, of course, rushed out and bought him the entire series.

At the Secondary Level

The shared reading experience looks a little different at this level, because you read aloud from a text, and each reader follows along in his own individual copy.

For students at the junior high or high-school level, finding appropriate literature does not have to be the exercise in frustration it used to be. Students who struggle with reading at this age are typically sensitive about being different from their peers; they are often reluctant to read books that they perceive are "for babies." However, there are many beautifully illustrated books with relevant material that will appeal to older beginners. Publishing companies that handle the ELL market have books with collections of stories for beginning readers at the junior-high and high-school level.

Another excellent resource for the busy secondary teacher is the school librarian. This professional will frequently know where to find additional resources if the school does not already have something on hand. There are also many resources available on the Internet as well as computer programs that generate lists of reading materials based on a theme.

The time and preparation required for choosing a book to read aloud necessitates as much energy as any other prep time, otherwise the reading will be a joyless enterprise for both listener and reader (Allen 1995). Allen offers key questions to ask in choosing appropriate books:

- **Is this the right book to meet the needs of these students at this time?** The interests of the students can play a critical part in your choice. For example, as we discuss on page 189, Melissa Ahlers' choice of *The Outsiders* was based on her students' fascination with gangs. These basic readers needed to be hooked before they would sit still and listen to a story, much less try to tackle it on their own.

- **Can I read this book in such a way that students won't see it as "boring"?** Not all books lend themselves to being read aloud. For those who are struggling or turned off reading, the book has to be "long on plot and short on description." *Sarah, Plain and Tall* is a perfect book for beginning literacy adult students, as well as for more advanced learners. The reading level is fairly low, but the themes of loss, change, and giving up what you know to make a start in a strange place are deeply understood by second-language learners. Therefore, even beginners can connect on many levels and get through the text without being frustrated or giving up.

- **Is this a book I enjoy?** Since reading aloud is a performance, bringing it to life is easier if it's one you can connect to. Include some personal favorites or some of your students' favorites—those books that have been around for years.

- **Does this book meet my instructional purposes?** You might use a story to introduce a unit or another text, to model a writing style, to demonstrate a genre, and so on. Barb used the hilarious picture book *Officer Buckle and Gloria* to teach about safety to a group of middle- and high-school Taiwanese summer campers. Using the pictures from the story and demonstrations by her son, Nick (thereafter known as "Danger Boy"), students learned key concepts and terminology (such as *safe* and *unsafe*). Both the story and the demonstration alerted them to potentially dangerous activities, such as the high-ropes course, mountain biking, and caving. The lesson was extended by picture drawings (figure 5.2a–c). What started as a read-aloud became a shared reading when the students took the book and the tape back to their cabins to play and replay.

Guided Reading

Guided reading has many of the same components as shared reading except that it is explicit, individualized, and focused on specific skills and strategies. This is one way of providing direct instruction. "Explicit teaching," writes Cambourne (2002), "refers to the practice of deliberately demonstrating and bringing to learners' conscious awareness those invisible processes,

Figure 5.2a–c A lesson on unsafe activities was extended by drawings.

understandings, knowledge, and skills they need to acquire if they are to become effective readers." He continues, stating that "by making explicit the invisible, often taken-for-granted processes and knowledge that effective literacy behavior requires" you are giving your students focused opportunities to learn something they might not understand or learn on their own.

Guided reading is an essential component of your reading program, because it allows you to pull together small groups of students for a particular purpose while at the same time fine tuning your teaching by pinpointing exactly what those students need. Because kids don't all learn in the same way or need the same things, here's your opportunity to work with them on vocabulary or comprehension strategies. You can do "think-alouds" to model the sorts of questions you ask as you proceed through a text.

Reading by the Student

Independent Reading

Independent reading

- Develops fluency
- Provides practice
- Builds confidence
- Builds vocabulary

A balanced program includes giving students ample time to read on their own. Because reading is a skill that needs practice, students need extended opportunities and long blocks of uninterrupted time just to read. Sustained Silent Reading (SSR)—or Sustained *Noisy* Reading, during which beginning readers read aloud to themselves, because they simply must be able to hear themselves (the skill of silent reading does not appear until they achieve a certain level of fluency)—is a profoundly more effective form of practice than drills in isolated skills. Sustained silent reading should be an integral part of every school day. Devote a certain amount of time to free reading, ranging from just 10 to 15 minutes with kindergarten children to as much as an hour or more (or an entire class period) with older or more experienced students. Allow students to select their own reading material during this time. No book reports, comprehension questions, or records should be required. The only requirement should be that they read silently from one book for a specified amount of time. Non-English speakers can profit from this time even though they might not yet be able to read any words. Steer your ELL students toward books you have read aloud in class or books that others within the class have written. The best books are those that are familiar, having been read and discussed prior to the ELL students' time alone with them.

Besides class time set aside especially for reading, students should be directed to read on their own whenever they finish daily work. Reading can be slotted into any spare 5 or 10 minutes of the day.

One key to success, write Forester and Reinhard (2000), is to have a large stock of reading materials available, both new and familiar. Fill your classroom with wordless picture books, catalogs, magazines, trade books, comic books, library books, class-made or individually-made books. The books you have read to the students in read-aloud or shared reading time are natural choices for them.

The other key is for you to read, too. Often SSR fails because the teacher uses this time to grade papers or converse with small groups about other school business. This defeats the entire purpose of SSR. It is important for you to read during that time, to model serious reading, and possibly to share what you have read after the reading time is up. Many students have never seen an adult read. By reading you are conveying the message that reading is important, as well as pleasurable.

Sharing Time

Build in time for readers to share what they have read. A classic study of second-language learners by Elley and Mangubhai (1983) found that when teachers flooded the classroom with books and allowed time for sharing, those children made significantly larger gains in reading than children in classrooms that used only basal readers or limited the reading to SSR *without* time for sharing. Students get excited about their friends' choices and are eager to read and share in the experience.

Specific Strategies for the Varying Needs of Your Students

Use Picture Books

Picture books are a good way to introduce reading to all levels of ELL newcomers. Because these books do not depend on text to tell a story, they can be used to stimulate talk and later, writing. At first, you can allow students to simply page through the books, perhaps during sustained silent reading time. But don't take for granted that they will know even such simple things as holding the book right side up, or starting at the front.

Figures 5.2a–c demonstrate our contention that using picture books is no longer appropriate only for children. This is a fallacy that needs to be expelled. What better way to introduce the theme of alienation than with *Crow Boy* or to introduce the concept of war than with *Faithful Elephants*? Even eighth graders, who may groan and sneer when you pick up a children's book, have been moved to tears by the wrenching story of the love the trainers had for their elephants and their anguish over their deaths.

Graphic novels, such as the *Bone* and *Naruto* series, are also very popular with students these days. Readers interested in Japanese series such as *Yu-Gi-Oh!* and *Dragonball Z* are very willing to learn how to read from right to left and immerse themselves in the manga worlds. New books continue to enter the young adult market, which include illustrations and graphics that propel the story equally with the text. *The Invention of Hugo Cabret* contains sections of story text, as well as other large sections of illustrations that develop the story without any text on the page.

Ask students to identify elements of the illustrations. Then, when they have acquired more English, you can ask them to tell you the story. You might have them make captions for each page, or you can transcribe their version of the story.

Encourage students to discuss these books in their own language with a peer, an aide, or at home with a parent. In this way they do not have to depend upon their fragmented knowledge of English to talk about what they see in the pictures. Picture books are important because they help students develop thinking skills. They challenge them to think about and articulate what they perceive. Read and Smith (1982) have identified other important skills that picture books can help develop:

- Sequencing – learning how to distinguish a sequence of pictures and develop vocabulary words such as *first, next, then,* and so on. Narratives in other cultures are often very different from our own; therefore, learning "story grammar" is a fundamental skill that should not be taken for granted.

- Identifying the *who, what, when, where* of the story

- Getting the main idea

- Making inferences

- Predicting what will happen next

- Drawing conclusions
- Establishing cause and effect

Make Your Own Library

If you have a limited selection of good picture books at the junior and senior high school you can—with the help of the librarian, the yearbook editor, and some enterprising photography students—make your own library. Printing is easy these days, if you can afford it. Mary's school has limited ELL resources, but they are fortunate enough to have a public library attached to the school library, so there are more children's and picture books available. Childish children's books are not always the best option when working with young adults, but if you need books to help develop vocabulary, public libraries often have wonderful travel books or other books with photos you can use. Also, your high school librarian might have high interest-low level books for young adult readers.

Here are some other things you can include in your personal library:

- **"Home-made" photo albums.** Take digital pictures of students involved in activities, such as building a parade float or doing an experiment. The content is familiar and can make ELL students feel they are a part of the school while learning vocabulary. Once students have mastered the basic vocabulary, go beyond the school into the community to take pictures.

- **Magazines.** Many how-to magazines, such as *Family Handyman,* show step-by-step procedures for building things. Pasted on wallboard and laminated, these can be used over and over.

- **Cartoon strips.** Cut out the frames, blank out the words in the speech bubbles, and have students fill them in with their own dialogue.

- **Pictures downloaded from the Internet.** Using an Internet image search can be helpful, but be careful, the filter is not always accurate, and some undesirable images may come up. It's best to do this kind of search with a peer or aide.

Use the Language Experience Approach (LEA)

The Language Experience Approach is one of the most effective reading strategies we have encountered. Simply stated, students dictate stories to the teacher, who records them to form the basic reading material. Teachers use the students' own vocabulary, grammar, and life experiences when recording the stories.

Steps in LEA

The experience consists of several discrete steps. You can vary them according to time, size of groups, and purpose.

1. Experience something together. This can be a field trip, a special event such as Valentine's Day, a shared story, a poem, a book, an activity such as

baking cookies, a movie, or even something as simple as examining and eating marshmallows. For example, one cold, rainy day, students arrived at Mary's school after a four-day weekend to find fire trucks and emergency vehicles out front. There was a propane leak in one of the buildings, and most of the school was off-limits to everyone. Teachers directed students to the gym until the all-clear was given. This experience was an excellent starting point for writing. Mary got her students started by asking questions such as: What did you think and feel when you arrived at school and the usual routine was disrupted? What would you have done if the emergency persisted?

2. Discuss the event together. This step is critical. Because the emphasis is on discussion as students describe or recall the event, they make gains not only in oral development, but also, as they analyze the event, in the intellectual growth needed for success in reading.

3. Write the story on chart or butcher paper, or, if your school has interactive whiteboards, type the words straight into the computer to be projected for the class.

   - Have each student contribute a sentence (unless you are working with a very large group, in which case you can elicit sentences from different children over a successive number of LEA sessions).

   - Write each sentence, saying aloud each word that you write. For example, "Mary said, 'I saw a giraffe,'" or "Mohammed thinks that kids' behavior is the hardest thing to adjust to in this country."

   - When you have written a number of sentences or completed the story, reread the sentences, moving your finger under each word as you read it to reinforce left to right progression.

   - Answer any questions that might come up.

   - Have the students read orally with you.

   - Have individuals read the particular sentence they dictated.

4. Have the students copy their own sentences or the entire story onto paper. If you haven't elicited a sentence from each student, you can now go around the room, and encourage each one to generate his or her own sentence on the topic.

5. Follow up on the activity. The experience does not stop with the writing. Other related activities can be included over the next few days:

   - Refresh students' memory by rereading the story; then, have individual students read it in its entirety.

   - Cut apart the words recorded on chart or butcher paper, and have the students put them in the correct order.

   - Reinforce specific skills and sight words by calling on individual students to, for example, "Show me a word that begins with *m*," or

Figure 5.3 First-grader Jeremy drew these characters from *The Nutcracker* after his class had read the story.

"Where does it say *giraffe?*"

- Ask, "What words do you know?" Underline these words, and have students place them in their word banks.

- Have students illustrate words or sentences, or even the entire story.

The Benefits of LEA

The Language Experience Approach has many features to recommend it:

- All the language skills are used at once—reading, writing, speaking, and listening.

- Words from the students' own vocabularies are used. Students have no trouble reading words like *hippopotamus* or *Lamborghini* when they come from their personal store of experiences.

- Skill building, such as sight-word vocabulary or letter identification, can be promoted within a meaningful context.

- Oral vocabulary is increased.

- Self-concept is enhanced. A student can look at a page or a book of collected stories with pride and say, "I wrote that."

- The approach is appropriate for all age levels, kindergarten through adult.

- Less proficient students can benefit from seeing text that more proficient students have generated about topics they understand.

- The students' points of view are valued.

- LEA can be done in the students' native language, which is especially useful when the students are illiterate.

- The content is authentic. Because the approach uses the students' own language based on their own experiences, it is immediately relevant; therefore, their interest and motivation will be high.

- The approach can be used in large groups, small groups, or with individuals, either as chart stories with the entire class, or as dictated stories written individually onto sheets of paper.

Do's and Don'ts with LEA

When using LEA with ELL students, there are several things to remember:

- **Do *not* use LEA to teach new concepts.** Use LEA to build and reinforce language already learned. Students' first stories might only be a few sentences, or even a few words long, such as *"Hmong house."* That's fine; it is still reading and is meaningful to your students.

- **Write exactly what students say, but do not reproduce their accent.** If a student says, "I lost my chooz," but he means "shoes," write *shoes.*

- **Do not make corrections to grammar, word choice, or organization.** For instance, after several rousing enactments of *Caps for Sale* (in which Barb always had to play the monkey), Zing and Ha wrote the following summary, partially reproduced below:

  > He wore them on his head. No one buy some hats. And he sat down on a tree, because no one buy her cap. Her leg were tired. He went to sleep. He wake up. He see no cap on her head. The monkeys had the hats. He looked up high and saw the monkey.

  While you are transcribing the story, it may be very tempting to change *some* to *the,* correct the pronoun to the masculine gender, and add an *s* to *cap* and *leg* to make them plural. There are several important reasons not to make corrections:

  - The goal of LEA is to make print meaningful for the students so that they can acquire reading skills. If you have made changes, and students attempt to read back their work as they originally stated it, they might become confused. In the writing example above, the teacher actually changed *buy* to *bought;* the students could not read the word, because they did not know it.

  - Your goal is to write a story that reflects the learners' thoughts and language, not to develop a perfectly stated essay. If you focus on surface errors rather than the meaning, you are not only missing the point of the lesson, you are giving the students the impression that correctness is the most important thing and that you are more concerned with form than with content.

Figure 5.4 A student's illustration of *Caps for Sale*.

- To change students' thoughts is to reject the legitimacy of those thoughts. It isn't their writing anymore, it's yours. Accepting what they say in English during these sessions does much to bolster their self-confidence.

Many teachers feel that if we don't correct students we reinforce their errors. However, put in the proper perspective, errors can be considered a reflection of a stage of language development—a transitional state that will eventually disappear. These errors are important for you as a teacher, because they give you a written record of what each student knows—and does *not* know—in English. The errors in the preceding example (*buy, her, leg*) show you what Zing and Ha need to learn in the future.

Once it has been written, you can go back over the story and ask students if they want to make any changes. At that point they might very well see the errors they have made and change them themselves. If not, you can point out the errors and give them the correct form—a much more valuable learning experience than making changes yourself during the writing process, and one that does not disrupt the students' train of thought while they are composing.

During the course of the school year you can return to these stories with the students to demonstrate just how much progress they have made in English.

- **Be extremely sensitive when including ELL students in large-group language experience activities.** Many ELL students are shy, feel hesitant about speaking (particularly in a group situation), and generally hover on the fringe of activities. LEA can be a great confidence booster if what the students have to say is important both to you as their teacher and to their fellow classmates. If each student is listened to attentively, the importance given to what they have to say can cause great gains in their self-image. Sadly, though, English-speaking students often laugh at newcomers for their poor pronunciation or sentence structure. More advanced students might say something like, "Don't call on Lagi, she doesn't know anything." Educate your students to understand that ELL does not equal stupid, and allow the newcomers the time and the opportunity to contribute to the best of their abilities.

- **At more advanced levels, or in the content areas, use LEA as a tool to elicit thoughts and brainstorm ideas.** You are not looking for perfection, merely ideas, and all students can participate.

Use Literature

The jury is in on the benefits of good literature for use in your reading program with students. Even Jeanne Chall, one of the foremost proponents of phonics and author of *Learning to Read: The Great Debate* (1996) noted that "few in the literacy community disagree with the need for high quality literature and writing experiences as the nucleus of literacy instruction." Routman (1996) discusses what literature does for readers:

- Literature allows meaning to dominate.

- Literature concentrates on the development of readers rather than the development of skills.

- Literature promotes positive self-concepts in beginning readers.

- Literature promotes language development.

- Literature promotes fluent reading.

- Literature deals with human emotions.

- Literature exposes students to a variety of story structures, themes, and authors' styles.

Bao, Fernando, and Salvador, for example, do not need to be excluded from literature studies, even though their proficiency and reading skills may be weak. Young children do not need to wade through basal readers before being introduced to literature. Older students need not be consigned to the high-interest, low-vocabulary books that were traditionally staples of the reading lab. Good fiction is available for all ages. Young adult fiction for middle-schoolers and high-schoolers can motivate poor readers and help bridge the gap between their current level of proficiency and the language competence they need for success in academic English.

Literature Circles

Talking about books with other readers gives students a chance to explore and refine their impressions and ideas, to increase their understanding of literature by hearing others talk about it, and to become critical thinkers. Literature circles encourage readers to give personal meaning to ideas presented in books.

Literature circles are particularly beneficial for ELL readers, because they capitalize on the social nature of learning. They provide structured opportunities for students to read, talk through the ideas they have, listen to others, and gain more insight into passages. Less proficient readers can learn from their peers and reread what they didn't understand the first time.

Many teachers still group students on the basis of reading ability. It is tempting to do this with ELL students. However, "Putting students into a group where instruction is slow paced is counter to what we know about effective teaching" (Rosenshine 1983).

Gunderson (1985) asserts, "placing ELL students in a group to hear and emulate poor oral reading is questionable at best." Literature circles are a way of including ELL students in groups that are not based on their reading levels.

According to the Literature Circles Resource Center (<www.litcircles.org>),

> *In literature circles, small groups of students gather together to discuss a piece of literature in depth. The discussion is guided by students' response to what they have read...Literature circles provide a way for students to engage in critical thinking and reflection as they read, discuss, and respond to books. Collaboration is at the heart of this approach. Students reshape and add onto their understanding as they construct meaning with other readers. Finally, literature circles guide students to deeper understanding of what they read through structured discussion and extended written and artistic response.*

Students, especially those learning English, need to become familiar with the structure and the routines before they can become productive members of literature circles. You need to set guidelines and teach them how to respond; they also need to see and hear how to respond. (For an extended discussion, see Fountas and Pinnell 2001, visit the Literature Circles Resource Center site, or Google "literature circles" for ideas and examples.)

Choosing who goes into what literature circle group must be judicious. Fountas and Pinnell note that you must take into account the reading abilities, the interests, and the experiences of your students. You also need to take into account the personalities. Keeping apart two boys who spend their time hitting each other is a no-brainer; keeping apart two students like Angel and Beverly—Beverly is less proficient in reading than Angel and uses Angel to do her thinking and speaking for her—is another type of situation you'll want to consider. Think it through carefully.

The book selections also must be judicious and take into account the needs, interests, and ability levels of the students. Although choice is an important part of literature circles, let's face it—ultimately, the choice is up to you. There are many important criteria that should guide your choice, but according to Monson (1995) you should ask yourself these three questions:

- Does the book succeed in arousing my emotions, and will it arouse (students') emotions?

- Is the book well written?

- Is the book meaningful?

In short, a good literature circle book has substance—something worth talking about.

McMahon (1997) says that the texts should meet your curricular needs. Sometimes teachers use themes to shape their choices. For one upper-level class working on the theme of immigration, Barb chose *Journey of the Sparrows*, *Thousand Pieces of Gold*, *Farewell to Manzanar*, *Enrique's Journey*, and *The House on Mango Street*. Another teacher chose the theme of survival and selected books such as *The Outsiders, Shiloh, Anne Frank: The Diary of a Young Girl, Hiroshima*, and *The Cay*.

Conducting literature circles is an approach that focuses on enjoying literature as literature, rather than on reading literature solely to learn reading skills. Reading becomes the end rather than a means to an end; the readers become better readers as a consequence of being engaged in reading and discussing a good book. In this approach, the teacher is a participant and a member of the readers' club rather than the source of knowledge and the inquisitor who asks questions to check up and test knowledge.

With this strategy there are multiple readings (at least two) of each book. The first is simply for pleasure and comprehension, to become familiar with the story line and to get a feeling for character and setting. The readers respond as readers, both to the story and to the enjoyment it brings them. The discussions and activities you set up after the reading are designed to help the students understand the story in more depth.

At least two readings are important for ELL readers. The first time they may struggle through the story with only partial understanding. This may be for a variety of reasons: they have insufficient background knowledge; the reading level is too difficult; and/or they are unaccustomed to the style of English language literature. On the second reading, the discussion and responses of other group members will help to increase understanding, and readers can go over the now-familiar material with added comprehension and enjoyment. Longer books don't necessarily have to be read again completely. Diving back into the book and rereading parts is often enough.

It is not necessary to require ELL students to read entire books or understand every word and every concept. You are simply working toward competency and skill. No high school student will be able to understand a book as well as you if you have read it six times and studied it in three college courses. We cannot expect depth and perception from beginners. We can, however, expect progress.

Here's one way of proceeding:

1. Choose a book, or several different books, and obtain enough copies for each student to have one. You can borrow from other teachers, or go to the library to cobble together a set.

2. Do a "sales job" to get the students interested in the book. Show a clip of a movie tie-in or the movie version of the story. Don't show the whole thing. Read the first page. Tell them snippets to pique their interest.

Gulliver's Travels

What happens when a man must chose between living with smart horses or stupid humans? Given the fact the man himself is stupid, which will he chose?

Wuthering Heights

Two tempestuous people not only destroy themselves, but the entire world around them. The original fatal attraction.

Figure 5.5 Here's how two teachers that Mary works with sell some of the literature they're going to be teaching.

3. Build background knowledge. Tell students what the story is about. This is a critical step for our second language learners who may not have the foundation or the knowledge base that we can assume in many of our mainstream students. If they don't have this background knowledge, they'll struggle and flounder. Show them how to tap into and connect with things they already know.

   For example, when Barb used *Sarah, Plain and Tall* with her class, she brought in want ads and personals she found online. In the story, Sarah is a mail-order bride, which is a concept unfamiliar to many students. The class wrote their own versions of the ad that the character, Jacob, might have placed. The students also talked about why they left their own birth countries, what happened, what was different from their home, and how they reacted to this new country. They could connect with Sarah's loneliness and homesickness. When Barb taught *To Kill a Mockingbird,* she talked about students' perceptions of race relations in the United States, stereotypes and prejudices that exist in their own culture, and derogatory words that exist in languages to put others down.

4. If you're using multiple books, have students choose which one they want to read. The selection should be based upon their interest, not your judgment of what is appropriate for the levels they are at. In this way reading groups are determined by students' interest, not by the built-in reading levels we were used to in the past.

5. Meet with each group, and set goals, such as how long it will take them to read to a certain point or to finish the book. Samway and Whang (1996) counsel that it is important to set goals and time limits for each section of reading, so that students don't get too far ahead or too far behind.

6. Do prereading activities. What you do before the students read can make all the difference in how much they get out of it when they do. Predict together what's going to happen. Preview the pictures, if there are any. Call the students' attention to things that might aid in their comprehension. Key them in to how the story is organized. Teach some important vocabulary that is necessary to be able to get through the text. Establish a purpose for reading.

7. Have students read independently. You may have to read a chapter or two to them so that they get used to the style and have a sense of the storyline. Complex novels such as *To Kill a Mockingbird,* written in a distinctive dialect with many words used in ways not easily explainable, need a great deal of "building into." The parameters of this reading are for understanding the text only. There will be no quizzes or chapter tests. You can have them respond to specific questions at the end, such as "Who did you relate to in the story?" "Tell me about one time in your life when you felt like this character did." Have students keep running journals of their reading. Post-it notes are especially useful for keeping track of interesting or important parts.

8. Peterson and Eeds (1990) call this next stage "The Grand Conversation," while Atwell (1998) calls it "dining room table" discussions. Engage in the conversation, contribute your thoughts and opinions, and point out your favorite parts, but don't let the class discussion follow the traditional teacher-led format. The object is for you to be a participant, not the ringmaster.

Grand conversations are not necessarily "grand" with ELL learners, at least at first. They often don't understand the story; they often don't have the vocabulary or the cultural background to get through the text; and they often have little or no practice in articulating their own ideas. But this stage is the most important, not only for ELL students, but for poor, or less-proficient readers.

Samway and Whang (1996) assert that

All children should have the opportunity to join an LSC [literature study circle], not just more fluent readers...they all prize these discussions. To deny a student access to these rich times of sharing because of a lack of fluency as a reader [or as an English speaker] is counterproductive. Therefore, struggling readers should be given help.

Students will be swept along by the discussion, which will help to clarify for them what they read, what they didn't understand, and the points they missed. They may not get much out of the book on the first reading, but after the discussion, they will return to the text for a second time with much more comprehension and enjoyment. When left open, these discussions are often lively and fun, with students bringing their own background experiences or interpretations of the text. Immigrant students often have different perspectives on experiences we take for granted and can offer interesting comments that enhance the discussion.

Dennis, for instance, who had grown up on a farm, took issue with one incident in *Sarah, Plain and Tall* that other readers enjoyed: Sarah and the children go swimming in the cow pond. He insisted that cow ponds were dirty, germ-filled cesspools and drew his representation of this part of the story (figure 5.6, right).

You may have to set up activities that give students the opportunity to deepen their understanding of the story. For example, Barb's class nearly gave up on *To Kill a Mockingbird*, declaring it was too hard. To help them understand the story,

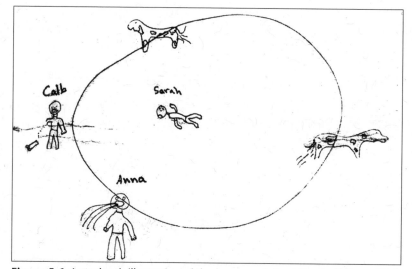

Figure 5.6 A student's illustration of the cow pond, from *Sarah, Plain and Tall.*

as well as to increase their confidence, she had her students draw maps of Maycomb, the town in which most of the action occurs (figure 5.7). In order for them to complete this assignment, they had to return to the text to find out where Scout lived in relation to Miss Maudie, downtown, Boo, and the schoolhouse. By talking together, reading for understanding, and graphically representing the town, they had a better sense of what the story was about.

Barb also gave periodic checkups, not for grading purposes, but to see what students understood and to give herself an idea of how much explaining or rereading was necessary. Randomly assigning characters, she had each student list facts about the character and then make inferences (figure 5.8). Then, each student was interviewed in character by other students in the class (figure 5.9).

There are few things more irritating and frustrating than hoping for a grand conversation and getting silence, downcast eyes, or blank looks in return. This doesn't mean that students didn't read; it often means they don't know what

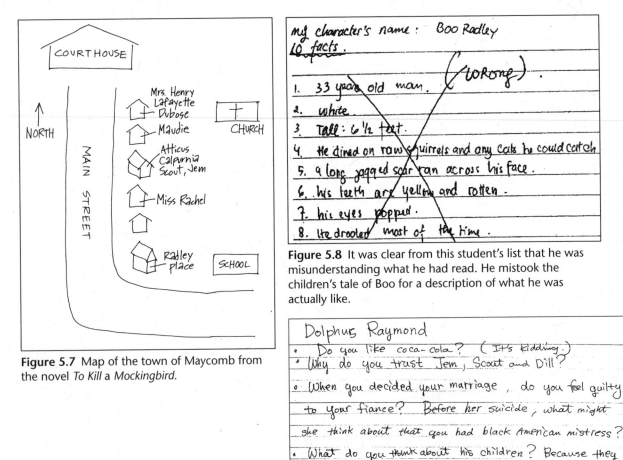

Figure 5.7 Map of the town of Maycomb from the novel *To Kill a Mockingbird*.

Figure 5.8 It was clear from this student's list that he was misunderstanding what he had read. He mistook the children's tale of Boo for a description of what he was actually like.

Figure 5.9 Questions posed to a student, in character, by "reporters" from the class. Note the depth of understanding it took to compose these questions.

to say. There are ways to jumpstart the conversation. One technique we've used successfully is having students record, on one side of a 3-inch x 5-inch card (or scrap of paper) one line from the story that they liked and their response to it on the other side. Then, they all have something to say. They can read their responses to each other in their circle, so they don't have to be intimidated by a large group, or you can put everyone in a circle to read their cards. This works for all levels with all genres, from literature to nonfiction, or political science and the news.

Another surefire way to get students going is to give them four response starters:

• One thing I thought…

• One thing I felt…

• This reminds me of…

• One question I still have….

Works like a charm. ELL kids and even middle and high schoolers have a lot of fun illustrating their responses.

9. Proceed to the second (analytical) reading using the students' comments you have written down such as, "The lady who spent all that man's money was awful. I just wanted to strangle her." There are always some students who are confident, outspoken, and more fluent than others. Barb remembers spending most of her high school and college years sitting in the back row waiting to be told what the story was about, because she didn't trust her own interpretation or was afraid it was different from the teacher's. Sometimes—and this is very true of many of our readers, not just second-language learners—she just didn't "get" what the story was about. The second reading, after the discussion, was always much more informed, and, in many cases, more enjoyable. This is an important step and should not be eliminated simply in the interest of time.

Figures 5.10a–b Here are some comments made by students about the story "All Summer in a Day," by Ray Bradbury.

Balancing the Needs of your Fluent and Nonfluent Readers

The perfect class would have all students achieving at the expected level at the same point in time. It never happens. Every class has its Ellies, its Spencers, and its Robbies. If you have second-language learners, you probably have your own Floriens, Francos, and Baos. Modifying your assignments for and expectations of them increases their chances for success. Here are ways to do it:

- **Implement buddy reading.** Having two students read aloud together is one way to improve the reading and language skills of both. They can alternate paragraphs or pages. Christina and Gloria, lively second graders, enjoy the challenge of reading aloud together, helping each other get through the "big" words. The simultaneous competition and cooperativeness motivate them to pick books that are at their level and to complete them with enthusiasm. Peterson and Eeds (1990) write, "The sharing of literature aloud anchors the sounds of the language of literature in the minds of the students."

- **Use audio books.** Many good books are now available on CD or as downloadable mp3s. Students can take them home, or use a listening center or a corner of the room during reading time. Don't think this is a cop-out or that it encourages laziness. Like read-aloud time, it increases students' chances of success, because it sidesteps the problem of struggling through a book that's too hard, it gives them a model of good reading, and it builds their vocabulary (their "story grammar" and their fluency).

- **Use books of different levels and reading complexity.** It doesn't hurt fluent readers to read easy books once in a while, especially if they're well written and appeal to the reader's interest. Many of Barb's students were put off at first by the simplicity of *Sarah, Plain and Tall* but enjoyed it once they got into it. Offering books that are simpler gives better readers a "breather" and less proficient readers a chance to get through a book on their own.

Working With Different Levels of Readers

Most of all, students need someone to guide them in their acquisition of English and reading skills. Following are strategies you can use for different levels of readers.

What do I do with the Baos in my class who are illiterate in their own language?

With illiterate students like Bao, you must start from scratch. She might not know things so basic to reading that we take them for granted:

- How to hold a book and turn pages

- That the markings on the page communicate meaning

- What a word is

- That in English, print moves from left to right

Unless she interacts with print, Bao won't learn any of these things; therefore, you need to involve her in as many activities as possible that include print. The foundation for students' readiness to read and write is their understanding that the language they hear and speak can be represented in print.

As noted in chapter 4, we strongly advocate an integrated approach. Instead of teaching word-attack skills and sight vocabularies, comprehension should be the priority. However, we recognize that there are certain things that your preliterate students need to know. As Bell and Burnaby point out in *A Handbook for ESL Literacy* (1984), people who know that a cow is a cow whether it is facing left or right do not automatically recognize that the differences between *p, b, d,* and *q* are significant. They need some training in prereading skills that involve shape recognition.

George Rathmell, in *Bench Marks in Reading* (1984), has listed the necessary prereading skills:

- Ability to recognize similarities and differences in shapes, letters, numbers, and words

- Ability to arrange items in a sequence, such as smallest to largest, beginning to end, left to right, including classifying items into categories and arranging pictures into a logical narrative order

- Ability to recognize letters and numbers

However, the teaching of prereading skills needs to be put in proper perspective and should not be allowed to take priority or become focused upon to the exclusion of all else. A balanced program of interaction with real texts, supplemented by practice in visual discrimination, is essential.

Use real manipulatives rather than photocopied exercises to teach prereading skills. For example, you can make a collection of articles such as

- Buttons, rocks, shells, leaves, flowers

- Stones, nuts, beans, marbles, metal objects

- Cloth, feathers, corks, bottle caps

- Ice cream sticks, straws, toothpicks, blocks

Possible activities include

- Sorting according to properties: size, color, shape, texture, flexibility, order, number of holes

- Math: weighing, measuring, graphing, adding, subtracting, counting, comparing, estimating, collecting, categorizing

- Language arts: describing, defining, sharing discoveries

These activities can be done individually or in small groups. Create a special corner where collections of various manipulatives are always available.

Where should I start?

First encounters with reading must be interesting and of practical value. Help students learn the most useful vocabulary:

- Start with their names. Children—and adults—derive intense satisfaction from seeing their own names in print and will copy them many times, learning the names of the letters as a matter of course. A Mexican woman once came into Barb's ELL night class. She was an illiterate migrant worker who wanted to know how to write her name. Barb wrote *Maria* on a piece of paper, whereupon Maria spent the next 45 minutes practicing. When she was satisfied, she left. She never returned; she had learned the one thing she had come for.

- Go on from students' names to the survival words they have learned. They can then make word cards for their desks, chairs, and so on, advancing to other items in the room.

First Encounters With Reading

At the Elementary Level

- Raid the preschool and kindergarten for shape, color, and number manipulatives and so on. Begin with very simple exercises, such as distinguishing between triangles and circles, then move on to more difficult tasks, such as matching letters or words.

- Stock your room with wordless picture books. During free-reading allow students to browse through these or have a buddy or aide discuss the pictures with them.

- Have students make their own books to read.

At the Secondary Level

Vocabulary should include

- Names of teachers

- Students' own addresses, telephone numbers, and other words they need to know to fill out forms (Note that although it is important for ELL students to learn and know how to write their own addresses, phone numbers, and so on, teachers should ensure students are aware of safety precautions such as not giving out this information to just anyone.)

- Common signs ("Men", "Women", "Help", "Exit")

- High frequency words, such as classroom objects, home objects, public transportation, names of businesses and public buildings, facilities in the community, and so on

- Basic subject-matter vocabulary including equipment terms, common instructions, and procedures

- Days, months, expressions of time

Figure 5.11 This picture is from a "storybook" a student made of her favorite story, *101 Dalmatians*. She "read" this book for days to herself and to anyone else who would listen.

When They Don't Know Their Alphabet

Perhaps your students are preliterate. Or maybe they can read, but in languages that use a writing system other than the Roman alphabet. They might read characters such as Chinese, or non-Roman alphabets such as Arabic, Hebrew, or Thai. How do you teach them our alphabet and writing system?

Students need to know the English alphabet and the words and shapes associated with each letter. The sequence of the alphabet, useful for dictionary work, can be learned much later when this skill has some purpose. At very least, students must be able to look at the written forms of letters and then trace, complete, and copy them. This raises a question of priorities. Having students learn the alphabet while delaying meaningful encounters with reading is a disservice. Don't spend large amounts of time teaching the alphabet while holding off on other learning. Students can learn the letters within the context of meaningful vocabulary.

For All Levels

- Begin with the suggestions for illiterate students.

- Use the language experience approach (LEA).

At the Elementary Level

- Practice or reinforce (don't teach) one letter a day. (That would waste 26 days just to learn the whole alphabet). For example, give each student a card with the letter *R* on it, and have them find all the words in the room or on the chart-stories they have elicited that begin with *R*.

- If you don't already have one, find a large chart of the alphabet, and display it prominently. You can also buy or make individual strips to tape to each student's desk for easy reference.

- Have "name banners" with the names of your students displayed around the room for the ELL students to refer to when practicing letter writing and letter recognition.

At the Secondary Level

- Begin using the suggestions noted for elementary students.

- Use high-interest, low-level reading books.

- Use picture dictionaries.

- Find books that the students are familiar with in their own languages. If you can locate stories translated from the students' first languages, the familiar content will guide their comprehension in the new language. Find a copy of a story Bible, or perhaps the Koran, or fairy and folktales from their home countries.

Accommodate the needs of your students. To illuminate the varying levels and needs of the students we have highlighted in this book, we have designed the following charts (figures 5.12–21), which focus on what each level of literacy looks like, what your primary objective(s) for that/those student(s) should be, and strategies you can use to achieve those goals. The beginners need a high level of support that gradually decreases as they grow in proficiency and fluency. It's a matter of withdrawing support as kids grow more independent.

> Ulises is given a list of spelling words to learn each week and a test. He flunks every time. Not only does he have problems distinguishing vowel sounds (*i* from *e* and *o* from *u*) and differentiating *b* from *p*, he also doesn't know how to use the words he learns in any context. What would you do with Ulises? What are your priorities?

Pre-Awareness/No English Skills—Elementary: Bao, Fernando

Characteristics

- Do not know that print has meaning
- Do not know what books are
- Have not held a pencil or pen
- Cannot look at pictures and see more than simple shades of color
- Cannot see drawings and identify them for what they are
- Do not know how to handle a book or turn pages
- May or may not be able to copy words
- May demonstrate understanding of a story by drawing a picture
- Cannot write own name

Objective

- Help them make the connection between print and meaning.

Strategies

- Read to them.
- Label items in the classroom.
- Use environmental print, picture books.
- Use the English they have to create language experience stories.
- Sing songs, recite rhymes and chants.
- Provide opportunities to draw, copy, and practice writing.
- If possible, get one-on-one help to:
  - Read to them
  - Assist during content learning
  - Learn basic vocabulary and sight words within real stories
  - Build background knowledge prior to lessons

When to include them in regular class activities

- Bao and Fernando can be included in most activities. They can "write" journals, sing songs, and listen to stories with the rest of the class.
- *Transition years*: Bao and Fernando can be included in most activities. During SSR they can read at their own level (picture books, little books). During literature circles they can either read on their own or have someone read a story to them so that they can be included in the discussions. Coordinate with the ELL teacher, aide, or other volunteer to dovetail tasks.

Figure 5.12

Pre-Awareness/No English Skills—Secondary[1] Bao, Fernando

Characteristics

Characteristics are similar to those in the preceding chart (5.12). As Bao and Fernando have few literacy and oral skills, it would be an exercise in frustration to place them in the regular classroom with no support or accommodations. They are unable to do the work productively yet.

Objective

- Help them make the connection between print and meaning.

Strategies

- Read to them.
- Label items in the classroom.
- Use environmental print, picture books.
- Use the English they have to create language experience stories.

- Sing songs, rhymes, chants.
- Provide opportunities to draw, copy, and practice writing.
- If possible, get one-on-one help to:
  - Read to them
  - Assist during content learning
  - Learn basic vocabulary and sight words within real stories
  - Build background knowledge prior to lessons

Where do they go?

- A Level 1 program if available
- Phys ed
- Keyboarding

Who supports them?

- You
- The ELL teachers

When to include them in regular class activities

- In activities that can be presented visually

Expectations

- Bao and Fernando will follow along with what has been modeled.

As they get older, these students' lack of knowledge about print and lack of experience become more and more serious. In fact, they increase exponentially at the secondary level. The lag is cumulative. The strategies listed continue to be useful for them; however, it becomes more a matter of *who* is going to deliver these services, than *what* is to be delivered.

Figure 5.13

Emerging Awareness—Elementary: Salvador

Characteristics

- Understands that print carries meaning
- Can demonstrate understanding of general terms like *read, page, storybook*
- Engages in "pretend" reading
- Can tell a story from pictures
- Can read and write own name
- Is beginning to read environmental print
- Is beginning to track from left to right
- Can repeat all or parts of predictable texts
- Has beginning familiarity with "story grammar" of English language stories, such as "Once upon a time…"
- Is beginning to write words
- Can copy with relative ease

- Is not fully aware of word boundaries
- Does not understand the concepts of letters, words, numbers

Objectives

- Reinforce the print-to-meaning connection.
- Build sight-word vocabulary.
- Build background knowledge.
- Reinforce sound/letter correspondences.

Strategies

- Follow strategies developed for Bao and Fernando.
- Read, read, read to him and with him.
- Use familiar patterned books for modeling and reading.
- Use frame sentences.
- Tailor the assignments you give him.

- Assess him orally for comprehension.
- Allow him to express his understanding through art or another medium.

When to include him in regular class activities

- Salvador can be included in all activities, especially all-class reading and teacher-initiated activities.
- He can read at his own level.
- Put him in a literature group he chooses by interest, or use the literature circle time to work with him individually on reading. Find ways for him to read the book, such as having someone read it to him, or having him listen to a recording.

Figure 5.14

---

1 Note that in charts representing secondary-level students (5.13, 5.15, and so on) we add the categories "Where they go," "Who supports them," and "Expectations," which are not included in the elementary-level charts (5.12, 5.14, and so on). This is because there are more variables for placement and classes at the secondary level.

Little Experience With Reading—Secondary: Salvador

Characteristics

- Has very little experience with reading
- Understands print carries meaning
- Can read and write own name
- Is beginning to read environmental print
- Has beginning familiarity with story grammar
- Is beginning to write words
- Relies on another person to read text
- Needs a great deal of support for guidance and strategies
- Ability to think and reason far outstrip his reading and writing capabilities

Objectives

- Reinforce the print to meaning connection.
- Build sight word vocabulary.
- Build background knowledge.
- Reinforce sound/letter correspondences.

Strategies

- Follow strategies developed for Bao and Fernando.
- Read, read, read to him and with him.
- Use familiar patterned books for modeling and reading.
- Use books on tape.
- Use frame sentences.
- Capitalize on his ability to think and talk by using verbal strategies to support written ones.

Where does he go?

- ELL
- Bilingual classroom
- Content classes
- Resource room

Who supports him?

- If you don't have enough students to build a program, you must hire someone to help him. One-on-one support is critical to make sure he knows what the assignments are and what he needs to do.

When to include him in regular class activities

- Group and pair him with supportive kids in English, social studies, and science.

Expectations

- Expect input and participation
- Verbal assessments

Figure 5.15

Emerging Readers—Elementary: Angel, Beverly, Newton, Spencer, Destiny, Andre

Characteristics

- Know that print records the story
- Can recognize words within a text
- Look at the text and words when reading
- Can spell a few words
- Understand that the sentence and pictures go together
- Are familiar with "story grammar"
- Are developing strategies to predict meaning
- Take information from a variety of sources
- Still read aloud
- Are aware of word boundaries when writing
- Are beginning to understand the conventions of punctuation

Objectives

- Learn strategies in reading: use pictures, graphophonic cues, context clues.
- Move reader along from dependence to independence.

Strategies

- Follow strategies developed for Salvador.
- Encourage independent reading.
- Use audio books and podcasts.
- Use stories in their first language.
- As their skills and oral proficiency develop, add:
  - Frame sentences
  - Content at a simpler level
  - Easy readers
- Stories translated from their first language
- Guided reading for specific strategies

When to include them in regular class activities

With support, include these students in all activities.

Figure 5.16

Inexperienced Readers—Secondary: Angel, Beverly, Newton, Spencer, Destiny, Andre

Characteristics

- Have limited experience with texts
- Can recognize some words within easy books, mostly in stories
- Choose to read very simple, familiar texts, if at all
- Very rarely read for pleasure
- Can spell a little
- Are familiar with story grammar
- Are developing strategies to predict meaning, but are usually very dependent on just one strategy
- Still read aloud or sub-vocally

Objectives

- Learn more strategies in reading.
- Move readers along from dependence to independence.
- Develop background knowledge in content areas.

Strategies

- Teach strategies for getting information from reference and nonfiction texts.
- Build background information.
- Expand vocabulary.

Where do they go?

- In-class support
- If ELL program, parallel program with SDAIE or sheltered English
- ELL resource room

Who supports them?

- Their peers
- ELL/bilingual teacher
- The reading teacher

When to include them in regular class activities

- In group work

Expectations

- Class work with modifications in *time* allowed for completion, in length of work turned in, and in the amount of ground covered

At this level, native speakers who don't read well have a high frustration level. Their spirits are flagging. The work they do can be the same as the work given to ELL students. Don't make it too simple! They have to understand the concepts, whatever their reading level. Make no assumptions.

Figure 5.17

Advanced Beginners, Gaining Fluency—Elementary: Abir, Nick, Robbie, Franco

Characteristics

- In the lower grades, many of our literate second-language learners are at a similar level to readers gaining proficiency in their native language.
- Reading is becoming more automatic.
- Are confident when reading familiar texts
- Pay attention to the words on the page
- Are growing in their independence
- Begin to read silently as they mature
- May use invented spelling
- Can read for a variety of purposes

- Select books that interest them
- Can retell stories they read in their own words
- Can extract the main idea from a text
- Use punctuation appropriate to the text and the difficulty of the purpose they are trying to achieve

Objectives

- Set wider parameters to experiment with and experience language.
- Encourage increasing fluency.

Strategies

- Read, read, read.
- Read in the first language.

- Provide structures and models to base writing on.
- Have students write responses to reading.
- Concentrate more on revision and editing in writing.
- Work on using the background knowledge they have.
- Encourage inferential thinking skills, such as prediction and sense of story structure to comprehend stories and new material.

When to include them in regular class activities

- All activities, with some modification for reading and writing levels

Figure 5.18

Increasing Experience—Secondary: Abir, Nick, Robbie, Franco

Characteristics

- Reading is becoming more automatic
- Are confident when reading familiar texts
- Are growing in their independence and stamina
- Still need support in content area texts

Objectives

- Wider parameters to experiment with and experience language
- Encourage increasing fluency.

Strategies

- Help them with unfamiliar material.
- Teach skimming/scanning skills.
- Encourage variety in length and difficulty of texts.
- Encourage inferential thinking skills, such as prediction to comprehend new material.
- Build background knowledge and vocabulary.

Where do they go?

- Content classes

Who supports them?

- Classroom teacher, ELL teacher, resource teacher

When to include them in regular class activities

- All the time

Expectations

- Content work with some modifications in activities, tests, and pace

The challenge for these students is finding appropriate material for the level at which they are reading. Walk them through the texts; it is counterproductive to ask them to read the passages and expect them to understand.

Figure 5.19

Increasing Fluency—Elementary: Rory, Jeremy, Ashley, Boris, Yoshi

Characteristics

- Can approach unfamiliar texts with more confidence
- Have good control of basic word analysis and self monitoring strategies
- Can apply their strategies in a wide variety of situations
- Begin to draw inferences from books
- Can use directories, such as a telephone book and table of contents
- Need support with cultural aspects of texts
- Can write quite sophisticated stories
- Pay attention to organization when writing

- Use context to predict meanings of unknown words
- Develop personal voice in writing
- Can self-monitor comprehension and strategies available when comprehension breaks down

Objectives

- Gain experience in tackling a variety of texts.
- Increase speed and fluency.
- Increase confidence.

Strategies

- Encourage self-selection.
- Promote shared reading.
- Use recorded books.
- Read to them and with them.

When to include them in regular class activities

- All the time

Some of these students, such as Yoshi, might be very good readers in their own language, but struggle through many types of text in the second. It is important to give them opportunities to read in the first language, but also to balance their skills by giving them easier tasks and texts from time to time, as well as challenging them with tougher tasks.

Figure 5.20

Increasing Fluency—Secondary: Rory, Jeremy, Ashley, Boris, Yoshi

Characteristics
- They read very well in their own language
- They need vocabulary
- They need background knowledge

Objective
- To keep up with the rest of the class

Strategies
- Provide content in their native language, if possible.

Where do they go?
- Mainstream all the time

Who supports them?
- You do

When to include them in regular class activities
- All activities

Expectations
- Same as others in the class, with some extra time allotted to keep up

The advantage Yoshi and Boris have is their strong academic skills in their own language. The solid schooling they had in their home country gives them the background knowledge needed to do well. They can look up vocabulary in their own language. You don't have to spend a great deal of time figuring out the steps to get them understanding.

Figure 5.21

Grouping

The question of grouping students is an issue that teachers have struggled with for many decades. Many of us remember when reading time meant sitting in small groups around a teacher doing round-robin reading while the rest of the class sat at their desks doing worksheets. Fortunately, this is a dwindling practice. However, with the range of needs and levels you will find in a classroom (such as our hypothetical one) grouping is a necessity. Bao needs a great deal of attention, as do Salvador and Fernando. Again, flexibility is key. There are times when you want to do whole-group activities, times when you want to do small groups, and other times when you want to work with individuals.

This is what one second-grade teacher has done to accommodate the different reading levels of students in her classroom. Sandy believes that reading should occur throughout the entire day. The students read during their content period. She reads to the entire group every morning and reads with them when they work in math and science. She gives them time for self-selected reading, and she has set aside a time specifically devoted to reading instruction. She uses a variety of methods to teach reading and takes advantage of ELL, Title I,[2] and bilingual help to assist her students. She conducts a variety of activities during reading time: students go to various centers, such as the computer center or the make-a-word center (where students play with magnetic letters and make smaller words from larger words), or they read independently while Sandy works with other groups.

- **Low-level language learners.** During reading instruction time, Bao, Salvador, and Fernando go to the ELL room to work on reading. There is no one good time for students to be pulled out of the classroom, but if this is an option, here is a time when the ELL teacher can work on reading and language skills in small groups with students of the same level.

---

2 Title I refers to the first section of the Elementary and Secondary Education Act (ESEA), an extensive federal statute that funds primary and secondary education. Title I is a set of programs set up by the United States Department of Education to distribute funding to schools and school districts with a high percentage of students from low-income families.

- **Intermediate language learners and emerging readers.** This group includes Angel, Beverly, Newton, Spencer, and Destiny. The Title I teacher comes into the classroom to work with these students. She works on building vocabulary, reading skills, and strategies at a level and using books with which they can succeed.

- **Moderately experienced readers.** Rory, Nick, Jeremy, Robbie, and Bounkham. These are students who are catching on to reading, or, in the case of the second-language learners, have learned some skills in their first language.

- **Strong, experienced readers.** Yoshi, Ellie, Kate, Ashley, Molly, Austin, and David. Even though they are good readers, solidly launched in reading and capable of working ahead on their own, these students still need individual attention and focused interaction several times a week so that they don't get lost in the shuffle of needs. They are beginning to get going in literature circles.

Sandy consults with the Title I teacher when she notices particular strategies that students need to work on. It doesn't happen as often as she likes, because it seems that the best readers need little help and the least fluent readers need help in everything.

During the hour to 90 minutes of reading time, while the least proficient and weakest readers are away working with the ELL teacher, Sandy reads aloud from a chapter book. She chooses books that are at a much higher level than the students can read on their own, but she believes that she needs to push and challenge all of them, including the best readers. They gather on the carpet to listen to and discuss a book chosen with the interests and personalities of the students in mind. The less-proficient students benefit from the conversations (which are very lively) and from the rich vocabulary of the literature selections.

Sandy also groups students during writing and content periods. The ELL teacher comes in during content periods, and twice a week a volunteer also works in the classroom. At first, the less-proficient students were grouped together, but over time students were divided in terms of personalities and level of proficiency, so that less-proficient students could benefit from the example and the language of students at a higher level. During writing period, a bilingual interpreter comes in to work with the Spanish-speaking students, reading to them, translating, and writing with them.

Brenda, a fourth-grade teacher, works in a similar fashion. Her higher-level students are launched more solidly into literature circles, but she does not have these working every day. She reads aloud to the students every day during the large reading/literature/language arts block she has set aside for the morning. During part of the week, she guides the class through the literature anthology. Bao, Salvador, and Fernando continue to work with the ELL teacher at this time. Right after lunch, the students do self-selected reading for 20 minutes. Brenda has brought in many books that are high-interest, low-vocabulary as well as picture books of all genres and reading levels that all students have access to. She does not use literature circles all the time. She works through one round of circles, then returns to a more traditional format so that she can work with different levels on different skills. This adaptation seems to help the lower-level students.

The Role of Phonics

Do I need to teach phonics?

The easy answer is yes, you do. But that's a qualified yes. If, and only if, your students need it, and for only as long as they do need it. Certainly not after students are reading at a third-grade level. No one will dispute that using the graphic configuration of words is one way to figure out what a word is. And, just as they need to know the alphabet, children need to know some basic sound-letter correspondences. They need to be familiar with the various sounds each letter can represent. Many of our words do follow consistent patterns. How *much* phonics to teach is the issue.

There is a place for explicit and direct help in developing a command of phonics. But this teaching must be strategic, selective, and based on the learning needs of your students. Kids don't care about skills. They care about stories. They want to laugh and cry and find out what happens next.

Polly, for instance, had several fifth and sixth graders who had very weak phonemic awareness. It would have been pointless to start with *A,* learn *B,* and so on. She pinpointed the letters they had difficulty with and, using the "Make a Word" strategy[3] devised by Cunningham and Cunningham (1992), she targeted these letters for students to practice within the context of real words.

Phonics instruction, write Galda, Cullinan, and Strickland (1997), "should never sacrifice comprehension nor should it replace independent reading activities." Teaching phonics exclusively ignores meaning. When introducing phonics, use only known words, not isolated sounds. Reading, writes Sarah Gudschinsky, author of *A Manual for Preliterate Peoples* (1973) should not begin with anything smaller than a word. Sound-letter correspondences can be learned and reinforced within the context of real reading.

In *Becoming a Nation of Readers*: *The Report of the Commission on Reading,* Anderson et al stated (1985): "Phonics instruction should aim to teach only the most important and regular of letter-to-sound relationships, because this is the sort of instruction that will most directly lay bare the alphabetic principle." This means teaching consonants that have only one sound, such as /m/. The report went on to state: "Once the basic relationships have been taught, the best way to get children to refine and extend their knowledge of letter-sound correspondences is through *repeated opportunities to read"* [emphasis ours].

Of course, in the primary grades children can learn basic sound-letter correspondences along with their classmates, but with older students, the more

---

3 As in the game Boggle, students are given a set of letters (for example, *d, m, e, a, r*) and are challenged to make words from them.

time spent learning these in isolation, the more time is taken away from reading itself—and constant drilling is tedious. Before they realize that the skills they are learning will eventually lead to reading, the students may become discouraged. Insistence on mastery of phonics may lead to more and more discouragement. The time allotted for phonics drill should be minimal in relation to activities spent encountering meaningful print. As pointed out earlier, while it is true that sounding out words is an important word-attack skill, it is not necessarily true that a word will be meaningful once it has been sounded out. For example, an English speaker might be able to read a Spanish text so that a Spanish speaker could understand what he's saying. However, if the reader's Spanish is so limited that he cannot understand more than the occasional word, he is only barking at print. The same principle applies to English words. Anyone with reasonable word-attack skills can sound out the word *calumniate*. However, knowing how it should be pronounced doesn't offer any clues about what it means. The meaning must either come from the context of the sentence or from a dictionary.

Good readers read for meaning. Poor readers are so busy decoding words they cannot concentrate on meaning and often lose the thread before they reach the end. Second-language readers, even though they may be fluent readers in their first language, tend to resort to poor strategies, such as reading word-for-word, working out every word laboriously. Thus, too much stress on sounding out words limits readers' strategies for getting meaning and also stresses correctness over understanding. Yoshi, for instance believed he had to translate each and every unfamiliar word in a sentence before he would even attempt to read it through. His skills were bogged down, because he was anchored to that dictionary. Mary knew he could read the material, but he was afraid to attempt it. Students must learn to focus on context and use syntax as a way of predicting meaning, rather than learning only to sound out words.

The task of learning sound-letter correspondences is particularly difficult for children whose first languages don't discriminate between sounds that are distinctive in English. We have all heard jokes about "flied lice" and "rotsa ruck." This is because Japanese and Chinese speakers hear one sound where English speakers hear two. Cree speakers don't have /sh/ in their language and will say *sip* for *ship*. Arabic speakers do not distinguish between /pl/ and /b/. Concentrating on these individual sounds when the student cannot distinguish between them is pointless. Even if Li can't say *rice* the way we might wish it or distinguish the /l/ and /r/ sounds, if he knows the difference between *lice* and *rice,* he will never make an error in the context of a story. Eventually he will be able to hear the difference, but until then you have better things to do than drills between minimal pairs.

There are many ways to embed phonics instruction within a meaningful context. Research has demonstrated that in classrooms where phonics are taught *in the context* of rereading favorite stories and songs and poems, children develop and use phonics knowledge better than in classrooms where the skills are taught in isolation (Routman 1996; Moustafa 1997; Cunningham 2000).

Here are a few ways to embed phonics instruction:

- Work on sound-letter correspondences using words elicited in a language-experience activity (LEA).

- Teach rhymes that focus on one particular sound. There are many books on the market that focus on particular sounds.

- Mary used tongue twisters with her beginners: *She sells seashells by the seashore.* It sounds corny, but her adult students loved it!

- Pick out known words that begin with the same letter, and have the students put them in their word dictionaries or on word cards with illustrations.

- Use your name banners (see page 175) to illustrate beginning and ending sounds.

- Use the student-made dictionaries to illustrate words that begin with certain sounds.

- Make alphabet books together.

- Make word lists and word banks.

- Emphasize certain sound/letter relationships during writing workshops.

- Give students plenty of opportunities to write, helping them write the sounds they hear in the words.

Working With Students Who Are Literate in Their First Language

Reading/Writing in the Correct Direction

What if the language in which students have first learned to read moves from right to left, or bottom to top?

Although languages such as Arabic, Farsi, and Hebrew use an alphabetic system, they are read from right to left. The problem of switching ELL students to left-to-right reading is resolved primarily through modeling. Students who are already literate will have learned proper eye-movement; now it needs to be reinforced in the proper direction.

Several methods can ensure that students move from left to right when they read or write:

- Monitor their initial reading experiences, making sure that they are reading correctly.

- When reading aloud, move your finger under the words you are reading.

- Provide a guide for the first few reading and writing experiences, such as arrows on the top of the page, or traffic lights showing green on the left and red on the right.

Developing Second-Language Literacy

My students are literate in their first language. Where do I go from here?

We used to believe that a person only learns to read once. It's not as simple as that. The skills of reading, true, are only learned once, but the cognitive demands that are placed on second-language learners are greater and more complex than those placed on first-language readers.

While many educators insist that it is essential to learn to read in the first language and to continue to read increasingly challenging texts in the first language, this is practical and possible in only a few languages. More book publishers have responded with texts in a number of languages, and there are more options available by searching the Internet. An ELL site will often have links to publishers, texts, materials, catalogs, and so on. If you do not have access to the Internet at your school, many local libraries have stations for public use.

Here are some pointers to begin developing second-language literacy:

- Start with material students already know. The school district in which Barb worked had a large number of Hmong students. For many years there was very little written in Hmong because it had been, until recently, an oral language. Finally, they were able to obtain the written versions of some of the favorite Hmong folktales, such as "The Plain of Jars" and "The Lady and the Tiger." Even beginning students, because they knew the stories already, were able to read them with comprehension.

- If at all possible, allow students to continue reading in their own language. This will help them master the skills and fluency needed to be efficient readers. The Internet provides newspapers in many languages.

- Encourage literate parents to read to their children in their own language; this is one of the best ways to support their child's intellectual development. Parents are often under the erroneous impression that they cannot help their child because they cannot speak or read in the new language.

- Augment use of translated materials (if available) with LEA (language experience approach).

- Have aides, peers, or older students read to them as often as possible, identifying known words and discussing content.

- Allow time for reading assisted by recorded text.

Aiding Comprehension in Both Language Arts and the Content Areas

Filling in the Gaps

What if students have a reasonable sight-word vocabulary, but still cannot comprehend simple materials?

ELLs face many difficulties in reading in a second language, including vocabulary, differences in style between written and spoken language, poor study skills, and lack of background knowledge.

Vocabulary: Lack of vocabulary can severely inhibit reading progress, as evidenced by this scavenger hunt form (figure 5.22), which was simple enough for English-speaking campers. Some vocabulary, such as essential vocabulary for content areas, simply must be taught directly, so that the students can understand the reading.

Differences in style: Narrative fiction is much different from content area textbooks, and students who do not know how to vary their strategies to suit the particular text often stumble and give up or gain nothing.

Study skills: Mary had two students who had weak educational backgrounds. One could speak English fluently, and while the other could understand a great deal and communicate his thoughts, his vocabulary still had many gaps. Reading was a problem for both, and they struggled with their history and English assignments. Mary showed them how to skim for the necessary concepts by helping them determine which paragraphs contained the important ideas and which material they could disregard. This took time, but by the end of the year, they could work independently.

Instructions:

Find the following nature items. We will be using these items in an art project.
Check off each item as you find it.
Have FUN!

____ A	*Acorn* 松果	
____ B	*Bark* 樹皮	
____ C	Something *Colorful* 很多 color	
____ D	Something *Dry* 枯葉	
____ E	Something *Evergreen* 任何 green	
____ F	Something *Funny* 快樂	
____ G	Something *Green* 綠	
____ H	Something that is *Hidden* 安佳	
____ I	Something that's *Inside* of something else 佳裡面……	
____ J	Something *Junky* 糖果紙	
____ K	Something *Kids* like 自己喜歡	
____ L	A *Leaf* 葉子	
____ M	Something *Many-colored*	
____ N	Pine *Needles* 針葉	
____ O	Something *Orange* or something *Oval* 橘色 橢圓形	

____ P	A *Pine* cone or a *Pebble* 松樹果	
____ Q	Something that *Quivers* 搖云动の…	
____ R	Something *Red* or something *Round* 紅色の…	
____ S	*Sand* or a *Seed* 種子	
____ T	*Twig.* 樹根	
____ U	Something that's *Under* something else 在…下面	
____ V	Something *Valuable* 不可能の東西	
____ W	Something *Wide* 長の…	
____ X	Something *eXciting* 興奮の…	
____ Y	Something *Yellow* 黃色の	
____ Z	A *Zig zag* in nature 青青の……	

Figure 5.22 This student's translation of items on a scavenger hunt form reveals his lack of English vocabulary.

Lack of background knowledge: Gunderson (1985) writes unequivocally that "a system that fails to give adequate attention to background and vocabulary teaching is destined to be unsuccessful with [ELL] students." Barb discovered, in one of her upper-level linguistics classes, that even though she stressed reading the assignments before the lecture, students were not doing so. Frustrated, she asked why. One of them explained that reading it after was easier, since they now had the background knowledge to understand what the text was saying. Barb realized, to her chagrin, that she was not practicing what she preached in other classes. How much more so is this true of our work with ELL students?

Cathy, from China, was assigned to read *Pilgrim's Progress* in her high school English class. She could read all the words out loud correctly, but with little comprehension, because the vocabulary, some of it archaic, was beyond her language experience and her background information was weak. As a Buddhist, she did not understand the concepts of *sin, guilt*, and *redemption*. Mary had to go to great lengths to fill in the basic information about Christianity (that we, in Western cultures, take for granted) before Cathy could begin to make sense of the text.

Getting Them *Into* the Text

Reading depends on knowledge—not just about words and sound-letter correspondences, but also about the world. The reader brings the sum total of his personal experiences to reading. Refugee or immigrant students, or those from remote reservations, may have either a very limited range of experience in terms of the school environment, or their life experiences may have been totally different from those in the stories they encounter. Those students who have spent most of their lives in refugee camps will not have the background knowledge to understand what we might consider a simple story about shopping in the big city. We cannot take for granted that just because the vocabulary is limited the story will be easy to understand. There must be a contact point—some core of knowledge to begin with, or they will not understand.

For instance, Miguel was struggling to read a story about pancakes. He was making many errors, and obviously getting very little from the reading. His teacher asked him, "Miguel, do you know what pancakes are?" With companions all around who had been remarking on how they loved pancakes, Miguel assured her that he did.

> *Do you eat them very often?*
> *Every day.*
> *What do you like on your pancakes?*
> *(He rubbed his tummy.) Salt. Yummy.*

Prepare for the Reading Assignment

Preparation for reading is a crucial part of the whole act of reading, whether at the elementary or secondary level, in language arts, or in the content areas. It should not be marginalized or skipped, because it often determines whether that day's lesson will be a success or a failure for the student.

Emphasize the prereading segment of any reading task. Anderson et al note that although prereading is the most important part of any reading lesson, it is certainly the most neglected. Prereading involves more than simply deciding which words will be difficult and discussing them beforehand. The prereading process can include

- Discussing the content first
- Reading the selection aloud to your students before they read it themselves, helping them with difficult concepts and words
- Showing a related filmstrip or movie
- Going on a field trip related to the subject
- Having students brainstorm and share what they know about a topic before introducing the text
- Predicting what will happen by looking at the pictures that accompany the text

For example, Melissa was faced with a difficult class of limited-English-speaking eighth graders. These students were a notorious bunch of poor readers with the attendant behavior problems. Many of the boys, if not already in gangs, were deeply attracted to the idea. They were becoming increasingly disenfranchised from what was happening in school. In thinking over what book to choose, Melissa decided on *The Outsiders*, because its plot centered around the theme of gangs. The two overarching questions she chose for the unit were:

1. Why do people join gangs?
2. What are the consequences of being in a gang?

She rented the movie and ran the recording forward to the scene where Johnny and Ponyboy are confronted by the Socs, and Johnny knifes one of them. The class watched, enthralled. Then, she abruptly turned the tape off, just as Ponyboy, his head being held underwater, loses consciousness. The class protested shrilly.

She began a discussion and, as a whole class, they brainstormed about gangs. Melissa, using a modified LEA, wrote their thoughts on the board. They discussed the following ideas:

1. What's the difference between a gang and a club?
2. Are gangs good or bad? First, the students voted. Then, they listed both good and bad qualities of gangs.
3. Gangs in the area. The students listed them.
4. How you can tell someone is in a gang.
5. What you need to do to become a member of a gang.

Very lively discussions about gangs ensued. The students were interested and engaged and had many thoughts to offer. Melissa took the chore of writing away by doing it for them, to keep the enthusiasm up and the conversation flowing.

The following day, she showed a little more of the movie. Some had seen it already and, with typical eighth-grade abandon, shouted out what was going to happen. Then, she read the first chapter of the story to the students, and for an entire class period, the students listened quietly. Over the course of the next several weeks, they continued to read the book, on their own, in small groups, as well as listening to Melissa read to them. Because she had chosen a topic that the students were intensely interested in and knew a great deal about, the students read with more attention and depth than at any other time she had that particular group of students. Although she taught this book to only ELL students, what she did would have carried over easily into a mixed class.

Making it Through the Reading With Comprehension

ELL readers often arrive at school with poor study skills. They do not know how to extract information from a text or how to read for the purposes demanded. They need extensive practice with the varied tasks of reading in the content areas. Here, again, the prereading segment of any reading task is critical. In addition to the suggestions above, we recommend the following strategies:

- Ensure that students know what they are expected to get out of the reading selection: the main idea, a general understanding, or specific facts to be recalled later.

- Ensure that students know what is required when answering any comprehension questions. If presented with a choice, do they need to pick out which statements are true, or must they put the sentences in order? Is there more than one correct answer?

- Walk the students through the reading selection, pointing out clues that aid comprehension, such as pictures, maps, italics, boldface print, and so on.

- Help them look at print configurations, such as the sizes and shapes of words or italics and boldface print, for clues to the relative importance of the information.

- Help them recognize what to look for. Often, readers get hung up feeling they need to know each word before they can go on to the next, thus spending an inordinate amount of time looking up words in the dictionary. Help them look for key words in a selection, such as the nouns and the verbs, then predict the meaning of the entire sentence based on these key words.

Apply Skills Learned *Beyond*, to Other Reading Tasks

It is imperative that students continue to gain in the vocabulary department, so give them ample opportunity to work with vocabulary. It's not enough just to be exposed to new words, or even for the student to be able to guess or infer the meaning of a word that is new. Their attention needs to be guided to the new vocabulary within effective contexts. Then, students need frequent opportunities to learn new words, to explore meanings, and to use the words they have acquired. Readers need to be engaged in focused work using the words by practicing them in various contexts. This can be as simple as matching the word to its definition, or as challenging as using them in sentences.

Election Unscramble

Unscramble the following words that are related to elections.

1. edaidnact   *There are few edaidnacts for governor.*

2. rpiyram   *I voted the rpiyram election.*

3. eisuss   *He read a eisuss about elections.*

Figure 5.23 This writer wasn't paying attention at all. What was he thinking? What does his writing say about the value of the assignment itself?

I was afraid but I talked to my friend.

Figure 5.24 Campers slept out under the stars. Their reflection assignment was written on paper folded into the form of a little sleeping bag.

Encourage Extensive Reading

Promote extensive reading at a level similar to or easier than English speakers. Find selections that will help promote competency in the strategies students have learned. In addition

- Have a class discussion about students' reading outside the classroom.

- Have students keep journals to record what they read.

- Allocate time to talk with each student individually about his reading. Get to know individual likes and dislikes so that you can steer students toward books that interest them.

- Have students read other works by the same author and books of the same genre or on the same topic.

- Retell the story through another medium, such as film, drama, radio drama, or through another literary form such as poetry or song.

- Write class (or school) newspapers, and/or magazines relating to the topic.

- After they've completed reading something, have a discussion to see if students' attitudes, ideas, and interpretations have changed.

Have a Supportive Environment

A supportive environment is one that is sensitive to the various needs of all members of the class. Franco needs different instruction than Kate. Austin likes to read adventure stories, Ellie is into high fantasy—what Nick distastefully calls "girl stories." Bao needs high-interest, low-vocabulary books, picture books, and audio books.

Ways to support reading include the following:

- **Promote flexibility.** This means that the class is open to change. Reading groups, the mainstay of much of reading instruction in the past, were often fixed. A redbird was always a redbird and an eagle was always an eagle, and the kids knew it. But Beverly can make gains in an astonishing amount of time, or she can plateau. Because learning spurts and coasting occur in every child, flexibility is a key strategy for adapting to the changes.

- **Be student-centered.** This means that the class is not a one-size-fits-all class, in which every student reads what the teacher assigns, takes the same tests, and gives only the right answer to teacher-initiated questions. Zemelman, Daniels, and Hyde (1998) write: "Making a school student centered involves building on the natural curiosity children bring to school and asking kids what they want to learn." It means active teachers who meet the students' needs by designing experiences based on their knowledge of the curriculum, of developmentally appropriate tasks, and of the students themselves.

- **Build on background knowledge.** Students *do* bring diverse background knowledge from their various cultures and experiences. Build on this.

- **Be supportive.** Accept and celebrate a variety of individual strengths.

- **Recognize and acknowledge the place for errors.** We often get hung up on correcting mistakes, particularly in reading. Some teachers have students read aloud as a way of checking their comprehension. When students are reading along and stumble over a word, it seems intuitively right to jump in and correct them, but this must be done with caution. We believe that asking individual students to read aloud without having a chance to rehearse is often not a good indicator of how well or how much he is comprehending. Reading aloud *to* someone is excellent practice, but not until readers achieve a certain level of fluency.

Some readers can read aloud perfectly—they sound wonderfully fluent, but comprehend little or nothing. Sixth-grader Jose, for instance, was turned over to tutors and classroom aides for two or three hours each day. The tutors were told that he needed practice in reading, and so he spent most of that time reading to them. He sounded good; he made few mistakes. However, when asked what he had read, he couldn't tell them. The enormous amount of time and effort spent was not furthering his comprehension at all. This time could have been better spent reading to him, with him, building strategies and background knowledge.

Other readers seem to stumble over every other word, making the task of listening to them particularly discomfiting. The temptation is to jump in and help. However, errors in reading aloud do not necessarily mean that the reader is not able to understand the text. Ken and Yetta Goodman, early on in their original research of reading, report that some errors are "better" than others. For instance, in the fifth grade, Maia read a short passage about elephants. This was her reading:

> *The elephant is the largest animal in the world that lives on land a full-found. Elephant may have a weight of about four tons and may be nine feet tall. Because elephants are so large, they have no natural enies other than man. Science elephants have so few enies, they are sually easy to get along with and almost always act friendly. Elephants usually live in heards(?)...A femaly, orladdy elephant is called a cow. During the hottest part of the day the herd will? Huddle?*

Teachers and other kids in the literature or reading group are often tempted to jump in, correct her immediately, or disrupt her thought processes by telling her to go back and sound out the words so she can get them right. She might be labeled as a disabled reader, and on the face of it, it seems she didn't get much out of it. In talking over the story, however, she didn't understand the key words *full-grown, herd,* and *huddle,* but she was able to pick up most of the story, and even though she mispronounced *enemies* she used the word accurately in her retelling:

> "The elephant don't got enemies. It's the largest animal. It usually herds with usually members of 30. They go a lake for drink water."

Most of Maia's miscues were not reading problems per se, but background knowledge. She could find the right information from the text when asked questions such as, "Why don't elephants have any natural enemies?"

Time

The most important element to emphasize in terms of a supportive environment is the significance of providing the time and opportunity to read, read, read. Peterson and Eeds stress (1990) that an essential component of a literature study program is "the provision of time for extensive reading on one's own. Children need time to read in peace, to just read without worrying about having to do things afterwards...Learning to read is a continuous, cumulative accomplishment." Allington (2001) goes further, suggesting

> The classroom teachers read to their students, but rarely give them time to read on their own and practice the literacy skills they've learned. Convince these teachers why it's important to make time.

that "one and one-half hours of daily in-school reading would seem a minimum goal." And this is time spent actually reading, not doing "reading-related" activities, such as completing worksheets. Research has shown that kids who were given more time to read performed better. Seems like a no-brainer, but in many classrooms kids spend time doing many things other than reading. Practice in reading means just that—reading.

This includes

- Being read to
- Students reading on their own
- Responding to the books read
- Discussing the books
- Conferencing about interpretations

This also includes time to grow in reading. With students who are non-native English speakers, like Bao, it takes a lot of time. Most preliterate students have a different learning curve. Sometimes it appears they learn very little for the first year. They can be very quiet, indicate little comprehension, and so on.

Don't be fooled. They are internalizing much and will respond quickly the following year. Time is important for these students. It is the lack of opportunity to read and be included in "real" reading and authentic literacy tasks that limits students' chances to learn to function in a literate world.

Conclusion

When we teach reading, these are our underlying assumptions:

- Reading must be for meaning.
- We learn to read by reading.

Reading does not happen in a vacuum. Readers need repeated opportunities to practice. They need a guide to help them over the rough spots and teach them strategies to get *into, through,* and *beyond* a text. And, they need a comfortable environment in which they can attempt to read without fear of being jumped on for their mistakes. By providing these essentials, we can move our learners from confused nonreaders, to competent readers able to tackle any reading text or task.

Reflections, Projects, and Projections for Discussion

- Write your own reading autobiography. When and how did you learn to read? Who taught you? Did you know how to read when you came to school? What did you know by the time kindergarten started? Did you love to read as a child? Do you consider yourself a reader, someone who reads all the time, or do you just read when you need to? When and why do you read nowadays? What kinds of books did you read during your early childhood, elementary years, middle, and high-school years? What was your most memorable (good or bad) experience with books as a child? Who is your favorite author now?

- Design the ideal classroom for developing reading in all your learners—ELL and English speaking. Consider either the students in the case studies on the following page, or some we have included in chapters 2, 3, 6, and 9.

  - What texts and materials would you like to have?

  - What can you add that will support beginning literacy students, or advanced speakers who are beginning readers?

  - How would you design your daily schedule?

- Consider what makes reading enjoyable for you. What can make it difficult or frustrating?

- Reflect on what you observe about your students who are better readers. What do you observe about the emerging readers?

- If you teach decoding skills, think about what the immediate goal of learning to decode is—to sound out words or to help students learn sight words to add to their repertoire? What's the difference?

- Think about the texts and other materials that you have in your classroom to support students' development of fluent reading. What can you add to your collection to support your ELLs?

- Reflect on how you select vocabulary to teach in all areas of your curriculum.

- Consider how much time you allocate to word study every day. Is this enough? Too much?

- Think about the routines for word study that you teach and encourage your students to use. Explore some variations that you could include.

- Reflect on the reading strategies you teach and encourage your students to use. Are there any other strategies that might work better for some students?

- Ask yourself how you differentiate instruction and tasks based on your students' needs.

- Think about when, during the school day, your students get to read books they can understand. How much time per day do you allocate for SSR? Is this enough?

Case Studies: Kirsty, Dave, Pa, Nou, Kou, Grace, and Charlie

Examine the case studies on the following page. Design a reading lesson that will support all the students in this class and enhance their reading ability. What texts can you use? What activities can you design that will engage Nick, Robby, Kate, Melody, and Destiny and help them to strengthen their reading, while also including Dave, Pa, Nou, and Kou?

Kristy

Kristy, 13, read the following, taken from the *Flynt Cooter Reading Inventory* (an informal reading assessment inventory for classroom teachers):

I dislike being the yougest.
(Text: I dislike being the youngest.)

I'm always gusting into trubby
(Text: I'm always getting into trouble.)

They sister on witching the shoe daily.
(Text: They insisted on watching the show daily.)

What does her reading of these sentences tell you, if anything, about her reading skills? Is this a valid assessment? How would you find out her reading level if you chose to use a different type of assessment? What sort of strategies is Kristy employing, and how would you go about helping her learn more useful strategies?

Dave, Pa, Nou, and Kou

Suppose the following four students are in your class:

Dave is repeating the grade you teach for the second time. He is in a reading group that is one year lower and with two English speaking students. Pa is outgoing, has a good command of oral language, and writes neatly. She is able to sound words out and guesses the letters she is not sure about. Her reading is proceeding, even though she is behind the English speakers in the class. Nou is Pa's twin sister. She is unhappy, because Pa has exited from the ELL program, and Nou resents the teacher for pulling her out of class, but she lacks basic vocabulary and therefore cannot comprehend sentences. Kou is bright and interested in doing his best to impress you. Although he seems to be able to comprehend grade-level material, he is very slow in doing his assignments.

- How would you choose texts for each of these students?

- How would you include them in the class?

- How would you accommodate them into the curriculum you must teach?

Grace and Charlie

Grace and Charlie are two new students from Korea. Grace is a level 5 and Charlie a level 4 (see chapter 2). They have been placed in your English class, which will be beginning *The Crucible* next week. Understandably, these students will need background information, but they might also have gaps that are greater than the historical material. Can you anticipate areas where students with a non-Christian background might have difficulties? How can you help them bridge the cultural gap? What other techniques can you use to help the students with the dual historical information, and how do you manage this with your other students?

Chapter 6
Writing—A Pig Broplem

In this chapter, we look at acquiring the skill of writing. We focus on

- Using a process approach to writing with ELL students
- What students need to become successful writers
- Commenting on student papers and assisting with revision
- How and when to correct errors

The Process Approach to Writing

Yesterday last night of the teacher Mary Eckes gaven would one to student all student in class-person doesn't get to have to know. This when student dd to get befor big one the squash all way came back to school at reach home family and neighbour. that right your are want to see becouse youre are doesn't have. doesn't know.

In the past several decades the emphasis in teaching writing has shifted from "product" to "process." The days when the only audience was the teacher—acting as judge, jury, and executioner—are long gone, and even lower elementary teachers are using the process approach now. But in many classrooms, particularly high-school classrooms, a piece like the one above often comes back bloodied with ink marks, graphically demonstrating just how far Cham falls short of the mark in approximating standard English. Although she may be given a chance to change her ideas or fix what is wrong, deciding what to fix and whether the final product will achieve a passing grade are other issues.

It is useful to use the writing process as a starting point for a discussion on writing with ELL students. We know that writing is not a linear process in which writers start at the beginning and work though, error-free, to the end; it is a cyclical process in which the writer continually circles back, reviewing and revising. Some of us start with outlines, others just start, discovering as they go where they're headed. Most writers plan, compose, then read what they've written, edit as they go, write some more, revise a little, and so on.

Genuine learning takes place during the process of putting thoughts down on paper. Writers, whether children or adults, do not become writers by simulating writing—filling in blanks on photocopied sheets, learning grammar rules, memorizing vocabulary, or practicing lists of spelling words. Writing authentic texts involves orchestrating all facets of language at once: a writer must consider the social and situational aspects of creating a piece of writing at the same time as he deals with decisions about meaning, spelling, grammar, and punctuation (Newman 1984).

With English language learners, it is tempting to focus first on vocabulary development, spelling, and grammar. However, this bottom-up approach returns to the use of such strategies as word drills, which have limited instructional value. It also neglects the main goal of writing: to create a meaningful text for a reader.

Who Is the ELL Writer?

It is impossible to come up with a simple profile of an ELL writer. There are many variables operating, as the following student examples show (students are roughly the same age):

Boris, in a journal response, writes:

Most people do not listen with the intent to understand, they listen with the intent to reply.

Although he just arrived in the U.S., Boris's English is nearly flawless, and his writing is better than many college students.

Yoshi, writing on the same topic, says:

The person who talks neither so important not interesting things, I've neve listens so hard. I've reacted at random. But it is a problem, even it is not important things for me. I have to tend to heare as much as I could. Becaseueven his/ her story is not important for me, it may so important for him/her. And I have to resonse sparsely. And we I don't have to wast of the time to hear ever which is not important or curious for me.

Yoshi has understood the reading and has good ideas, but he can't yet express them fluently. There are many grammatical errors that slow the reader considerably.

Andre, after viewing the movie *Charlotte's Web* writes:

PIG:
Thes store abayt a pig. He don't want to pepele eat him and he don't want to die. Spider halp him and safe his life. Spider tiche him howe to dans. And he wini the ftrst plase on a scow. And hese ownar sad I willliwe hime a lift.

Andre has had limited schooling in both his first language and English. His writing has many grammatical errors and is very simple.

The name below was signed by Bao, who had no prior schooling.

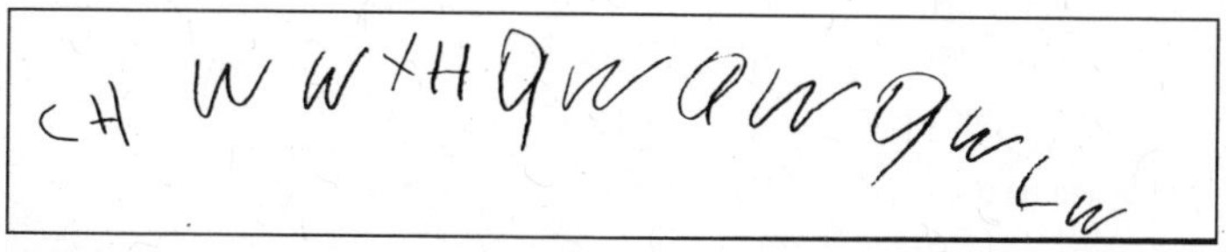

Figure 6.1 This signature shows the student's inexperience with print.

But writers are writers, and all writers face two challenges:

- What to say
- How to say it

Moreover, all writers

- Have a purpose or intent when they write
- Make mistakes
- Have crummy first drafts (Lamott 1995)
- Must orchestrate many things when they write, making complex decisions about such things as audience, form, organization, as well as punctuation, word choice, spelling, and so on (Newman 1984)
- Must operate simultaneously on two levels: composing (creating ideas, putting their thoughts in logical, articulate form), and transcribing (physically writing a text) (Barrs et al 1989)

This is precisely why kids, especially language learners, often fear and avoid writing. A group of Syrian second language learners brainstormed why they find it easier to talk and harder to write. Here's their list.

Why we like to talk:

- Listeners can tell you they don't understand. You get instant feedback.

- Listeners make eye contact and give you cues, such as facial expressions, body language, and voice tone to tell you whether you are making sense, or boring them, or entertaining them.

- There is no control on speaking. You can express yourself freely.

- There's a feeling of excitement.

- You exchange information that is not necessarily correct or incorrect.

- It's a shared experience. You're a partner.

- It's enjoyable.

- You don't make spelling mistakes.

- We have an intrinsic need to relate to others.

- You can make corrections and additions to add to your point.

- You can pause, think of words, ask for help if you can't think of the right thing to say.

Why we don't like writing:

- We make mistakes that everyone can see.

- We have to connect information, with all the proper transitions and the precise words in a specific order.

- We have to supply all the information.

- Sequencing is hard.

- Thinking is hard.

- We never seem to have enough time.

- There's an unknown reader.

- We may not know enough grammar to write correctly.

- We need training.

- We need special knowledge.

- We can't find the right words.

- Writing requires discipline.

- It's not spontaneous.

- We're afraid of criticism.

- Poor assignments that are boring, tedious, too difficult.

This list is pretty complete, and we all suffer from one or all of the above challenges at some time or another. ELL writers, some of whom are learning to write for the first time and others who are accomplished writers in their own native language, must cope with the challenge of using words, grammar, and structures that are unfamiliar to them to formulate thoughts.

Helping Students Become Successful Writers

To learn to write well, every beginning writer needs

- To be immersed in writing

- A supportive environment

- Feedback from interested readers and guidance from knowledgeable teachers

- Time

Immerse Students in Writing

Being immersed in writing means not only frequent opportunities to write, but frequent opportunities to read—both finished products and the ongoing work of other writers. This idea of immersion has recently been at the forefront even more than it was in the past. Graham, MacArthur, and Fitzgerald (2007), in their studies of effective writing practices, state that the writing is literally on the wall:

> The most effective and engaging teachers had classrooms that were overflowing with writing materials, books and other tools for literacy learning and instruction...Bulletin boards were covered with student work, and all of the furniture and areas around the room were designed for student access and learning. Classroom libraries were stocked with quality children's literature as well as student-created texts.

Allow your students to write. Does "allow" sound like a strange concept? We have seen many teachers who do not believe that children should be allowed to write on their own until they have control over forms, have what the teacher deems is sufficient vocabulary, or sufficient command of the English language. We vehemently disagree with this viewpoint. Zemelman, Daniels, and Hyde (1998) concur, stating that

> All children can and should write...writing should not be delayed while reading or grammar is developed first; rather, experimenting with the ingredients of written language is one of the prime ways of advancing reading achievement and mastering the conventions of language.

And Samway and McKeon (2007) state that "grammar, spelling, and vocabulary (as well as other aspects of writing, including organization, style, and content) can all be developed in the context of the student's own writing."

Cathy Tegen, an ELL teacher, was team-teaching a summer program with a teacher who believed that the limited-English-speaking children in the class should not be allowed to write. Cathy persuaded the teacher to give them a chance. Figure 6.2 shows what one student, who had hitherto never been allowed to write, produced.

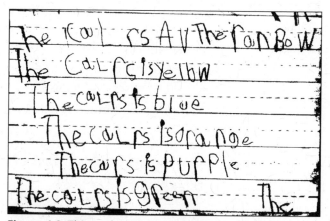

Figure 6.2 This student's writing displays a good deal of knowledge about words, sound-letter correspondences, and English grammar. In addition, he had something he wanted to communicate.

Encourage the Writing Process

The writing process has been researched in detail over the past few decades, beginning with Emig's groundbreaking work, *The Composing Processes of 12th Graders* (1971), and has helped us align what we do in the classroom with what real writers do. Allow students time to work through the stages of the writing process, which can be divided into the following stages:

1. **Prewriting:** This is the thinking stage, also called the "percolating" stage or the "get-ready-to-write" stage. This is when students pull their thoughts together and make the initial decisions about where to start, points of view, characters, as well as the information they want to include.

2. **Drafting:** In this stage, students put their thoughts on paper. This tentative, exploratory stage can often be the hardest part; articulating what one is thinking can be a long and sometimes arduous process. Putting pencil to blank page is a major step.

3. **Rereading:** Students should be encouraged to reread what they have written throughout the writing process, to determine if they have conveyed the message they wanted to convey in the best possible way.

4. **Revising:** Revision means "seeing again." At this stage writers clarify and refine their ideas, adding, subtracting, and moving text around.

5. **Editing:** Editing is putting a piece into its final form. The focus changes from content to mechanics. Writers polish their writing by correcting spelling, punctuation, sentence structure, and so on.

6. **Publishing:** In this final stage, writers share their writing with an appropriate audience.

Working with limited-English writers presents special challenges, particularly at the earlier stages. Not only are many older students at very low proficiency levels and beginners to the entire schooling process, ELL writers are often what Tompkins (2000) refers to as "novice writers," that is, unaware of audience, purpose, and form. They have few strategies at their disposal, they are more concerned with mechanics than ideas, and they view writing simply as putting words on paper. Thus, for them, revising means "fixing," or making their piece longer, not better.

For instance, Joaquin wrote a paper on the Titanic (figure 6.3a). Although this paper has many grammatical errors, it is lively and filled with strong details. It demonstrates Joaquin's understanding of what happened when the Titanic sank, and it shows his sense of humor (a whale ate him). There is much good in this paper.

Yet note Joaquin's revisions: he simply made it neater and made a few grammatical changes (figure 6.3b). He did not seem to know what needed to be added or how to improve his writing. In helping him, his teacher focused on correcting the many errors in spelling. This is understandable, because these are the most obvious mistakes, and they obscure much of the meaning.

> I pade to go no the Titank
> at the Man iroon it that the
> ice brg there was a hole on Fitak
> the wootr came roohn in.
> The Pepel sremn and I said
> "What." A dog strd brcn at me.
> I wht to chak whqt Wes get on I
> saw a hbole and it was big !
> + strd croing be cou I dided
> wot to gron. Jomt out of
> the Tytanic and then
> I get eat an by a whale.

>   paid   on   Titanic
> I pade to go no the Titank. At the
> mens room   hit   iceberg
> man room, it hat the icebrg. There was
>   Titanic   water   rushing
> a hole on Titak. The wrotr came roshn
>   people   screaming
> in. The pepel were sremn and I said
>   started barking   went
> "What?" A dog strd brcn at me. I wat
>   check   going
> to chak what was get on. I saw a hole
>   started crying because
> and it was big! I strd croing be cous I
> didn't want   drown jumped
> dided wot to gron. Jomt out of the
>   got eaten
> Titanic and then I get eat an by a whale.

Figure 6.3a–b There is little difference between Joaquin's first draft (a) and his second draft (b).

Six-trait writing[1] helps both mainstream students and writers like Joaquin improve their writing. Rather than overwhelming students with too many tasks on too many fronts, selecting one trait to work on helps students focus. For example, Joaquin has good ideas. He could make this story more vivid by adding details about what he saw and how he felt when the water came rushing in. He might choose to work on word choice. Setting reasonable goals for him puts success within his grasp and takes much of the burden of improving the writing off your shoulders.

Working with beginners such as Joaquin is not a quick-fix operation. It's a long, involved process of working on many fronts: teaching writing skills and problem-solving strategies, allowing students to write freely and frequently so that, over time, the writing becomes more fluent, less error-ridden, and less problematic. Working with such writers is very labor-intensive: simply put, you have to do a lot of the work for them, because they can't do it themselves. What's more, we have to be judicious about doing things for students all the time, because this can lead to reluctant or disabled writers. We need to encourage risk-taking and push students beyond what is safe and easy.

At this point, we'll describe ways to support the writing process and give examples of what students produced. At the end of the chapter, we will describe, in more detail, how to help students become competent at the revising stage.

---

1   Six-trait writing is a model that originated in Beaverton, Oregon in 1984, coined by the Northwest Regional Educational Laboratory (NWREL). "Traits are simply qualities that are noticeable to others and that help us define whether performance—any performance—is strong or not" (Colorado Charter Schools). The six traits of writing are: ideas (main point or storyline), organization (structure), voice (the writer behind the message), word choice (vocabulary), sentence fluency (how the writing sounds), and conventions (mechanics). See <uscharterschools.org/cs/codeg/view/cs_bmsg/347> and Spandel (1997) for further discussion.

Prewriting

Prewriting is perhaps the most important step for writers in both the first and subsequent languages. Yet it is often the most neglected step. Prewriting is a time for students not only to generate ideas, but to pool their collective knowledge of vocabulary and grammatical structure appropriate to the lesson. All students, and ELL students in particular, need to have a great deal of stimuli before they write. As a lead-in to writing, provide as much opportunity as possible for students to listen to and participate in discussions relating to the topics they will be writing about. Make prewriting an important part of every writing activity. Here are some ideas for engaging students in their writing topic:

- Read stories and poems to them. This is effective for kindergarten through high school. Reading aloud provides students with models for story writing by giving them a sense of story form, characterization, plot, drama, and so on. It also sparks their imagination, giving them ideas to write about.

- Brainstorm as a class, generating lists of ideas and possible topics.

- Take field trips.

- Listen to speeches.

- Show films, videos, or filmstrips.

- Allow students to talk about their work with you or with each other.

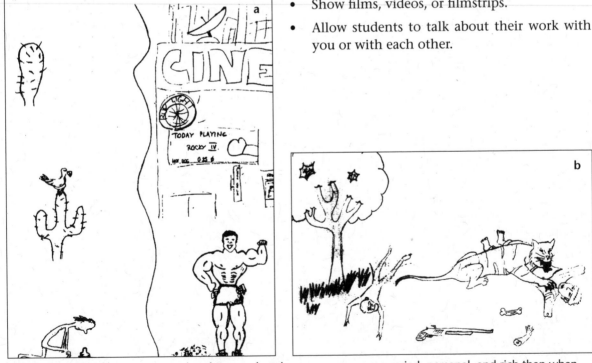

Figure 6.4a–b When encouraged to draw, students' responses are more varied, personal, and rich than when simply given fill-in-the-blanks on lined paper. Stan vividly captured the difference between life in rural Central America and life in the U.S. (a). Rhody's drawing depicts the Hmong folktale "The Lady and the Tiger" (b).

- Allow students to draw, either as a preparation for writing or as an enhancement to their writing. Drawing is a valid form of communication and often gives students time and ways to formulate their thoughts before they set words to paper. Drawing also lets them demonstrate what they are thinking but cannot yet articulate.

- Supply appropriate vocabulary, making it explicit and visible. One of the toughest parts of writing is finding the right words. And lack of vocabulary is a huge hindrance for second language learners. Part of making a rich environment is making sure that they have access and exposure to the words they need. Brainstorming words to put on the walls, or having students make their own dictionaries makes the process easier.

Drafting

Everyone produces crummy first drafts. For beginning writers in any language, this stage often generates a great deal of what can only be called "junk." Students are often far afield of what they need and want to say and need careful guidance through this process.

What is the Americans?

Since the Americans have diverse culture, ethnicity and broadly widened land, I cannot find any specific definition of the Americans. In the urban area like New York, Chicago, or Los Angeles, people seem not to be afraid of meeting foreigners because of many opportunities to see them on streets. On the other hand, in the rural area, the Americans are conservative, ignorant and friendly. The average Americans are conservative and ignorant about world geography and words news, contrast to the recognition by the other countries that the United States is the only super power in the world.

This rough, unedited draft was written using notes taken from the board. Students had listed their perceptions of Americans, which included the ideas that Americans are ignorant and conservative. Noboru was simply writing without thinking through what had been stated. The paper is filled with unsupportable generalities and vague prejudices. Most of the essay needed to be heavily edited, substantiated with examples, or just plain thrown out.

Beginners often copy straight from the text. This is *not* plagiarism. It is a useful strategy for thinking through what it is they want to say. As students get older and more proficient they can begin thinking about paraphrasing, consolidating information, and putting thoughts into their own words. Enforcing it at the beginning stages is counterproductive.

Advanced beginner and intermediate ELL language learners can be especially vulnerable to copying information when attempting to work on content-based essays for assignments. Trying to locate and then juggle information gleaned from text or reference material can be overwhelming to a student not fluent in English. Students at this level are proud to assemble the information they have found and may simply not have the ability to reformulate it for their essays.

a

PG

I BELEIVE THIS NATION SHOULD
COMMIT ITSELF TO ACHEIVE
A GOAL BEFOR THIS DECADE
IS OUT, OF LANDING
A MAN ON THE MOON
AND RETURNING
HIM SAFLEY TO EARTH. SO
SAID PRESEDENT JOHN
F. KENNEDY IN AN ADRESSE
TO CONGORES ON MAY 25
1961, HIS WORD'S
POSED A CHALLENG TO THE
AMERICAN PEOPLE, AT
THAT TIME, AMEICAN SPACE
EFFORTS LAGGED FAR
BEHIND.

b

Apollo 11 Facts

Apollo 11 was the 11 group to go into space but the 1st group of men to set foot on the moon.

The men who set foot on the moon were Neil Armstrong and Buzz Aldrin. Michael Collins stayed inside the rocket ship. Apollo 11 took off on July 16 1969 and made it to the moon 4 days later on July 20.

The Rocket was built by 300,000 workers and had five million separate parts. Apollo had three parts: a command module, the Columbia, the Lunar module, the Eagle and a service module. The two space ships separated and Neil Armstrong said, "The Eagle has wings."

Figure 6.5a–b One can only wince at the enormous amount of effort put in by this small boy. He clearly did not understand what he was reading and did not know how or where to start when confronted by the assignment to "write an essay on Apollo 11" (a). He went on doggedly to fill seven pages by copying. He should not have been allowed to go on that long in the wrong direction. In the end, Barb asked the student to tell her what he had learned about Apollo 11, and typed his ideas into the computer (b). (At that late stage of the game, when his frustration was very high, this approach was the only way of salvaging anything from the assignment.) Through careful questioning and showing him where the essential information was, he could read for meaning and write an adequate paper.

Here's another writer who is struggling in his first draft to put his own thoughts into a paper using support from outside sources. The copying is blatant and very apparent in the sudden shifts in style and sophistication of prose. He needs direct instruction in paraphrasing.

The tree element of african culture is food soul food in the south of u.s. is very similar to food in africa and dance is same like african s africa america. throughout the narrative,music to place in socio cultural context,which include the author perspective on how cultural implerialism particulary in the united states has excted a toll on person of african descent and negatively impacted the culture of the larger societ.although recognize that african american music is a syncretic creation primary involving african and european roots,she stresses both the importance of the african heritage author perspective,then offers a distinct contribution to our understanding about the essence of african music.

There is a certain point, however, when writers need to become aware of the concept of plagiarism. This cannot be left to chance. Raimes (1999) writes that in Western society we take the "ownership of works and text" very seriously and therefore it is important for students, as they grow accomplished and fluent, to know what plagiarism is, when it occurs, and how to avoid it.

Reid (1993) notes that it is our responsibility to give students "frequent, carefully monitored opportunities to practice the skills of paraphrase summary, quotation and citation" so that they can develop an awareness of other authors and texts.

Rereading

At every step in the process, students need to be encouraged to reread what they have written. This "is the glue that connects the stages of writing," advise Fletcher and Portalupi (2001). Things that seemed great when you put them on paper can seem really cheesy and lame when you reread them after a day or two. Rereading is one way of having your students review what they have read. It also is a way for them to become critical readers and thinkers. Is this what I really want to say? Is there a better way to phrase this?

Revising

Revising is very hard for many students. Spandel (1997) asks, "Why is revising so repulsive?" For one thing, many beginners, either first- or second-language writers, "have enough trouble getting the copy written in the first place. They're still working on motor skills, pacing, balance, margins, letter orientation, and other complex skills which come naturally and automatically to older writers." For second-language writers, finding the words they want, groping in a language they're not yet fluent in, can be an exhausting enterprise. Many beginning writers believe that once they have put their thoughts down on paper, they have reached the end; they are finished, and aside from correcting a few spelling errors they have nothing more to do. Students need to learn that authors often write passages many times before they are satisfied. Intervention by the teacher at this stage is critical. This is the stage when changes should be made that affect meaning. Guide your students by making suggestions for changes, by asking for clarification, and so on. Later in this chapter, we provide writing examples and discuss ways to help students revise their work.

Yet, not everything needs to be revised! Spandel advises: change things *only* when the piece is going to be formally published and when the student writer has gone as far with the editing as his skills permit. For many of our ELL students who are novice writers, getting the words on paper is enough. As we demonstrate below, the purpose of the writing determines whether it needs to be revised or not.

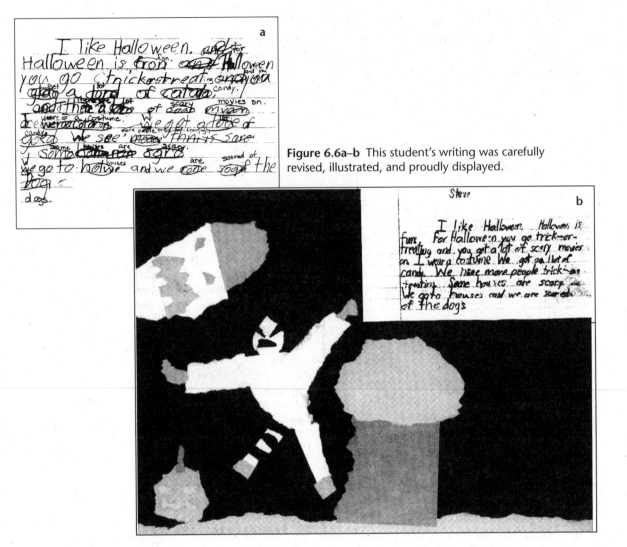

Figure 6.6a–b This student's writing was carefully revised, illustrated, and proudly displayed.

Editing

As difficult as revising is for students, editing is just as difficult; it demands close attention to details such as grammar, punctuation, and spelling that they have not mastered yet. As teachers, we have to resist the temptation to correct everything on every paper. We discuss editing in more detail on page 229.

Publishing or Bringing the Writing to Closure

Closure can be achieved by

- Posting work
- Taking it home
- Checking off that something is completed
- Having due dates

This may or may not actually involve publishing. Spandel (1997) writes, "Do not feel compelled to publish everything. It's exhausting for everyone and completely unrealistic. No one publishes everything she or he writes. Encourage students to be selective about what goes all the way through the process."

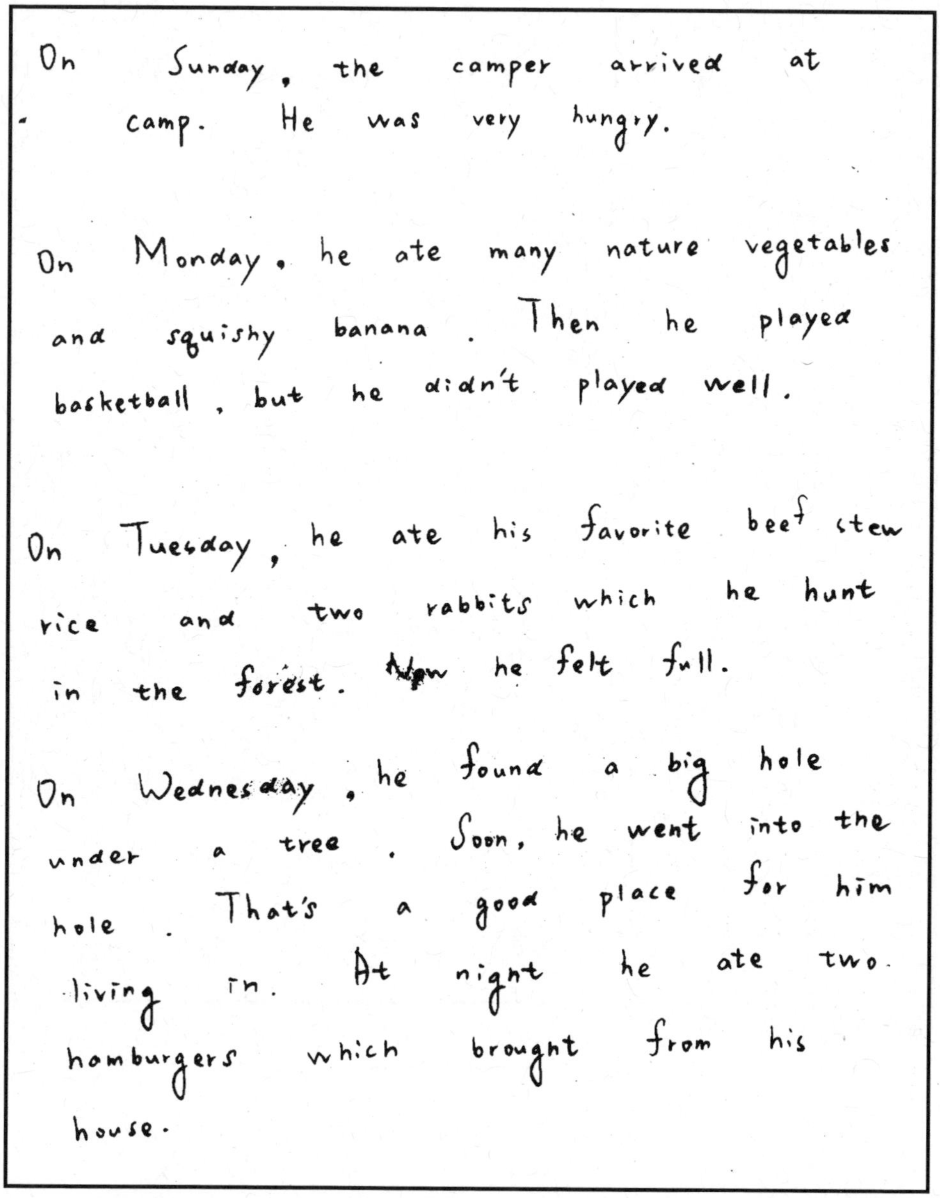

On Sunday, the camper arrived at camp. He was very hungry.

On Monday, he ate many nature vegetables and squishy banana. Then he played basketball, but he didn't played well.

On Tuesday, he ate his favorite beef stew rice and two rabbits which he hunt in the forest. Now he felt full.

On Wednesday, he found a big hole under a tree. Soon, he went into the hole. That's a good place for him living in. At night he ate two. hamburgers which brought from his house.

Figure 6.7 Unlike the younger and less proficient students who wrote *The Very Hungry Camper* stories, Hunter did not want to illustrate his. However, he still enjoyed writing his own version and displaying his considerable skill with the language. There would be no point in editing this, unless he, or his teacher, wanted to display it somewhere, which he chose not to do. Compare Hunter's story to the other versions of *The Very Hungry Camper* examples in this book (see chapter 4, page 130). It serves to illustrate that a well-chosen task can be fun and appropriate for many ages and levels of proficiency. (Figure continues on the next page.)

On Thurday, he got up very early and investigated the dragonfly. Then he went back to the hole and will cook his lunch. He haven't ate breakfast. At lunch he ate five packages of instant noodles. /taisty

On Friday, he went into the forest again, but he got lost. He didn't ate anything all day. He was very very hungry again.

On Saturday, he found some bird eggs on the top of the rocks.
He try to climb on there. But he was lose. Finally, he fell on the ground and got die. The End.

Figure 6.7 – continued

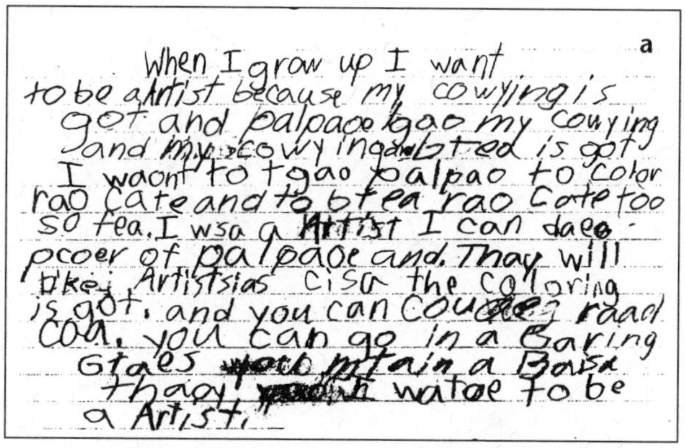

When I grow up I want to be a Artist because my cowying is got and palpaoe bao my cowying and my cowy ing batted is got. I waont to tgao palpao to color rao Cate and to btea rao Cote too so fea. I wsa a Artist I can daeo pcoer of palpaoe and. Thay will like; Artistsias cisa the coloring is got. and you can couqes raad coa. you can go in a Baring Gtaes mtain a Boisa thaay watae to be a Artist.

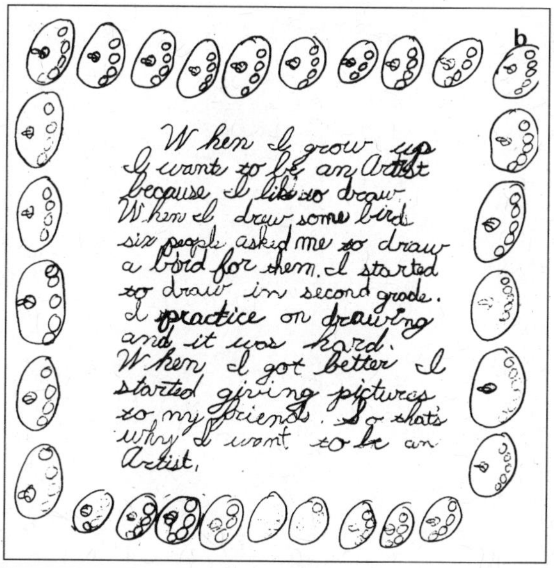

Figure 6.8a–b This paper was revised with a great deal of effort and help from Laura, the student's teacher. The finished product was something that this child could be proud of.

When I grow up I want to be an Artist becouse I like to draw. When I draw some bird six people asked me to draw a bird for them. I started to draw in second grade. I practice on drawing and it was hard. When I got better I started giving pictures to my friends. So that's why I want to be an Artist.

I am going to talk about when they tooke me to the U.S. When they tooke me to the u.s. they tooke my in a big boat. When they tooke me to the u.s. it was bad becaose ther was not enough of room for all people in a small boat. I the ship ther wher a lot's of frinds from different trib's and one day I ran in to a family having a pick nick and I saw a girl. And that girl I seen her on the ship to. Ther is a afew people from the village like my best frinds ho work whit me. No I didn't almost now one until we talk to each other when we laid a plan to kill the white man. In the ship is very stuffy because we didn't have a bathroom we have to use the bathroom were we wher. We didn't have enough space we wer dunch upand we didn't have enough food for along time travelling on the ship. The ship is taking use to the U.S. We didn't stop nowere we when't strat ther. The white man treat use very bad because we are black. I get sick for a little whil but most of the other people did.

It is so nasty on the boat because they have childern that have dirty pants. Some people are dead, and some people don't have clothes. Some slaves are sick and throwing up on their people. I have a friend that is on the slave ship with me. She was raped by men and she was crying. We eat some bread and salt water. We didn't have much space until a lot of people died. The ship is going to South Carolina. We stopped in Florida before we got to South Carolina. The white men were hitting us. They broke the skull of a little girl that was crying. I am so sad because I am going to another country.

Figure 6.9a–b Examples of students' writing about slavery from a sheltered social studies class. These students wrote journal entries as if they had actually been slaves. The writing gave them opportunities to showcase what they had learned and practice their writing.

Writing: An Everyday Activity

Make writing an everyday activity. For learners to advance their writing skills, they must have constant opportunity to practice. Setting aside a block of time each day or several class periods per week for reading, revising, and seeking feedback is critical to learning advancement. Embed writing in every part of the day, or at the secondary level, into every subject. Here are some suggestions for doing this:

- Make writing "real." The purpose for the writing must be authentic, with real audiences.

- Write letters to the principal, to real authors, to heroes.

- Produce newsletters, or even full-fledged newspapers, about class or school activities.

Figure 6.10 When Maddy Hutter and Janet Mason's English classes finished reading *Beowulf*, they challenged their students to illustrate the story in comic book form. This is a page from Mei-Hua's comic.

Figure 6.11 This masterpiece in salesmanship was written by a fourth grader.

- Prepare invitations to parents' night and school concerts.

- Maintain two-way journals with other students.

- Keep records of events, such as field trips, pet care, growth charts for plants, daily schedules, and so on.

- Make writing meaningful. In other words, find topics your students can "sink their teeth into," frequently allowing them to choose their own topics. All students write best about things they care about. Everyone knows how boring the "My Summer Vacation" assignments are, and how little one has to say. But students who are captivated by the need to say something about a topic that interests them will be carried along by their enthusiasm.

  At both the elementary and secondary levels, some teachers have collected stories their students tell from their homeland. Old folktales, legends, and myths have special meaning to the students who write them and give their fellow students a greater understanding of the rich cultural heritage the newcomers have brought to their adopted country (figure 6.13).

- Encourage students to explore all forms of writing, from poetry, to persuasive essays, to advertisements. Audience, topic, and purpose change with every new composition, as do form and style. Academic writing differs

Cool dude baby part 13
cool dudes first advencher

cool dude was on vacation to zombie island for two days but he didint no that it was a hontid   Island kas it loot like all the other islands but there are sand monsters and ghools also dragons to wen cool dude got thar he sat down in the sun on the beech to rest from the long trip to zombie island well he was lying on the beech he herd somthing creeping up behind him then he jumped up swung his arm around and hit the sand monster writ in the head and killed the sand monster but he herd another sound behind him and he peeked in back of him and he sawe a sand dragon uh no said cool dude the sand dragon is the powerfullist monster alive it bloos any heart full thing at you to kill you im getting off this island whit now so he flu off zombie island but when he was in the air he saw another island so he flu down to get on that island but he didint no that that island was called ghool island when he landed all these ghools came charging at cool dude yikse said cool dude now I got to get off this island to so he flu off ghoul island. And flu to Hawaii where there is not that much troubel to spend the weekend resting from the long trip to Hawaii The end.

cool dood baby herd on the news that a kide got shote by a cowboy in black stone canyen so he floo over thar at the speed of light and he saved the kide he put the coyboy in jale. once again cool dood baby will never end.

Figure 6.12 This third grader wrote very little, and resisted writing, until he found a computer program in which he could superimpose a small baby upon a series of different scenes. With the picture in front of him, he could invent a story about the scene. His stories grew increasingly complex as the saga of *Cool Dood Baby* developed. In all, he wrote 22 stories.

Day by day the weeds grew bigger and bigger. The farmer didn't take care the corn. And the weeds hurt the corn.

On the fourth day, the farmer didn't came and a cow came. So the weeds asked, the corn. And the weed said, "Is that your owner?" So the corn answered, "No."

On the fifth day, the farmer didn't came and a wolf came to the field. So the weed asked, the corn. And the weeds said, "Is that your owner? "So the corn answered," that isn't our owner"

On the Sixth day, a chicken came and a Chicken look around everywhere then the weeds said, "Is that your owner?" "The Corn said, "no!" On the seventh day, there was the farmer came. He had his a big hat and his pipe with a long knife. And the farmer cut the weeds down. The corn was so happy "oh, Mr. Farm You really helped us much! Thank you, Thank you!"

Pao Moua
&
Kong Meng

Figure 6.13 Hmong students retell a Hmong folktale in their own words.

from writing in personal journals, as a letter to a friend differs from a letter complaining about problems in the school. Skilled writers know about writing, about rhetorical styles, about methods of reaching their audience. Students need practice in all areas.

The example of a persuasive letter found on the next page is written tongue-in-cheek. It was written by a student on a student visa who would be sent back home if he didn't stay in school. The letter exhibits a very strong voice as well as the linguistic and mental dexterity of the writer.

Figure 6.14 This freshman's Grecian urn depicts a scene from Homer's *The Odyssey*.

Dear Mr. Detwiler,

I am sorry I was unable to come to school last week owing to mental illness. My constitutional defect didn't prevent me from yielding to a disease. I also enclosed herewith a certificate from the doctor, who is attending me. Yesterday he said to me "Health is the most precious. Without health, you can not work or study to the full. In order to maintain health, it is important to take moderate exercise and to take a fresh air" and then he wanted to go with me to the shopping center. For this reason, I visited a shopping center and met you, but you didn't give me a chance to explain my situation. I think that something seems to have gone wrong with us, you and me. For mercy's sake, don't misunderstand my position. In addition, I was very busy last week because of taking three exams. This has been my first time.

Therefore, I was afraid that I made a bad record in exam, and then couldn't get a sleep all night. So I couldn't go to school. If I go to my country according to your unreasonable demand, I won't come back to America to study for good. The reason is that Korea is something of a stern country. If you give me a chance once more, from now on, I will study without absence and concentrate my energies on only studying English. I humbly ask for you pardon.

Sincerely yours, Kibong

Dear teacher:
Hope you likes
this present.
thanks your teach.

your student: Wade's pen

FOR DEAR Barb:

We're so happy for your teaching
Katie and Nick are both good childre
we're all love them.
You must a good mom.
And a good teacher.
Thanks for your teaching.
We are all love you!

singnature:

Molly Hsueh. July. 98'.   Tim Ann 98.9.10.   Benjomin 7.10.98
Amy   Alice   Allen
Jacky   Joseph   Leo
Andy
June   Jason   Mars   Victor Lee
Debby   Rex   Angel
Clark   Susan   Denny   David
   KEVIN
   10 JUL 98'

Figure 6.15a–b. These letters, unsolicited, were written from the heart.

- Provide time for both intensive and extensive writing. *Intensive writing* is structured and written for a specific purpose. This is writing to be revised, writing where the specific skills of organization, mechanics, and editing can be taught. *Extensive writing* is not to be revised or corrected; it is used to articulate thoughts, explore ideas, and gain fluency without the need to stop and worry about correctness. Journals, diaries, and learning logs are all examples of extensive writing.

Here are two journal entries, written as exercises to promote fluency. They are full of errors, but the point is to get the students writing freely—*extensive writing.*

> *I like take this class cause I am learning to much so now I can do this journal. She gave os a lot of homework that is the bad part, but and the real is good to learn more.*

> *Guess what I am? I' am made of stain steel. I am kept in a drawer of the kitchen. I' am used every day; the Children's uses me every morning in company of a bowl of cereal. I can be in different shapes I can be a round or oval my size can be small, medium or large. Each time did you sit at the table I can not miss.*

Use of Technology in Your Writing Program

New technology, computers in particular, can be very helpful to beginning writers. For some ELL students, it's easier to practice writing on a computer than on paper. Word-processing programs print the letters of the alphabet perfectly, in straight, neat lines. Students' compositions, no matter how short, can be printed in a professional manner.

All steps of the writing process (prewriting, drafting, and so on) can be learned and practiced on a computer by individuals or groups. For example, a small group of both ELL and native-English speakers can work cooperatively on one computer. After brainstorming for prewriting ideas, they can write their story without fear of making mistakes, not only because errors are seen as part of the writing process, but also because their errors will be so easy to correct. Revising and editing, when it is possible to delete and/or rearrange words, sentences, and paragraphs simply by pressing keys, is simple, and most students find it satisfying and fun. Writing a second or third draft of a paper is no longer tedious. Students are usually proud of their professionally printed final product and eager to start the next one.

If we return to the list at the beginning of the chapter generated by second language learners about why it can be harder to write (in a new language) than it is to speak (see page 199–200), we can see how many of these problems and roadblocks can be eliminated. On wikis and discussion boards, readers can tell the writer they don't understand, and they can get instant feedback. They can express themselves freely, and the technology enhances the excitement. The shared experience makes it enjoyable, not a tedious, intimidating chore.

We have found that students, particularly language learners, are avid users of technology as an aid to writing. They are more willing to struggle at the computer than when they are faced with a blank sheet of paper. We've also found that students are better behaved when at the computer. Using technology enhances their motivation and willingness to produce. They can hide behind the computer. When their work is sent by email either as text or an attachment, there is a buffer between them and what they've produced, and they do not feel put on the spot.

We have also noticed that students don't cut corners when they're using computers. When the possibility of creating something beautiful or eye-popping is attainable, they work extra hard, more motivated to do a better job than if they were simply drawing or producing something handwritten. Book reports, for instance, used to be snoringly boring. With technology, they can be beautiful, creative, fun to read. There is no limit to what students can do.

PowerPoint is an example of a computer program that can be very helpful to beginning writers. Although many people disparage PowerPoint, we have found that students who are required to do PowerPoint projects do a better job of presenting than those who simply stand up in front of a class and talk. Here's why:

Hung and His Hobbies
My hobby is Karate or Taekwondo. It is my life, but my mother hate those and she thought those a bad things. I really try to learn, become actor or at least a hero of in my country. When learn karate or Taekwondo my was crying why I don't understand she those bad. My mother is more than every things, deeper than pacific Ocean and highest than Everest mount. Then I was listening always her words. My mother is more than my hobbies.

My Future
I future will be finishing College or my law School. I really want to go Harvard University. It is my future dreams. Also I want to married nice girl.

- PowerPoint forces students to be more articulate. They need to think through exactly what is going to go on that slide instead of bluffing. Their work needs to be precise and specific.

- They have a guide with which to proceed through their presentation.

- The audience has something to focus on, so they're not horsing around, more likely to be paying attention. An attentive audience is more supportive and less distracting to the presenter.

Figure 6.16 Kee's personal brochure

Preprogrammed templates can also function like PowerPoint frames. To the right, for instance, is part of Kee's personal brochure. The entire class enjoyed uploading their own photos or downloading picture art to jazz up their productions.

Provide a Supportive Environment

It is important to consider not only the act of writing itself, but also the setting in which students write and the response to their writing. Cunningham et al

(2000) write that feeling is the energizer of reading and writing: "Thinking is the essence of what we do when we read or write, but feeling determines how much and how often we choose to read or write, and whether we will persist in reading or writing when we have difficulty." Students must feel that they *can* learn to read, write, and speak English better. They must feel self-confident in their ability to use strategies. The more you can do to motivate them, to encourage them to try, and to help them believe that they can be good writers, the better they *will* become. Reading and writing must be pleasurable, not something that causes anxiety or pain. We can help make this possible in the following ways:

- **Create a comfortable atmosphere.**

  - Set up a climate of trust in which students believe that writing is important and that their writing is valued.

  - Encourage students to take risks as writers, to experiment with different forms and styles without fear that their mistakes will be punished.

  - Give students authority over their writing by allowing each of them to choose their topic and style.

  - Encourage students to exchange ideas and share drafts, to get feedback and ideas from each other.

  - Help students to understand that writing is a meaning-making event.

  - Make reasonable demands to help students become better writers. Calkins (1994) writes that we should not set up editing expectations that put extraordinary demands on writers who are beginners, or who are second-language learners. "If these children know they must find

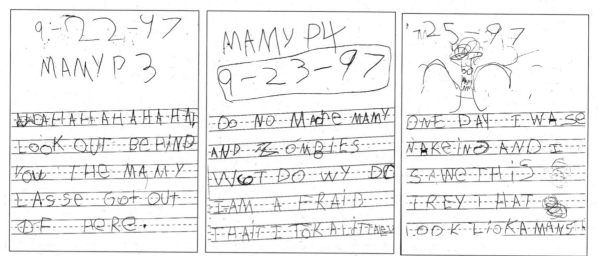

Figure 6.17 This is the first time Nick sat down and seriously wrote something that showed a discernible structure. He had been fascinated with the *Goosebumps* series, and each page of writing was in an episodic, cliffhanger style that clearly showed attention to the structure of the *Goosebumps* books.

every single misspelled word in a dictionary, they will write with safe words, choosing *big* when they wanted to say *enormous*."

- **Make reading an integral part of the writing program.** Opportunities to listen to and read good-quality literature is a critical component of becoming a competent writer. "The interconnectedness of reading and writing is profound and inescapable," write Fountas and Pinnell (2001). "Fragmenting these complex literacy processes interferes with the greatest goal of literacy education—the construction of meaning from and through text. Using reading and writing together in harmonious concert enables learners to draw on these complementary processes at the same time they work to construct meaning." Only those who have been exposed to good models can become good writers. You can see the reading reflected in the writing of students. Galda, Cullinan, and Strickland (1997) write, "If children spend time exploring and discussing books, if we help them notice the structures and patterns they encounter, and if you let them know that many writers experiment with innovations, they will borrow from their reading when they want to."

- **Make writing a collaborative act.** There is a myth that writing is a lonely act, done in solitude; this isn't necessarily true. Language is a social act and writing can be too. In observing writers truly engaged in writing, researchers have noted how they talk while they write, sharing their thoughts and their writing with other writers to get more ideas. Bilingual and non-native-English speakers often talk and write more when allowed to interact with their peers. Galda, Cullinan, and Strickland write, "Beginners talk to themselves to guide their writing and to others to seek and get help or to collaborate. They also use talk to get ready to write, exploring ideas to write about with peers or simply saying them aloud to themselves. They also frequently read aloud as they write." New technology, like wikis and discussion forums offer students instant feedback and support this collaboration. Encourage this interaction by promoting collective writing of stories, science and social studies projects, even the invention of new worlds.

  Barb was continually frustrated by a class in which a research paper was required. By the end of the semester, she didn't have a class anymore; she had a bunch of frustrated individuals mooning about the library searching for information, slogging through the process of shaping their ideas into a coherent text. To keep the class together, to demonstrate the need for revision, and to bring out one of the hardest traits to learn—voice—she introduced dramas. The students wrote plays together. They brainstormed a list of possible settings, voted on one, chose and developed characters, then, in small groups, wrote dialogue. The collaboration produced an electricity she had never experienced in a writing class, and the ideas generated together were beyond what any an individual could have produced. Even the titles were inspired.

  And although Barb announced up front that she was not going to be in the plays, somehow she always ended up being the worst bad guy. In

Layla comes in, starts talking. She doesn't want them to hurt the Pres.

Layla: I don't want to do this.

Alex: Okay, okay, calm down. Listen to me. Whos the bad guy here? The president, right?

Layla: But I really love him. I don't want to hurt him.

Stan: (He grabs her arm.) Shut up, you bitch!

Alex: It's okay (He pushes Stan away)

David: Listen xayla, either your with us or against us whats it gonna be ??

Jasiel: (Walks towards layla) Maybe we should get rid of her first (grabe her)

Milos: Calm down guys, if we are gonna do this, lets do it right

Isabella: Darlin will you? Hmmh no more queen ha ha ha! Kick her butt !!

Tamaki: Hmmh saves me alot of trouble get her out the way! First! (countejumper)

Jiro: Let's make this quick men, I have business to take care of back home.

Pablo: Hmmh, (nodding head)

Alex: (puts his arms around layla). Don't worry lay a, everything is gonna be alright.

Stan: I don't know why you bother with that bitch anyways.

David: All this conflict won't get us anywhere. Lets get down to some serious work

Jasiel: Yea, it o time for action

Milos: Guys, now we are set. (Pres. walks in)

Bart: Hey, can I play this? (He picks up a sax and starts to play)

Jasiel tries to get near him to tell him and talk to him.

Figure 6.18 Here is a piece of the script from *A Time to Sing*. The parameters for the play were that everybody had to have an equal role, there were no stars, and no goldbricks. At this point, the general plot had been formulated, and class members were writing dialogue for each other (to forego one-word answers from shy violets).

Air Force II: Disaster in the Skies she played Tiffany, the flight attendant who planted guns in the bathroom for a mere $50 thousand so the terrorists could take over the airplane. In *A Time to Sing,* she played Layla Love, an intern who, jilted by the president, let the bad guys (disguised as a rock and roll band called "The Bomb in the Guitar Case") into the White House so they could blow it up. In *Sometimes Evil Has to Win,* she was the first to die.

- **Provide time for sharing writing and ideas.**

- **Encourage and train peer editors.**

- **Celebrate students' writing.** Students need an appreciative audience to read their writing and to offer encouragement. The feedback they receive in response to their writing has a significant impact on how they perceive the writing process and how much they improve. Edelsky (1986) noted that writing assignments that emphasize quantity alone, with no honoring of the writing by publishing or discussion, could be destructive—promoting the idea that quantity is more important than quality. To recognize student writing, we suggest you employ some of the following strategies:

  - Display students' writing on the wall for everybody to read.

  - Have an "author's chair" (where student authors sit and read their work to classmates) as the seat of honor.

- Have "Author of the Week," during which one student's writing is celebrated and displayed on a special area of the wall. Have other students interview the "author."

- Publish the writing in the form of books, with hard covers the students make themselves.

- Create a special library of books written by students.

- Provide a time for public reading of students' writing. At both elementary and secondary levels, students need to have the opportunity to be recognized and applauded for their efforts.

- Produce "readers' theater," using excerpts from students' writing.

- Build in time for students to read their work aloud. This gives them a chance to practice their reading skills, as well as the opportunity to proudly display their stories to an attentive audience.

- **Allow students to write in their own language.** If they speak and write in a language you don't know, then of course, you cannot read it. However, as with reading, writing in one language improves writing in another. Encourage students to write in English, but allow them to start in their own language, making the transition to English as they grow more confident in their abilities. Researchers such as Edelsky (1986) have noted that there is often no clear break from the ELL students' native language to English. Often these students will write in both languages within the same piece of writing for a while, until they feel safe or confident enough to write totally in English. Even fluent English speakers will substitute words in their own language during first drafts.

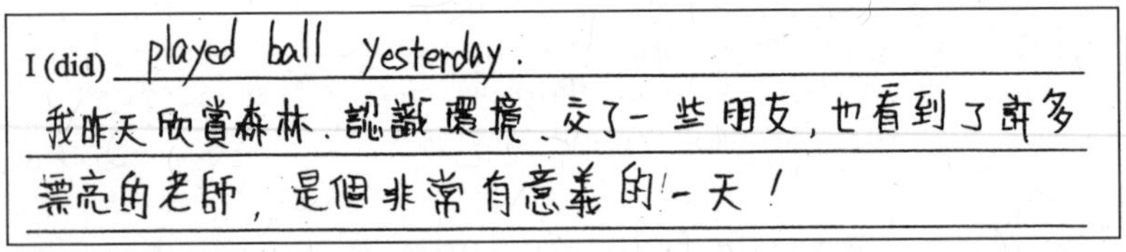

I (did) _played ball yesterday._
我昨天欣賞森林．認識還虎．交了一些用友，也看到了許多漂亮的老師，是個非常有意義的一天！

Figure 6.19 This student seemed to need to express what she had done the previous day in Chinese.

- Provide mailboxes for students to write letters to you, or to each other.

Ensure Guidance and Feedback from Interested and Knowledgeable Readers

All writers—beginning, developing, fluent, and experienced—need help with the writing process. They need guidance in making some of the larger decisions including such things as topic, style, and form. All writers need feedback on how effectively they are communicating, direction as to how they can improve, and help with specific points such as mechanics, spelling, and punctuation. Your role in implementing a supportive environment and helping writers grow is critical. That means you have to know as much as possible about what can make you effective as a teacher, what works with students, and what promotes the most growth.[2] Students who don't know writing strategies, who don't understand the writing process, who experience failure at writing, or who don't grow as writers, learn to hate it, fear it, and ultimately stop writing.

Provide Good Writing Models

One way of supporting students' writing is through good modeling. Just as we can't expect a child to learn to swim by simply throwing him in the deep end of the pool, we can't expect students to become good writers simply by placing a sheet of paper in front of them and telling them to write.

Beginning writers need to see that writing is more than just worksheets and outlines, a chore to get through; writing is a wonderful way to articulate thoughts, one that can be enjoyable and exciting. Watching a teacher working on a draft of a letter or essay can demonstrate that writing isn't a tedious task or a meaningless activity, but a satisfying, creative act.

Atwell (1998) writes, "We need to find ways to reveal to students what adult, experienced writers do—to reclaim the tradition of demonstrations that allows young people to apprentice themselves to grown-ups. Observing adults as they work is an activity of enormous worth and power when it illumines what is possible." By modeling the writing process, you give students insight into how to formulate ideas, how to take an idea and move through the process from start to finish, how to organize the writing, how to make it interesting, how to provide an ending, and how to punctuate. You also demonstrate how all writers reread what they have written, and how to add the necessary changes to improve it.

Not all writers need the same amount or kind of support. "Effective, engaging...literacy teachers provide just enough support so that students can make progress, with the purpose of encouraging students to accomplish as much as possible on their own—to act in a self-regulated fashion" (Graham, MacArthur, and Fitzgerald 2007). As writers gain independence, strategies, and skills, they need you less and less to show them how to start, write, revise, and edit.

There are five levels of writing support you can give your students (Fountas and Pinnell 1996; Tompkins 2000). These levels don't necessarily mean that beginners are limited only to shared writing, or skilled writers to the process of writing. You can use all levels with all grades, depending on what you are teaching.

1. **Modeled writing.** You write in front of students, composing and transcribing, while you think aloud about word choice, organization, and ideas. When you are writing for beginners, you are demonstrating all the literate behaviors that they must learn in order to write: left to right with a return sweep, shaping letters, and so on. Modeling writing can reinforce print concepts, decoding skills, spelling, mechanics. It helps students hear the sequencing in sounds and words.

---

2 **Note:** For help in evaluating student writing, we have included the Test of Written English (TWE) Scoring Guide as Appendix H on page 342. The guide prioritizes the elements of good writing, making assessment easier.

2. **Shared writing.** This level of support includes the Language Experience Approach (see chapter 5, page 160). You and your students create a text together. Everyone is doing the composing, you are doing the transcribing. Students add ideas but also contribute to word choice, spelling, and so on as they are able.

3. **Interactive writing.** This level is much like shared writing, but you are letting students take more control of the transcribing side of the writing process, as well as the creating side. You and your students create the text together, sharing the pen or the chalk. At the lower/elementary level, students take turns writing the words and letters they know. At the upper levels, students are equal partners in writing text with you. This can be true collaboration. When you allow yourself and your students freedom to experiment, this method can be very exciting. You never know where you'll end up. The results can surprise everyone.

4. **Guided writing.** Guided writing is an important tool in your kit. Like reading, a lot of the elements that make up skilled application are not self-evident. The task of writing is so complex, that kids often don't automatically figure out how to do things on their own, especially when they are not avid, advanced readers. With this level of writing support you present a structured lesson, then the students write as you supervise. This can include teaching one of the rhetorical modes, such as how to structure a compare-contrast essay, or how to formulate poems. It also means teaching a writing strategy or a skill, such as the functions of punctuation, literary craft, or conventions of writing. Guided writing works as an interim step between dependent and independent writing. It also works for explicit teaching in small groups. It provides an opportunity for targeting weaknesses or for giving students specific tasks, such as organizing, enhancing style, tackling different genres, time for brainstorming or reflection.

5. **Independent writing.** At this stage, if not before, students work through all the stages of the writing process independently. Students do all composing and transcribing, while you monitor and help revise and edit.

Working With Beginning Writers

Modeling at Work

My students are illiterate. They don't even know their alphabet much less how to write a whole text. What do I do to help them?

Here is where modeled writing comes in—write for them. Many students have never held a pencil before. The fine motor skills required for writing demand much effort on the part of beginning writers. Often just the act of trying to put letters on paper is so taxing it frustrates their efforts to express coherent thoughts. The temptation is to have them practice their ABCs until they have learned them correctly; however, these skills should be practiced only within the context of real writing. Practicing meaningful phrases, rather than words in isolation, reinforces meaning as well as skills. Don't wait until students can form sentences before allowing them to write. Even though they can't write, students have plenty to say; everyone has a story to tell. Encourage them to jump right in.

Researchers studying first-language learners have noted that children pass through a sequence of broad stages when learning to write: scribbles; only a few letters, words, and illegible squiggles; a sentence or a series of several unrelated sentences; two or more related sentences (Clay 1975; Teale and Sulzby 1986; Reutzel and Cooter 2004). While we cannot apply these stages on a wholesale basis to non-English-speaking students, we can be aware of them and allow our students the freedom to experiment and learn, without imposing the need for perfection and precision immediately.

Figure 6.20 Translated, this means, "I love hopscotch because of the kids. I love soccer because of the kids."

In chapter 5 about reading, we discussed the Language Experience Approach (LEA), in which you write the students' thoughts first, then have them copy what you have elicited. The word *fireman* might be a whole text for one student; accept it as such. After you have recorded students' thoughts, they can copy your writing onto their own paper. They will make the transition to writing on their own when they are ready—when they have gained enough confidence to try, when they have learned some vocabulary, or just simply when they have learned that writing has meaning.

First-grader Rebecca, for example, did not seem to understand the basic speech-print connection. After many months of watching LEA in action, she began to copy the words the teacher provided on the board as springboards to thought. One day her teacher wrote the words *playground, soccer,* and *hopscotch* on the board. Figure 6.20 shows what Rebecca wrote.

For a first try at a real story, her piece is impressive. She shows that she understands the functions of print and that she is aware of syntax, sentence structure and boundaries, as well as punctuation. Rebecca is also making a personal and lively statement about the topic. She loves soccer and hopscotch because of the kids who play the games with her. There is much to be praised and encouraged.

Scaffolding

My students are novices. They don't know where to start; or, if they do, they aren't organized. What can I do?

A scaffold is a framework on which students can hang their ideas. Scaffolds allow students to concentrate on content. Since scaffolds provide the forms, they help students learn how to organize at many levels: the grammatical level, the sentence level, the paragraph level, and the text level. Students model the scaffold, imitate it, and gain control over their writing.

There are many different types of scaffolds. Two of the more common ones are

- Patterned poetry, such as haiku, cinquain, diamante, and sonnet

- Frame sentences. In one elementary school classroom, after a unit on occupations, students made little books about themselves, each in occupational roles they thought they might enjoy. They wrote sentences according to the framework worked out together on the board:

  "I am a _____. I wear a _____ uniform. Here is where I work. This is me working."

Students illustrated their books with pictures of themselves in their various roles (figure 6.21).

Figure 6.21 Yoshi, in second grade, choosing an occupation.

A more sophisticated frame used Whitman's poem "I Hear America Singing." The students filled in blanks; instead of "I hear America singing," for instance, they wrote about their home country. Below is Igor's remarkable picture of Russia through his word choices. (Underlined words and phrases were blanks to fill in.)

> I hear _Russia_ singing, the varied _anthem_ I hear.
> Those of _government,_ each one singing his _song_ as it should be.
> The _President_ singing his _song_ as he _making a new constitution._
> The _deputy_ singing his as he makes _some new laws and orders._
> The _Prime Minister_ singing _as he sits on his throne, the new taxes singing as he_
>   _stands._
> The _unemployment song_ of the mother, or of the young wife _without_ work, or the
>   girl _unemploying or boy unemploying._
> The day what belongs to the day – at night the party of young _oppositions_
> Singing with open mouths their _controversive_ songs.

Here are a couple lines from Roberto's version:

> I hear _Cuba_ singing, the varied _songs_ I hear,
> The _rafter_ singing what belongs to him in his _raft the reason why he_
>   _leaving his land..._

Models are especially important for scaffolding in the upper grades and for the content areas, as writers need examples of good writing in order to write well themselves. Find constructive examples of text for students to use as guides. Provide them with positive models, such as sample research reports or science results. With some instruction on how the sample is organized, students can follow the same format for clearer, more readable papers.

We discuss the use of creative copying and mimicry in chapter four. Here's another example. Using models as starting points for writing stretches students beyond what they would ordinarily be able to accomplish by giving them sophisticated syntax and providing a structure on which to hang their own ideas. To follow is part of Ricardo's poem. His model was the poem

"Fifteen," in which the author, William Stafford, ends each verse with the sentence, "I was fifteen":

> *In Central America I found myself in the mountains of Guatemala. In a summer time where I can see the mountains around the village where I live nice and beautiful in the morning you can see the foggy on the villages and at night you can see the stars which is incomparable the nice view of it. I was fourteen.*
>
> *When a heard that my oldest brother got here in the U.S. the first one in the family here. I was fourteen.*
>
> *And than I thought about coming here to, and I picture myself here in the United state driving a car and succeed in life I was fourteen.*
>
> *Back than I didn't have anything not even a bicycle but I was Happy with my life because I live in a wonderful village with humble people. I was fourteen.*

This is what a student can accomplish when he has a framework on which to base his ideas. How many chances do you get to use the word *incomparable* in your writing? He knew the word and used it brilliantly.

Some writing-process advocates feel that teaching structure, such as the rhetorical modes (narrative, descriptive, argumentative, comparison and contrast, and so on), removes students' control over their written work. However, we believe that for ELL students, it is important to focus directly on organization. Most students born in North America have been exposed to writing from early childhood. After many years of reading stories, magazine articles, newspapers, and so on, they have internalized the organizational patterns that are common to each type of writing. So, when we ask them to write a story or to compare two objects, for instance, they can do it with little difficulty.

Many ELL students have not had the benefit of these years of reading and writing. While we can hope that our students will learn these patterns incidentally, without explicit instruction, we cannot leave this to chance.

In addition, many cultures and non-Western societies have different ways of organizing essays and stories. Students from these backgrounds need to be shown directly that, while their patterns are not actually incorrect, the structure can be confusing to English-speaking readers searching for a familiar pattern of organization. Form should not be imposed arbitrarily without regard for purpose or audience (for example, "Today we're going to write a five-paragraph essay"), but neither should we leave organization to chance.

Here's a step-by-step example of a model lesson:

1. Use Total Physical Response (TPR)[3] and games to teach prepositions. Have students practice prepositions by going over, around, through, between (and so on) objects.

2. Go for a walk through the school, through the neighborhood, or anywhere students can practice walking, running, jumping, and crawling, over, around, through, and between things. (In our summer ELL program, part of the day included a challenge course that involved students climbing into a deep hole in some boulders, crawling over and around the

---

3 For a detailed explanation of Total Physical Response please see chapter 7, page 257.

boulders, and then sliding down a long rock face to be caught by an instructor. It was very scary and exhilarating.)

3. Reinforce the prepositions and the sound-to-print connection by having students read each preposition and demonstrate what it means.

4. Read the book *Rosie's Walk* several times through.

5. Provide large sheets of paper folded in half for students to make their own books.

6. Instruct students to write about their own walk, using at least five prepositions.

Figure 6.22 Using the book *Rosie's Walk*, by Pat Hutchins, as a framework, Jeff and Mimi wrote about their own day using prepositions they knew. Note how each one used vocabulary at their own level of proficiency to write their own books, extending the basic sentences to tell about their day.

7. Have students read their books to each other.

8. Display the books for others to read.

Students in our program made paper dolls of themselves attached to a string to fit into a pocket on the cover page of their book.

Giving Constructive Feedback

Correcting Errors

My students make a lot of grammatical errors. What should I do?

The answer to this question depends on the students' level and the purpose of the assignment. With younger children and newcomers, it is, at first, best to accept any effort on their part. Even if the language is totally garbled, the essays unstructured, and the main ideas obscure, don't correct the grammar. Instead, talk to the students about their ideas to help clarify what they really want to say.

> *Yesterday last night of the teacher Mary Eckes gaven would one to student all student in class-person doesn't get to have to know. This when student dd to get befor big one the squash all way came back to school at reach home family and neighbour. that right your are want to see becouse yours are doesn't have. doesn't know.*

How would you find out what Cham is trying to say in the preceding example? After questioning Cham, Mary figured it out: Cham was telling a story about a squash. Mary used to bring in produce from her garden and hold a lottery to determine which student would get the vegetables; no one knew who was going to win. Cham won on that occasion, and the prize was such a large squash that she shared half of it with her neighbor. With a little prompting, the story became clear, and Mary could help her focus and clarify. Pointing out Cham's grammatical errors at this point would have been harmful because she would have been discouraged.

This does not mean that errors should be completely ignored. We cannot focus solely on the process at the expense of the product. We must show a clear concern for mechanics. Quality and correctness are important issues because, ultimately, we are writing to be read—and understood! Here again, it is a matter of priorities. As with reading, accuracy and skills should be secondary to meaning. We've all read the story or essay that is perfect mechanically and yet says nothing, while we've read others that are riddled with errors and yet are sprightly and creative.

Stress content more than correctness. Initially, getting the ideas out is the important thing; then they must be shaped until the writer achieves what he wants to say. Students need the chance to rewrite—nobody writes the first draft perfectly. If students are worried about perfection, they will be afraid to be creative and experimental, sticking only to what they are sure of. Ammon (1985) noted that writers who feel they need to invest much of their time and energy to spelling and other component skills tire quickly and eventually give up before they have finished. If your students are concerned both with mechanics and getting their ideas out, they may be forced into a trade-off, paying more attention to one to the detriment of the other. In other words, as Frank Smith writes in *Reading Without Nonsense* (1997), "Emphasis on the elimination of mistakes results in the elimination of writing." Allow students plenty of time to make tentative efforts and sort out their ideas before asking them to wrestle with the problems of getting their writing to look and sound like native English.

Other than careless or accidental ones, most errors are not random; they are strategies students employ when they have not yet learned or mastered a new form or concept. They show courage in trying something new. Celebrate mistakes; applaud students for daring to do something difficult. Errors can demonstrate both what the students know and what they have not yet learned. As with reading, we can view errors as valuable insights into the students' development and use them to pinpoint areas they need to work on. For example, if Wei Xia writes, "I am a youngest student in the class," it is clear that he needs to learn more about articles.

Publishing students' work in the form of newsletters and so on will motivate them to correct and revise. If they have a stake in what is written, if their names are noted as authors and their work is out there for the world to see, they will be more concerned with perfection.

What should *I correct?*

Limit yourself to correcting one type of mistake only, and ignore the rest for the time being. This is called focus correction errors (FCE) (Collins, 1997) and is a sound method for insuring that writers don't get overwhelmed. Marking every error students have made can be defeating; they won't know where to start and will get so bogged down trying to correct all their errors that they may give up, and any momentum gained will be lost. If you limit what you're going to correct, students can spend more time working on the content of the paper, rather than trying to fix all the surface errors—which may not improve the quality even if it were error free.

Ravi Sheorey (1986) lists a hierarchy of error categories:

Along the way there were many families camping by side of road.

These families were either resting due to long hours of traveling, or they were simply stuck because of the car trouble.

Figure 6.23 These two sentences are from an essay on *The Grapes of Wrath* written by Annie, a proficient speaker. Yet, she still struggles with the article *the*—when to use it and when not to. Care to explain the rule on this one?

1. The most serious errors are verb forms (agreement, tenses, and so on).

2. Next in importance are word-choice errors.

3. Less serious errors are articles and prepositions.

4. Spelling errors are the least serious of all.

We shouldn't expect total perfection, nor should we expect that if we correct a type of error once, it will never reappear. Unfortunately, it isn't that simple. Mastering English is a long, often slow process. The English article system, for instance, which native English speakers take for granted, is a second-language learner's nightmare. What seems to work in one sentence is totally inappropriate in another. Often prepositions make no logical sense at all, so they must simply be memorized. For example, we speak of *in the street* as well as *in the box,* and *on the table* as well as *on time.* Before they can master English forms, English language learners need a great deal of exposure to the range of structures and meanings possible.

When allowing time for revision, remember the law of diminishing returns. When we are striving for fluency, working for perfection on each paper fosters frustration. Many times it is appropriate to allow the student one or two rewrites, then go on to something else. Give students many opportunities to write for fluency alone, without correction, such as in journal-writing.

At what stage should I make corrections?

If it is done at all, correcting must be done with the idea that the student will continue to work on the paper. Proett and Gill (1986) write, "Correcting involves pointing out students' mistakes; if it is done by the teacher with no further response from the student, it is probably a useless activity." Instruction and correction in mechanics are most effective at the editing stage, in response to a particular need. For ELL students, error correction too early in the process (for example, during the first revision) is liable to curtail their creativity, because they feel forced to concentrate on being "right." Gadda, Peitzman, and Walsh, in *Teaching Analytical Writing* (1988), point out that correcting the mechanical points of a paper is like fine-tuning an engine, something you do only after you have replaced and repaired the major parts. Why should someone work hard to fix something when it may be completely overhauled or even scrapped altogether? If they correct the language first, they will be unwilling to change the content. Only after the paper is clear, well-organized, and thorough, should the student work on fine-tuning grammar, spelling, and so on.

Revising and Editing With ELL Students

The most logical way to make corrections is to allow two revision stages, one for content, the other for mechanics. Thus, the writing process for ELL students would look like this:

1. Students compose.

2. Teacher or peers respond. This first response is for content alone. Ideas, organization, and clarity are the priorities here. You can train your students to work as peer editors for this stage, to respond to the impact of the work, ask for more ideas, clarification, and expansion. If you have access to an interactive whiteboard, students can send you their drafts to be displayed on the board for all to see. The entire class can comment, and you can demonstrate ways to respond and offer suggestions.

3. Students revise to clarify, add detail, and reorganize.

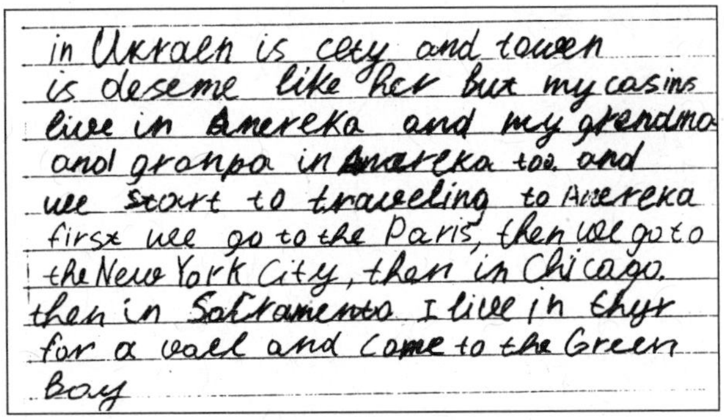
in Ukraen is cety and towen
is deseme like her but my casins
live in Amereka and my grendma
and granpa in Amareka too. and
we start to traveling to Amereka
first we go to the Paris, then we go to
the New York City, than in Chicago.
then in Sakramento I live in thyr
for a vael and come to the Green
Bay

Figure 6.24 Andre's first draft.

MY JOURNEY

In Ukrain cetys and towen deseme like her. But my casins, Grandma and Grendpa live in Amereka. and we start to traveling to Amereka. ferst we go to paris. Then we flie to tha New York City.Then in Chicago. And after we flie to the Sacramento. and live in ther for a vael, and com to the Green Bay.

Figure 6.25 Andre's second draft.

4. Teacher or peers respond. This response is for mechanics. What has not been cleared up through a second reading and self-editing can be worked on here, on a specific topic (such as articles or verb tense) agreed upon by you and the student.
5. Teacher teaches grammatical points as necessary.
6. Students edit for mechanics.

With this sequence, students know when you will be focusing on the form of their papers and won't be wasting their creative energy trying to remember the rules of grammar at stage 2 (although they can ask for and receive help in grammar at any point of their writing).

Andre, for instance, was writing about what it was like in his country. He wrote a paragraph about his journey here from his country (figure 6.24). The link between the sentences—that he came because his cousins and grandparents already lived in America—are only inferred by their juxtaposition, and his use of the word *but.* He gives a quick travel itinerary and ends up where he is living now. His errors are mostly in grammar and spelling. He spells *deseme (the same)* and *a vael (a while)* phonetically, according to how he has perceived the words.

Andre's revision (figure 6.25) consists simply of retyping what he had written before. (Note that he makes mistakes in the retyping, such as *ferst* [*first*] and *paris* [*Paris*], which he did not make in his handwritten draft.) This is typical of novice writers, who, without direct intervention, do not know how to improve. He does not seem to have a sense of form or purpose. If the purpose of the second draft was to get Andre to practice typing, then it can stand as is, with some lessons on how to use the spell check and some help with grammar. Should his teacher ask him to revise, they could focus on why he came to this country, and specifically what the journey was like. The teacher could help him brainstorm a list of details to use in his next try. Or, he could focus on why he came here if the cities and towns are comparable to those in the Ukraine. What did America have to offer?

Responding to Students' Written Work

Abdullah wrote the following text in response to the question, "Which English language skill is the hardest one for you?"

Which english language skill has been the hartest on. English is funy longuage that we sey some the and read o the such as secret, sure or surprise. That meen riting is the hardest one for me so I thik that I'm still week in spilling and I need riting coure, also I don't knew much vocapulary that hard for me, spilling or riting needs memorise t learn but my memory is not good so it is hard to rite will wheth outrong in spilling or problems. If I tell about the easiest one, I sey listening is more easy for me I have good improvment in it so not prob in it also me gramar is good one easy enough for me to learn but the pig broplem is vocapulary and spilling onthing is easy I can speek will and understand will with proctes every thing become easy sometimes I rite pregraph to improve my riting but still need it might be next term it becom brety good any how I don't like this laguage

An understandable first reaction upon seeing such text is shock, followed by a feeling of helplessness, if not despair. How does one respond when the problems are of such magnitude, when the spelling is clearly out of hand, the punctuation practically nonexistent, and the meaning, in many places, is obscure? How does one untangle the various problems without overwhelming Abdullah and destroying whatever self-confidence he has?

Many of his errors may be performance based—errors made because he was inattentive, careless, or preoccupied with getting the meaning out. For instance, Abdullah writes *language* once, then *longuage,* and further on *laguage;* also, *hartest on* and then *hardest one.* Upon rereading, he will probably correct these errors.

One strategy you might employ is to have your students read their writing aloud to a peer or have the peer read it back. Many times they will correct themselves, because what they write does not jibe with what they hear. Abdullah may hear where the sentences should begin and end and put periods in the appropriate places. If he doesn't, you have an indication of where the gaps are in his knowledge. Those errors are the competence errors—made because he has not learned a particular grammatical point, word meaning, spelling, or rhetorical form.

Once he has had a chance to rethink his writing, it is your turn. Your response is critical and, at this point, should be on content alone. Ideas, organization, and clarity are priorities. There is a logical order of thinking, which leads to clear statements. In answer to the question, "Which skill has been the hardest one?" he answers that writing is and gives a graphic example of why: we say things one way, and then we write them another. (There is an /s/ sound in *secret,* a /sh/ sound in *sure,* and a /z/ sound in *surprise,* and yet we write them all with the letter *s.)* He states that he has trouble with spelling and vocabulary, an accurate assessment of his problems. Through his examples, one can sense his frustration at learning this difficult language. There are two important ways to respond to his writing, and you should employ them both:

1. **As a reader:** It is important for Abdullah to see how his writing has an impact on you personally. You can make interlineal comments, such as "I have trouble with spelling, too!" and "Good examples!"

2. **As a teacher.** On a separate sheet of paper make specific suggestions as to how to improve.

Guidelines for Written Responses to Students' Writing

Gadda, Peitzman, and Walsh (1988) give guidelines for commenting on students' writing:

- **Skim the entire piece of writing before recording comments.** Otherwise, you may make comments, only to find that the student has answered your suggestions further on in the piece.

- **Address students by their names.** With each communication, you are responding to a real person, and starting out this way establishes a connection between the two of you.

- **With each student, begin by stating a strength of the student's written work, then pinpoint the nature of the weakness(es).** But don't negate your praise with *but* or *however.* Praise without reservation.

- **Be supportive in tone.** These pieces of writing are true accomplishments for those who are struggling to articulate their thoughts in a new language. Don't dampen their enthusiasm. Students are likely to try harder for someone whom they know understands and is in their corner.

- **List text-specific questions and suggestions for change.** Note the places that worked particularly well. Notes at the bottom of their papers like "tighten" or "reorganize" will not help them. If the students knew how, they would have done so.

- **Phrase your comments tentatively when appropriate.** Students need to understand that there are often many ways to solve problems. On occasion you may mistake the intent of a student, and if you make rigid pronouncements about changes required, you could be destroying the entire paper and its worth. And, most important, remember that these are the students' papers, and they need to maintain authority over their own writing. They need to have the right to change as they see necessary to make their papers fit their plans.

- **Don't solve students' problems for them.** Direct them, help them to find the problems, but let the students work at solving them.

- **Close with encouraging remarks.** Show that you have confidence in their abilities. For example: "Abdullah, your examples of the problems we have with spelling are very vivid. English is a funny language that frustrates many first-language English speakers too. Your writing would be more readable if you reorganized it. Your thoughts jump from spelling to writing to vocabulary to listening and back to spelling again. Why don't you look for your weaknesses in spelling and writing first, and try to figure out why you have those problems. Then, move on to what you are good at. End on a positive note! You are very accurate when you look at your own problems, and your examples demonstrate just how difficult English can be."

- **Give the student a chance to revise again.** On this draft you can edit for grammar and mechanics. This does not mean doing the work for him.

Show Abdullah what is wrong, why, and then direct him in the most productive way to give him a better understanding of English usage.

- **Don't correct every error he has made.** (With writing like Abdullah's, you would wind up marking nearly every word, and he would be so defeated he might give up altogether.) Choose one type. If, for example, he has not corrected his sentence boundaries by inserting periods and starting the next sentences with uppercase letters, that might be a good place to start.

Many students want—in fact, insist on having—every error corrected. If this is the case, it is often fruitless to mark the spelling errors and tell them to look up the words. If they don't know how to spell the words in the first place, looking them up won't help. How can you tell Abdullah to look up *with* when he has spelled it *wheth*? Telling students how to spell words is not cheating, nor is it encouraging them to be lazy. You can incorporate the worst errors into each student's personal spelling plan, as discussed below.

Spelling

My students' spelling is terrible! If it is a low priority, should I ignore it altogether?

The examples to the right (figure 6.26a–c) show how third-grade first-language English speakers spelled the word *policeman*. And here's how second-language learners spelled the same word (from the Language Assessment Scale): *palesman, polisoe, polcole, offsur, plecoman.*

Poor spelling is one of the most noticeable errors that writers make, and it is also one that we are most inclined to condemn. Thus, many teachers feel that teaching spelling is important, and perfection is critical. Many educators also feel that allowing children to spell spontaneously and incorrectly will lead to bad habits down the road. Experts, however, emphatically disagree. Robert and Marlene McCracken (1987) state:

> If conventional spelling is required initially, the [writing] program will fail, because the children will be inhibited from expressing their ideas in writing. They will fail to learn the alphabetic principle of written English, because conventional spelling obscures the sound-letter relationships.

A computer spell check does not necessarily help. Having misspelled words highlighted can paralyze beginning writers so that they lose all their creativity and willingness to go on. Other writers simply choose whatever is suggested, resulting in silly sentences that aren't even remotely what they meant to say.

A good reading program, again, complements a writing program, and vice versa. It is in both the acts of reading and writing that learners figure out the sound-letter correspondences.

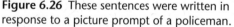

Figure 6.26 These sentences were written in response to a picture prompt of a policeman.

Figure 6.27 Sabina's picture.

Figure 6.28 Mike was one of those kids who couldn't say his *r*'s and substituted *w* in both his speaking, and his writing. He is writing to his brother's friend, Raed. This says "Raed is really really really really really really stupid. Really 100% dumb is his brain." When he was able to make the /r/ sound, the *w* disappeared from his writing.

Susan Sowers (1988) writes,

Inventive spellers' errors don't interfere with their learning to spell correctly later. Like early attempts to walk, talk, and draw, initial attempts to spell do not produce habits to be overcome. No one worries when a child's first drawing of a person is a head propped up on two stick legs. As the errors become more sophisticated, two stick arms protruding from the head where the ears should be—no one fears this schema will become a habit, though it may be repeated a hundred times…[These errors] are greeted as a display of intelligence and emerging proficiency.

Most errors in spelling are not random. They are based on a student's stage of understanding of sound-letter correspondences. As with any other skill, children begin with gross approximations, improving their accuracy as they go. For example, when Rania draws a silly picture of Atosa and labels it *I am cucu*, or when Enrique writes *chack* for *chalk*, or Sabina writes *wich broom* under a drawing of a witch (figure 6.27), they are demonstrating that they know a great deal, if not the finer points of English spelling.

The McCrackens (1995) advocate making a chart of "doozers," words that are very common and yet resist phonetics, such as *once, the, of*. Keep this list displayed on the wall for easy reference.

Some schools use the "guess and go" approach, in which the child writes an approximation of what he wants to say, and comes back later with the correct spelling. This is what Rebecca (see page 223) used. *Bksakids* was a very good try at *because of the kids*, and she wasn't hampered by the necessity to get it perfect the first time.

Some methods that teachers use to support spelling development include

- Daily opportunities to write

- Word walls

- Personal dictionaries

- Personal spelling demons. We all have words we constantly misspell, and keeping a list near us can help in times of doubt.

Conventional spelling *is* important. As time goes by and a student's competence increases, conventional spelling should be expected. By the time English-speaking students reach the fourth grade, they should be conventional spellers. Teachers in the mainstream tend to be much stricter and intolerant of errors than ELL and English-as-a-second-language teachers are.

Thus, at some point we need to emphasize and demand correctness, because sooner or later we won't be there to correct their errors for them, and they will be held accountable, and knocked down for their lapses. Writers will only be taken seriously when their work is error free. And ultimately, they will be held to the same expectations as their native-English-speaking counterparts. Such an expectation cannot always be held out for ELL students who enter school with varying levels of literacy; however, we can and should expect them to reach for that goal.

The most important things to remember when looking at a student's writing are: (1) there is often a logic to the errors, and you can frequently see through them to the meaning if you look hard enough, and (2) the student usually knows what he is trying to say, and can tell you if you ask.

Guidelines for Conferencing

Written responses to writing are well and good. However, they only go so far. How many times have teachers given up on an entangled piece and simply written, "See me," on the bottom, because there is no way to make headway in the paper without talking to the student?

Conferencing is not for writers who have finished their pieces. It's for writers in the middle of their work, and its purpose is to help with ideas, language, format, and so on. Atwell (1998) writes,

> *Young writers want to be listened to. They also want honest, adult responses. They need teachers who will guide them to the meanings they don't know yet by showing them how to build on what they do know and can do. Student writers need response while the words are churning out, in the midst of the messy, tentative act of drafting meaning.*

When conferencing with students, it's important not to take ownership of their work. It's very easy to fall into that trap, and it often happens because they are hesitant about their work. In a conference

- Sit next to the student, not across, so that the conference is personal.

- Let the student keep the paper in his hands. It's his paper.

- Begin with a general open-ended question. Calkins (1994) suggests, "How's it going?"
- Ask the student to comment on the parts he is struggling with, or on the parts he is proud of.
- Listen.

Most of the time students don't make errors or write poor papers because they're lazy. They just don't know how to make it better, and they need someone to sit next to them and talk through how they could improve it. To refer back to the list on page 199, we can build in the elements that make talking enjoyable in order to make writing more bearable. Brainstorming with someone, bouncing ideas off each other, reading aloud, and saying "Hey, try this," helps approximate the pleasure of talking over problems with someone else, with the goal of improving the written work.

Using Peer Tutors

Peer tutors can be a valuable asset in a writing classroom, because they provide real audiences for students' work. They are also less threatening than the teacher. Kids are much more likely to open up to their peers, and the social aspect of writing can be heightened, leading to excitement and improvement. At the elementary level, students can simply share their writing with each other. At the middle- and high-school levels, the feedback can be much more explicit and sophisticated.

But peer responses can often fall flat or fail altogether because students don't know what to say: they can't get beyond "I liked it," or they can find nothing but fault. This is why training is necessary; beginning writers don't know much about how to make their own writing better, much less a peer's writing. Their responses and critiques might be pretty lame at first, but don't give up. They need the practice of "seeing." You want them to become independent writers, and working through editing others' writing moves them in that direction. They need to be exposed to how others tackled the same assignment. They need a wider range of audience than just you.

Train your students to know what to look for, and how to give specific suggestions. Have them look at the content, not the grammar, finding parts that are well written and parts that confused them or could have been written in more detail. It may help to give them a worksheet with specific tasks for them to complete, or questions to answer when reading the draft. Here are some instructions for upper-level students in reviewing drafts of an argument paper.

Content Editor: Read the paper carefully. Is there a clear thesis? Has the writer presented enough evidence to support his/her claim? Has the debate been presented in an impartial way? Has it been explained so that you can understand both sides of the issue? Are there any examples of faulty reasoning? Make comments for your writer.

Organization Editor: Read the paper carefully. Has the paper been organized in such a way that it is clear which sides have been presented? Are the paragraphs ordered to develop the topic logically? Does the content of each paragraph help develop the writer's claim? Have the differing positions been presented with equal weight and clarity? Is there a different organization that would make it clearer?

For lower-level students, you can have them answer such prompts as:

I didn't understand _____.

I thought the most descriptive words in your paper are _____.

When you revise, you could do the following to make your paper more effective: _____

Academic English—Achieving on Par with English Speakers

We discuss academic English in chapter 8. Here, we discuss, specifically, the issue of helping ELLs achieve at the same level as peers in the mainstream classroom. Academic language is "the kind of language used in classrooms, lectures, textbooks, and tests [and] is different from the everyday spoken language of social interaction" (<academiclanguage.org>). Using the academic terms and discourse features of the disciplines is a critical factor in the success of our students. Fostering and nurturing it in writing is one way to move our students to their ultimate goals.

To follow are two writing samples from students who have been mainstreamed. These are both serious and competent students. Hector, from Guatemala, wrote a research paper on trafficking of children, a very big problem in his country:

Countries with out many resources for example, poverty and low salary people do horrible things in order for them to survive. There are places in Guatemala and Mexico where people sell their kids. ...Is sad that people do this bad thing but still happen every single day in our time somewhere out there especially in countries that don't have law again children trafficking. Many of these things that are happen in countries like Mexico and Guatemala part of it is the government fought. The government has the authority to change laws and put new laws. Trafficking children should be big grime in Guatemala. But is not they only charge a 450 Quetzales fine. This is one the issues that concern me.

Hector has done a lot of research, and his paper has a strong voice and the force of personal conviction behind it. But the errors are multiple, and he would be penalized harshly if he handed it in to a mainstream teacher untrained in ELL methods or insensitive to ELL students' needs. Some researchers argue that schools should be more tolerant. Zamel and Spack (1998) as well as Valdez (1999) have promoted "leniency" among instructors, suggesting they should "learn to read more broadly, with a more cosmopolitan, less parochial eye" (Leki 1992). Having worked in language labs for years now, and seeing the intense dismay on both English-speaking and ELL students' faces when they see their grades knocked down because of grammar, spelling, and punctuation errors, or worse, documentation errors, we are not optimistic that this will change soon, if ever. We do our students a disservice by letting them believe they might be given leniency.

Here's an excerpt from a self-reflection by Anh. With some explanations and help from the teacher, he managed to master most of the content of the course.

> *I'm relevant with working a group of student because I can express myself and share what I know, I also learn thing from them. The experience they have like treasure to me because it could be a lesson for me to learn. To completing assignments and reading first I have to prepare what should I start because the reader is not only a person knows how to read a book but also a person who understands what the book said that is a reader.*

Anh's writing is understandable if not free from errors. He has sophisticated syntax and complex sentences. Again, it's easy to focus on the errors, and many teachers outside ELL pounce immediately and give up on the student. Anh needs continued practice at the higher levels of writing as well as reading in the content areas so that he masters the content and vocabulary of these fields.

Hector and Anh need help in growing toward the ambitious goals of English fluency and mastering content at the same level as English speakers. Multiple drafts means simply that: multiple. Barb grieves her students by not putting grades on papers until they achieve at least a *B*. Students are willing to take their lumps and get by with a *C*, or sometimes worse—if a grade is put on their papers. But Barb just hands it back and says, "Not good enough. Write it again." Or, "Getting better, but here's what you can do to make it a WOW! paper. Now go try again." So they write and rewrite and rewrite until it qualifies as a competent or superior paper. They're not happy about it, but when it's good enough, they know it. And they know how it got that way.

As teachers, we need to pay attention to the demands of other courses and make sure our students can navigate the tricky waters of academic discourse. This area of academic literacy and fluency is something we cannot leave to chance.

Time

One of the most important things we can give to our second-language learners is time: time to write and time to learn at their own pace. The only way to become a better writer is to practice, practice, practice, and ELLs need the opportunity and the time to do so. One of the "bad" things that happened to good ideas, writes Hoffman (1998), is that the writing process became "proceduralized, i.e., that on Monday we do prewriting, Tuesday we draft, Wednesday we revise, etc." Beginning or limited-English writers need a lot of time to grapple with all the complexities of the writing process, and it can take much longer for some than for others. Students need time to learn the rhetorical structures, to learn spelling, and to learn strategies. And, more than anything, students need you, the teacher, to spend time talking and writing with them.

Conclusion

The major assumptions we operate under when we teach writing are:

- We learn to write by writing.

- All writing must be done for real purposes, with real audiences.

- Writing involves the emotions as well as the brain, and we need to take care of our writers by engaging, motivating, encouraging, and cheering for them.

Writing is an important part of the school day. Writers learn by interacting with print and by experimenting with thoughts and forms, without being forced to worry about correctness. Younger or newer ELLs should not be excluded from writing merely because they have not yet mastered orthography, sentence patterns, or a large vocabulary. They need to be allowed to practice communicating thoughts, expressing feelings, and learning how to organize their thoughts on paper through the process of writing whole texts. Spelling and grammar will be learned during the act of writing. By providing a rich and supportive environment for students, you can help them grow as writers.

Reflections, Projects, and Projections for Discussion

- Do you consider yourself to be a writer or a teacher of writing (or both)? How does this influence what you do in the classroom?

- Who are your favorite authors? How has reading the writing of your favorite authors influenced your own writing?

- If you dislike writing, why is this so?

- Think back to a time when you were successful at writing something. What contributed to that success? For example, who helped you, and how? If you had no help, what did you do to achieve that success? How can you make that possible for your beginning or apprentice writers?

- When, during your school day, do students get time to practice the whole skill of writing?

- Look at the writing samples we have supplied in the case studies for chapter 2 (Bao, Vianney, Richard, Yoshuane, Liz, and Tommy).

    - What daily writing activities could you develop for each of these students to promote growth in his/her writing?

    - What is the next goal for each student to master?

    - What are your priorities, as an educator, for working with each student on writing development? What will you focus on?

    - What are reasonable demands and goals for each student?

    - In what ways could you help each student learn to self-assess and edit?

- Develop an LEA (Language Experience Approach; please see chapter 5, page 160) for a book you have read to your students. Take it the next step with them. For example, if you are working with secondary students, use students' contributions to develop a paragraph or essay about the book.

- Reflect on all students in your class. What are reasonable demands for them (both for writing development and for keeping up with the rest of the class) given their age and the grade you teach?

- What does your writing class or the writing portion of your school day look like now? Do you use the writing process approach? What is the rationale behind your answer? Would a writing workshop approach (including the writing process, student feedback, the rewriting process, and so on) work for your class? What steps could you take to move toward this method of teaching writing?

- What steps do you need to take to prepare your students for the responsibility of writing workshops (that is, reading and commenting on class-mates' papers)?

Case Studies: Yung Tae, Alejandro, Duong, and Jessica

Yung Tae

Here's one of our favorite writers, Yung Tae, responding to the question: What do you consider to be your greatest strengths and weaknesses?

> *The fact that my oneself afraid cannot throw away a spontaneous habit is the point. It fears the fact that it goes back in spontaneous life and the fact that with in my oneself at falls from light it tears. The weak point which I am having with the will power which it omits to the different person it is disregarded the fast that unpleasantly.*

What in the world is he talking about? Where would you start? What sorts of questions would you ask Yung Tae in order to untangle the meaning behind his words? What would be your plan for helping him improve his writing? Respond to his writing in order to clarify what he means.

Alejandro

Here is Alejandro's writing

> *I am born on New Jersey. I stared the school in United Sates but went I was eight year I moved with my parents to Dominican Republic that is one of the reason do I forget write an English.*

What would you correct in Alejandro's writing? How much assistance would you give him in correcting his errors? In which direction would you steer him to help him find the errors himself?

Alejandro gets extra help from his teacher on his papers. When she reviews his writing, she puts a ^ mark where something is missing, but she does not suggest what needs to be inserted. She also underlines parts that are wrong (for example, the word or phrase is unclear, or he has used the wrong verb agreement). When his teacher marks something as questionable, she does not explain why. He is supposed to know (or figure out) what is wrong and fix it by himself. Why could this be a problem for Alejandro? What would be a better way to help him?

Common Issues for Alejandro and Yung Tae

Several issues crop up with Alejandro and Yung Tae:

- Should you make them change their writing?

- With effort (much more with Yung Tae), you can figure out what they're trying to say. Is it worth the effort to split hairs on every slightly skewed word or phrase each one came up with?

- Would you ban dictionaries for these two students? How could you help your students find the correct words if some words, such as *go*, or *do*, have over 400 meanings?

Duong

How would you help Duong correct and improve this writing?

> *My name is have a lot of meaning, abou power, strong, deer, rich so I like my name when I was my country but when I came here my name begin by "D" so different sound here. They also call wrong my name. Some people Vietnam told me my name If they call me wrong sound so my name will become bad word. I think I have to chage my name. Duong.*

Jessica

Jessica is a high intermediate level 5 in English proficiency. Her family is ethnic Chinese; when she was a little girl they escaped from Vietnam by hiding her in a suitcase for two days. Jessica works in her family's restaurant, but they don't pay much attention to her otherwise. Her father gambles the family's money, so they struggle financially. She has very low self-esteem and apologizes constantly.

Jessica's classroom performance is good. She understands the material, but she has trouble with the work when she needs to grasp more than the literal meaning. This is evident with symbolic text or subtext. Jessica's writing has many errors in grammar and syntax, and she worries she cannot improve. She is disorganized, and sometimes she is her own worst enemy. Frequently, she actually has a completed assignment in her messy backpack, but she fails to turn it in because she thinks she left it at home.

Jessica has an excellent English teacher, but the teacher penalizes Jessica for her nonproficient errors. This discourages Jessica and makes her reluctant to turn in her work. This is Jessica's senior year, and she is starting to fall behind.

- How would you handle Jessica's issues?

- What are Jessica's strong points? Where is she weak?

- How can you help her to improve? How can you show her progress?

- What can you do to help the classroom teachers understand how to help Jessica?

THE GREAT OCEAN

Ocean is a mass body of salt water that covers three fourth of the Earth. I, too, have an ocean between my father and I. My father had tried to swim across the ocean many times, but every time he tries, I would finds some ways to make him drown, forcing him to retreat. He, therefore, would wait awhile, until the storm is over, and tries again, and I would be there waiting for him; stopping him from reaching the surface. My hatred for him is deeper than the deepest depth of the ocean. My sister would often ask me, "Why can't you be like me, forgive and forget? Don't forget, he's our father." And I would often reply, "But I'm not you."

Figure 6.29 The rest of Jessica's essay can be found in Appendix J.

Chapter 7

Speaking and Listening—
Winning the Rottery

In this chapter, we look further at the listening and speaking components of acquiring a language that we began in chapter 3, which included a detailed discussion of how you can provide meaningful and useful input. We focus on

- The importance of oral language in learning and personal growth

- Phases of language acquisition, and what these look like in the classroom

- How to treat errors

- How to develop the skill of listening—an end in itself

- Talk in all areas of the curriculum—opportunities to talk and listen

The Importance of Oral Language in Learning

Franco, who took his name from a Franco-American truck driving by when he and his brother were choosing new names, was 12 when he arrived from Taiwan and was enrolled in junior high. His family owned a Chinese restaurant in a nearby shopping mall. Although Barb—who worked with him three afternoons a week—and his classroom teachers were conscientious and patient, Franco's progress seemed very slow. Conversations with him were usually one way; he seldom managed more than a phrase or two here and there. More often than not, his response was either a shrug or an "I don't know." He could not do the regular work in his content-area classes. He hardly seemed to be learning at all.

And yet outside the classroom, things were different. He consistently beat Barb at Monopoly and Risk. These are, by no means, easy games, and Barb explained the rules painstakingly in English. She would read out the Chance and Community Chest cards that Franco drew, and more often than not, he could follow the instructions without further explanation. At the end of each session of Monopoly, they each kept their property and money so that they could continue the next session where they had left off.

Although he was not a break-in artist, Franco gained the respect and admiration of the eighth-grade boys by demonstrating that he could open any combination lock in the school. Another demonstration of his ability to understand was when the other students would bid him, "Go tell Mrs. Mitchell, 'F____ you'." And, with a wide grin on his face, Franco would obligingly go to Mrs. Mitchell and say, "F____ you, Mrs. Mitchell," to the howls of his classmates.

Franco was a lot smarter and knew a lot more than he let on. He used his English (and his lack of it!) to his advantage. He selectively misunderstood what he didn't feel like doing by pretending he didn't know what he was saying, but clearly comprehended things that were important to him, such as the rules of games and instructions from classmates.

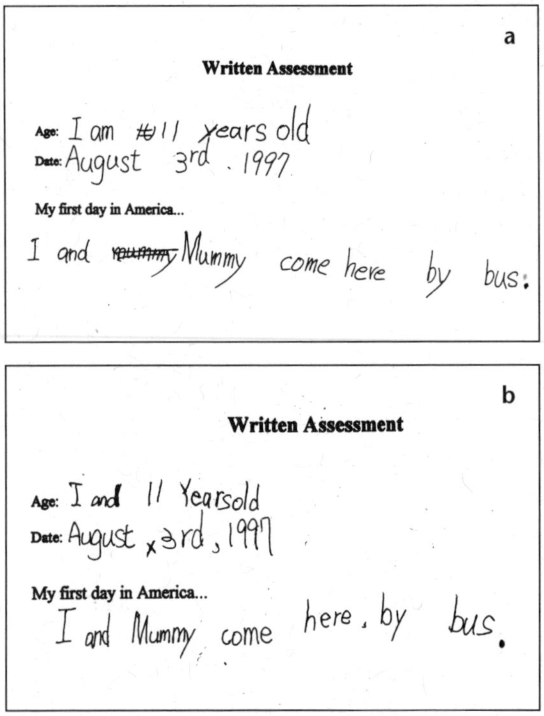

One of the most interesting things about Franco was his intelligent use of strategies to increase both his status and his friendships that more than made up for his lack of fluency and proficiency. If he had so chosen, he could have used interactions to increase his learning as well. His teachers could have placed him in situations that took advantage of his natural social nature and increased both his proficiency and his ability to function throughout the curriculum.

Not all of our students are as outgoing (or as naughty) as Franco. Shyer or quieter students may not be so willing.

Angel and Beverly, both also from Taiwan, are at the opposite end of the spectrum. Angel is very shy and will not attempt to speak English at all. She and Beverly converse together almost entirely in their native language. It is often difficult to gauge how much they actually understand or are learning; they never raise their hands or volunteer, and they only speak to each other. This is frustrating for their teachers, and it also presents a dilemma for them. They want to encourage the use, growth, and maintenance of the girls' home language. The teachers know that allowing Beverly and Angel the chance to talk things over in their first language aids significantly in their comprehension. But, because no adults at the school speak Chinese, the teachers cannot distinguish between real learning and idle chatter.

Because of Angel's shyness and Beverly's protectiveness of her, as well, perhaps, as Beverly's loyalty that prevented her from reaching out to others, these girls did not use the language they had (English *or* Chinese) to learn more. They were a closed circle.

As with reading and writing, competence in both speaking and listening is best acquired in a setting that encourages students to talk and experiment with

Figure 7.1a–b It was impossible to tell from Beverly and Angel's writing who had generated the work and who had copied.

language, and that respects and values their contributions, however slight, hesitant, or faltering (Brock 1997; Martinez-Roldan and Lopez-Robertson 1999-2000). The environment Franco was immersed in was conducive to learning. He was not isolated in a language lab, learning, "Hello, Mrs. Mitchell, how are you?" and "Please pass the pencils." He was surrounded by people using English for real purposes—to further relationships, to get homework done, to harass poor Mrs. Mitchell. Franco was strongly motivated to make friends and used the language skills he had to further that end. Having him spend his time working on pronunciation and grammar would not have helped much.

Beverly and Angel need to be encouraged to open up to others. However, you have to accept the fact that some students simply aren't ready. It is important not to fall back on drills to get them to open up, or force them to speak English to each other. It is very easy to simply give up, overlook them, and decide that they are nonparticipants in conversations and discussions. This is a trap we cannot allow ourselves to fall into. As we state numerous times in this book, there are multiple means other than speaking to demonstrate competence and understanding.

But we also have to keep the door open for Angel and Beverly. Sooner or later, when they are ready, one or the other will begin to talk in English. Bao, for instance, had been silent the entire autumn. One day, she was informed that girls from the fifth-grade class were going to come in and perform an ethnic dance. Suddenly, loudly and clearly, she said, "Aw, I already know. I don't wanna do that. I know how to play that," surprising her teachers.

It is easy to undervalue the importance of oral language use in learning, because we spend so much time inside and outside the classroom doing just that. However, we need to recognize the centrality of talk and capitalize on this natural tendency. Both talking and listening, write Barrs et al (1989) "cut across the curriculum...Within the classroom contexts, the quality and range of oral language opportunities will significantly affect the child's progress and development as a talker, listener and learner...Opportunity for oral language use across a full range of informal as well as formal contexts must be afforded throughout the day." These authors go on to assert that how children use language to explore experience and how they express what they understand "is at the crux of learning."

In fact, the California State Board of Education went so far as to state that "speaking and listening skills have never been more important. Most Americans now talk for a living at least part of the time. The abilities to express ideas cogently and to construct valid and truthful arguments are as important to speaking well as to writing well" (1998).

To develop competency in both the listening and speaking areas of English, newcomers need

- Teachers who understand the stages of language acquisition and adjust their input to fit each student's level

- Teachers who are tolerant of errors, enabling students to learn without being labeled or punished for their pronunciation or word-choice errors

- Many opportunities to talk, listen, and interact with others—real talk, real questions, rather than inquisitions with a predetermined answer that the teacher owns

- Time

Language Acquisition and Classroom Input

While acquiring a language is an individual process, we can make generalizations about the phases the learner goes through. Comprehension often precedes production. What Franco, for instance, said—or was able to say—was by no means indicative of the learning that was taking place. He could understand the complex rules of Monopoly, and while he would never have been able to explain them back, he could certainly follow the directions well enough to win time and time again.

We see this with our own children learning their first language. Children recognize their names at five months and phrases such as "Here's your Mom," and "Wave bye-bye" at about seven months, long before they say their first word. By the time they speak, they have had nearly a year of listening, and their ability to understand spoken messages far exceeds their ability to produce.

For second-language learners, our priority as teachers should be fluency before accuracy. Getting things done supersedes getting things right. As they gain competence and confidence, students will work out the details of grammar and pronunciation.

The Three Stages of Language Acquisition – A Continuum

Researchers Burt and Dulay (1982) found that language learners progress through three general stages as they gain communication skills. These are not necessarily discrete stages; they represent more of a continuum from no language to full participation:

Stage 1: One-Way Communication. The learners listen to the target language but are not able to speak it.

A common question we hear from teachers goes something like, "Beverly and Angel aren't saying anything. What can we do to make them talk?" Some researchers, such as Stephen Krashen (1982), claim that language learners go through a silent period, which can last from between one and six months. Others have questioned this idea and found the timeframe to be closer to two weeks. Still others say there is no such thing. But teachers often tell us of students who have been in their classes for weeks without saying a word, leading them to believe that these students aren't learning.

This silent period can be the result of several things, or a combination of things. It could be a period of silent non-comprehension during which the new language simply seems like a stream of sound to the learner. It could be due to psychological withdrawal as a result of culture shock. Or, it could simply be due to a particular student's personality; perhaps he or she is a shy person.

The student's learning style could also affect production. This student may prefer to learn by rote memorization of rules, remaining silent until a number of structures are learned, rather than relying on intuitive knowledge and making the most of the skills already acquired. He or she may have come from a culture in which asking questions indicates misunderstanding, and is an insult to the teacher and a dishonorable thing to do. Or, possibly, the conversation is going so fast that inserting a comment is like drinking from a fire hose—by the time they think of something to say, the opportunity is long gone.

Mai Lor, for instance, came to Cinda's classroom when she was in the third grade. Records from her former school informed Cinda, the ELL teacher, that Mai Lor had said but two words throughout her schooling thus far; in fact, the kindergarten and first-grade teachers had both remarked that she never said a word in school. Following up on what she observed with Mai Lor, Cinda had conversations with Mai Lor's mom. She found out that Mai Lor spoke only in Hmong at home.

Whether your students are silent for six months or begin to communicate on the first day, they need to be allowed "listening time," without being forced to speak. Research has shown that the emphasis in learning a new language should be on listening first, and that forcing a student to speak can be detrimental to his learning. Granted, waiting until your student is ready to speak can be difficult. Going day after day speaking to a student who doesn't respond is frustrating; the temptation to force this student to say something—*anything!*—just to see if you are getting through can be strong.

It may be easier to resist the temptation if you are aware that this is a passing stage. And it doesn't mean they're simply vegetating. Speaking and listening happen all day long. Having expectations—expecting that the student *is* taking in the language, even if he isn't producing it yet—is so important. Just because a student doesn't produce much in the way of speech doesn't mean he isn't learning. Continue to talk to the student, and acknowledge he is in the class. Igoa (1995) remarks that "there is a lot that goes on in the silent stage. Beyond our comprehension, they comprehend."

Stage 2: Partial Two-Way Communication. The learners listen to the communication and respond with either gestures or in their native language.

Students can demonstrate comprehension in ways other than by speech. Allow them to respond by nodding their heads, pointing, drawing, gesturing, or pantomiming.

Over the course of the year, Mai Lor began to join in with the rest of the students while in a small group outside of the mainstream classroom. It was a big day when, in science, Mai Lor pointed to pictures of the full moon, the quarter moon, and the crescent moon, to indicate she understood.

Stage 3: Full Two-Way Communication. The learners listen and respond effectively in the target language.

In addition to learning single words, people learn language in chunks. Their first utterances often consist of unanalyzed wholes, such as "What's the matter?" or "That's mine." What these chunks do is allow a learner to participate in a conversation or game without having completely mastered the grammar of the language. From these chunks, they can move toward complete sentences as they figure out the rules of the new language.

By the end of the year, Mai Lor would even volunteer to read aloud: "I want to read. Can I read first?" The mainstream teacher insists that Mai Lor still does not know how to speak English, but Cinda has observed her in many different situations and knows better.

Burt and Dulay state that the three phases of language acquisition are important for the classroom teacher to understand for a couple of reasons:

- By understanding these stages you won't be overly concerned if your students' production does not match their ability to understand.

- Students are best able to succeed if the level of activity matches their current stage of development. Therefore, if your students are capable of uttering only simple sentences, use activities that require minimal language skills.

Four Levels of Questioning

In chapter 3, we discussed ways of adjusting your speech to make it easier for your students to understand. Good questioning techniques also encourage students to respond in English, at their own levels. Here are four levels of questioning with some examples:

Level A. The teacher asks questions that require only *yes* or *no* answers. For example: "Are you standing?" "Can you hear me?" "Did Maria open the window?"

Level B. The teacher asks *either/or* questions, and the students respond with one-word answers using either a noun or a verb. For example: "Are you walking or standing?" "Is she sitting on the table or on the chair?"

Level C. The teacher asks questions using *where* or *what,* and the students are able to respond with a single word or a partial phrase. For example: "Where is Baldo sitting?" Answer: "On the floor." "What is Rocio doing?" "Sitting."

Level D. The teacher uses no content vocabulary to ask questions, and the students are able to respond in full sentences. For example: "What is Sabina doing?" "She's dancing." "What will Salvador do?" "He's going to shut the door." "What did Anna do?" "She climbed on the chair."

This hierarchy of questions is an important concept to remember. In the teacher's rush to communicate with a student, it is easy to overlook the complexity of question-asking. Yet, questions that are above the students' comprehension levels can be confusing for them. When the students' problem is the grammar used, not the vocabulary, rephrasing the question often creates more confusion. For example, you might start out with the question: "What time is it?" Then, when the students fail to understand, you may try rephrasing the question, "What time do you think it is?" or "What do the hands on the clock say?" believing that stating it another way might help. If the students understood the concept, however, they would have been able to answer the question in the first place. If they didn't, rephrasing would only confuse them further, because they are hearing three questions they don't understand, not one. If students are confused at one level of questioning, revert to the previous one. For example, if the student doesn't understand "Where are you going?" revert to "Are you going home or to Mrs. Smith's class?"

Tolerance for Errors

Perfect comprehension and production are not realistic goals for second language learners. Students need to be encouraged to express themselves. A casual attitude toward oral mistakes, in which one accepts all attempts at communication and does not pounce on errors, will foster confidence and the willingness to speak up. However, this doesn't mean ignoring mistakes altogether. Grammatical and pronunciation errors often do get in the way of communication. The goal, if not to eradicate a foreign accent, is to move the student toward speech that a listener does not have to struggle to understand.

Grammatical Errors

My students make a lot of mistakes in grammar. Should I correct them or not?

Just as we discussed in the chapters on reading and writing, emphasize communication and meaning, not correctness. Most parents recognize that acquiring language is a process that takes several years. A two-year-old does not come out with perfectly formed grammatical sentences. His speech is apt to be limited to only one or two words at a time, such as *Mommy, juice,* or *big dog.* Instead of looking for mistakes, parents focus on the meaning and content of the child's speech. They are confident that these "mistakes" will disappear as the child matures and communicates. Parents don't correct their children for their linguistic inaccuracies. If a child says "Daddy goed to work," the mother accepts this as communication and responds to the truth of the statement. However, if a child points to a dog and says "cat," the mother will correct this error in fact. Parents will also use correct language in response, thereby modeling correct usage.

As teachers, however, we often feel it is our responsibility to point out errors. We feel constrained to correct every mistake the student makes, feeling that if we don't, the student will continue to make that error.

If we view second-language learning as a process that takes a number of years and recognize that students need time to hone and refine the rules of our language, we can view these mistakes not as faults, but as stages of development the students have reached on their way to mastering English. Whatever they say, and however they say it, we need to recognize, understand, appreciate, and support their attempts to communicate by responding to the message.

Research has shown that pointing out mistakes seems to do very little for language learners and may serve more to distract them from their meaning than to help them get meaning across. Pointing out mistakes may even impede their progress, because this approach focuses more on form than on meaning and also undermines their confidence in their attempts to communicate.

Krashen (1982) advises that the focus of language should be on communication, not on grammatical structure. As you observe your students relax and begin to make attempts at communication with you and with other students, encourage them to move beyond silence and focus on continued language interaction. This focus relieves you of the expectations that students must produce "perfect English" and allows students to make their own generalizations. Gradually, through time, practice, and the process of error-making, they will come to approximate the English they hear spoken around them every day.

Use errors as benchmarks to a student's progress, and use your knowledge of these errors for subjects to work on at other times. In chapter 4, we discuss how to use patterned language to focus on specifics such as tenses. Another option is to give brief mini-lessons on these specifics during the editing stages of writing.

Modeling, as parents do, is another way of giving students input about their speech. For instance, if Lupe says, "I no like broccoli," you can respond with, "Oh, you don't like broccoli. What *do* you like?" Thus, she can hear the correct form in the context of a statement that has immediate relevance to her.

If a student has expressly stated the wish to have his grammar corrected then it is best to do so, but only *after* he has finished talking. You can say, "You said 'losted.' The correct form is 'lost.'" But make these corrections only if invited. The long-term efficacy of corrections is dubious and usually only satisfies the individual student's need to know.

We want to emphasize that error correction is not a one-shot solution; you cannot correct or work on an error once and expect the student never to make the same error again. Sorting out the grammar of a language is a long, slow process. For this reason, we reiterate that a lenient attitude toward errors in grammar is the wisest course to follow while the students sort out the intricacies of grammar for themselves.

Trouble With Pronunciation

My students have difficulties with pronunciation. Shouldn't I work on these with them?

Pronunciation is another matter altogether. While we still advocate that saying something is more important than getting it right, there are times when you may have to take steps to help a student with pronunciation.

It is not good practice to assume that language learners will correct pronunciation problems later in the acquisition process. We believe that some language learners are not able to do this. Frequently, students whose native language has tones (such as Chinese, Vietnamese, or Thai) or a different stress and pitch system (like Korean or Burmese) have great difficulty speaking English that can be easily understood. Because they respond to tones, when speaking they often drop the endings of words. For example, "You like some bread?" will sound like "You li' so' brea'?" or "His wife is at home," will sound like "Hi' wi' a' ho'." The focus for teaching pronunciation should be on helping the students to communicate—to get their meaning across accurately—not on the correct reproduction of minimal pairs (sounds produced in the same place in the mouth, in the same way, but that nevertheless differ, such as /p/ and /b/, /f/ and /v/).

Every language uses a certain number of sounds to make up words, and they are not always the same from language to language. Some languages have sounds we don't have. Spanish, for instance has two /r/ sounds: the rolled /r/ in *perro,* and the /r/ in *pero.* Farsi and German have the guttural /h/ as in *khosha-medi* and *ich.* Other languages don't have sounds that we have or "hear" only one sound where we hear two. Arabic speakers, for instance, do not distinguish between /p/ and /b/; Spanish speakers don't distinguish between /sh/ and /ch/. Speakers of the Navajo language do not distinguish between /p/, /b/, and /m/. Often these speakers cannot hear the difference.

Differences are not only confined to different languages, but to different dialects within a language as well. In her speech, Mary, a Northern California native, doesn't distinguish the difference between the vowel sounds in *cot* (kat) and *caught* (kat). To Barb, from the Midwest, this is incomprehensible. Barb can hear it; why can't Mary? How pointless it would be for Barb to stop everything and drill Mary in this difference! If Barb said, "I was sleeping on a cot in the tent when my husband caught two fish on Lake Oroville," no one would have any doubt about which word Barb was using when. To label Mary as stupid or slow because she can't hear the difference would be ridiculous. And yet this has been done time and again to students whose dialects or languages do not contain certain sounds we use in our own dialect. One of Barb's student teachers, for example, discovered that the students he was tutoring couldn't distinguish between /f/ and /v/ and spent an entire week helping them articulate the different sounds. Drilling them endlessly on sounds they cannot distinguish is pointless, and more often than not extremely frustrating. What's more, in the face of the whole task of learning English, it is a waste of time.

But we must address the problems created when students use correct English structures in their speech but still have problems being understood because of their pronunciation. Mary had a student, Thien, who went to a fast-food restaurant and ordered "free hamburgers." He immediately got a lecture on how "We work for things in this country; if you think you're here for a handout then go back where you came from." What Thien really meant to order was *three* hamburgers, but because he was not able to articulate the aspirated /th/, he was misunderstood. This particular sound is difficult for students of many language backgrounds. These students compensate by using /f/ or /t/ in the place of /th/.

Working with minimal pairs within the context of words—*hit* versus *heat* for example, *free* versus *three,* or *very* versus *berry*—is often not very productive, but it can work more effectively if the minimal pair work is part of a natural sentence structure. Try using, as examples, idioms that students find useful or puzzling and want to know the meaning of, such as "save your breath" and "through thick and thin," or common phrases like "Thanks a lot."

Mary found it helpful to alert students to the problems they would encounter when they tried to pronounce English words. Some students preferred to be told that it would be difficult for them to say certain sounds; they were then able to spell, write, draw, and so on in order to communicate.

Pronunciation is more complex than simply mastering minimal pairs. Students from other countries often have a difficult time with the stress and pitch system in English speech. As a result, these students can often sound angry, excited, or emphatic to a native-English speaker, when to their own ears they are being solicitous and polite.

Another facet of pronunciation that eludes many ELL students is the clipped, de-emphasized English spoken in informal conversation (often referred to as "reduced English") in which we drop endings and slur our words together. Mary once spent a period of time with her students explaining the *have + to (havta)* construction, when one of her students asked, "When are we going to learn about *gotta*?" Imagine how frustrating this type of language is to students who, when speaking in their own language, were rewarded for consistent clarity!

Activities to help improve students' sensitivity to the nuances of English can be enjoyable. Focus their attention on listening to differences in pitch patterns by comparing the pronunciation of words that occur in several languages, like *chocolate* or *coffee*. Have students pronounce their names with you, pronouncing them the way North Americans would tend to. This helps them focus on the differences in pitch or minimal sounds. Sometimes students discover that a word they have heard frequently but didn't understand is actually a North American approximation of their own names!

Poetry is a good way to help with pronunciation that can involve the whole class. Shel Silverstein and Jack Prelutsky are great fun for both reading and pronunciation. Kids will tolerate reading them aloud again and again. They also teach phrasing and cadence.

Try, for instance, *Homework! Oh, Homework!* by Prelutsky. That one seems to pop up at the end of every class period when the homework is being assigned. Others, such as *Be Glad Your Nose Is on Your Face* and *Bleezer's Ice Cream* are such fun you can return to them without boredom for quite a while. Try round-robin reading with some of these poems.

Songs are another fun way to practice pronunciation. You can use YouTube to find just about anything these days, and song lyrics can be found with the tap of the keys.

Students' inability to hear sound differences often show up in their writing as well as their speech:

However, we should take notice there are not only regal immigrants, but also illegal immigrants.

In addition the taxes which are corrected from American workers control the welfare that sustain poor illegal immigrants.

After the war Japan became to most successful minority grope in the U.S. because of Pearl Harver.

These examples show how reception and pronunciation spill over into other areas of students' work and skew the meaning of what they are trying to communicate.

We believe that drilling on sounds in isolation is counterproductive; pointing out troublesome sounds and having students practice them within words is more helpful. Work on pronunciation only when students express a wish to focus on improving their language delivery or when their pronunciation of certain words gets in the way of being understood.

Listening and pronunciation practice are facets of language learning that can be turned over to technology. Students can tap into the computer individually with earphones so that you can work with others. Authentic online materials to listen to include those found on NBC, ABC, BBC, NPR, Al Jazeera, and Voice of America sites, as well as major news magazines, such as *Newsweek*. As well, the British Council maintains an English learning website for students called LearnEnglishCentral (<www.britishcouncil.org/central.htm>). Start there.

There are many expensive computer programs on the market, but there are also many free websites devoted to pronunciation practice that you can take advantage of instead of spending the money. If you have the technology available for students to access what's available online, by all means use it. Students can practice on their own and get instant feedback about whether they were correct or not. To get you started, check out

- California Distance Learning Project (<www.cdlponline.org>)
- The English Listening Lounge (<www.englishlistening.com>)
- The Internet TESL Journal (<iteslj.org>)
- About.com (<www.about.com>)
- Manythings.org (<www.manythings.org>)

Using Talk to Explore and Gain Understanding

Talk is an important part—a critical part—of learning. Students need to talk in order to learn and to become competent language users. Barnes (1986) states: "Talk is a major means by which learners explore the relationship between what they already know and new observations or interpretations which they meet." We should, as Barrs et al (1989) emphasize, promote the social aspect of talking as an important dimension of learning and development.

Cullinan (1993) points out several of the roles that talk plays in and outside the classroom:

- **Students learn by talking, because talking helps clarify thoughts.** Have you ever found yourself talking out loud to yourself when you're trying to figure out something that's hard? Putting something into words helps us give form and shape to the thoughts we have in our heads.

  For example, when working on this book, we email chapters back and forth to each other to read. But it isn't until we actually sit down and talk through each paragraph within each chapter that we can be sure what we have been saying is what we really mean.

- **Talk aids comprehension.** Students who talk about a topic understand it better than students who don't talk about it. Talking in their own language is especially important for second language learners. They can go straight to the subject matter, unimpeded by their lack of mastery over English. For example, Barb began a lesson involving animals. She brought in a large number of picture books on animals and allowed students to peruse them. Then, she handed out three-by-five-inch cards onto which the name of an animal had been printed; one student had *ant*, others had *octopus, deer, lizard,* and so on. Students who could not identify their animal rushed back to the books to find out what it was. Other students knew more English and could help identify and explain. When students were asked to group themselves according to classifications such as height, number of legs, eyes, omnivorous/carnivorous, nocturnal/diurnal, and so on, they could discuss these different traits in their own language. To force them to speak entirely in English would have been pointless; it would have lessened the learning experience as well as diminished the fun, since the object was learning, not necessarily simply learning English.

- **Talk provides a window into students' thinking.**

- **Talk supports reading.** Peterson and Eeds (1990) write,

  The spirit of collaboration is essential in constructing meaning [in reading]. Teachers work together with children, and children with children, to initiate responses, share interpretations, and construct meaning. This messy process involves a certain amount of groping, questioning, and putting forth of promising beginnings in the hope that others will contribute to the completion. This way of working encompasses both inquiry and critique as the basis for comprehending a text is broadened. Children practice making meaning as they make personal connections to the text and benefit from the insights of others.

  We know that when we read, another reader might have a different interpretation of the story. Book clubs, literature circles, and dramatic readings are all means of increasing both our enjoyment and our understandings of the books we have read. For example, Kari wrote in her journal:

  When I read the book, I wasn't impressed with it. It wasn't that I hated the book, it was more of a feeling that I could take it or leave it. Listening to the other class members' feelings about the book gave me a greater acceptance of it. I think if I read it again and thought about it more I would appreciate it in a new light.

- **Talk supports writing.** Galda, Cullinan, and Strickland (1997) write, "Talk that explores ideas can have a profound effect on learning...exploratory talk creates and transforms knowledge."

  Second-language learners who are not strong writers can tell us what they mean and the point they are trying to get across when faced with essays or stories that they cannot get the thread of. Talking with students before, during, and after they work on a piece of writing helps writers clarify their thinking, decide where to go, and furthers their options and choices.

For example, Enrique was a competent English speaker but could not read or write well in either English or Spanish. Mary helped him prepare to write an essay about "Sir Gawain and the Green Knight" by being his scribe. As Enrique related what the story was about and articulated what he understood, Mary wrote what he told her. Telling it out loud allowed him to clarify his grasp of the story; then Mary typed up exactly what he had said and printed it out. Reading it through gave him successful practice at reading and an opportunity to review the story. He then felt more prepared to tackle the actual writing of the assignment.

> One problem Mrs. Mason faces with her ELL students is their use of dictionaries. She finds the oddest, most peculiar words in their papers. For example, Han used the word *perish* in this way: "children perish their original rules of language and adopt new ones." What could you do to remedy this problem?

It is often necessary to sit and talk with the author about what it is he is trying to convey. Sometimes ELL students' writing is so impenetrable that this is the only way to get the meaning. Barb once received a composition from a student that was supposed to be a descriptive piece. It was a jumble of "I saw..." sentences that seemed to have neither a central theme nor cohesion. Puzzled by the essay, she returned to the author. The student said she was using, as a model, an essay by a famous author about what he saw in Central Park. Only then did the student's paper make sense to Barb; together, they looked at the original and shaped her essay in ways that made it better.

Glory wrote:

I felt swimming can learn a/the bull's eye a target still more to befond of. I would like to shopping as can buy very oneself like a/ the bull's eye a target east to west.

Jim wrote:

Communication is a system formed by the relationship of emotion. Thus, if a partner is the strong silent type, the result of conversation may often be useless or formalistic. Because, the conversation partner feels the simultaneously uncomfortable. In general, the silent moment in conversation comes from the many aspects: the indifferent issue, the linguistic problem, and the unfamiliar relationship with the partner, for example. However, the moment came from such a reason is the instant or temporal problems, perhaps.

In Glory's case, we can simply ask her what she meant and go on. In Jim's case, however, we need to untangle with him exactly what he wants to say so that it comes out in a coherent way, understandable to readers. It is obvious that this writer has sophisticated and deep thoughts about the problem, even if what he writes is not altogether clear.

How many times have we heard a student tell us easily and succinctly what they meant to say that did not come anywhere close on paper? And when we ask, "Well, why didn't you write that?" they shrug helplessly.

- **Talk supports growth in the content areas.** "Collaboration to solve problems and make sense of new information is supported by talk. And, because as we talk we become aware of what we think and know and wonder about, talk provides that foundation on which we can build by relating new information to existing knowledge and ideas" (Wollman-Bonilla 1989).

  Brenda's second-grade class was studying matter. For several weeks she set up a variety of experiments. Students, working in pairs, added effervescent tablets to water and to vinegar, mixed salt in the water, and then evaporated the water on the windowsill. Water was always spilled, and arguments about who got to do what were rampant, but the second graders were intensely interested and engaged, predicting what was going to happen and writing up the results. A silent classroom, in which everyone was expected to sit still and keep their mouths shut, would have been a sterile atmosphere with the learning curtailed.

- **Talk supports growth in academic language.** Students hear the way words are pronounced, the stress and intonation of academic words such as *medical* and *medicinal*, words they would never be able to sound out on their own, such as *silhouette*. Talking to them at the level they are producing will limit them to the level they function at without pushing them further.

Opportunities to Talk and Listen

Studies have revealed that second-language learners and others from diverse backgrounds can engage in meaningful talk; they benefit a great deal from being included in discussions, whether they contribute or not (Brock 1997). Therefore, we need to create as many opportunities for them as possible.

Rashid wrote in his journal:

It is no doubt that my surrounding has far fecting implication on a person. I strong believes that morden to learn a language fluently you have to go there to live by so doing you apply the language daily learn new vocabulary your proficiency in the language is test and over all your command in the language is refined on a daily basic. I realised that my english improve by socializing with different english speaking people. I had a good incident were a girl asked me if it was first time to see snow, I responded back by saying that it may my second time to see snow, I explained to her that I hae seens now before in london. The bad incindent was when I was telling my friend about the fin I had in altant he did not understand me, although I repeated what I wanted to tell him twice. From these two incidents I concluded that I have to learn the american accent well enough and try to keep my accent from interfealing. I hope that by the time I graduate I will master well in my english.

We need to give students as many opportunities to interact with their English-speaking peers as possible. It is sometimes difficult for older students to overcome the shyness and awkwardness to make attempts, but it's worth the effort.

We also feel it is important to promote listening as an end in itself, not merely as a means to speaking. We spend much of our time listening; we listen to conversations, radio, TV, and so on. Listening is a critical skill, particularly in the content classes, where sophisticated listening skills are necessary—following directions in a science lab, listening to lectures in history and government class, learning rules of a game in phys ed, or receiving explanations of procedures in math.

To follow are some strategies you can use to promote listening and speaking skills.

> Ze, talking about her weekend, said, "The my family won't go yesterday night 'cause of the bunch of clouds in the sky."
>
> What could she possibly mean by this? What would prompt her to use the word "the" at the beginning of this sentence? What could you do to clarify?

TPR – Total Physical Response

Total Physical Response, developed by James Asher (1965), is one of the richest and most successful activities you can use and can involve anywhere from one student to the entire class. The underlying premise is that listening to and understanding the English language must come before the actual attempt to speak. The strategy is based upon the belief that language acquisition can be greatly accelerated through the use of body movement; therefore, each lesson includes commands and actions that help the student learn through doing. By listening and responding physically to instructions or commands, students are involved to a greater extent than when they respond only verbally. They are thus not required to respond orally, they are simply asked to follow the directions given by the teacher. In the fun, relaxed atmosphere of a TPR lesson, students learn very quickly and efficiently. You can turn the responsibility for this activity over to an aide, a native-English speaker, or even a proficient student.

A typical TPR lesson proceeds as follows:

1. The teacher gives a command, modeling if necessary. For instance, say "Stand up," and, at the same time, stand up yourself. Remember to speak in a normal tone of voice and at normal speed. Do not speak too slowly, or students will quickly become bored and inattentive.

2. Students respond physically by standing up. Slower learners can watch and imitate the actions of others who have caught on more quickly.

3. When a number of commands have been given and learned, you can combine them to form a series. For example, "Mario, stand up, walk to the window, and open it."

As students pass through the stages of language acquisition, and their ability to speak English develops, TPR gives them the opportunity to take control and use their newly acquired vocabulary by acting as the TPR leader. You can now have them give the series of commands to the class, motivating them to speak clearly and enunciate correctly. You can use this time to pinpoint pronunciation problems your students might have. You have a natural opportunity for working on strengthening those points within a meaningful context.

Use TPR to introduce important survival verbs such as *walk, go, stop, turn, close, open, lock, unlock, sit, stand.* You can embed other important vocabulary within the commands in sentences such as, "Francisco, pick up the blue book, and put it under the fire extinguisher."

TPR is primarily a listening activity, but it can become a very rich and enjoyable activity involving all four language-arts skills (listening, speaking, reading, and writing). You help language learners to make the speech-print connection if, once a series of commands is mastered, you write the series on the board for students to read and, if possible, copy for themselves. Realizing that the words they have just heard and responded to are the words they now see on the board is an important step.

TPR can be adapted to a variety of different situations. For example, if you find your high school students are reticent about marching around the classroom, or you think that the TPR activities described above would not be appropriate in your class, then adapt TPR to your specific situation.

If you are working with a small group of ELL students within a larger class setting, try working with manipulatives. For example, place cut-outs of a square, circle, diamond, star, and triangle in front of the group of students. Point to a shape, and say, "This is a star. Now, you point to the star." Do the same with another shape, then review with the star.

As students understand what you are doing, you can vary the activity by having them pick up the shapes and give them to each other. Or, you can extend this activity to a string of directions whereby students listen to your commands and draw the shapes on a piece of paper. For example: "Draw a star in the upper right-hand corner, draw a triangle in the middle," and so on. Next, have them circle, underline, check, or cross out the items they put on the paper. Then, show students a model of your instructions, repeating what you said so they can check their papers to see if they followed the instructions correctly. In this way, students are learning listening skills without having to respond verbally. They are also learning to follow a sequence of directions with vocabulary they will be expected to know.

You can use these types of modifications in the content areas, such as in science and math, to help students learn to follow instructions or master basic vocabulary. Have your native English-speaking students model the appropriate actions. Pair a newcomer with a native-English speaker when following maps or a procedure in science.

Games

Use games to review content-area knowledge with students as well as to promote listening and speaking skills. Games are very useful for encouraging student participation and, ultimately, language growth. Students' inhibitions are lowered when they're having fun. Best of all, with games, the focus is on the activity, not on language structure. Here are some easily adaptable games to play with students:

- **Bingo.** If it is played with words instead of numbers, bingo is appropriate for all levels and classes, since you can target any important vocabulary that students need to learn. Record target vocabulary for students to see on the board or on a piece of chart paper. Have each student choose which of the target vocabulary to list on a prepared blank grid, much like a bingo card. Note that there should be several more words to choose from in the target vocabulary list than there are available spaces on the grid; each student chooses his or her own words, so that all students have a different combination of words on their grid. Also, record each of the target vocabulary words on a separate slip of paper, and place the words into a bag. Give students bingo chips or something similar (kidney beans or even small slips of paper also work). Have one student pull out one word from the bag at a time, and read it aloud. Have the rest of the students use the bingo chips (or other) to cover the words on their grids. Decide ahead of time whether players need to cover one line of words or their full grid in order to call out, "bingo!" If you choose one line only, it's not necessary to have more words to choose from in the target vocabulary list than there are available spaces on the grid, as students' word choices will be in different orders, and they won't all get bingo at the same time.

- **Go Fish.** This game is good for reviewing content vocabulary by having students match pictures to new vocabulary or simply by having students supply the vocabulary words from memory when shown the pictures. You can make the game cards out of index cards. If you do not have the time, have an aide, a native-English speaker, or even an ELL student make the cards. You can use this game as an icebreaker for new students; along with the vocabulary, students can learn each other's names in a relaxed setting.

- **Categories.** For this game, have students write a word that is relevant to a particular category (topic) across the top or down the side of a sheet of paper. Then, have them list words related to the topic that begin with each of the letters in the word(s) listed across the top or side. For example, a lesson in nutrition could require students to think of food words beginning with each of the letters in the words *good health*, as in figure 7.2.

  This activity is a lot of fun when done as a group. It can last as long as students can think of words to fit into each column or row. The exercise works best when the category topic is a very general one, and the word or words listed across the top or side of the page has a variety of letters.

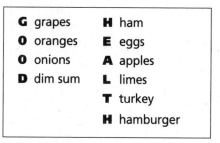

G grapes	**H** ham
O oranges	**E** eggs
O onions	**A** apples
D dim sum	**L** limes
	T turkey
	H hamburger

Figure 7.2 "Good Health" was the category topic used for this word game.

- **Hangman or Password.** Always favorites with students, these are both good games for vocabulary review and also to help reinforce spelling. You can use either simple or difficult words to play these games.

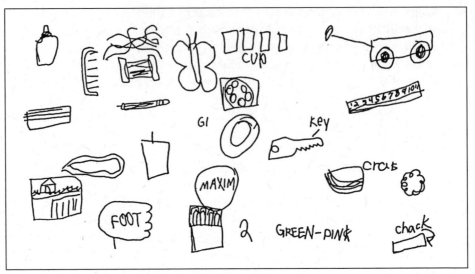

Figure 7.3 This student drew these objects from memory and labeled items he knew the words for.

- **Memory.** For about two minutes, show the class a detailed picture of a place or an event, or a tray filled with items. After students have studied the picture or tray, remove or cover it, and ask questions about the contents to see how much they remember. (How many cats were in the picture? What color was the one by the door? What was next to the spool of thread? How many crayons were on the tray?) Or, have students draw the objects, labeling them when they know the words (figure 7.3).

More Talking Activities

Other talking-based activities to help you review content-area knowledge with students and to promote listening and speaking skills include

- **Interviews.** Make a list of about 20 statements. Draw a line in front of each statement. For example:

  _____ has been to Disneyland.

  _____ wears glasses.

  _____ has a sister.

Have students interview each other to find out whose name(s) is/are appropriate for each blank. Set a time limit for this activity. Students enjoy finding things out about each other and have an opportunity to use English in the process.

- **Silent Films.** With silent films, students do not need to struggle with language to understand what is going on; this is a purely visual experience. After viewing a film, have students respond to questions about it. If showing an action film, stop the projector at a critical turning point in the plot, and ask students to suggest their own preferred endings, orally and/

or in writing. You can do this activity with beginning, intermediate, or advanced students.

- **Tongue Twisters.** Students enjoy tackling the old favorites such as "She sells seashells by the seashore," "Peter Piper picked a peck of pickled peppers," "How much wood would a woodchuck chuck if a woodchuck could chuck wood?" or "Rubber baby buggy bumpers." You can target minimal pair issues quite effectively with tongue twisters.

- **Drama.** Again, we feel that drama is central to any curriculum, whether it be primary, secondary, or adult. One of the strongest contributions that drama can make to the education of your English language learners is in oral language proficiency. Good communication skills are essential in today's workplace, and therefore more attention is being given to the mastery of fluency and clarity as well as sensitivity (Zhang 1995). Participating in dramatic exercises can give students opportunities to practice in each of these areas.

  Barb, always up for the spontaneity and laughter that drama brings, uses it often. She throws out scenarios such as "You want to get a job after school. Convince your family," or, "Your neighbors have complained about the noise in your apartment. Go apologize to them," with hilarious results. No one knows what will happen or what will come out of peoples' mouths. Often personas emerge miraculously. Abdi became infamous for being a tough, unsympathetic boss or manager. Juan declared himself a police officer in one impromptu skit, and thereafter, Officer Juan was called upon again and again to mediate in disagreements or loom over disgruntled tenants or customers.

  The facets of oral language facility that drama encourages are

- Spontaneous speaking

- Basic listening skills

- Understanding paralinguistic elements such as pitch, stress, and juncture

- Vocabulary development

The beauty of drama is that the vocabulary, the discussion, and the listening are embedded within a real context. The learner is engaged in accomplishing a task as well as solving a problem, such as "Where do I stand?" "How should I move across the stage?" "How do I say this sentence to give the desired effect?" Students must attend to what is going on in order to say or do whatever comes next.

For days before the production of *Lon Po Po,* Eve could be heard practicing, "Be sure and lock the door, and do not open it while we are gone," while shaking her forefinger in warning. Tommy labored over the word *unfortunately.* And even as the cast was assembling onstage, Jim was whispering, "How do you say this?" while pointing at words such as *bought* and *built.* He wanted to make sure he had them right. The necessity and desire for clarity and correctness was unmistakable.

Conclusion

The major assumptions we operate under concerning speaking and listening are:

- Learners acquire language in an environment that is full of talk that invites response.

- Students will speak when they are ready.

- Fluency precedes accuracy.

- An acceptance of all attempts, whether correct or incorrect, will promote confidence.

Provide opportunities for your students to develop these skills. Present lessons consisting of content that is meaningful, while asking questions appropriate for your students' levels in an atmosphere that encourages them to take risks. The interaction you encourage allows for language experimentation and, ultimately, leads to language acquisition.

Reflections, Projects, and Projections for Discussion

- Were you a front-row person in school and in college or a backbencher? Why? What prompted you to be a part of discussions or to sit on the sidelines and listen?

- Think of teachers you have known who were successful at getting all students to talk. How did they do it? How could you change the dynamic in a classroom so that all students feel free to add their input?

- If you have had any experience learning a second language, are there any sounds that you found difficult to pronounce? How hard did you work at perfecting that sound, or didn't you care?

- How good are you at listening through for the meaning in what second language learners say, or do you get tired and give up?

- Have you ever been embarrassed or humiliated in front of a class for some mistake you made, or have you observed this happen to someone else? How and why did it happen? What did the teacher do to repair the situation, or did they cause or exacerbate it?

- Newton is so shy he never speaks. It's hard to tell what he knows. Think of ways to interact with him or with an NEP (Non-English proficient) student such as Bao.

- If Bao refuses to speak and she has been classified as a level 1, preliterate student, what ways could you find to assess what she knows?

- What technology can you access to support a student in your class who has minimal speaking skills?

- Which students in your class could you use as buddies to help support students with minimal speaking skills?

- What techniques can you implement to support an NEP/LEP (limited-English proficient) student?

Case Studies: Chung, Beverly, and Angel

Chung

Chung is from Korea. Although his grammar is very precise—he knows the rules better than most teachers—and he is holding his own academically in the classroom, his pronunciation is abysmal. The other teachers refuse to try to understand him, giving up as soon as he opens his mouth, and continue to insist on correct pronunciation, which is very embarrassing for Chung. He can't hear the difference between certain sounds. The sounds /f/ and /v/ do not exist in Korean, so he says things like "pinally," for *finally*, and "berry" for *very*.

How could you help him? Should you concentrate on the sounds he finds challenging? What are the priorities for him? If you decided that you should work on pronunciation, what exercises would you choose? What do you do about the other teachers?

Beverly

Beverly has been here for one year. She understands much of what she hears in class, and reads and writes at a much higher level than you would think, because she is very reluctant to participate in any way in classroom dialogue. She is also very cautious about making mistakes in front of the class and when she is in a group. She simply will not try if there are any risks. When you observe her in a one-on-one with another English-speaking student, you can see she understands what the other student is saying, but she takes a long time to respond, because she is always looking for the exact word.

- Where can you start with Beverly?

- How can you give her the confidence to talk?

- What sorts of situations would you provide for Beverly so that she can feel comfortable speaking?

Angel

Angel is Beverly's best friend. When the two of them are allowed to sit next to each other, they speak Chinese to each other. Angel is extremely shy and will not attempt to speak English at all. She uses Beverly as the buffer between her and the rest of the world. This is beginning to present several problems. The first is that, with Beverly translating for her, Angel's exposure, need to understand, and opportunities to practice English are being limited. It also is becoming a problem for Beverly, because she seems to want to make friends with some of the other students, but she feels obligated to be with Angel.

At first, Angel would not answer any questions on her own, even questions like "What is your name?" or "How old are you?" Now, even though you are sure her receptive English is improving, she has grown totally dependent on others, particularly Beverly, for help. If you ask her questions, the other students tend to prompt her and whisper loudly, so she hears them. After long, uncomfortable silences, she will put her hand up in front of her mouth and whisper the answer everyone is telling her to say. Then she'll say, "No, no, no," as if she's made a mistake and wants to erase all those words. Sometimes you only know she's speaking because you can see her lips moving.

- Should you separate Beverly and Angel?

- How can you help Angel become comfortable enough to speak, or is it better just to leave her alone?

- What steps can you take to shut up the other students so they don't constantly fill in for her?

- How long should you allow Beverly to speak in Chinese with Angel, or do you think it's a good idea just to let them keep on with it? What will you base your decision on?

- Are there any ways you can give Angel opportunities to practice speaking in English that will not exacerbate her shyness?

Chapter 8

Content-Area Instruction—
The Impotance of Science

In this chapter, we discuss some of the problems ELL students face in content-area classes and, through the experiences of two teachers, show how they

- Approach curriculum, standards, and benchmarks

- Develop overall learning plans

- Present lessons in an organized, comprehensible way

Kelly Sturm, a science teacher, was faced with teaching the concept of simple machines to a class of sixth, seventh, and eighth graders who had minimal English and literacy skills. Written materials consisted of definitions such as the following:

"Lever: There are three basic types of levers, depending on where the effort is applied, on the position of the load, and on the position of the fulcrum..."

This material was too difficult for Kelly's students to read on their own and took a great deal of explaining. The school provided realia in the form of packages of plastic gears. The students were led through a series of exercises: Put gear *A* in the slot. Place gear *B* so that it interlocks with gear *A*. Predict what will happen when you turn gear *A*. Put gear *C*... Boring! The students were learning little more than that if they turned gear *A* as fast as possible it would fly through the air and clatter loudly as it hit the floor. Or, worse—they may have been learning to hate science. The hours Kelly spent making overheads to explain the various machines seemed an exercise in futility.

Sandy Maxwell's class of fourth and fifth graders had 28 students, only four of whom were native-English speakers. The proficiency level of the second-language students ranged from no English at all to fluent, but reading several years below grade level. The social studies and science curriculum for these grades included units on Wisconsin and climate. For the latter, Sandy had skipped the lesson on heat the previous year; concepts such as *therms* seemed to be beyond the range of the students' abilities and her ability to get the ideas across. Even the general introduction seemed too technical:

> *Heat is a form of energy. Atoms and molecules, the tiny particles that make up everything that exists, are constantly moving, and the amount of heat within any substance depends on how much and how fast its atoms move. When more heat energy is given to something its temperature rises, it expands, and it may change from a solid to a liquid or from a liquid to a gas. Heat can be transferred from one place to another in three ways, conduction, convection, or radiation, but it can only move from a hotter area to one that has a lower temperature.*

At the same time, Sandy recalled what a struggle it was every year to get winter clothes for many of the poorer children; parents from subtropical or tropical countries simply did not understand the dangers of frostbite and hypothermia. Winters are particularly severe in Wisconsin, and one year school did not close until the temperature reached –35°F. Despite repeated warnings, working parents were often forced to drop their children off at school, sometimes an hour before classes started. Sandy decided that a lesson on heat was a priority.

The type of situation each of these two teachers found themselves in has become increasingly common in North American schools. In a class of 25, many teachers—particularly those in inner-city, urban classrooms—have seven or more ELL students. As more and more non-English speakers flood the border states and provinces, just as many are moving away from these port-of-entry points into the midlands and heartlands. This means that more and more mainstream teachers are teaching curriculum content to ELL students.

Content-area learning begins in earnest in the upper-elementary grades. In the lower grades science is often embedded in thematic units, but it becomes increasingly compartmentalized as students get older. From about the fourth grade onward, students are no longer only learning to read; they are reading to learn. This means they must have the requisite fluency and skills in reading and the background knowledge required to gather information from a text.

Research has shown more and more clearly just how important that academic knowledge is. In fact, Scarcella (2003) asserts, "Learning academic English is probably one of the surest, most reliable ways of attaining socioeconomic success...today. Learners cannot function in school settings effectively without it." She goes on to note that many teachers don't even know what academic English is, and therefore do not stress its importance.

Because many of our non-English-speaking students come to us with poor reading skills and many gaps in the kind of background knowledge and language that we take for granted with our college-bound, mainstream students, these requirements pose special problems for teachers of the upper-elementary grades. The problems are even more acute for those junior high and high school teachers who specialize in one subject. Having this background knowledge allows

---

Mai is failing art. She is uncoordinated, cannot hold a pencil correctly, and needs total structure. Her teacher resists modifying the class expectations for her, because "art is supposed to be creative!" How would you intercede, and what can you do to help Mai pass?

students access to the people, the experiences, and the ways of functioning in distinct domains that they otherwise would not have access to. The lack of this language and knowledge can relegate smart, promising, and ambitious ELL students from achieving their goals of higher education and advancement in the professions.

In the past several decades, teaching English to ELL students has shifted from treating it as a subject, to teaching English *through* other subjects. This is an about-face from when students had to learn the English language first; only when they had enough oral proficiency could they begin learning content in earnest.

One supervisor recently visited the high-school English classroom of one of her student teachers. Khae, a Southeast Asian student, sat in the back of the room. Khae was not given anything to do and did not participate in classroom activities. The supervisor asked why he was not included. The student teacher replied that she had been told by the school counselor not to worry about trying to include Khae until he had learned English. (How this was supposed to happen had nothing to do with her!)

Imagine Khae's progress. He is allowed a year of oral development: listening, speaking, working on his language competence. If all goes well, within that year he might learn to speak fairly well, be able to communicate his needs, relate to his friends, and produce a passable English sentence. Along the way, he might begin to read and may even be able to write a few sentences. He might be promoted to the next grade.

In the meantime, his classmates are reading and writing at grade level, taking the content classes such as history, geography, math, and science required for graduation from high school. As the years go by, Khae will be left further and further behind. The gap in background knowledge will become wider; study skills will not be learned. The lag is cumulative: success breeds success, but failure breeds failure.

Integrating Language and Content

The above scenario does not have to happen. Research has shown that students can learn content and language at the same time. In fact, we know that integrating language and content—learning the content material and the language needed to understand the content at the same time—is more effective than simply learning language and only then trying to learn content (Short 1991; Crandall 1995). There are several important reasons for this:

- Integrated instruction brings both cognitive development and language.

- Content provides real meaning, not just structures of language that are abstractions and may seem to be of little value to the learner. "Rather than introducing a series of isolated units, language instruction is most effective if it teaches language that provides access to subject matter texts, discussions, and class activities" (Echevarria 1998).

- When students learn subject and language together they are more motivated because the content is interesting and valuable to them.

- The language used in school is different from the language used outside the classroom. James Cummins (1981) distinguishes between basic interpersonal communication skills (BICS) and cognitive academic language proficiency (CALP). Within a year or two, a student might have mastered the BICS. He might be a competent speaker, have friends, and be able to carry on conversations in English. But, while these interpersonal communication skills are important, they are not enough to succeed in school. They do not carry over into the content areas where other kinds of language demands are made, for a couple of reasons:

  - Basic interpersonal communication skills are inadequate to attain the higher-level skills of problem solving, inferring, analyzing, synthesizing, and predicting—skills required for academic success in the content areas.

  - Conversations are embedded in meaningful context. Students can pick up clues (body language, gestures, facial expressions) to gain meaning. They can also ask for clarification if they don't understand. But academic language is usually "context reduced"; a student is often asked to obtain information by reading texts that have few pictures to help guide comprehension. Cummins suggests that these cognitive academic skills (CALP) require five to seven years to acquire.

The distinction between BICS and CALP is a dichotomy that many researchers of academic language (Scarcella 2003, Wiley 1996) reject as being too simplistic, because many students acquire academic language early, and some kids never acquire the basic interpersonal skills that allow them to read the subtle nuances of the language. In addition, this dichotomy can also lead teachers to think that learning academic English can be delayed until their students have acquired BICS. This is a big mistake. Many students come out of ELL or bilingual programs with good oral skills, but have either undeveloped academic language skills or need help transferring to English the content knowledge they have acquired using their native languages.

Potential Problems With Academic Language for ELLs

The academic language of content-area classes can pose many problems for ELL students. Knowing what these problems are will assist you in helping your students bridge the gap between their first language and the linguistic demands of the lesson.

The core content areas are built around certain concepts and essential vocabulary. Students often can't understand lessons without knowing this vocabulary. Bobbi Jo Moore, for example was teaching a sixth-grade science unit on matter. Her students had heard the word *matter* before, in sentences such as "What's the *matter* with you?" and "It *matters* to me." Introducing the concept of *matter* was difficult, especially the idea that air can take up space and have mass.

Students in content-area classes are likely to have problems in the following areas: vocabulary, syntax, differing systems and thought processes, and pragmatics.

Problems With Vocabulary

- Each subject has its own particular set of terms that students may not yet have learned, such as *synthesis, microorganism, abolitionist, impeach, coefficient, addend.*

- Many words used in everyday language have a specialized meaning within specific content areas, such as *product* or *square* in math, *kingdom* and *energy* in science, or *primary* and *inflation* in social studies.

- Many words are abstract and can't be explained simply, such as *democracy, justice.*

Problems With Syntax

Textbooks commonly use the passive voice, reversing the normal word order, a form students come to understand and use only later on in their acquisition of English. For example, "This polarization is reinforced by the mass of contradictory evidence that seems to lend support to both sides." (Many native-English speakers will have trouble with that one!)

Texts often use complex sentences whose meanings hinge on transition words like *because, nevertheless, consequently* or *although,* which students may not understand or notice. For example, "Both the Puritans and the Pilgrims left England because they felt the Anglican Church should become more like the Catholic Church," or "Although her business was unfinished, she left."

Problems With Differing Systems and Thought Processes

Haynes (<everythingESL.net>) points out that math is often a big challenge for ELLs, because they may use different recording systems than we do. They may use commas instead of decimal points. They may form their numbers differently. They may be accustomed to simple rote memorization and not used to reaching their own conclusions or forming their own opinions, much less expressing them.

Students may also be used to the metric system. Ricardo confessed that he finds the idea of feet and miles baffling: "It's so much easier to work in metric, because *kilo* always means a thousand, and *centi* always means one hundred." Students find that certainty comforting as well as easier to work with.

Long is in fourth grade and is a level 2 in English proficiency. She does not know her multiplication facts or the division process. After going over the process three times and working through problems together, no light goes on. What now?

Loua is working on long division. Although he knows his multiplication facts, he doesn't know that you need to multiply the first number by each digit—he ends up with only one or two rows of numbers, not three if he's multiplying by three digits. How would you explain the right way if his English is very limited?

Problems With Pragmatics

Pragmatics involve the larger units of discourse beyond the word, phrase, and sentence level, such as the text itself and your lectures. Students may encounter the following challenges in this area:

- They may not have enough English proficiency to understand the textbook or your lectures.

- They may not know how to read difficult material for various purposes or have strong enough study skills to extract information from their textbook or reference materials. Many times they read narratives the same way they read expository prose or editorials—as if they were facts.

- They may not have the general knowledge we assume with our North American students. For example, they may not understand the concept of *democracy* or the meaning of *ecosystem*; or, they may be unfamiliar with animals such as mountain lions and armadillos; or, they may not have learned of the Challenger space shuttle.

> John, a level 3 in English proficiency, is struggling with social studies. The topic is latitude and longitude and its effect on temperature and the effect of Gulf Stream waters on a city's temperature. How would you explain these ideas to John? What strategies would you use? What materials would you need?

- The text may be structured in ways they are unfamiliar with.

- They may not be familiar with tasks such as "drawing conclusions, analyzing characters, and predicting outcomes" (Haynes).

- The directions are often "multistep and difficult" (Haynes).

- They may not understand the idea of scientific inquiry or how to go about it.

- They may think that the use of manipulatives is babyish and an invitation to play or goof off, because they don't take it seriously.

Bridging the Gap

Bobbi Jo Moore, an ELL teacher (as well as a student), wrote in her journal:

> *If there is one thing I learned while agonizing over this unit and discussing it in class, it is that I need to set up more of a bridge from where the kids are to where I want them to be. As of now, I am standing on the other side of this huge chasm yelling, "JUMP!" hoping they are strong enough to make it.*

A typical period in a traditional content-area classroom consists of a lecture, discussion of the assigned textbook readings with students, and then tests based on these lectures and readings. Until they achieve full proficiency in English for academic purposes, ELL students simply cannot succeed in such circumstances. In order to succeed in the content areas, ELL students need

- Clearly defined goals

- Comprehensible input
- To be engaged as learners and as investigators

Your Goals

Your overall goals for teaching are

- To help your students learn English. This means helping them "to use English to achieve academically" in content areas (TESOL 1997). They need to learn the specialized vocabulary of your particular discipline and have the opportunity to learn such skills as explaining, informing, describing, classifying, and evaluating.
- To teach your content area
- To teach the higher-level thinking skills
- To teach the procedures and systems unique to your field
- To promote literacy. No longer is teaching reading and writing solely the job of the English teacher. These teaching skills belong in every classroom where students need help understanding lectures, making presentations, reading for information, and writing reports.

Standards and Benchmarks

With mandated standards and benchmarks in most content areas, skills and bodies of knowledge have been laid out in detail. How to operationalize these standards and benchmarks for students who have not mastered the language and may have huge gaps in their learning is a unique and complex challenge. Yet, the standards and benchmarks are an advantage to ELL teachers—we can set up opportunities for students to learn *by doing* rather than by listening to lectures and retrieving facts.

As states implement standards and benchmarks, teachers must begin to consider what these mean for ELL students. Standards are "broad curricular goals, while benchmarks are specific knowledge and skills identified at grade levels or grade ranges. They are the 'what' we are seeking to impart to our students" (Sargent and Smejkal 2000).

For example, for sixth-grade physical science Kelly Sturm was teaching toward the following four standards for science in Wisconsin:

- Standard 1: Understands the nature of scientific inquiry
- Standard 2: Understands the interaction of science, technology, and society
- Standard 3: Understands personal and social perspectives of science
- Standard 4: Understands the history of science, people, and technology

Given what we know about the nature of inquiry and our beliefs about how students learn best, simply manipulating gears was pointless for students without reference to the "why's" and the "what's." Kelly searched for a new approach—which we illustrate in a few pages.

What to Do

The big challenge is to make the content-area lessons comprehensible while meeting the needs of both your mainstream students and your ELL students—challenging the native-English speakers while making content meaningful and accessible to the English language learners. At the same time, you need to align your teaching to the standards and benchmarks set for your particular grade level.

The following strategies will help your ELL students and, at the same time, enrich learning for your mainstream students. Strategies to make content easier for ELL students often achieve the same result with *all* students. Again, good teaching is good teaching, and good teaching techniques are especially important for teachers of ELL students.

You can embed content within meaningful context by involving all four language arts skills—reading, writing, listening, and speaking—in active ways. Strategies include grouping, modifying textbooks, and setting priorities.

Before You Teach

When you're faced with ELL students and hardly know where to begin, it's easy to get bogged down in the day-to-day problems and lose sight of the overall picture. Here are some steps to help you manage:

- **Assume nothing.** Don't assume they understand abstract concepts such as free will, processes such as how to conduct a science experiment, or strategies such as how to determine what's important or not important in lectures, discussions, or textbooks. Don't assume that they understand cross-academic terms such as *compare and contrast, interpret, suggest, define, analyze.* Don't assume they know the vocabulary of your field, even if they are advanced learners.

- **Choose a topic of study.** This may or may not be chosen for you. Some teachers have more leeway than others in specifying the topics they are going to focus on. When making your choices some issues you may wish to consider include:

  - Importance in the curriculum. Is this topic so esoteric or so abstract that no matter what you do, your ELL students aren't going to get it? If it's not absolutely central to the curriculum, you might want to discard it.

  - Is the concept big enough? According to Wiggins and McTighe (1998) there are four criteria to determine whether a concept is worth studying in any depth:

    1. Is it enduring, in other words, will it add value and meaning to your students' lives?

    2. Is it at the heart of the discipline, or on the periphery?

    3. Does it need "uncoverage," that is, exploration in any depth?

    4. Is it potentially engaging? Will your students be actively involved?

For instance, in the book *American Journey: The Quest for Liberty to 1877* author James Davidson includes, in the table of contents:

- "Unit One: The Americas: Geography of the Americas; The First Americans, European Exploration.
- Unit Two: The Colonies Take Root: Colonizing the Americas; The 13 English Colonies; Colonial Life."

Knowing these ideas is undoubtedly important in an overall understanding of the nation's history. Whether your students can handle them at the level they have attained is another question altogether. You need to carefully select what they can understand in any depth.

- Possibilities for extension into other areas of the curriculum. Not every topic has to be theme based and include math, history, social studies, and so on, but if you can bring in other areas and make connections, so much the better.

- Richness. The possibilities inherent for language use and learning that extends beyond the narrow topic itself.

- Latitudes for "ups and downs." Can the lesson be tweaked so that all levels of learners in the class gain something from the lesson and succeed? Can the assignments be adapted so that each student is working to his or her linguistic and intellectual capacity?

- **Develop a plan.** If you have established an overall plan for the course, as we suggested in chapter 1, you are way ahead of the game. You have goals and learning targets for your students, competencies they must develop to succeed, and themes to build the course around so that with each successive spiral, the students better understand the material. Now, you can go on and work out the fine points of your particular subject matter.

  When looking at the standards and benchmarks, it's easy to think you have to abandon everything you have taught. Don't. That's throwing the baby out with the bathwater. Sargent and Smejkal (2000) caution that "vital connections are lost when benchmarks are taught in isolation. Students end up possessing isolated skills, without the larger concepts and skills to apply them...For students to construct meaning, the benchmarks must 'fit' together in a way that makes sense to them." Much of what you did before naturally fits under these standards and benchmarks. Don't think that all those years of training and teaching were lost and you have to start over.

- **Analyze the textbook.** You may or may not use one. For many classes a textbook is the main resource for classroom learning, and reading this book is integral to understanding the content of the course. But what you expect when you say, "Read the following pages for tomorrow's class" and what your students actually do are often very different. For this reason we discuss the use of textbooks, including some strategies for modifying the text to meet the needs of your students.

For instance, the first paragraph in the book *History of the United States,* by Robert Field, (1993) begins, "An early scholar to think seriously about the origin of the Indians was Thomas Jefferson. The man who would become the third President of the United States had a consuming interest in all things far and near, past and present." This passage would prove difficult for many students because of the complexity of the sentences, the implied knowledge of Jefferson and his presidency, and the vocabulary such as "consuming interest."

We are not in any way suggesting that textbook publishers are at fault. They have, in the past several years, incorporated substantial use of literature, media tie-ins, and extension activities. Many of our students, however, simply do not have the skills to read this sort of text.

You can't take for granted that the students in your class have either adequate study skills or sufficient language proficiency to meet the objectives you have laid out for them. Many students, English speakers included, are poor readers and have poor study skills. Many texts assume that students are all reading at grade level, which often is not true of ELL students (or many others). They may take the book home, they may not; they may skim it with comprehension, or they may read every word and still not understand what they have read.

When reviewing a textbook, consider the following points:

- Does the subject matter covered match the priorities you have set? When you check this match, decide what to cover and what you will be able to gloss over. If a chapter or section doesn't fit into your scheme, skip it.

- Analyze the textbook from the ELL students' viewpoint. What problems might your students have? What concepts and vocabulary might be new and unfamiliar to them?

Textbooks presume a great deal of background knowledge. For instance, most North Americans know a lot of history. We may not know all the facts behind historical incidents, but most of us have a general idea of our history: we have watched countless westerns, mini-series, and dramas on television and in films, trudged through museums, and visited historical sites on field trips.

We cannot, however, presume ELL students have this background knowledge. Many students from other countries were extremely successful in school and have rich experiences to bring to the learning task. Others know of nothing outside their refugee camp or their village. Knowledge of their native country's role in world affairs may be nonexistent, much less their knowledge of American or Canadian history.

Marcus poses a problem for his ELL support teacher. When he has homework in his metal shop class, he has no problem; he pays attention to the material and can handle the answer sheet by himself. Not so with history or English; he can't focus and won't do the assignments without a lot of "hand-holding." What is his problem, and what steps can you take to help him improve?

But they *do* understand the concept of immigration and change. Many have firsthand knowledge of war, many are now experiencing cultural conflict and the challenge of adjusting to new technology and new ways to make a living. They all understand the concept of freedom. These are critical issues in their lives. You can capitalize on these things by using what they *do* know as a starting point.

Goals for your Students

Goals for your students consist of both language and content objectives. Decide what, specifically, they need to know. From this list of requirements, you will have a clear idea of what they have attained.

When teaching English-language learners, you need to support their language development, including essential vocabulary. "Vocabulary is critical for English language learners because we know that there is a strong relationship between vocabulary knowledge in English and academic achievement" (Echevarria 2000). Every subject has its own special content vocabulary. For example, the words *population, community, ecosystem, biosphere, tissue, cells* are fundamental vocabulary to science. This is vocabulary you cannot simplify easily and which must be specifically taught. Students need to know these words to read the text and to go on to more specialized or broader knowledge in that particular field. For instance, your language objectives may be that by the end of the lesson your students will be able to

- Understand the essential vocabulary for the unit (for example, *solid, liquid, gas, matter, mass, space*)
- Follow directions accurately in conducting experiments, such as
  - Tie string to the middle of a straw to make a hanging balance scale
  - Blow up two balloons, and tie a piece of string to each balloon
- Write the results of their findings:
  - What did they observe?
  - What does the experiment prove?
  - Was their hypothesis correct?
- Present findings orally

Content objectives are what students should know and be able to do at the end of the lesson. Kelly, for example, wanted her students to

- Practice observation and recording skills
- Demonstrate an understanding of the basic concepts of the unit (the simple machines and their functions, forms, and uses)

When You Teach

Provide Comprehensible Input

Help your English language learners to understand the content you teach by

- **Modifying your strategies for teaching.** In other chapters, we have discussed how to change your speech for English-language learners. Ditch the lecture format.

- **Actively involving learners.** This means providing as many hands-on materials and/or manipulatives for students as you can think of. Simply asking students to write the list of vocabulary words in their notebooks and looking up definitions for the words is not actively engaging them. Echevarria (2000) writes,

    Although all students benefit from guided practice, English language learners make more rapid progress in mastering content objectives when they are provided with multiple opportunities to practice with hands-on materials and/or manipulatives...Practicing by manipulating learning materials is what is important for ELLs, because it enables them to connect abstract concepts with concrete experiences.

    Nobody forgets the time they had to dissect a frog, a cat, a baby pig, or a cow's eye. Years after, we can still recall the excitement (or being grossed out yet captivated). We also will never forget Mr. So-and-So droning on for an entire semester about government—we don't remember the content, simply the drudgery.

- **Teaching vocabulary.** Scarcella (2003) maintains that it is not possible to "do" science, economics, or mathematics with only ordinary language. One must "do" discipline-specific work with academic and discipline-specific language.

- **Organizing the material into easily attainable and sequential steps.** You can organize your lesson in a structured way so that you can teach study skills at the same time as content. We demonstrate how in the next section.

- **Providing many opportunities for interaction.** This promotes language development and supports development of content knowledge, especially for language learners. If you do not have bilingual support teachers, there may be other students in the class who "get it" and who can explain concepts in the ELL student's native language. Set up group configurations and class projects that promote peer interaction and talk.

- **Giving students the chance to apply the knowledge they've gained.** This is the way they learn best: building, practicing, performing, and doing. Kids never forget the plays they put on, the store they owned in *SimCity*, the edifice they built with toothpicks or Popsicle sticks, or the boat they designed out of aluminum foil. Nanci Smith, a high school special education teacher, is a master at drawing students into the material. When she teaches the concept of *slope* for her algebra students, she uses PowerPoint to make it visual, but she adds a Total Physical Response component by having the students get up and sing Y=MX+B to the tune of "YMCA." The kids form the letters and the symbols with their hands. Everyone gets silly, but they learn the equation.

Expanding on the familiar "preview, view, and review" format, Chamot and O'Malley (1986), who developed the Cognitive Academic Language Learning

Approach, suggest teachers take the following five steps in teaching any lesson:

1. Prepare
2. Present
3. Practice
4. Evaluate
5. Expand

We suggest that you follow the same procedure for each segment or unit of any discipline you are teaching.

We demonstrate these five steps by returning to Kelly Sturm's lesson on simple machines. Kelly knew she had to give up on the prepackaged gears lesson and start over. While keeping the five steps in mind, she focused on the following benchmarks for standards 1 to 4:

- Identifies questions that can be answered through scientific investigations

- Designs and conducts a scientific investigation

- Uses appropriate tools and techniques to gather, analyze, and interpret data

- Develops descriptions, explanations, predictions, and models using evidence

- Thinks critically and logically

- Designs a solution or product

- Implements a proposed design

- Knows the potential for accidents and the existence of hazards

- Knows that scientists use observations, experiments, and theoretical and mathematical models to formulate and test their explanations of nature

1. Prepare

What Kelly did first to prepare her students is what Bybee (1997) terms "engage" them. We are particularly attracted to this term, because it embodies the idea that students (particularly middle-schoolers) need to be engaged and interested in a topic before they learn it. To engage her students Kelly showed the first long, marvelous scene from Charlie Chaplin's *Modern Times* (1936): his day in the factory. The kids were so enchanted with the movie they talked the substitute teacher (Kelly happened to be away the day of viewing) into showing it three times. Since *Modern Times* has the barest minimum of words, they could understand everything. They talked nonstop about the movie when Kelly returned, a total about-face from the silent, disengaged class who had woodenly put gears together.

2. Present

Kelly gave a quick overview of the simple machines—wheel and axle, pulley, screw, inclined plane, wedge, and lever—to show students what they were and how they worked. She defined their functions and taught the vocabulary that was necessary to understand the unit. The students' job, on the next viewing of *Modern Times,* was to identify as many simple machines as they could in the movie.

The next step was to have the students look around their environment. The class took a tour of the school. They went down to the boiler room and up and down halls looking for simple machines. It was hilarious to hear someone shout, "Look! A wedge!" as if he had discovered gold. To reinforce the concepts, students were judiciously divided into groups (more proficient students with less proficient ones, calmer students among the more rowdy) with each group in charge of finding as many examples of their simple machine as possible—one group looked for wedges, one for pulleys, and so on. Students were given a worksheet to complete to keep them on task and responsible for recording what they saw, as well as to promote reading, writing, and oral skills (figure 8.1).

Homework consisted of going home and finding, in their own environment, as many examples as possible of the seven machines.

3. Practice

In the same groups, the students were given the task of inventing their own mini-carnival ride using at least three simple machines. Kelly brought in scraps of wood, metal, cloth, string, and so on. She priced the different materials so that the "contractors" had to budget their money and buy their supplies. The "contract" students had to fulfill is shown in figure 8.2.

4. Evaluate

In this case, Kelly's baseline evaluation was simple: Did the ride work? She added specific criteria on how to judge the rides. She also gave the students responsibility for evaluation by having them judge both the other groups' rides and their own rides (figure 8.3).

The key component of the final evaluation was having a Polly Pocket doll ride in the machine. If "the baby died" (in other words, flew out of the ride and landed on its head), the ride was not safe. During this evaluation, one student, Kong, tested the performance of each ride. After placing the doll in the seat, Kong would shout, "Hey, man, see if she flies out!" There were several occasions where the "baby" soared across the room, and the students had to rethink not only how to keep her in her seat, but also how to keep the seat from spinning so fast that she was inclined to fly out in the first place.

5. Expand

The class went to the carnival and rode all the rides. Nobody flew out.

The unit was a resounding success on several levels. Not only did Kelly set up a situation in which the students were deeply engaged in what they were doing, it was a rich situation: rich with talk, inquiry, and the need to understand, in a very real way, the principles they were talking about. The concepts and vocabulary were embedded within the situation and were learned by carrying out the assignments. In addition, less-proficient students could use what skills they had in their own language and culture in the project. One student in particular, whose English proficiency was very low, was extremely gifted in math. Yang could visualize what needed to be done and implement tasks in ways other students couldn't. He brought in a motor and battery from a remote control car. Kelly watched as he hooked it up to his ride, made a few adjustments, and turned it on. It worked! When asked how he knew to do this, Yang replied, "I just, you know, experiment with stuff."

We can see how Kelly prepared for and achieved her goals in a natural way. She gave her students a problem—build a ride—that could be answered through scientific investigation. Only through careful planning and trial and error could the students build a ride that worked and was safe and structurally sound.

Simple Machines

Date: _____

Names: _____ _____ _____

1. In your group, brainstorm where in the school you might find the simple machines we have been studying. What form will they take?

   _____

   _____

   _____

2. Take a tour around the school. You must find three examples of each.

Pulley: _____ _____ _____

Lever: _____ _____ _____

Wheel and axle: _____ _____ _____

Screw: _____ _____ _____

Inclined plane: _____ _____ _____

3. Report back to the class.

What did you find? _____

_____

Where did you find it? _____

_____

What was it used for? _____

_____

_____

Figure 8.1 Worksheet for simple machines.

Building Contract

CONTRACTOR'S CURRENT JOB   Date: _____

Your job is to design a carnival ride.

The carnival ride must use at least three simple machines.

The ride must have a name. your team must agree on the name.

Each member of the team must be able to explain how the ride works.

PROPOSAL

This is what we are going to build: _____

_____

We will also provide a drawing of what the completed carnival ride will look like.
Here is a list of the parts we will need:

Part	Amount Needed	Price Per Part	Cost
Part 1:			
Part 2:			
Part 3:			

                                      Estimated Cost $ _____

PROPOSAL

Names of Building-Team Members:

1. _____

2. _____

3. _____

We will build_____
(name of carnival ride)

It will have these three simple machines: _____ ,

_____ , _____

Cost for labor and materials: $ _____

Upon completion:

Signatures: _____ , _____ , _____

Figure 8.2 Carnival-ride assignment student contract.

Carnival Ride Evaluation

Every member of the class will judge each ride. The rides will be evaluated based on the following categories: quality, creativity, safety, structural strength, fulfillment of the assignments, uses three simple machines, functioning of the ride, the ride's name, and whether each member of the constructing team can explain how the ride was made and what it does.

The rating scale will work like this:

3 = Wow! Great job!

2 = Pretty good!

1 = Needs improvement

0 = This step was not completed

DIRECTIONS: For Each category, circle the number you think best fits the carnival ride you are judging. Use the rating scale above.

Quality	3	2	1	0
Creativity	3	2	1	0
Safety	3	2	1	0
Functioning of the ride	3	2	1	0
Structural strength	3	2	1	0
Uses three simple machines	3	2	1	0
Fulfillment of the assignment	3	2	1	0
The ride's name	3	2	1	0
Each member can explain the ride	3	2	1	0

Figure 8.3 Assessment criteria for carnival rides.

On their own, the students

- Designed and conducted a scientific investigation
- Used appropriate tools and techniques to gather, analyze, and interpret data
- Developed descriptions, explanations, predictions, and models using evidence
- Thought critically and logically
- Designed a product
- Communicated their design plans and their evaluations based on established criteria

- Considered the hazards and potential dangers of poorly designed rides
- Tested out their theories in real ways

Meanwhile, Sandy Maxwell was searching for ways to make the concept of heat operational. As discussed earlier, the definition of *heat* was too difficult and complex for most of her students to understand. So, Sandy looked through several books about climate and temperature and settled on the following goals for her students to understand:

- What is heat?
- Why is it necessary?
- How do we measure it?
- How does it affect us? How do we notice it? How do we feel it?
- What are the consequences of heat (or lack of it)?
- How do we adapt to it (getting warm and keeping warm)?

Here is how Sandy used the five steps to teach her students about heat (climate), as well as to cover the unit on Wisconsin:

> During a social studies test Dayna answered quickly and finished about the same time as the English-speaking students did. She received a score of 5 out of 20. She explained that she did not know what the teacher was even asking, so she might as well guess and be done with it.
>
> What should the teacher have done before the test? What could he have done during the test? What should he do now?

1. Prepare

Whole-class preparation: Sandy began with a whole-class discussion about what it takes to survive in winter. Students made lists of the kinds of clothes they needed to wear when it's cold. Sandy read aloud from *On the Banks of Plum Creek,* from chapter 35 to the end: Pa, returning home from town, gets lost in the snow. He survives for several days, within sight of the house, on melted snow and Christmas candy.

Some of the less-proficient students did not quite understand the story, so the class did process drama, in which more-proficient students reenacted Pa's days in the snow.

Small-group background building: Sandy coordinated with the ELL teacher to work on background knowledge with the English language learners. The ELL teacher found books on the students' native countries; then the students looked at picture books, she read stories to them, and they discussed the kinds of houses they lived in and the kinds of clothes they wore. The beginner groups did language experience activities in which they drew pictures of their homes in their native countries and told about their lives there (figure 8.4).

Figure 8.4 Amparo's picture of her home.

2. Present

Whole group consideration and discussion: Students were asked to respond to the question, "If you were stuck in a blizzard for four days, what would you want to have along with you?" Sandy brought in props (matches, candy bars, water, blankets, coats, pillows, a map, a flashlight, a book, a cell phone, canned meat) so that students could see the items they had to choose from and select the ones they thought were the most important. In cooperative groups (carefully selected to include beginners surrounded by more proficient classmates), students listed five things they would want or need. The group had to decide unanimously and justify their choices. A good deal of rich discussion resulted.

3. Practice

Pair work: Pairs of students were assigned to monitor the weather across the nation, graphing the temperatures on a chart designed to show temperature ranges in different climates.

Individual work: Sandy had students become scientists, observing local weather daily. Students kept a daily record of

- Temperature changes
- What they saw and felt outside
- What changes they noticed
- How they adapted to the weather that day

The expectations for the assignment varied according to the proficiency and skill level of the individual student. For example, beginners were expected to complete frame sentences, such as:

The temperature is _____ today.

It is _____ degrees outside.

I am wearing _____, _____, and _____.

More proficient students were expected to write complete sentences. Native-English speakers were required to write at least a paragraph.

Large group work: The class took periodic tours around the school and school-yard, making predictions, such as which areas were likely to be warmest, which were likely to be coldest, what animal tracks they might find, and so on.

4. Evaluate

Large Group/Small Group/Individual: Sandy set up scientific experiments that led students to develop their own theories of heat, how it changes, and how it is transmitted (figure 8.5). She circulated constantly to evaluate how well the students could understand the concepts, based on what they wrote and did.

Continuing with the science theme, Sandy asked these questions: "Why is winter hard for animals?" "What are some of the ways animals deal with the hardships?" The class brainstormed a list of ways animals adapt. Each student chose an animal indigenous to Wisconsin and researched how it adapts to the cold, where it lives, and what it eats during winter. Students wrote reports and drew pictures of their animal in its habitat on a huge winter mural.

Sandy had many books on winter in her classroom. Her students used the books to learn facts about their chosen animals. Sandy also made available as many easy readers, picture books, and books in the ELL students' native languages as she could.

While students worked on their individual projects, she worked with small groups, reading to beginners, teaching specific skills, and rereading language-experience stories.

From there, Sandy branched out into social studies—she had her students study different climates. She found resources for hot, cold, and temperate regions.

5. Expand

The long unit on heat culminated in a beach party in the gym in mid-winter.

Sandy's units on Wisconsin and climate were successful for the following reasons:

- She decided beforehand what she wanted her students to know. By doing this, she eliminated a lot of the useless tangents we can find ourselves getting mired in. She was clear about her goals.

- She made the units relevant.

- She was flexible in her grouping strategies, assignments, and expectations based on the proficiency levels of her students. She balanced group work with independent work.

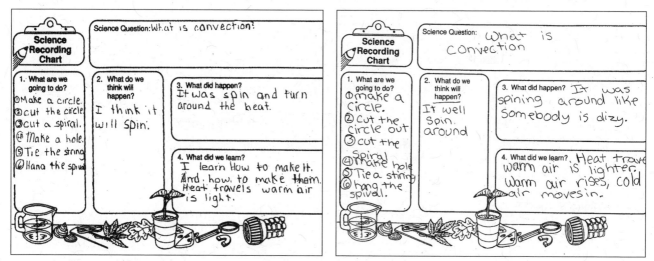

Figure 8.5 Two students record their experience with convection.

- Her focus for the lesson was to understand the concept of heat, not to memorize rote facts.

- She used a variety of materials.

- She varied her assessment of the students: students who were more proficient and verbal made oral presentations, others simply displayed their work.

- The students practiced and learned many of the procedures necessary for scientific inquiry by asking questions, conducting experiments, gathering data, and using this data to give explanations.

- Not least in importance, students learned the value of protecting themselves from the elements and adapting to the climate they now lived in.

Being Flexible

It is not necessary to always be as ambitious as Sandy and Kelly were. Sometimes we don't want or need to develop an entire lesson. Regardless, you have to ask yourself two basic questions:

1. What content do you want your students to learn?

2. What are the necessary vocabulary words students need to know?

For example, we taught ELL in a summer camp program in the mountains of California for several years. When we began planning for our first summer, we chose, as a main theme, the concept of stewardship for our environment and ourselves. When the students arrived, we realized this idea was too ambitious without interpreters and more complex than we had time to develop. We didn't carry through with this part of the curriculum the first year, but we didn't give up on the idea. It struck us how many of our students commented on how clean it was in the mountains and how fresh the air and the water were compared to the dirtiness and pollution in their own country (figure 8.6).

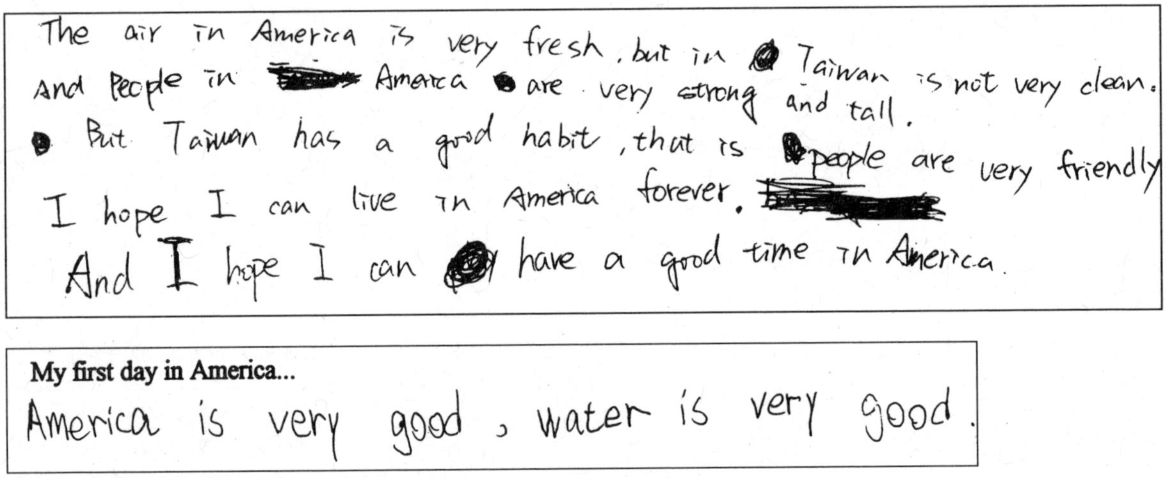

> The air in America is very fresh, but in Taiwan is not very clean. And People in America are very strong and tall. But Taiwan has a good habit, that is people are very friendly. I hope I can live in America forever. And I hope I can have a good time in America.

> My first day in America...
> America is very good, water is very good.

Figure 8.6 Taiwanese students commenting on the air and water in California.

Over the course of the next two summers, we built more science into the curriculum. After all, we reasoned, we were in the mountains, the kids were from the city, and this was probably one of the few chances they would have to camp in the wilds. We wanted to make the most of it. So, revisiting our idea of stewardship (and being more realistic), and keeping in mind that camp was supposed to be fun and lighthearted, we had our students focus on the following goals:

- To wonder
- To investigate their surroundings in a focused way
- To learn about nature by experiencing it
- To care about the environment

These were modest goals, but we were successful in reaching them. The students enjoyed themselves. They learned a great deal about habitats, about the animals that lived in that particular area, and the accompanying vocabulary. They had the chance to read, write, talk, and be out in the sunshine (figure 8.7a–c). We also made the most of an expressed interest of our students and channeled that interest in appropriate ways.

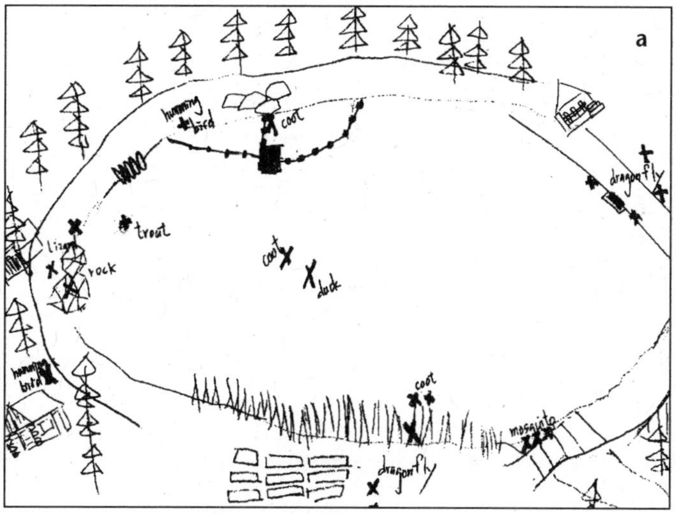

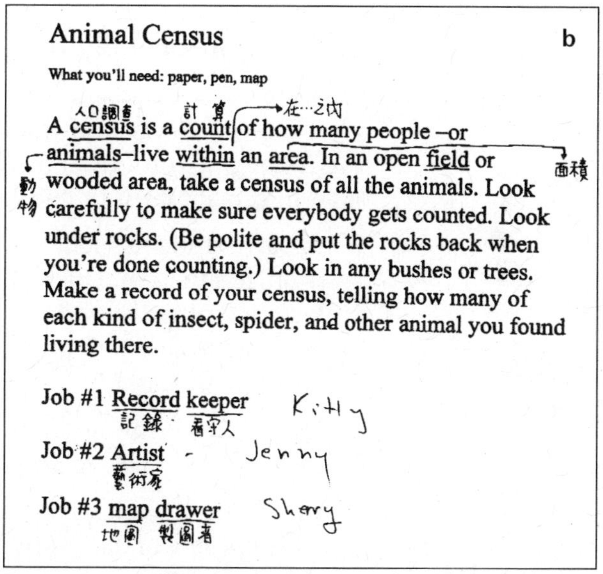
b

Animal Census

What you'll need: paper, pen, map

A census (人口調查) is a count (計算) of how many people –or animals (動物)–live within (在…之內) an area (面積). In an open field or wooded area, take a census of all the animals. Look carefully to make sure everybody gets counted. Look under rocks. (Be polite and put the rocks back when you're done counting.) Look in any bushes or trees. Make a record of your census, telling how many of each kind of insect, spider, and other animal you found living there.

Job #1 Record keeper (記錄 看守人) Kitty
Job #2 Artist (藝術家) Jenny
Job #3 map drawer (地圖 製圖者) Sherry

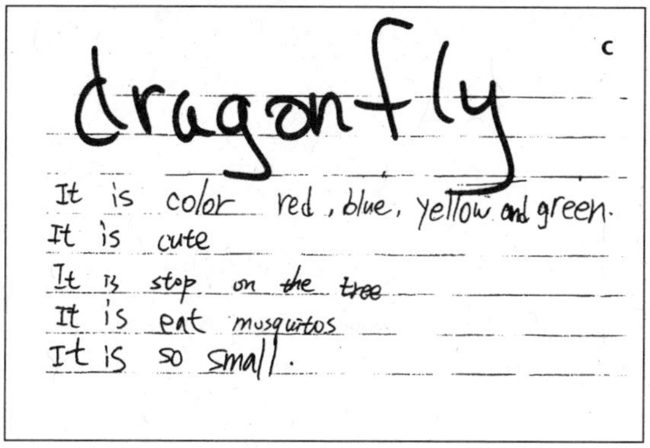

Figure 8.7 a–c We took the students on a hike around the lake to identify what lived there. The less-proficient learners drew maps and pictures of what they saw (a). The higher-functioning groups were handed the animal census paper (b) and were encouraged to read it and figure out the meaning themselves. As an extension, they wrote simple reports (c) and made 3-D representations of the animals in their habitat.

Each year we tried again: We looked at what we did, figuring out what worked and what didn't; we decided what our next step would be in making students conscious of their personal role in preserving natural habitats; and, keeping in mind our vision, we got closer to our goal.

We included this example to stress that it's okay to stumble, to fall a little short of the mark, to rethink strategies, and try again. It's also okay to go where the interests of the students themselves take you. And, not the least in importance, if your students are thinking and learning something, the time is not wasted. Whether what they learn is what you stated expressly in your goals is only part of the issue. You're adding to their understanding of the world, to their fund of knowledge. Don't beat yourself up about what you didn't accomplish. Analyze it, tweak it, and try again.

Testing for Mastery of Concepts

Testing is a tricky area. Sometimes students' inability to write in English makes it difficult to determine just how much they have learned. Or, they may not have enough English proficiency to understand the question, even though they may well understand the concept.

Checking Informally for Understanding

There are less stressful and more accurate methods of evaluating student progress than tests. Many of the tasks you set in the evaluation component of each lesson can give you a truer picture of what each student knows. Here are some other informal means of checking for students' understanding:

- Observe students' behavior while they work and interact with others in a practice situation. Does Saif participate, or does he sit back and let others take the initiative and do the work? Does Lupe make meaningful contributions? How often, and how many? Does Shinsuke look lost and bewildered by the task?

- Talk with students about their work. Discuss what they've done. Often students are better able to articulate their understanding verbally than in writing.

- Examine the work students have produced. Give credit for any input they have made, whether nonverbal or verbal.

Testing the ELL Student

If tests are an integral part of your course, here are some suggestions for making them easier for ELL students:

- Give the test orally. Arrange for a bilingual parent or aide to interpret.

- Simplify the language you use in the test. Unless you are testing vocabulary that is important to your field of study, avoid words you have not taught.

- Simplify the structures. Make the instructions easy to understand, and give straightforward commands, such as "Complete the following."

- Avoid complex sentences.

- Test only the specific skill or concept you have taught; don't test language. For example, here is eighth-grader Chantamala, in response to the test question, "Would you like to move to the New World? Why? Give reasons."

  New world my father like to go to the new world because you can do every-thing like the way that know. We can go at the jungle, and cuting the wood to make a house, hunting, killing, growing crop or other thing that you want-ed to do best for your life or family, then you can do everything that you want by your own.

It is easy to get lost or overwhelmed by the errors in an ELL student's paper. At first glance, Chantamala's composition might seem incoherent and disorganized, but the student has actually understood quite a bit of the discussion. The class had just studied the colonization of America. This student gives very specific reasons why the New World was better. Even with her garbled language, she has conveyed the message that people could do anything they wanted: build their own homes, cut wood, kill animals—rights denied in many Old World countries. She has understood that the New World offered freedom from the harsh, restricted life of common people in the Old World. If Chantamala were to be graded on her command of English, her many errors would count against her; however, she has learned some of the basic concepts and demonstrated her understanding of them.

Your criteria for grading might look like this:

- Did she understand the question?

- Did she answer the question?

- How well did she develop her thoughts?

- How thoroughly did she present her case?

- Is she performing to the best of her ability, given her stage of language competency, or is she just goofing off?

With these factors in mind, you can weigh this student's performance against that of other students in the class and give her a grade that is fair.

Be realistic and honest in your assessment. If your students accomplish less than the basic goals you have mapped out for them, don't give "pity grades." High school teacher Mary Delie stresses that it doesn't help students in the long run. They may pass the assignments and their grade level, but if they haven't mastered the content, they can't move on to the next level and succeed. It is better to assess students fairly and know up front where the gaps are.

When Mary Eckes received a certain ELL student at her high school, it was evident he had fallen through the cracks throughout his elementary and junior high years. Tomás was a kind, gentle boy, and while his spoken English was excellent, he had many serious reading problems. Mary wondered how he had gotten as far as he had, but suspected, due to his sweet nature, teachers were reluctant to fail him. As a result, he was in high school but unable to manage in his content classes. He needed attention, he needed work, and time was running out.

Grading English language learners is difficult; the key is to have goals and expectations for your students and to understand what English language learners can demonstrate.

Using Technology in the Content Classes

The possibilities for using technology in service of content learning are practically limitless, from math tutorials, to interactive vocabulary-development websites and programs, to graphic organizers, to digital scrapbooks. Viewing streaming video on a particular period in history before reading the text can help fill in the gaps for all students, not just ELLs. The immediacy of the web gives teachers access to resources that were rarely available so easily before the Internet. Students can use PowerPoint in a variety of ways; they can make videos, create brochures, and so on. Your creative mind and the technology you have available can expand the content material beyond paper and pen assignments.

a

Briefly define or describe the following terms:

Sea Dogs *they were slaves*

Golden Hind *sailed th raysn't the strait of magellan*

Charter *it document the rules*

Armada *a warship*

Joint Stock Company *a Company*

House of Burgesses

Royal Colony *under complete contral*

puritans *were reformers*

separatist *new churches*

pilgrims *or religious travelers*

Fundamental Orders *plans of the goven.*

proprietors *charters and own eq.*

patroons *'religious groups*

Quakers

Frame of Government *gave the colonists a representative*

Pennsylvania Dutch *unvchmeans Bermans*

b

U.S. HISTORY
CHAPT 6. pages 121-124

1. Name two Indians that helped the early English settlers.
chief Powhatan ara Squanto

2. What was the attitude of the Indians toward land ownership?
they had lot of Culturals

3. How were the Indians beliefs about land different from the colonists?
the Indians belived that the land belonged to no one person or group

4. What is a pagan?
or people who worshipped many gods rather than one

5. Why were the Indians destined to lose the conflict of cultures?
becausa thire dieing out and poeples are moving in to their land.

6. What was the middle passage?
a voyage across the Atlantic Ocean

7. What were the slave codes?
it made slaves their owners property

8. Describe three of the slave codes?
a. *they could not vote*
b. *if they run away they would be hit or whipped*
c. *they could not own they things*

9. Who led one of the earliest slave rebellions in the colonies?
did Cato

10. Why was life so difficult for free blacks?
they were not welcome into white coloial society. they had to live in a sepaate neighbornooads. the even had black pews in church and they had their own black school.

Figure 8.8a–b This student defined key terms (a). What grade would you give her for this test? How well did the student answer the short-answer questions (b)? Would you include any "fudge factors" in your grade?

There's no question that students need to learn how to use the technology that is available. ELL students often have to be taught explicitly how to use calculators and computers. Don't assume they know how. The big question we need to ask ourselves first is whether the technology we're using is skill and drill transferred to another medium. Do we want to spend a couple hours putting together a PowerPoint on cloud types, or can we simply take students outside and look at clouds?

Conclusion

The two major assumptions we operate under when teaching the content areas are

- Language can be effectively learned through content.

- Content language provides students with both useful language (in terms of knowledge) and usable language.

Time in a content-area classroom can be productive time for ELL students, even before they become as proficient in the language as their English-speaking peers. They can gain English competency by and through what they learn in class, and even though they cannot always articulate as well as their classmates, there are many alternative ways they can demonstrate their mastery of the concepts.

Reflections, Projects and Projections for Discussion

- Think of a class such as science or social studies that you really loved in school. Why did you love it? What did the teacher do to make it so exciting or interesting? What qualities did the teacher exhibit? What did you do in class that so enthralled you?

- Think of a class you hated or possibly even flunked. Why did this happen? What was the teacher like, and how did that teacher deliver the material that made it so repugnant or boring or impossible to master?

- Think of a time when you were faced with a learning situation where the teacher was so abstract that everything went right over your head. How did that make you feel? What strategies did you use to learn the material? If you got help in the class what did your tutor or teacher do to make the material accessible to you? If you managed to succeed, what did you do? If you gave up and bailed, at what point did you decide it was too much for you?

- Choose a class you are teaching, or one you are planning to teach, for instance, fifth-grade science.

  - What are the bottom-line competencies your students will need to achieve in order to succeed?

- Design a lesson based on the information from the preceding bullet.

- Develop a vocabulary list or an activity/lesson to provide background information your students will need to succeed.

- Develop an overall plan for these same students: what are the goals; what are the ups and downs—the methods you will use to either make the material more challenging for the more proficient students or native language learners, or to modify for less proficient learners?

- What are the benchmarks for achievement in your class or subject? How will you assess this to show progress in students? Make a checklist of benchmarks, and note how you will assess each student to demonstrate progress.

- Review the writing and the proficiency levels of some of the students showcased in previous chapters. Think about how they would function in your content area. Do you know what background information will be missing for these ELL students? Will you need more materials to support what your students don't know, in order for them to succeed? What would these materials consist of? Who will you need to collaborate with so the students have what they need to progress?

- What technology can you access that will help your students to better master the material in your subject?

- What should you do when some of your students just don't get it? What questions should you ask? If they don't understand, is that reason to move on, or to re-teach? How many of your students have to fail to understand the concepts in order for you to worry?

Case Studies: Mrs. Dickinson, Alem, Kamiko, Kayo

Mrs. Dickinson

Mrs. Dickinson is going to teach a lesson in matter to her third-grade students, which includes the classic, exciting vinegar and baking soda volcano. The vocabulary students need to know includes *matter, dissolve, evaporate, crystal.*

- What types of prelistening work might be done in order to prepare students for the task?

- What additional vocabulary would be needed to understand this lesson?

- What sort of background information will Mrs. Dickinson need to supply for students such as Bao, Salvador, Angel?

- What types of concepts are presupposed with this lesson, which Mrs. Dickinson may have to explicitly teach?

- How might student comprehension be checked?

- What alternative methods would Mrs. Dickinson use to evaluate students such as Bao, who are low level literacy, or Newton, who can understand the concepts but cannot write fluently or competently enough to demonstrate his understanding?

- What level of accuracy should she expect from Boris?

- How can Mrs. Dickinson partner students to make this lesson more comprehensible?

- What types of printed texts might Mrs. Dickinson select for the differing levels in her class?

- What types of synthesis activities might she use in order to integrate the ideas?

Alem

Alem is having trouble in his history class. His English is pretty good, but he is still lacking in some of the content vocabulary. He hears a word, looks it up in his dictionary, and writes it in English. By the time he finds the word, Miss Beuler has launched into something else. Alem talked to Miss Beuler, but she said Alem needed to find a friend who will lend him a copy of the notes. This teacher speaks with many breaks and "eh"s, so Alem loses track of what's going on. Miss Beuler thinks that it's Alem's problem that he doesn't understand, and she refuses to make any adaptations to her lectures.

- What can you do to help Alem succeed in his history class?

- Is it a reasonable strategy for Alem to get the notes from someone else?

- How much time should you spend helping Alem understand the material?

- How will you know what's important for him to learn in this class or what is possible to skim over?

- What suggestions do you have to intervene with Miss Beuler, or should you bypass her and simply help him?

Kamiko

Your class will be studying the American Civil War, culminating in an essay on causes and consequences of the war. Kamiko is a level 4 in English proficiency and is new to the United States.

- What kind of background information will Kamiko need before she can even do research for her essay?

- What vocabulary will she need to understand as she starts?

- What materials can you find that will help her fill in the gaps?

- How can you accommodate Kamiko during class discussions?

- What additional tools can you use to help Kamiko manage the material?

- How can you break down the assignment into smaller tasks?

- When it is time for Kamiko to assimilate all the material she has gathered or completed, what is the best way for her to approach writing the essay?

Kayo

Kayo is an upper level ELL student, and she is having trouble keeping up with the class. She takes notes in her native language, which is difficult, because she doesn't know how to translate these words, and by the time she figures it out, she's missed something else that was said. She spends a lot of time trying to understand her classes in both languages. This, too, takes a lot of time because she is constantly going back and forth between languages. In addition, her notes are faulty when she translates them, because she writes words such as *bivrate* instead of *vibrate* and *valoon* instead of *balloon*.

- What can you do to help Kayo?

- What recommendations would you have?

Chapter 9

Resources—Earnestly Extract the Lesson

In this chapter, we discuss how to best use the resources in your school and the community. We give suggestions on how to

- Coordinate with support personnel, such as ELL, bilingual, and reading teachers as well as paraprofessionals so that you can use them to both your and their best advantage

- Use buddies and tutors

- Encourage your students' parents to participate in their children's schooling

- Use interpreters

- Make best use of the technology that is available to you

Cherie works in an inner-city school that has received a block grant limiting class size to 20. She has ten Hispanic students, three Hmong, two African American, a Native American, and four native-English speakers in her grade 2 class. She meets every week with the other second-grade teachers to plan. They coordinate their efforts, talk over problems, and modify the curriculum together to meet the needs of their students. During the day, the lowest-proficiency ELL students leave the classroom to go for ELL help during language arts. The ELL teacher comes into the classroom during content science and social studies, the Title I teacher comes in to work with several small groups during reading time, and a bilingual support person comes in to work with the Hispanic students during writing and math time in the afternoon.

Cherie is trying to make the most of the support personnel in her school. While aligning all her core work to the curriculum and the state's model standards, she is giving ELL students the maximum support during the time they need it most and giving her more proficient students challenging material to work with.

What Cherie has going for her is her willingness—and confidence—to allow other teachers into her classroom to share the load. She also has the support of her principal and other professionals who adapt their schedules in creative ways. This is as it should be.

But things are not always as they should be. And it is easy to focus on the things that get in the way of collaboration; pull-out ELL programs, push-in ELL programs, and ELL centers (where students come for extended periods of time) all have their attendant problems. Sometimes the politics of special interests, such as ELL programs, take precedence over the needs of the whole. Other times, budget considerations eliminate the most needed programs or personnel.

Solving the major issues concerning placement and configuration of services is not the point of this chapter. For every district, each with its own particular problems, populations, and politics, there are unique answers.

We have decided to sidestep these issues in favor of presenting a model of what *can* be. If you break down how these issues are configured, you have some sense of the choices you have and what you can lobby for. A collaborative model, in which responsibility is shared among the various professionals, is best. And again, flexibility is the key. We cannot promote one ideology, because everything might change tomorrow anyway.

We have always stressed that ELL is everybody's responsibility. Just because Bounkham has been assigned to your class does not mean that you should shoulder the entire task of educating him. Nor does it mean that if there is an ELL teacher in the classroom, Bounkham is her responsibility alone. He is in your class for the majority of the day. In addition to the help he gets from the ELL teacher, you need to modify your classroom and your teaching to make the curriculum accessible to him.

Meeting the needs of your English-speaking students is a challenge in itself. Teachers of ELL students are often frustrated, because they cannot give their ELL students the time and attention they need. How can you make the most effective use of the resources available to you, so that you can meet the varying needs of all your students—English-speaking and ELL alike?

The ELL Teacher

The ELL teacher is your prime source of support. She has expertise in both language acquisition and in modifying instruction to meet the needs of your students. She is also an extra pair of hands and eyes—another adult to watch, reason, and evaluate what's going on in the classroom. She can teach and reinforce the vocabulary and the concepts so necessary for your students' success.

The ELL teacher is also your best ally. Many of us who became ELL teachers fell into the job, not by design, by default. But once we had a taste of working with English learners, we never looked back. Nothing else comes close. Teaching ELL is a passion. The job is never the same, because the populations, the needs, the classroom makeup are always changing. We never know what we're going to get and that's half the fun. We work in a constantly shifting political and situational milieu that demands flexibility, optimism, and the ability to meet all comers at their level.

ELL teachers, often relegated to corners, broom closets, orchestra rooms, often the ones to whom the sole responsibility for students has been given, are the ones who fight on. Use them to your best advantage.

Making the most of your time with the ELL teacher maximizes the learning your students get. But it takes coordination and careful planning. Debbie, the ELL teacher at Cherie's school, comes into the classroom for science and social studies. Recently, she arrived in the classroom 10 minutes after school had started, and science was about to begin. She had no idea what Cherie had planned for that day and spent most of her time bending and pointing. This was not the best use of her time, and she and Cherie were both frustrated and grouchy.

Cherie thought back to her own days as a bilingual teacher. She was primarily responsible for working with first- and second-grade teachers, and with one teacher in particular, Sherry. She and Sherry planned for one hour each week. They discussed content and reading in terms of who was going to be in charge, and who was going to do what. When Cherie came into the classroom, they already had their game plan worked out and they were on the same page. "It takes time and it takes commitment," says Cherie. But it worked.

Cherie's school devised a Team-Teaching Checklist (figure 9.1). We believe this list captures what needs to be done to take full advantage of an ELL teacher's skills.

Team-Teaching Checklist

_____ Define your teaching roles.

_____ Establish common class goals and individual goals:
- Grouping (how and where)
- Modifications
- Enrichments

_____ Divide responsibilities for subjects.

_____ Make time for planning.

_____ Decide on who will do grading and report cards.

_____ Agree on common discipline system.

_____ Build in time for parent communication.

_____ Set your routines:
- Daily teacher tasks
- Ordering materials
- Copying lesson plans

_____ Work to maintain consistency in schedules and plans while allowing for flexibility.

_____ Do ongoing assessment of past lessons.

_____ Keep lines of communication open.

Figure 9.1 Team-Teaching Checklist

"But I don't have time!" you say. Make time. It's that simple. You are not maximizing your time when, for example, an aide or ELL teacher asks, "What are we doing today?" and learns, on the spot, what you have planned for that day, or, you respond, "I don't know." Planning together up front ensures that

- You will not use the ELL teacher as an aide

- The ELL teacher knows what students are expected to know

- You will not duplicate services

- The ELL teacher does not have to guess what to teach, will teach things that are relevant and useful, and will not undermine what you do in the classroom

Communication is the most important factor in establishing a good relationship with the teachers who work with you and your students.

Flynn (1992) recommends that ELL teachers team with a limited number of classroom teachers (or content teachers, in secondary school). This allows them to work with the classroom teachers to plan the curriculum for the entire class. They can then concentrate instruction on the needs of the low-English-proficiency (LEP) students as they relate to the instruction in your classroom.

This is the ideal, and is, perhaps, unrealistic. Bad principals, bad administrators, bad policies, lousy allocation of dollars, and poor planning all get in the way. But the ideal is worth working for. When it works, as it did for Sherry and Cherie, it's wonderful. The kids get the best of both of you.

Nowadays, more and more schools are doing the "push-in" method of ELL support, where the ELL teacher works with the students in their classroom. This is an ideal practice in theory, but take care that the ELL teacher doesn't become a glorified aide. One ELL teacher, Erin, reports that when she works in the high school science class, the teacher tells her she doesn't know what to do with the students and sends Erin off to make copies of worksheets. What a waste of Erin's and the students' time! Personalities, teaching styles, and philosophies can clash, so having someone work in your "territory" takes work.

Classroom Paraprofessionals—Teacher's Aides

Classroom aides and/or ELL aides are often hired in response to a sudden influx of students who speak a language that no one else in the school can understand or speak. Often these aides have no education training; they are hired simply because they can speak both English and the language of the new student(s). In some districts, the minimum requirement for hiring bilingual aides is that they can speak English. Even this criterion is sometimes difficult to meet. If you can't find a bilingual aide who is proficient in both languages, you are probably better off with an aide who is simply a good aide.

The Ideal Aide

The ideal classroom aide has all of the following characteristics:

- Good English-language skills—not just "some" English, but proficiency in reading and writing

- A positive attitude

- A working knowledge of classroom management: how to motivate students, how to discipline, how to reinforce what you teach

- Cultural savvy; enough understanding of both cultures to work, at ease, with both

- Patience

An aide with all these qualities would be wonderful, but you may not be able to find someone matching this description in your district. Certainly, the decision to hire an aide should not be based solely on his or her knowledge of the ELL students' language. Good English skills are far more essential. Other useful skills are a working knowledge of reading theory and some knowledge of basic ELL principles.

Although most of our discussion relates to working with paid aides, parent or bilingual volunteers may also be used in the same capacity.

Using Your Classroom Aide

You must first decide whether the classroom aide is there merely to be a clerk or will have a more responsible role within the classroom. We believe that your aide is a valuable resource, and though keeping records, grading papers, and running off photocopies are all useful tasks, your aide can be used to advantage in many other areas.

Some teachers give their aide complete responsibility for their ELL students. This may be tempting, as you have many other students to work with, but the aide, who lacks both training and experience, is not the teacher. Your aide should be there to complement your role, not to take over and work exclusively with ELL students. You, the teacher, must be the driving force and role model, give clear directions, set expectations and parameters, and use the aide to your advantage, capitalizing on his or her strengths and personality.

The Teacher's Role

Your main role with regards to an aide is to offer guidance and supervision, as well as to provide an environment that is conducive to rapport and open communication among you, your aide, and your students. Here are some suggestions for going about it:

- Find out the strengths and weaknesses of the aide and what he or she feels most comfortable doing. Ask your aide for written (rather than verbal) responses to the following questions:

- What do you—or could you—do especially well in this classroom?

- What do you feel unprepared to do in the classroom?

- Clarify your expectations of the aide. We suggest that both you and the aide respond, in writing, to the following four-part question (provide space on the paper for four or five different thoughts):

   What do you see as each person's responsibilities in the following relationships:

   - Teacher's responsibility to the teacher's aide

   - Teacher's responsibility to the students

   - Teacher's aide's responsibility to the teacher

   - Teacher's aide's responsibility to the students

   The answers to these questions will alert you to your aide's expectations of you and to possible differences between your two sets of expectations. It will also help you define your perception of your own role and responsibilities. There is nothing as destructive to a good working relationship as two people operating under different assumptions about their roles. If these aren't spelled out and clarified at the beginning, frustration and resentment can lead to job dissatisfaction, unhappiness, or an inability to work together, which may lead to the aide resigning his or her position.

- Clearly define duties and responsibilities for both yourself and the aide, and draw up a written contract that outlines these. This contract can be renegotiated from time to time and referred to throughout the term. In "The Aide's Role" section, found on pages 302–303, we give suggestions for appropriate tasks.

- Before school begins, meet with the aide (let's call him Mr. Chun), and help him to become familiar with the classroom, the materials, and textbooks. Make sure he also knows the school jargon, such as what CTBS, and SAT, and so on mean.

- Give Mr. Chun a complete tour of the school, and introduce him to support staff, the secretaries, the principal, the nurse, the counselor, and so on.

- Introduce Mr. Chun to the students. Use the same title they use for you, to demonstrate that they are to treat him with the same respect. If you are known as Mrs. Burton, he will go by Mr. Chun, not Martin.

- Make sure he knows the philosophy of North American education, as well as your own personal educational philosophy. Many aides come from countries that have philosophies much different from ours. To an immigrant from Japan, for example, American classrooms can seem overly noisy and chaotic, children rude and disrespectful, and discipline nonexistent.

- Make sure Mr. Chun has at least a basic knowledge of the principles of ELL teaching and learning. When Barb taught in a self-contained classroom, she welcomed the assistance of an ELL intern from the local university. He worked two days a week for 10 weeks, participated in planning sessions, and carried on many conversations with Barb concerning learning styles and philosophies of education. But after he had left his internship, his final report to his professor stated unequivocally that there should have been many more drills and that the teacher should have been focusing on grammar. Even after 10 weeks of involvement, he was unable to accept established second-language teaching theories and continued to compare Barb's teaching methods unfavorably to those methods used when he was a student in his own country. As a result, Barb was never quite sure how much he had tried to undermine what she had been doing while he was working with her students—a discomfiting feeling.

- Discuss lesson plans, objectives, and the implementation of your long- and short-term goals. Make sure Mr. Chun knows exactly what you want him to do, either in conjunction with what you are doing in class, or as extension and enrichment. Figure 9.2 provides a sample planning sheet you can use with either paid or volunteer aides. The "comments" section is to be used for observations and perceptions of how the day went, who did particularly well, and who had difficulty with the material. These

---

Teacher-Volunteer (or Aide) Planning Sheet

Name of volunteer (or aide) _____

Name of teacher/grade level _____

Name(s) of student(s) _____

Skills to be reinforced or tasks to be completed by volunteer (or aide):

Time frame _____

Materials to be used _____

Location of materials _____

Procedures _____

Comments of volunteer (or aide):

_____

_____

_____

_____

Figure 9.2 Teacher-Volunteer (or Aide) Planning Sheet (reproducible master – Appendix I)

comments are particularly useful if your time is limited, or if the aide leaves each day before you have a chance to discuss work with him. His assessment will also be useful when planning new activities.

- Make sure your aide knows the *why* as well as the *how to*. Often good ideas go awry because the aide doesn't know the reasoning behind the lesson plan. For example, if you ask Mr. Chun to do TPR (see page 257) with some students and, without understanding the principle behind it, he has the students repeat every command after him, he is defeating the purpose of TPR.

- Clarify when it is important to use the first language. Having someone who is able to jumpstart comprehension by explaining in the first language, build background knowledge, clarify misunderstanding, and affirm the validity of the first language is an invaluable asset in a classroom. But there is a fine line between being an asset and being a crutch—one that you and the aide need to work out between yourselves.

- Ask for input. If your aide works consistently with small groups of ELL students, he may know them better than you do and may have a clearer insight into their strengths, weaknesses, and possible reasons for behavior problems.

- Capitalize on his strengths. Find out if he has any special talents. For instance, Barb's aide, Emma, had abundant artistic talent and enjoyed making posters, wall displays, and awards for the students. Midori was a librarian and could always find a book appropriate for each child.

- Tap his knowledge of his own culture, traditions, and values. He has the special perspective of a member of a specific culture and can bring an understanding and richness to the classroom that would be lacking otherwise. He can help you and your students understand how culture influences people's way of perceiving things, and how different behaviors result from language or cultural differences. For example, when Mary was teaching a lesson on body parts, the students were not responding as enthusiastically as she had hoped. This was suddenly made clear when her aide pointed out that she was touching them on the head and shoulders, sacred areas to Buddhists.

- If he is comfortable with it, allow him to assume responsibility in his area of expertise. Some aides enjoy responsibility, others prefer to be led. Still others are very conscious of what-is-aiding and what-is-teaching and will not cross that line.

The Aide's Role

Your aide's principal role is to complement you in the classroom, helping to carry out your lesson plans, and supplementing and enriching what you have taught. The most helpful areas are

Translating (if the aide is bilingual)

- When there is a breakdown in communication or a problem, acting as interpreter to explain or sort out the difficulty

- Translating school notices, permission slips, and so on
- Providing initial orientation, and explaining school and classroom rules and regulations to students and parents

Working with individual or small groups of students

- Developing LEA stories (see chapter 5, page 160)
- Developing reading readiness skills
- Reading to students
- Working on math concepts that ELL students may not understand
- Breaking down activities into smaller, more comprehensible units for students who need extra explanation
- Coordinating with content-area teachers, previewing a lesson, then recapping it for ELL students in their language
- Reviewing and reinforcing concepts taught to the class as a whole

Acting as a bridge with the community

- Attending parent-teacher conferences and acting as translator
- Getting permission slips signed
- Accompanying parents to school

Community Aides

Community aides, who liaise between the school and the community, play quite a different role from classroom aides. They can be a powerful force and can exert much more influence on parents and community than you can, so English-language skills are not as important for community aides as the ability to command respect. In many Asian neighborhoods, a man who has status as a respected member of the community is far more influential than someone whose English might be better, but who has no status. One elementary school in northern California has an older Hmong man as a volunteer. He is a clan leader and so receives great respect and deference from the local Hmong population. When there is a discipline problem, Mr. Lee steps in, and the problem no longer exists. He is the community liaison, interpreter, and elder, and is, by all accounts, a man to be reckoned with. His pervasive influence is invaluable to the school; he is an ally they both appreciate and depend upon.

Buddies

We discussed buddies briefly in chapter 1; now we would like to look at the topic in more depth. Rather than arbitrarily assigning a buddy student to help out a newcomer and leaving the buddy undirected and to his own devices, it is wise to be more systematic. One school has instituted a carefully planned and executed buddy system that has seen great success. This system, as with most successful programs, has strong administrative support. It involves the careful selection and training of ELL buddies, as well as parental involvement and the use of contracts:

- Only good students, who are patient, mature, tolerant of differences, and wise enough to know when to help and when to let the ELL student work on his own, are selected as buddies.

- A training workshop is given at the beginning of the year to sensitize all student-buddies to the challenges ELL students face and to help them learn ways to assist their buddies. Parents of student-buddies are given a form to sign, giving permission for their child to be a buddy.

- Each buddy is matched with a student in his class and given a list of fun and friend-making things to do. Students sign contracts, which detail things they will do with their buddies. Some suggestions include going to McDonald's together, calling their buddy on the phone every day, inviting their buddy home once a week.

- Special recognition is given to buddies for their service. There is a friendship picnic at the end of the year, and a "buddies poster" (photographs of each of the buddies with his/her newcomer friend) is displayed in a prominent place in the school.

This program makes everyone in the school aware of the ELL students, not as a problem to be overcome, but as a special opportunity for learning and friendship. Being appointed a buddy is seen as an honor. This buddy program is a systematic, well-planned way to ease the transition for new students.

Tutors

For additional one-on-one help for students, tutors are invaluable. A tutor may be another student in the class, a more advanced ELL student, a student aide, a senior citizen, or a National Honor Society student interested in gaining service points. A tutor does not have to speak the language of the ELL student he or she works with. According to high school teachers Debbie Angert and Jan Booth, in a CaTESOL (California Teachers of English to Speakers of Other Languages) conference workshop in 1987, the best candidates for peer tutors are those who

- Exhibit a willingness to help others

- Are not overly grade conscious

- Are not excessively shy

- Will be good models for appropriate behavior and good study habits

Working before or after school or during study time, tutors can

- Take notes during each class, giving copies to the ELL student

- Explain directions

- Clarify vocabulary

- Read textbook material to the ELL student

- Make sure the ELL student is following directions and working on the task at hand

- Give you feedback on the ELL student's progress and problems

Parents

Parents are central to the success of their children's education. Your partnership with students' parents can enhance their children's school experience profoundly.

Contrary to the perception of many teachers, most parents are anxious and willing to help at home and are extremely concerned about their children's success at school. The major hindrance is that they often don't know how to help. You can help them help their children by showing them specific ways to encourage and enrich their children's learning experiences. Here are some suggestions for including the family in literacy and language learning. The title of these activities, "home fun," is important. According to Scott Enright and Mary Lou McCloskey (1988), who developed the activities that follow, home fun activities should

- Be engaging and fun

- Integrate language learning into all activities

- Necessitate participation of both parent (or other older person) and child

- Respect and use the family's native language

- Allow adequate time for completion

- Be presented by the teacher with preparation and follow-up

- Provide variations based on the student's language-proficiency level

The most basic and important activity literate parents can do is read to their children. It doesn't matter in what language—whether in their first language or English; reading in one language helps reading in the other. It doesn't even have to be literature; food labels, newspapers, letters, bulletins anything in print will do. If parents are not literate, other family or community members can help.

Home Activities to Promote Literacy

Enright and McCloskey list other activities to promote literacy and an understanding of the value and use of literature:

- Record the different ways family members use reading in a day.

- Record examples of environmental print (street signs, bumper stickers, and so on) that students can recognize.

- Collect food labels and/or containers to be used in classroom activities.

- Give ELL students assignments to help them learn about their families.

- Make family trees.

- Make personal "what-happened-when" timelines.

- Collect funny stories about students' childhoods.

- Collect family stories in a certain category—humor, superstition, ghost stories.

- Interview family members to study the history of the family.

- Study a particular aspect of the parents' lives when they were children.

- If parents have moved around, make a map of their migration.

- Give students assignments to help them learn more about their culture.

- Write stories about holidays and special events in students' culture or homeland, such as New Year's, Bon Dances, powwows, fiestas, and so on.

- Record recipes for ethnic dishes.

- Illustrate traditional costumes.

- Collect traditional fairytales.

- Interview others to find out traditional ways of doing things, such as how to conduct a Japanese tea ceremony.

- Interview others to find out about special skills they performed in their homeland, such as carving, hunting.

- Illustrate life as it was in their homeland.

- Involve family members in projects to learn about their communities.

- Sketch their rooms, their houses, their blocks.

- Make a map of the student's street.

- Make maps of routes commonly traveled, such as from home to school and to the store.

Interpreters

There are times when it will be absolutely essential for you to have an interpreter—when things go wrong and you need to clarify why and how to rectify the situation; when you need to discuss with parents how their child is doing in school; when a student is sick or hurt and in need of medical attention. For these occasions, it is important that you have located and approached at least one person who is a fluent speaker of your student's language.

Interpreters are valuable assets to any teacher. If they are from the same ethnic group as your student they know the culture of the person you are trying to communicate with and can provide a bridge between your culture and theirs. They can advise you, for instance, that in their culture it is very impolite to be direct, that one communicates by beating around the bush; or, they can tell you that it is typical to flee from the police when you've been stopped for a violation, because people in their country are often jailed for long periods without knowing why. While the interpreter is explaining something to the student in his language, you have time to think through your next question. Most important, interpreters can verify that you and the other party are actually communicating with understanding.

When you require an interpreter, do not use a child in this role. It may be alright to collar a fellow student occasionally in a casual situation, when you simply need to get a point across or understand a student's question, but for major interviews or problems, children should not be used for several reasons:

- Children don't have the experience, wherewithal, or training to ask appropriate questions.

- Using children robs adults of their authority. This is particularly true with parents from traditional patriarchal societies. Giving children such power strips adults of their authority.

- If something goes wrong, you don't want the child to get the blame.

- The child may not be old enough to understand the concepts or problems you are trying to discuss, especially when they involve a medical situation.

- Some concepts are not directly translatable, and the child may not have the cognitive maturity to explain in other words.

Using Interpreters

Here are some suggestions for using interpreters and the procedure to follow in selection, training, and employment:

Choose the appropriate interpreter for the situation.

- Know your students, and have some understanding of their cultures. For example, if you have a suicidal teenage girl, you should not use her father as the interpreter. Be aware of the ethnic antagonisms that exist between groups. Remember Barb's student who slept with a knife under his pillow for an entire year (see chapter 3), because his roommate was a student from a country with which his own country shared a mutual hatred? This was in spite of the fact that they liked each other. They made it through the year, but his learned distrust simmered below the surface. The tensions or discomfort between certain family members or cultural groups can short-circuit any efforts you make.

- Select someone you're comfortable with, someone who you think is reliable, who you can trust to translate your ideas accurately and not undermine what you are saying. For instance, if you are telling a student that keeping a handgun in his locker is a very serious offense, you don't want your interpreter saying, "Don't worry. I have one myself. I'll show you how to use it."

Meet with the interpreter beforehand to talk about the situation at hand.

- Explain the purposes and the goals of the meeting. You don't want to shock the interpreter with discussion of a sensitive subject when the client is already present. For example, an interpreter may feel extremely uncomfortable discussing personal issues, such as gynecological issues or other concerns that are inappropriate, in his culture, for him to discuss with the other party.

- Make sure he knows that he should not ask questions for you or answer questions for the student. His job is simply to interpret what each of you say; he is not your voice or theirs, but the conduit through which you both talk.

- Make sure that the discussion that transpires will be absolutely confidential.

- Make sure you know how to pronounce the names of the people you will be meeting with.

- Establish such basics as

  - How you will be introduced

  - Where you will sit—behind your desk or with the others, in a circle? (What is the least intimidating arrangement?)

  - If it is appropriate to touch the other person (parent, sibling, or other)

  - If it is appropriate to make eye contact with the other person

  - If the interpreter will paraphrase or interpret word-for-word, and if he will interpret in short phrases or paragraphs

  - If the interpreter will give you feedback about the other person's feelings and reactions (for example, "He's sad") during the meeting, or afterwards

When the student arrives

- Make introductions.

- Establish immediately that your interpreter is there simply to interpret, not level charges.

- Look at the student, not at the interpreter.

- Establish your student's degree of English proficiency if this is your first meeting with him (you don't want to be shocked or embarrassed to find out that your student has understood many of the comments you have made to the interpreter that were not meant for his ears).

- Avoid long discussions with your interpreter while the student waits.

- Simplify your language.

- Plan your next statement while the interpreter is relaying your message.

- Watch your student's nonverbal cues carefully for signs of frustration, discomfort, or anger.

After the session

- Discuss whether you solved the problem or if another meeting is required. How did the student respond to your decision?

- Pay the interpreter. Even if it's a nominal fee, make it worth his while to have come. Schools usually have some kind of fund to pay for this, and you must compensate him for his time and effort.

Technology

The use of technology inside and outside the classroom is exploding, and with it is our increasing dependency on this very technology to conduct our ordinary lives. This phenomenon leaves us, as teachers, running to keep up.

In the current euphoria over the promises and possibilities of technology in the classroom, it's important to get a clear picture of not just the possibilities but the pitfalls too. Technology is continually evolving. Consequently, we must constantly figure out what we need to do and how to use what's available. Unfortunately, there's always a lag between what's out there and what schools can afford. If a computer is obsolete by the time it hits the shelf at the store, then how do we, as teachers and school systems, keep up?

In addition, there is a constant tug-of-war between those who see computers and other technology as essential and those who believe that it gets in the way of learning and detracts from those very essentials. Grants and government resources flood us with new equipment, then dry up. Gung-ho teachers, who lead the technology way, retire or move on. Administrators flog us for not integrating technology more, for not being more up-to-date, then don't provide the faculty with the professional development, the support, or the time to do it.

To assess the value of any technology device the first question we need to ask is whether it gets us farther down the road toward our ultimate goal of educating our students. We can return to the list of skills 21st century youth need, discussed in the Introduction, and ask whether technology enhances and promotes these skills:

1. Be able to use multiple literacies. Technology, of course, is what drives many of these multiple literacies, therefore, it is important that we provide our students with opportunities to engage in them.

2. Be able to work collaboratively with others. Today's technology gives students opportunities to work together. Do they *need* technology to do this? No. Technology broadens the horizons, expands the possibilities, but not having it doesn't mean they can't learn to collaborate.

3. Master problem-solving skills. Again, do they need technology to do this? No.

4. Possess communication skills. Technology, in this case, facilitates the learning in ways that simply reading a book does not. But nothing beats talking face-to-face with another person, or being in a classroom where students are engaged and excited.

5. Be able to access data, and decide how to use it. Here, again, is where technology becomes every educator's dream. When one is limited to the books on hand, particularly in the poorer schools, one's access to information is seriously limited, and the digital divide grows wider. Going to a museum sure beats taking a virtual tour, and planting a garden or watching a butterfly emerge from a cocoon beats reading about it online. But, if your school can't afford a field trip, at least having the opportunity to watch a butterfly emerge from its cocoon beats just looking at a picture of it. And streaming a video of a choreographer's dance style beats just describing it. So don't beat yourself up if you're not as far along the technology continuum as you'd like to be, or if you don't have the up-to-date equipment that other schools do. The basics are the basics, and they come first.

6. Be able to sort the junk from the important data. No matter how technically advanced students may be when using a computer, most of them are inexperienced at distinguishing authoritative websites from those whose information is questionable. Students are often quite happy to land on the first website returned in their search results just to get the assignment finished. It is up to the teacher to either narrow the search for the students, or give them specific guidelines on how to assess the information they find.

Benefits of Technology in the Classroom

There are multiple ways that technology can enhance learning:

*   **Equity of access.** Rural schools, in particular, which don't have the numbers to budget for an ELL or foreign-language teacher, can benefit from distance-learning capabilities.

*   **Variety.** With modern technology, you have many more resources at hand with which to veer away from the old skill-and-drill or pencil-and-paper methods we were limited to just a few years ago.

*   **Real-world skills learning in both language and technology.** Students need to know how to use what's out there, and it's often the school that must provide these opportunities, particularly for students from low-income or rural areas.

*   **Teamwork and effective collaboration skills.** Students learn how to communicate electronically using blogs, chat, or email. If they are producing a multimedia project, they learn to delegate the workload, manage video, sound, and text. They have to know how to work on one project in multiple locations, (classroom, library, home). Ultimately they need to know how to complete a quality project and turn it in on a deadline.

*   **Communication with different types of audiences.** Trying to relate to others through key-pal (email pen-pals) communication, instant messaging, and such affords students practice with audiences besides just you.

- **Immediate connection to the outside world.** News and information searches provide students with instant feedback, giving them the opportunity to question and discuss their results as they research.

- **Keeping parents in the loop.** Many schools provide teachers with school webpage options. Teachers can post homework, calendars, assignments, handouts, and so on. If students are absent or need to review material, a school webpage can be a one-stop shop for information or help. In addition, more and more districts are moving to online grading and attendance record keeping. Parents can go online to see if their child is keeping up with assignments or needs help at home.

Constraints to Technology in the Classroom

It's important to acknowledge the things that hold us back from using technology as completely as we'd like or as organizations such as the ISTE (International Society for Technology in Education) suggest is necessary.

- **Technology availability in your building.** Even though they may have a computer in every classroom, not every school has servers, technical support personnel, or the budget to constantly upgrade.

- **Your knowledge, skill, and comfort level in using what's available.** Not all of us are able to negotiate the gadgets and programs with ease. The time required to learn how to use the newest innovation, incorporate it into our classroom, and get it going is not just significant, but can be formidable and daunting. We have to face the fact that often this task can detract from what we're supposed to be doing. This is why participation in training sessions, professional development, and support are critical.

- **Breakdowns.** It's disconcerting, frustrating, and certainly disruptive to be planning on using a certain type of media only to find that it's not available, or it's not working. It takes a great deal of fast footwork and a plan B to get back on track.

- **Time required to plan, implement, design, develop, and evaluate.** Most new technologies are front loaded. For instance, you can't learn how to use Blackboard and implement it on the fly in the middle of the semester. You have to have everything set up beforehand, because it's just too labor intensive to do it last-minute. The Internet can also be an incredible time-waster. You can spend hours looking for things that would take 10 minutes at the library, or waste precious minutes (instead of 10 seconds in the phone book), because of the sheer volume of "stuff" online, which is constantly shifting according to who pays what fees to the search engines.

- **Information overload.** The sheer amount of information available can be so overwhelming that it can have the unfortunate backlash of restricting rather than expanding students' experience, because they get overwhelmed and can't take it all in. Fewer choices can lead to more language processing.

Pitfalls of Technology

There are also some serious issues we have to face when we consider how, when, and where to use technology:

- **Technology implements should not be used all the time.** They are not babysitters; they can't replace you. The bottom line is that a human being sitting in front of a computer can't learn as much as a human being interacting with other humans.

- **Technology puts distance between you and your student.** This factor is a double-edged sword. Certainly, we want to create independent thinkers and learners, who take charge of their own education, but some kids can hide behind the computer and recede into anonymity if you let them. We can also get so caught up in the technology that we forget to get out from behind the monitor once in a while. This can lead to the loss of personal relationships with our students. Online classes, which some high school students have access to, are faceless. Lazy instructors who set up the courses and then go off to do their own thing are worse than useless.

- **Shifts in power structure.** Kids are always on the cusp of the new technology; they may know more than you and have more confidence in navigating the newest wave. They use technology constantly to enhance their social networks and their lives, while we may be limited to checking our email. Having students who know more can lead to students who value and respect you less.

And, probably most importantly,

- **Most of the technology and the information that is available is not focused on language learning, or even on learning in general.** It's your job to make it so. How you make it serviceable in your goal to help your students learn English, how much time you have available, and your own teaching philosophy all impact that factor more than what is actually out there. Songs, videos, or podcasts that replace rather than support solid language learning by offloading the content in favor of the media itself simply have to go.

This last pitfall is why many teachers, as well as universities, are backing away from technology. Math teachers are finding that students know how to punch the correct buttons to compute a problem, but they don't know how or why they reached the answer they did. Students can click through tutorials and pass quizzes without learning any of the material. Universities that have spent hundreds of thousands of dollars on remedial programs are discontinuing them, because students cannot make the leap from what they learned in the program to actually solving the equations, or writing the essays demanded in grade-level classrooms. Universities that once offered online classes have moved in the direction of hybrid or blended classes that offer a mix of in-seat and online teaching. This is because kids need teachers. They need a person— a real face—in front of them. They need the interaction of a classroom, where ideas are bandied about, and the magic of the group makes the sum of the students equal more than the parts.

Technology does not replace good teaching. Teachers all over the world are working in crowded, poorly ventilated or heated rooms, with 50 or more students to the class, few materials, and little technology beyond pencils and a board. And yet, they continually and consistently produce capable, proficient speakers of English. The bottom line: a human being in front of a computer can never learn as much as a human being interacting with a group of other humans.

Ways to Use Technology Effectively with English Language Learners

- **Decide**. How does this technology-focused or technology-facilitated task support language learning? Are students learning to read, learning to write, or are they simply being entertained? Are they learning the concepts that lay out the framework for the subject, or are they simply learning how to use a machine?

- **Prepare, prepare, prepare**. Nothing invites chaos better than simply plunking students in front of computers. While one can't get his machine going and wants a different one, another has forgotten his password. Three are already into chat rooms (that are most likely wildly inappropriate), others have logged onto Facebook, and still others are playing loud games or running to see what their friends are doing. You must have the links already set up and the task ready for your students. You alone can decide whether the time at the computer is worth the time and effort expended in getting it ready.

- **Hold their hands, and expect nothing**. You can't rely on students to know what they're supposed to do, to check what the assignment is, to know how to go on to the next step.

- **Train them**. Show them specifically how to use a calculator, how to find the appropriate websites, what to do if they get lost. You need to be certain they are trained in every single element they are expected to participate in. At very least, this reduces the time you spend running from station to station, helping them get up and running or find their way back to the task at hand and get down to the real learning.

- **Model**. Demonstrate high-quality homework assignments and discussion postings on threads. Collect examples of excellent student work to show your students, so they have attainable goals in mind when they begin.

- **Require a product at each computer session**. Students work most effectively when they know what is required at the end of their computer sessions. If the assignment is a project, break it down into segments that they must be responsible for at the end of each class. For example, if students are doing research for a project on the Great Depression, break down what it is you want them to accomplish each time they visit the computer lab. They will stay focused and be less likely to go off surfing and wasting time.

- **Have a backup plan.** If your computers crash, or someone else is using them, or for some reason you can't access the site you wanted to use, you'd better have something else to do.

How to Evaluate Technological Resources

The first questions we have to ask are the ones we've been asking all along:

- Is the task for which you are using this technology whole?

- Is it real?

- Is it meaningful?

- Are errors a helpful component of the learning, or is the program or task designed in such a way that if the student makes a mistake he is taken all the way back to the beginning to run through the material again? Many video games send players back, but there are other intrinsic rewards that compel the player to try again—which may not be present in many of the tasks we set for them.

In addition, we want our students to

- Experience (see and interact with) the world in a new way

- Gain the potential to join and collaborate with new groups

- Develop resources for future learning and problem solving

- Learn how to think about what they're doing so that they gain new strategies to build on (Gee 2007)

The activity must

- **Encourage active learning.** No point and click. No free answers whereby the student can simply bypass the reading or listening activity to get the task done.

- **Reward their efforts through achievement of meaningful success.** Exercises that are pointless, which the student can finish without some feeling of mastery, will lose the students somewhere along the way.

- **Increase their mastery of a specific skill.** Do they understand how to use order of operation? Can they use the vocabulary that the task required of them? Can they produce a better quality paper? Have they learned a specific reading strategy that they can employ when they read a text?

Conclusion

Teachers often express their frustration at the monumental task of meeting the needs of all their students. We wrote this chapter to help you tap the resources available for succeeding with this task. You're not in this alone. Using available resources helps make your job easier, reinforces the things you do in class, and helps you establish what you are doing right, as well what needs improvement. The main benefit you gain is support for your efforts.

Reflections, Projects, and Projections for Discussion

- Think of a time when, as a teacher, you felt sabotaged by a parent. What happened? How did you resolve it (or didn't you), and what was the fall-out from that situation? What could you do to forestall this from happening again?

- Recall a time in your life when there was a communication breakdown between home and school. What happened? How did you resolve it (or didn't you), and what was the fallout from that situation? What could you do to forestall this from happening again?

- Recall a time when you needed resources and couldn't obtain them. What did you do? How did that affect your ability to function? What could you have done to forestall this situation, and what can you do to eliminate the possibility that it might happen again?

- Think about the resources you have within your school (bilingual personnel, parent organizations, and so on). What can you do to supplement your resources if you don't have extra help?

- List the people and places outside of school that you can enlist for help. Is there a community center of the language group of your ELL(s)? Are there churches that host services in the language(s) of your students? Are there free or low-cost legal services for low-income or immigrant residents? Compile a list, so you can refer your students and their families if the need arises.

- What are the trends in immigration for your area? Has your city or town been targeted for relocation of refugees, or are certain language groups moving in? Who can you access to be ready for an influx?

- Craft letters to parents about yourself, your classroom, and your expectations of your students. Translate, or get help in translating the letters into the languages you expect arriving students speak. If you expect some parents to be preliterate or not comfortable with written correspondence, devise other methods for communicating with them.

- Lay out a set of expectations and tasks for parent classroom volunteers so that you won't be stuck scrambling if they appear. What's the best use of that parent's time? When and how can they be used to best advantage?

- Lay out a set of expectations and tasks for a paraprofessional (aide) in your classroom. What's the best use of that aide's time? When and how can he or she be used to best advantage?

- Lay out a proposal for how to work as a team with either a classroom teacher or an ELL teacher so that there is wise use of their time and talents and no hard feelings or disagreements. What's the best use of that teacher's time? When and how can they be used to best advantage?

Case Study: Elias

Elias is absent from class for the fifth time this month. When you try to question him, he shakes his head, lowers his eyes, and lifts one shoulder in a shrug. His English-proficiency skills are barely a level 2, even though he has been here for a year now. He's friendly and sociable, and by this time has some close friends who don't seem to care that his English is rudimentary. You know a little about his background but need more. Between you and the counselor, you compile the following profile:

Elias was the oldest of five when his family was sponsored by a church to come to America. His mother and father had spent their entire lives in a refugee camp. The church rented a house for his family, which, due to requirements laid out by the resettlement agency, was much larger and more expensive than they had bargained for or the family needed. The church furnished the house and paid the rent for six months. They were optimistic that the family would be on their feet and self-sufficient by the end of those six months.

But it wasn't that simple. Neither parent could read nor write. They had none of the most rudimentary survival skills. They had to be taught the most basic tasks, such as how to use a washing machine, how to turn on the stove. Because a car was out of the question, the family needed rides everywhere.

Elias' father got a job that didn't require him to speak English, but he missed work often, because he was not used to responsibility and was fired. Elias' mom lives in a haze, looking bewildered and shell-shocked. Overwhelmed by too many demands and the pace of life in this new country, she accomplishes little and never smiles. Dad has become morose and sometimes, you suspect, violent toward Elias' mother.

English language lessons for the family are progressing with painful slowness. The church has continued to support them, but, as with many churches, the core members at the heart of the church family are a small group, and they're becoming exhausted by the family's neediness.

Elias and his sisters have been making gains in school. These gains are very slow, however, which puts Elias increasingly further behind. To compound matters, because his parents are often helpless, Elias has to be taken out of school often to translate, as best he can, for his parents at the store.

As the ELL teacher, you've been at this school for six months. Originally you believed that you should be teaching the ELL curriculum, but over time you have begun to realize you are totally responsible for your students' reading and writing development. The teachers in charge of Elias and his sisters have fallen into this trap, and leave the bulk of the work to you. You can say, in confidence, that the only consistency in the district is inconsistency.

- Where do you start with a student like Elias? What are the prevalent factors in his situation? What can you do to help ease his transition? What are the priorities if he's five years old? Eight years old? Ten? Twelve? Fifteen?

- If you were actually his ELL teacher, how far would your responsibilities to Elias extend, as well as to your other students? What would be the limits to your responsibilities?

- If you were Elias's classroom teacher, how far would your responsibilities extend? What would be the limits to your responsibilities?

- In what ways can you collaborate with other teachers and supports to make sure Elias gets what he needs? When, where, and how will you find the time to do this?

- What resources beyond the school can you tap and pull in that would benefit Elias?

- Think back to the discussion in chapter 3 on appropriate programs for ELL students. What sort of program would benefit your school, its makeup, and the students, which would suit Elias's needs?

- The stakes get higher and higher as Elias gets older. What are your priorities for each age? If he's 10 when he arrives, what can you realistically hope to accomplish? If he's 15 when he arrives, what can you realistically hope to accomplish, and how do you keep from just giving up?

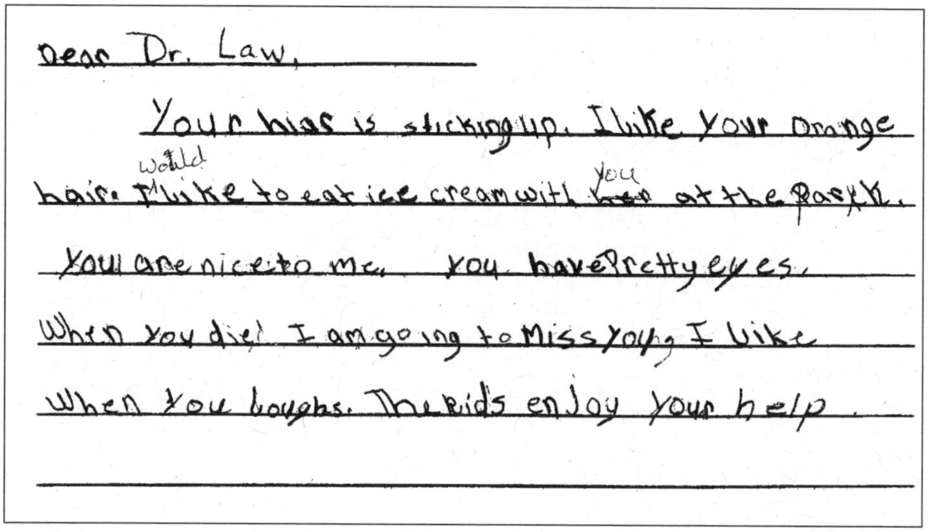

> Dear Dr. Law,
>
> Your hiar is sticking up. I like your orange hair. I would like to eat ice cream with you at the Parkk. You are nice to me. You have Pretty eyes. When you die, I am going to Miss you. I like when you loyghs. The Kids enjoy your help.

Figure 9.3 Christina's letter highlights the service that ELL teachers make to their students.

Thank you

Thank you for having me ☆ Thank you very much for every day. I enjoyed really every day ② I hope t see you some time. I hope you will come to Japan some day. **Very** ⑩⓪ Thank you.

Mary You made breakfast, lunch and dinner very delicious I think want to eat mothers cook.

John Thank you! Thank you! Thank you!!! Big eye very much. Don't forget ☆

Elise very enjoyed. Thank you for **present**. I really enjoyed every day. Japanese very much.

Jeremy kanji very much. Long hair is the best. 最高

EVERYONE
TANK YOU.
I'll never forget
to FAMIRY

March. 17. 2004

Figure 9.4 Suki, a Japanese student who stayed with Mary's family, wrote this thank-you letter to the family.

Appendixes

Basic Information For Parents

To the parents of _____

The following information will help you to understand your child's new school. Please share this information with your child so that he or she will feel more comfortable at school.

If you have any questions, please call _____
and we will be happy to answer them.

Date _____

Identification Information

Name of school _____

School address _____

School telephone _____

Name of principal _____

Name of teacher _____

Grade _____   Room number _____

Other Information

Schedule of School Day

First bell for morning session _____   First bell for afternoon session _____

Tardy bell _____   Afternoon recess _____

Morning recess _____   Dismissal time _____

Lunch options

☐ Eat hot lunch provided at school   Cost: _____

☐ Eat sack lunch provided at school   Cost: _____

☐ Eat sack lunch brought from home

☐ Purchase milk only, to drink with   Cost: _____
   sack lunch brought from home

☐ Return home for lunch

Transportation Options   ☐ Bus   ☐ Walk   ☐ Parents provide transportation

Portage & Main Press, 2010, black line master, ISBN 978-1-55379-232-1

Illness   If your child is ill please do not send him or her to school.

If your child is too ill to be able to function in class or if his or her temperature is 100°F (37.8°C) or above, we will send him or her home. (If no one is at home during school hours, please make other arrangements with the school in case your child becomes ill.)

Absence   If your child is ill or for some other reason will not be at school, please phone the school secretary or principal at _____

Portage & Main Press, 2010, black line master, ISBN 978-1-55379-232-1

Home Language Survey

Note: This form is used for assessment and placement purposes. Obtaining this information is required by law in the U.S.

Date _____

School _____

Teacher _____

Dear Parents,

In order for us to help your child, we need to know the language(s) you speak at home. Please answer the following questions. Thank you for your help.

Name of student _____
                        Family name   Given name

Years of school completed _____   Age _____

Native country _____

1. What language did your child learn when he or she first began to talk?

    _____

2. What language does your child use most frequently at home?

    _____

3. What language do you use most frequently to speak to your child?

    _____

4. What language is most often spoken by the adults at home?

    _____

Signature of parent or guardian_____

Portage & Main Press, 2010, black line master, ISBN 978-1-55379-232-1

Student Vocabulary Test

Note: To be completed when new student is admitted to school. You may wish to use photos from magazines or catalogs to make flash cards for this purpose. Drawings are not recommended.

Teacher _____ Student _____

School _____ Grade _____

Have student identify using English vocabulary. Use check marks to note those words the student knows. Leave others blank.

1. Colors

☐ red ☐ blue ☐ green ☐ yellow

☐ orange ☐ black ☐ purple ☐ brown

2. Numbers—Kindergarten

☐ 1 ☐ 2 ☐ 3 ☐ 4

☐ 5 ☐ 6 ☐ 7 ☐ 8

☐ 9 ☐ 10

Grades 1–3, as above plus

☐ 11 ☐ 12 ☐ 13 ☐ 14

☐ 15 ☐ 16 ☐ 17 ☐ 18

☐ 19 ☐ 20

3. Shapes

☐ circle ☐ square ☐ triangle ☐ rectangle

4. Alphabet (present in random order)

☐ A ☐ B ☐ C ☐ D

☐ E ☐ F ☐ G ☐ H

☐ I ☐ J ☐ K ☐ L

☐ M ☐ N ☐ O ☐ P

☐ Q ☐ R ☐ S ☐ T

☐ U ☐ V ☐ W ☐ X

☐ Y ☐ Z

5. Personal Information

☐ name ☐ age ☐ address ☐ phone number

Portage & Main Press, 2010, black line master, ISBN 978-1-55379-232-1

6. Body parts

☐ eye	☐ nose	☐ cheek	☐ mouth
☐ neck	☐ chest	☐ shoulder	☐ arm
☐ hand	☐ stomach	☐ leg	☐ knee
☐ foot	☐ finger		

7. Spatial orientation

☐ left	☐ right	☐ in front of	☐ out
☐ over	☐ above	☐ beside	☐ behind
☐ in	☐ near	☐ far	

8. School vocabulary

☐ recess	☐ hall	☐ washroom	☐ auditorium
☐ playground	☐ locker	☐ office	☐ lunch
☐ teacher	☐ lunch room	☐ principal	☐ secretary
☐ tardy slip	☐ school	☐ science	☐ phys ed
☐ math	☐ school bus	☐ language arts	
☐ drinking fountain		☐ library	☐ gymnasium

9. Classroom words

☐ desk	☐ books	☐ paper	☐ board
☐ crayons	☐ notebook	☐ pencil	☐ glue
☐ chalk	☐ clock	☐ eraser	☐ page
☐ rug	☐ scissors	☐ seat	☐ chair
☐ table	☐ window	☐ wastebasket	☐ computer

10. Clothing

☐ coat	☐ dress	☐ jacket	☐ hat
☐ gym shoes	☐ mittens	☐ pants	☐ shirt
☐ shoes	☐ skirt	☐ socks	☐ sweater

11. Safety terms

☐ stop	☐ go	☐ walk	☐ don't walk

12. Time

☐ morning	☐ noon	☐ afternoon	☐ night
☐ day	☐ today	☐ tomorrow	☐ yesterday
☐ week	☐ next week	☐ month	☐ year

13. Other vocabulary

☐ first	☐ last	☐ big	☐ little
☐ small	☐ smaller		

Portage & Main Press, 2010, black line master, ISBN 978-1-55379-232-1

14. Money

☐ penny ☐ nickel ☐ dime ☐ quarter

☐ cent ☐ cost ☐ dollar

15. Transportation

☐ bus ☐ car ☐ truck ☐ plane

16. Everyday directions

☐ wait ☐ sit down ☐ stand up ☐ sit on the floor

☐ come here ☐ line up ☐ pick up ☐ open book

☐ touch ☐ cut out ☐ wait ☐ copy

☐ wash your hands ☐ raise your hand

17. Home words

☐ address ☐ brother ☐ sister ☐ father

☐ mother ☐ home ☐ sofa ☐ chair

☐ table ☐ bed

Portage & Main Press, 2010, black line master, ISBN 978-1-55379-232-1

Basic Student Information

Note: This form is to be filled out at time of student's admission to school, with the assistance of parents and/or interpreter. (Health information is retained separately.)

Name of student _____

Address _____

Telephone _____ Birthdate _____ ☐ M ☐ F

Father's name _____

Place of employment _____

Business telephone _____ Cell phone number _____

Mother's name _____

Place of employment _____

Business telephone _____ Cell phone number _____

In case of emergency, if parents cannot be reached, call

Name _____ Telephone _____

Other Information Native country _____ Native language _____

Other languages spoken _____

Arrival date in U.S./Canada _____ Arrival date in state/province _____

Number of years in school in first language _____

Number of years in school in second language _____

Previous school enrollment in U.S./Canada _____

Previous English instruction before arriving to this country _____

Comes from rural/country background _____ urban/city background _____

Additional Information _____

_____

_____

_____

Portage & Main Press, 2010, black line master, ISBN 978-1-55379-232-1

Checklist for Assessing Emerging Readers

Student Name_____ Date_____

Age _____ Grade _____

	Not Yet	Emerging	Yes
Listens to story, but is not looking at pages			
Tries to read environmental print			
Demonstrates book-handling knowledge (right side up)			
Looks at pictures as story is read aloud			
Makes up words for picture			
Demonstrates directionality of written language (left to right, page order)			
Pretends to read			
Recognizes some words from a dictated story			
Participates in reading by supplying rhyming words and some predictable text			
Memorizes text, and pretends to read story			
Looks at words, and tracks words when reading or is being read to from a familiar story			
Recognizes words, in a new context			
Reads word for word			
Reads familiar stories fluently			
Reads unfamiliar stories haltingly			
Uses context clues, phonic analysis, sentence structure, to read new words and passages			
Reads easy books fluently			
Chooses to read independently			
Reads fluently			

Portage & Main Press, 2010, black line master, ISBN 978-1-55379-232-1

Writing Sample Score Sheet

SKILL AREAS	DESCRIPTION	SCORE
Content	☐ theme developed	Fluent
	☐ related ideas and examples supplied	
	☐ thought development adequate	Intermediate
	☐ some unrelated ideas used	
	☐ uneven (or no) theme development	Beginner
	☐ many unrelated ideas included	
	☐ few (or no) examples given	
	☐ insufficient writing for evaluation	
Organization	☐ good topic development	Fluent
	☐ opening sentence or introductory paragraph included	
	☐ concluding sentence/paragraph included	
	☐ ideas well organized, clearly stated, and backed-up transitions included	
	☐ topic or opening sentence included, but no closing sentence provided	Intermediate
	☐ weak organization	
	☐ inadequate back-up information provided	
	☐ few transitions included	
	☐ no topic sentence development	Beginner
	☐ no opening or closing sentence included	
	☐ little or no organization	
	☐ no back-up information provided	
	☐ no transitions included	
	☐ ideas confused or unrelated	
	☐ insufficient writing for evaluation	
Vocabulary	☐ correct use of word forms (prefixes, suffixes, etc.) and idioms	Fluent
	☐ sophisticated word choice	
	☐ meaning clear	
	☐ generally correct use of word forms and idioms	Intermediate
	☐ word choice correct	
	☐ meaning clear	

Portage & Main Press, 2010, black line master, ISBN 978-1-55379-232-1

	□ many errors in word forms and idioms	**Beginner**
	□ ineffective word choice	
	□ words selected though direct translation	
	□ meaning confused or obscured	
	□ insufficient writing for evaluation	
Language Skills	□ correct use of verb tense	**Fluent**
	□ good sentence variety and complex construction	
	□ good control of agreement, number, word order, parts of speech	
	□ most verb tenses correct	**Intermediate**
	□ simple sentence construction	
	□ errors in agreement, number, word order, parts of speech	
	□ frequent errors in tense	**Beginner**
	□ forced sentence constructions	
	□ many errors in agreement, number, word order, parts of speech	
	□ insufficient writing for evaluation	
Mechanics	□ few errors made in spelling, punctuation, capitalization	**Fluent**
	□ occasional errors in spelling, punctuation, capitalization	**Intermediate**
	□ many errors in spelling, punctuation, capitalization	**Beginner**
	□ handwriting unclear or illegible	
	□ insufficient writing for evaluation	

Portage & Main Press, 2010, black line master, ISBN 978-1-55379-232-1

Individualized Educational Plan

Note: This form is to be completed by the ELL teacher, the resource teacher, or the classroom teacher three or four weeks after the new student has been assigned to the class, or whenever an IEP is to be updated.

Student's name _____
                                Family name   Given name

Birth date _____ Age _____ ☐ M ☐ F
              Mo   Day   Year

Grade level _____ Assessment test _____

Date given _____ Primary language _____

Assessment test given in primary language? ☐ yes ☐ no

Supplemental Testing Observations

Oral production _____

_____

_____

Comprehension _____

_____

_____

Reading skill _____

_____

_____

_____

Written skills _____

_____

Summary of observed testing performance _____

_____

_____

_____

_____

Portage & Main Press, 2010, black line master, ISBN 978-1-55379-232-1

Particular Learning Needs   ☐ Spoken language   ☐ Reading   ☐ Written language

☐ Other _____

Comments _____

_____

_____

_____

_____

Short-Range Goals _____

_____

_____

_____

Strategy for implementation _____

_____

_____

_____

Long-Range Goals _____

_____

_____

_____

Strategy for implementation _____

_____

_____

_____

_____

Portage & Main Press, 2010, black line master, ISBN 978-1-55379-232-1

Individualized Educational Plan

Note: This form is to be completed by the ELL teacher, the resource teacher, or the classroom teacher three or four weeks after the new student has been assigned to the class, or whenever an IEP is to be updated.

Student's name _____ Ruyshchenko _____ Boris _____
                        Family name   Given name

Birth date __ January 13 _____ Age __ 13 _____ ☒ M ☐ F
              Mo   Day   Year

Grade level __ 8 _____ Assessment test __ LAS _____

Date given __ January _____ Primary language __ Russian ____

Assessment test given in primary language? ☐ yes ☒ no

Supplemental Testing Observations

Oral production __Level 5 English proficiency in conversational skills.__
__Could converse easily, without hesitation, on familiar topics.__

Comprehension __Understood everything he was asked, and could__
__answer easily.__

Reading skill __Records from Russia show reading in Russian was at__
__grade level. Reading in English is approximately two years lower,__
__with significant gaps in academic vocabulary. Will not be able to__
__function on par with English-speaking classmates in content areas.__

Written skills __Could write in English, but had many non-native__
__errors.__

Summary of observed testing performance __Boris talked incessantly.__
__He couldn't sit still, answered with questions, trying to get you__
__to give him the answers. Very busy even when sitting. Seems to__
__have a chip on his shoulder about the inferiority of schools in__
__America.__

Portage & Main Press, 2010, black line master, ISBN 978-1-55379-232-1

Appendix G—Example 1

Particular Learning Needs   ☑ Spoken language   ☑ Reading   ☑ Written language

☐ Other _____

Comments Continue to develop content vocabulary. Continue to develop reading skills in both English and Russian. Work on fluency. Work on social skills. Specific rules set out concerning proper classroom behavior. Monitor group work to encourage appropriate interaction with peers.

Short-Range Goals Work on content vocabulary in all skill areas. Help Boris adapt to classroom structure. Work on social skills with peers.

Strategy for implementation Assign Boris an adult mentor to work with with him on adapting to new school situation and routine, help with feedback on school assignments, and work on content.

Long-Range Goals Continue to develop cognitive academic vocabulary. Continue reading in Russian. Develop reading content material in English, and work towards fluency in written English.

Strategy for implementation Work on specific assignments with Boris to focus on vocabulary. Get appropriate books in Russian from home, newspaper articles on Internet. Review reading in English. Monitor Boris for success in group activities.

Portage & Main Press, 2010, black line master, ISBN 978-1-55379-232-1

Individualized Educational Plan

Note: This form is to be completed by the ELL teacher, the resource teacher, or the classroom teacher three or four weeks after the new student has been assigned to the class, or whenever an IEP is to be updated.

Student's name _____Thuyen_____ _____Newton_____

                       Family name   Given name

Birth date ___March 4___ Age __16__ ☒ M ☐ F

        Mo   Day   Year

Grade level __10__ Assessment test _LAS_

Date given __January__ Primary language _Vietnamese_

Assessment test given in primary language? ☐ yes ☒ no

Supplemental Testing Observations

Oral production _Minimal. Frequently unintelligible because of pronunciation. Inaccurate grammar, halting speech, simple vocab. Level 2. Minimal conversational skills._

Comprehension _Knows a few words. Can retell a story on basic level. Can follow two- and three-step directions._

Reading skill _Unable to fill out home language survey. Could read sentences at grade-3 level. Can retell a story on basic level._

Written skills _Can write name. Shows limited knowledge of simple vocab. Syntax irregular. Simple writing on concrete and familiar topics. Unconventional spelling._

Summary of observed testing performance _Newton was born in this country and should be farther along in English than he appears. Seems to have an excellent ability for drawing as he drew a few pictures while waiting for testing to be completed. He is withdrawn._

Portage & Main Press, 2010, black line master, ISBN 978-1-55379-232-1

Particular Learning Needs

☑ Spoken language ☑ Reading ☑ Written language

☐ Other _____

Comments Newton needs reinforcement in all four skill areas. Beyond academic skills, Newton will need help interacting with peers.

_____

_____

_____

Short-Range Goals Involve in group activities. Capitalize in artistic area. Read simple texts. Build fluency and understanding. Increase vocabulary.

_____

Strategy for implementation Place in art class. Work with mentor for reinforcement and mediation with content area teachers.

_____

_____

Long-Range Goals Work on social skills, monitor closely. Continue to develop skills in reading and writing. Observe and develop performance in Vietnamese.

_____

Strategy for implementation Work closely with mentor, particularly as this type of student can fall through cracks easily. Foster work with art projects inside and outside class, encourage a buddy in particularly difficult classes, try to develop a small group for this student.

Portage & Main Press, 2010, black line master, ISBN 978-1-55379-232-1

Individualized Educational Plan

Note: This form is to be completed by the ELL teacher, the resource teacher, or the classroom teacher three or four weeks after the new student has been assigned to the class, or whenever an IEP is to be updated.

Student's name   Luckner   Spencer

                Family name   Given name

Birth date   November 2   Age   6   ☒ M   ☐ F

        Mo   Day   Year

Grade level   Kindergarten   Assessment test   Print awareness

Date given   April   Primary language   Non-standard English

Assessment test given in primary language?   ☒ yes   ☐ no

Supplemental Testing Observations

Oral production   Very oral and fluent

Comprehension   Good

Reading skill   Could not pick out his name from a list of five names.

Written skills   Wrote 3 letters of his name and random letters in response to spelling test.

Summary of observed testing performance   This boy tried very hard to do a good job. He was charming and capable of holding a conversation. He displayed intelligence and was quick to find ways to "survive" the test. Didn't know the names of all his brothers.

Portage & Main Press, 2010, black line master, ISBN 978-1-55379-232-1

Particular Learning Needs ☑ Spoken language ☐ Reading ☐ Written language

☐ Other _____

Comments <u>This child will need support in all areas. Spencer wants</u> <u>to achieve, so this desire needs to be reinforced with success.</u>

Short-Range Goals <u>Assimilate into class and routine. Make the most of the time</u> <u>left in the year.</u>

Strategy for implementation <u>Strong one-on-one support for this</u> <u>student. LEA, word banks, frame sentences.</u>

Long-Range Goals <u>Resist tempation to give into shortness of time left in school</u> <u>year, use what time is left. Build self esteem through reading</u> <u>and writing successes.</u>

Strategy for implementation <u>Paired reading, mentor for one-on-one,</u> <u>sound/spelling correspondence. Establish home/school</u> <u>connections.</u>

Portage & Main Press, 2010, black line master, ISBN 978-1-55379-232-1

Individualized Educational Plan

Note: This form is to be completed by the ELL teacher, the resource teacher, or the classroom teacher three or four weeks after the new student has been assigned to the class, or whenever an IEP is to be updated.

Student's name _____ Bill _____ Charlie _____
                              Family name   Given name

Birth date __February 20__   Age _6_   ☒ M   ☐ F
            Mo   Day   Year

Grade level __Kindergarten__   Assessment test __LAS__

Date given __August__   Primary language __Unknown__

Assessment test given in primary language?   ☐ yes   ☒ no

Supplemental Testing Observations

Oral production __Minimal__

_____

_____

Comprehension __Difficult to know__

_____

_____

Reading skill __Could not pick his name out of field of five names.__
__Does not demonstrate any knowledge that print has meaning.__

_____

_____

Written skills __Could not write name, does not know alphabet.__

_____

Summary of observed testing performance __Shy and hesitant, did not__
__seem to have experience with print. Did not attempt to read/__
__write, spoke little, seemed unfamiliar with school.__

_____

_____

Portage & Main Press, 2010, black line master, ISBN 978-1-55379-232-1

Particular Learning Needs

☐ Spoken language   ☐ Reading   ☐ Written language

☐ Other _____

Comments _Help Charlie become comfortable with school and_ _begin reading and writing._

_____

_____

_____

Short-Range Goals   _Help Charlie feel part of group in order to participate._

_____

_____

_____

Strategy for implementation _Pair with friendly buddy to get_ _connected. Work on affective objectives first._

_____

_____

_____

Long-Range Goals   _Focus on familiarization with print. Continue to work with Charlie_ _on feeling comfortable at school. Learn about home language._ _Encourage family to build skills._

_____

Strategy for implementation _Focus on Charlie's participation at all_ _levels, work with LEA, frame sentences, and reading books_ _of his interest areas. Meet with parents._

_____

_____

Portage & Main Press, 2010, black line master, ISBN 978-1-55379-232-1

Individualized Educational Plan

Note: This form is to be completed by the ELL teacher, the resource teacher, or the classroom teacher three or four weeks after the new student has been assigned to the class, or whenever an IEP is to be updated.

Student's name ___Xiong___ ___Bao___
Family name   Given name

Birth date ___June 10___   Age ___9___   ☐ M ☒ F
Mo   Day   Year

Grade level ___3/4 split___   Assessment test ___LAS___

Date given ___October___   Primary language ___Hmong___

Assessment test given in primary language? ☐ yes ☒ no

Supplemental Testing Observations

Oral production ___Didn't say anything___

Comprehension ___Very little demonstrated. Would not, or could not follow simple directions.___

Reading skill ___None demonstrated. Would not pick up a book. Did not demonstrate any knowledge of print.___

Written skills ___None demonstrated___

Summary of observed testing performance ___Bao was very shy and reluctant to respond to any questions. Avoided eye contact and seemed very uncomfortable with the process. Shrugged her shoulders in response to questions.___

Portage & Main Press, 2010, black line master, ISBN 978-1-55379-232-1

Particular Learning Needs

☑ Spoken language ☑ Reading ☑ Written language

☐ Other _____

Comments _Need to develop a social vocabulary first. Start with print has meaning, environmental print, labels in classroom. Begin with lists, name, environmental print. Bao will need intensive work in all areas._

Short-Range Goals

Develop survival and social vocabulary, introduction of reading skills, help with assimilation into classroom and school routine.

Strategy for implementation _Read to Bao, label items, use English to create LEA stories, provide opportunity to draw, copy, and practice writing._

Long-Range Goals

Participation in classroom work, develop content vocabulary, incorporate Bao in classroom routine, continue work in four skill areas.

Strategy for implementation _Continue to provide appropriate books for reading, place Bao in groups to encourage social English. Use LEA stories to reinforce vocabulary and reading skills in content area, use Hmong aide to foster primary language development._

Portage & Main Press, 2010, black line master, ISBN 978-1-55379-232-1

Test of Written English (TWE) Scoring Guide

SCORE

6   **Demonstrates clear competence in writing on both the rhetorical and syntactic levels, though it may have occasional errors**

A paper in this category

- Effectively addresses the writing task
- Is well organized
- Uses clearly appropriate details to support a thesis or illustrate ideas
- Displays consistent facility in the use of language
- Demonstrates syntactic variety and appropriate word choice

5   **Demonstrates competence in writing on both the rhetorical and syntactic levels, though it will probably have occasional errors**

A paper in this category

- May address some parts of the task more effectively than others
- Is generally well organized and developed
- Uses details to support a thesis or illustrate an idea
- Displays facility in the use of language
- Demonstrates some syntactic variety and range of vocabulary

4   **Demonstrates minimal competence in writing on both the rhetorical and syntactic levels**

A paper in this category

- Addresses the writing topic adequately but may slight parts of the task
- Is adequately organized and developed
- Uses some details to support a thesis or illustrate an idea
- Demonstrates adequate but possibly inconsistent facility with syntax and usage
- May contain some errors that occasionally obscure meaning

3   **Demonstrates some developing competence in writing, but it remains flawed on either the rhetorical or syntactic level, or both**

A paper in this category may reveal one or more of the following weaknesses:

- Inadequate organization or development
- Inappropriate or insufficient details to support or illustrate generalizations
- A noticeably inappropriate choice of words or word forms
- An accumulation of errors in sentence structure and/or usage

Portage & Main Press, 2010, black line master, ISBN 978-1-55379-232-1

SCORE

2 **Suggests incompetence in writing**

A paper in this category in seriously flawed by one or more of the following weaknesses:

- Serious disorganization or underdevelopment
- Little or no detail, or irrelevant specifics
- Serious and frequent errors in sentence structure or usage
- Serious problems with focus

1 **Demonstrates incompetence in writing**

A paper in this category

- May be incoherent
- May be underdeveloped
- May contain severe and persistent errors

Portage & Main Press, 2010, black line master, ISBN 978-1-55379-232-1

Teacher-Volunteer (or Aide) Planning Sheet

Name of volunteer (or aide) _____

Name of teacher/grade level _____

Name(s) of students(s) _____

_____

Skills to be reinforced or tasks to be completed by volunteer (or aide):

_____

_____

Time frame _____

Materials to be used _____

_____

_____

_____

Location of materials _____

Procedures _____

_____

_____

_____

_____

Comments of volunteer (or aide): _____

_____

_____

_____

_____

_____

Portage & Main Press, 2010, black line master, ISBN 978-1-55379-232-1

Jessica's "The Great Ocean"

Note: The first paragraph of this essay also appears on page 242.

THE GREAT OCEAN

Ocean is a mass body of salt water that covers three fourth of the Earth. I, too, have an ocean between my father and I. My father had tried to swim across the ocean many times, but every time he tries, I would finds some ways to make him drown, forcing him to retreat. He, therefore, would wait awhile, until the storm is over, and tries again, and I would be there waiting for him; stopping him from reaching the surface. My hatred for him is deeper than the deepest depth of the ocean. My sister would often ask me, "Why can't you be like me, forgive and forget? Don't forget, he's our father." And I would often reply, "But I'm not you."

What has happen to cause such distant and hatred between my father and I, went all the way back when I was a kid. As a kid, I remember how poor my family were. My mom would often buys dozen trays of eggs in substitute of meats and vegetables. Back then, eggs are extremely cheap, and my family would eat it three meals a day. Because my family is in desperate needs of money, my father went up to Reno to look for jobs. Every week my father would come home bringing couple packages of steaks for us.

But every time he leaves, we would become poorer, and I would always wonder why. Later on, my parents decided to move to Reno, and there my puddle of water formed, and as years goes by, it keep expanding until the puddle became an ocean. At first, my dad would only takes his salary to the Casino, but pretty soon he began stealing money from my mother. Relatives and friends looked down on us. The Casinos became my father's home, and when he ran out of money, he would shows up on our doorsteps, treating us sweetly, slowly tricking my mother into

Continues on next page

Portage & Main Press, 2010, black line master, ISBN 978-1-55379-232-1

handling him her money, then he would go back to his Black Jacks, Pokers, and slot machines. My sister at the tender age of thirteen were forced to look for a job to help out our mother. When we moved to Tahoe, my father changed for awhile, but not before long he changed back into his old self and start spending his nights at the casinos again.

As we got older, my father realized his mistakes and tried to make it up to us, but he did not realized trying to cross the ocean is dangerous. The sharks would prevented him from reaching the other end of the ocean. But my sister is right, he's my father and no matter what did, right or wrong, a part of me would always love him but a part of me would also hated him. I saw my father's mistakes and I know my family comes first before anything. I will not be like my father, uncaring and selfish. I pity my father because I know he is lonely and wishes we would filled him with loves but the ocean could not shrink, the sharks would not go away. I do not know when I could finally forgives him for what he had done to us. The ocean are just too big.

Portage & Main Press, 2010, black line master, ISBN 978-1-55379-232-1

Glossary

BICS—Basic Interpersonal Communication Skills
The skills involved in everyday communication—listening, speaking, carrying on basic conversation, understanding speakers, and getting one's basic needs met.

CALP—Cognitive Academic Language Proficiency
The skills that are needed to succeed in the academic classroom, which include problem solving, inferring, analyzing, synthesizing, and predicting. They go beyond the BICS, demanding much greater competence in the language.

Context-Reduced Language
Language that has few visual and/or aural cues to help the learner understand. This is demanding language because the learner's ability to understand the spoken or written message depends solely on his proficiency in the language. Examples of context-reduced language situations are lectures without demonstrations or visual aids; math word problems without illustrations; textbooks without charts, diagrams, or photos.

Context-Embedded Language
Language that is most easily understood is embedded in a context that is rich in cues such as concrete objects, gestures, facial expressions, art, music, phys ed, face-to-face conversations, games, hands-on activities (as with science), math computation problems, and TPR.

Emergent Literacy
Literacy is viewed as the development of the association of print with meaning, something that begins in early childhood and is acquired over time, rather than as skills students are formally taught and learned when they go to school. Most children who grow up in Western society have experience with print long before they come to school. Not so with a host of newcomers. Teachers cannot assume that these students know such things as how to hold a book, or what reading and writing are for.

Explicit Instruction

Instruction that directly explains the what, why, when, and how of certain skills, such as how to write a paragraph, skim a text, sound out a word, or use context and other clues to figure out meaning.

FEP/FES—Fully English Speaking/Fully English Proficient

Students who are able to participate fully in regular classroom activities. ELL students are usually designated FEP after scoring beyond a designated percentile on a standardized proficiency test. Educators must keep in mind that students should not be considered FEP on the basis of their oral language alone—the FEP designation does not necessarily mean that the student will be able to perform successfully in the content areas. Many FEP students struggle with the cognitive academic language in the content areas and may continue to need some support. In addition, many students, no matter how proficient, still write with a foreign accent; in other words, their syntax and word usage show many traits of their first language.

Guided Reading

One way of providing direct instruction, guided reading is explicit, individualized, and focused on specific skills and strategies. Guided reading allows you to pull together small groups of students for a particular purpose while at the same time fine tuning your teaching by pinpointing exactly what those students need.

Input

The language the student hears and encounters on a daily basis. This includes directed input in the form of language lessons and ordinary conversation.

Intake

The language the student actually processes and learns and is able to use and understand when he reads it or hears it spoken.

Integrated Approach

An approach to literacy instruction that links reading, writing, listening, and speaking skills, rather than considering them separate skills.

LEA—Language Experience Approach

A method of promoting reading in which the teacher begins with the experiences the students bring to class (or experience together), and then develops oral and written activities around these experiences. The teacher uses the students' own words to write stories, which are then used in a variety of ways.

LES/LEP—Limited English Speaking/Limited English Proficient

Understands some English, but is not fluent enough to compete academically with English-speaking peers.

Literature Circle

Discussion group based on self-selected books for reading; each group consists of students who independently read the same book (or different titles by the same author, or books with a common theme), rather than the lock-step reading approach where the teacher selects the reading, or the students go on to the next story in the basal reader.

Miscue Analysis

A miscue is defined as the difference between the oral response of a reader and the actual words printed on the page. Miscue analysis, developed by Kenneth and Yetta Goodman, is a method of evaluating reading comprehension using a detailed analysis of the types of errors made when reading aloud. Particular strategies are then used to help the reader correct his comprehension errors.

NES/NEP—Non-English Speaking/Non-English Proficient

Speaks little or no English.

Pull-Out

Students are "pulled out" of the classroom to work with the ELL teacher. Often, the ELL teacher supplements or prepares the students for what is going on in the regular classroom. At the high-school level, ELL teachers act as a resource, helping students get through their content classes by explaining homework and with understanding the readings. Often, ELL teachers teach vocabulary that we assume students know: shapes, telling time, colors, parts of the body, or beginning reading skills.

Push-In

In this model, the ELL teacher comes into the classroom to work with the students. In an ideal world, this is a terrific option especially if the ELL teacher is bilingual. The teachers team together to work on content. It's here that the bilingual teacher can translate, add insight into cultural issues or special problems that arise.

Sheltered English

Sheltered English is an approach to teaching the content of science, social studies, and so on through modified language and methods in order to make the information comprehensible to the students.

TPR—Total Physical Response

Introduced by James Asher, this method uses physical actions to develop language skills in second-language learners. Students are asked to respond physically to commands or directions, often in a game-like situation.

Writing Process

The activities involved in producing writing, including prewriting, drafting, rereading, revising, editing, and publishing.

Bibliography

Academiclanguage.org website, "Academic Language" (definition). <http://academiclanguage.org> (accessed January 26, 2010).

Alatis, Penelope et al. "Learners, Teachers, and Aides/Volunteers: Bermuda Triangle or Synergy?" (paper presented at the 21st International TESOL Conference, Miami, FL, 1987).

Alberta Learning. *English as a Second Language, Senior High School Guide to Implementation.* Edmonton: Alberta Learning, Learning and Teaching Resources Branch, 2002.

Allen, Janet. *It's Never Too Late: Leading Adolescents to Lifelong Literacy.* Portsmouth, NH: Heinemann, 1995.

Allington, Richard L. "Fluency: Still Waiting After All These Years." In *What Research Has to Say About Fluency Instruction*, edited by Alan E. Farstrup and S. Jay Samuels. Newark, DE: International Reading Association, 2006.

_____. *Big Brother and the National Reading Curriculum: How Ideology Trumped Evidence.* Portsmouth, NH: Heinemann, 2002.

_____. *What Really Matters for Struggling Readers: Designing Research-Based Programs.* New York: Longman, 2001.

_____. "The Schools We Have, the Schools We Need." Albany: National Research Center on Literature Teaching and Learning, 1994.

Alsop, Ron. *The Trophy Kids Grow Up: How the Millennial Generation is Shaking Up the Workplace.* San Francisco: Jossey-Bass, 2008.

American Federation of Teachers. *Where We Stand: English Language Learners.* Washington, DC: American Federation of Teachers, 2006.

Ammon, Paul. "Helping Children Learn to Write in English as a Second Language: Some Observations and Some Hypotheses." In *The Acquisition of Written Language: Response and Revision*, edited by Sarah Warshauer Freedman. Norwood, NJ: Ablex Publishing, 1985.

Anderson, Richard C. et al. *Becoming a Nation of Readers: The Report of the Commission on Reading.* Washington, DC: National Institute of Education, 1985.

Angert, Debbie and Jan Booth, CATESOL (California Teachers of English to Speakers of Other Languages) conference workshop, 1987.

Armstrong, Sally. *Using the 8 Step American Management Association (AMA) Problem Solving and Case Analysis Process.* Grant Rapids, MI: Davenport University, 2005.

Asher, James. "The Strategy of the Total Physical Response: An Application to Learning Russian." *International Review of Applied Linguistics* v3, n4 (1965): 291–300.

Atwell, Nancie. *In the Middle: New Understandings About Writing, Reading and Learning with Adolescents,* 2nd edition. Portsmouth, NH: Boynton/Cook, 1998.

Au, Kathryn. *Literacy Instruction in Multicultural Settings.* Fort Worth: Harcourt Brace Jovanovich, 1993.

_____. "Participation Structures in a Reading Lesson with Hawaiian Children: Analysis of a Culturally Appropriate Instructional Event." *Anthropology and Education Quarterly* v11, n2 (1980): 91–115.

Au, Kathryn and Alice J. Kawakami. "Research Currents: Talk Story and Learning to Read." *Language Arts* v62, n4 (1985): 406–411.

August, Diane and Timothy Shanahan, eds. *Developing Literacy in Second-Language Learners: Report of the National Literacy Panel on Language-Minority Children and Youth.* Mahwah, NJ: Lawrence Erlbaum, 2006.

Barnes, Douglas. *Language, the Learner, and the School,* 3rd edition. New York: Penguin, 1986.

Barrs, Myra et al. *The Primary Language Record: A Handbook for Teachers.* Portsmouth, NH: Heinemann, 1989.

Bell, Jill and Barbara Burnaby. *A Handbook for ESL Literacy.* Toronto: OISE Press, 1984.

Benedict, Susan and Lenore Carlisle. *Beyond Words: Picture Books for Older Readers and Writers.* Portsmouth, NH: Heinemann, 1992.

Benesch, Sarah, ed. *Ending Remediation: Linking ESL and Content in Higher Education.* Alexandria, VA: TESOL, 1988.

Biological Sciences Curriculum Study (BSCS). *Developing Biological Literacy: A Guide to Developing Secondary and Post Secondary Biology Curricula.* Colorado Springs, CO: BSCS, 1993.

Blachowicz, Camille and Donna Ogle. *Reading Comprehension,* 2nd ed. New York: Guildford Press, 2008.

Bliatout, Bruce et al. *Handbook for Teaching Hmong-Speaking Students.* Folsom, CA: Folsom Cordova Unified School District, Southeast Asia Community Resource Center, 1988.

Briggs, Sandra et al. *Guidelines for Working with Limited-English Proficient Students.* San Mateo, CA: San Mateo Union High School District, 1985.

Brinton, Donna, Marguerite Snow, and Marjorie Wesche. *Content-Based Second Language Instruction.* New York: Newbury House, 1989.

Brock, Cynthia. "Exploring the Use of Book Clubs with Second Language Learners in Mainstream Classrooms." In *The Book Club Connection: Literacy Learning and Classroom Talk*, edited by Susan McMahon and Taffy Raphael. New York: Teachers College Press, 1997.

Bunch, George. "'Academic English' in the 7th Grade: Broadening the Lens, Expanding Access." *Journal of English for Academic Purposes* v5, n4 (2006): 284–301.

Burton, R. *Everyone's Child; Education: The Changing Face in the Classroom.* <www.nwrel.org/nwedu> (accessed March 16, 2009).

Bybee, Rodger. *Achieving Scientific Literacy: From Purposes to Practices.* Portsmouth, NH: Heinemann, 1997. ·

California Department of Education. *Reading/Language Arts Framework for California Public Schools, Kindergarten Through Grade Twelve.* Sacramento, CA: California Department of Education, 2007.

California State Board of Education. *English-Language Arts Content Standards for California Public Schools, Kindergarten Through Grade Twelve, 1997.* Sacramento, CA: California Department of Education, 1998.

Bibliography

California Teachers of English to Speakers of Other Languages (CATESOL) website. "Position Statement on Literacy Instruction for English Language Learners, Grades K–12" (1998) <http://catesol.org/literacy.html> (accessed January 26, 2010).

Calkins, Lucy McCormick. *The Art of Teaching Writing,* revised ed. Portsmouth, NH: Heinemann, 1994.

Cambourne, Brian. "Holistic, Integrated Approaches to Reading and Language Arts Instruction: The Constructivist Framework of an Instructional Theory." In *What Research Has to Say About Reading Instruction,* 3rd ed, edited by Alan E. Farstrup and S. Jay Samuels. Newark, DE: International Reading Association, 2002.

_____. "Conditions for Literacy Learning: Explicit and Systematic Teaching of Reading—A New Slogan?" *The Reading Teacher* v53, n2 (1999): 126–127.

_____. *The Whole Story: Natural Learning and the Acquisition of Literacy in the Classroom.* New York: Scholastic, 1998.

Cantoni-Harvey, Gina. *Content-Area Language Instruction: Approaches and Strategies.* Reading, MA: Addison Wesley, 1987.

Cappellini, Mary. *Balancing Reading & Language Learning: A Resource for Teaching English Language Learners, K–5.* Newark, DE: International Reading Association, 2005.

Capps, Randy. "Hardship among Children of Immigrants: Findings from the 1999 National Survey of America's Families" (number B-29 in series, "New Federalism: National Survey of America's Families"). Washington, DC: The Urban Institute, 2001.

Capps, Randy et al. "The New Demography of America's Schools: Immigration and the No Child Left behind Act." Washington, DC: The Urban Institute, 2005.

Carbo, Marie. Carbo Recorded-Book Method™. Syosset, NY: National Reading Styles Institute, 1992.

Carr, Kathryn S. et al. "Not Just for Primary Grades: A Bibliography of Picture Books for Secondary Content Teachers." *Journal of Adolescent & Adult Literacy* v45, n2 (2001): 146–153.

Carrasquillo, Angela L. *Teaching English as a Second Language, A Resource Guide.* New York: Garland (Routledge), 1994.

Center for Applied Linguistics. "Indochinese Students in U.S. Schools: A Guide for Administrators" (Language in Education: Theory and Practice, No. 42). Washington DC: Center for Applied Linguistics, 1981.

Chaffee, John. *Thinking Critically,* 8th ed. Boston: Houghton Mifflin, 2004.

Chall, Jeanne. *Learning to Read: The Great Debate,* 3rd ed. Fort Worth, TX: Harcourt Brace, 1996.

Chamot, Anna Uhl and J. Michael O'Malley. *A Cognitive Academic Language Learning Approach: An ESL Content-Based Curriculum.* Washington, DC: National Clearinghouse for Bilingual Education, 1986.

Charter, Patricia F. "Special Education/Bilingual Education: A Collaborative Model." *Thrust* 18 (1989).

Chen, Linda and Eugenia Mora-Flores. *Balanced Literacy for English Language Learners, K-2.* Portsmouth, NH: Heinemann, 2006.

Chips, Barbara. "Using Cooperative Learning at the Secondary Level." In *Cooperative Learning: A Response to Linguistic and Cultural Diversity,* edited by Daniel Holt. McHenry, IL: Delta, 1993.

Churchill House School of English. "Classroom Language" lesson activities worksheet. <www.churchillhouse.com/english/classlang.pdf> (accessed January 11, 2010).

Clay, Marie. *What Did I Write? Beginning Writing Behaviour.* Portsmouth, NH: Heinemann. 1975.

Cobb, Thomas and Michael Gallagher. "Adapting Real Web Content for Adult Learners with Real Needs." North York, ON: *The Canadian Modern Language Review / La Revue canadienne des langues vivantes,* Journals Division, University of Toronto Press, 2005.

Collier, Virginia. "How Long? A Synthesis of Research on Academic Achievement in a Second Language." *TESOL Quarterly* v23, n3 (1989): 509–531.

Collins, J. J. *Selecting and Teaching Focus Correction Areas: A Planning Guide.* West Newbury, MA: Collins Education Associates, 1997.

Colorado Charter School page (Announcements). "Help To Improve CSAP! Six Trait Analytical Assessment Model." <uscharterschools.org/cs/codeg/view/cs_bmsg/347> (accessed January 5, 2010).

Cooper, J. David. *Literacy: Helping Children Construct Meaning,* 3rd ed. Boston: Houghton Mifflin, 1997.

Cooter, Robert B., E. Sutton Flynt, and Kathleen Spencer Cooter. *Cooter Flynt Cooter Comprehensive Reading Inventory: Measuring Reading Development in Regular and Special Education Classrooms.* Boston: Allyn & Bacon, 2006.

Corder, S. P. "The Significance of Learners' Errors." *International Review of Applied Linguistics* 5 (1967): 161–9.

Cramer, Ronald. *Writing, Reading and Language Growth: An Introduction to Language Arts.* Columbus, OH: Merrill, 1978.

Crandall, JoAnn. *Developing Content-Centered Language Learning: Strategies for Classroom Instruction and Teacher Development.* Thailand: Chulalongkorn University, 1995.

_____, ed. *ESL Through Content-Area Instruction.* Englewood Cliffs, NJ: Prentice-Hall, 1987.

The Critical Thinking Community. "Our Conception of Critical Thinking..." <www.criticalthinking.org/starting> (accessed January 11 2010).

Csíkszentmihályi, Mihaly. *Creativity: Flow and the Psychology of Discovery and Invention.* New York: HarperCollins, 1996.

Cullinan, Bernice, ed. *Children's Voices: Talk in the Classroom.* Newark, DE: International Reading Association, 1993.

Cummins, James. "The Role of Primary Language Development in Promoting Educational Success for Language Minority Students." In *Schooling and Language Minority Students: A Theoretical Framework,* edited by Charles F. Leyba. Los Angeles: Evaluation, Dissemination, and Assessment Center, 1981.

Cunningham, Patricia. *Phonics They Use: Words for Reading and Writing,* 3rd ed. New York: Longman, 2000.

Cunningham, Patricia et al. *Reading and Writing in Elementary Classrooms: Strategies and Observations,* 4th ed. New York: Longman, 2000.

Cunningham, Patricia and James Cunningham. "Making Words: Enhancing the Invented Spelling-Decoding Connection." *Reading Teacher* v46, n2 (1992): 106–115.

Daniels, Harvey. *Literature Circles: Voice and Choice in the Student-Centered Classroom.* York, ME: Stenhouse, 1994.

Davis, Deborah et al. "How Northwest Region States Are Supporting Schools in Need of Improvement." Portland, OR: Northwest Regional Educational Laboratory, 2007.

DeCristofaro, Dina. "Author to Author: How Text Influences Young Writers." *The Quarterly* v23, n2 (2001) 8–12.

Delpit, L. "The Politics of Teaching Literate Text." In *Negotiating Academic Literacies Across Languages and Cultures*, edited by Vivian Zamel and Ruth Spack. Mahwah, NJ: Lawrence Erlbaum, 1998.

Denton, David. "North Carolina Strives for Balanced Reading Instruction." Atlanta, GA: Southern Regional Education Board, 1998.

Dierking, Rebecca. "Creative Copying, or in Defense of Mimicry." *The Quarterly* v24, n4 (2002): 7–10.

Duke, Nell and P. David Pearson. "Effective Practices for Developing Reading Comprehension." In *What Research Has to Say About Reading Instruction*, 3rd ed, edited by Alan E. Farstrup and S. Jay Samuels. Newark, DE: International Reading Association, 2002.

Dulay, Heidi, Marina Burt, and Stephen Krashen. *Language Two*. New York: Oxford University Press, 1982.

Duncan, Sharon E. and Edward De Avila. *How to Administer the LAS*. San Rafael, CA: Linguametrics Group, 1985.

Dunn, Sonja with Lou Parmenter. *Butterscotch Dreams: Chants for Fun and Learning*. Portsmouth, NH: Heinemann, 1987.

Dyson, Anne Haas. "Symbol Makers, Symbol Weavers: How Children Link Play, Pictures, and Print." *Young Children* v45, n2 (1990): 50–57.

_____. "Appreciate the Drawing and Dictating of Young Children." *Young Children* v43, n3 (1988): 25–32.

_____. "Transitions and Tensions: Interrelationships between the Drawing, Talking, and Dictating of Young Children." *Research in the Teaching of English* v20, n4 (1986): 379–409.

Echevarria, Jana and Anne Graves. *Sheltered Content Instruction: Teaching English-Language Learners with Diverse Abilities*. Boston: Allyn & Bacon, 1998.

Echevarria, Jana, MaryEllen Vogt, and Deborah J. Short. *Making Content Comprehensible for English Language Learners: The SIOP Model*. Boston: Allyn & Bacon, 2000.

Edelsky, Carole. *Writing in a Bilingual Program: Habia Una Vez*. Norwood, NJ: Ablex, 1986.

Elley, Warwick and Francis Mangubhai. "The Impact of Reading on Second Language Learning." *Reading Research Quarterly* v19, n1 (1983): 53–67.

Emig, Janet. *The Composing Processes of Twelfth Graders*. Urbana, IL: National Council of Teachers of English, 1971.

Enright, D. Scott and Mary Lou McCloskey, *Integrating English: Developing English Language and Literacy in the Multilingual Classroom*. Reading, MA: Addison Wesley, 1988.

Entertainment Software Association. "Industry Facts." <www.theesa.com/facts/index.asp> (accessed January 11, 2010).

Field, Robert J. *History of the United States*, revised ed. New York: Booklab, 1993.

Fillmore, Lilly Wong. "Research Currents: Equity or Excellence?" *Language Arts* v63, n5 (1986): 474–481.

Fletcher, Ralph and JoAnn Portalupi. *Writing Workshop: The Essential Guide*. Portsmouth, NH: Heinemann 2001.

Flickinger, Gayle Glidden. "Language, Literacy, Children's Literature: The Link to Communicative Competency for ESOL Adults" (paper presented at the 12th annual meeting of the International Reading Association [IRA], Texas State Council, Corpus Christi, TX, March 1–3, 1984).

Flower, Linda and John Hayes. "Writing Research and the Writer." *American Psychologist* v41, n10 (1986): 1106–1113.

_____. "Problem-Solving Strategies and the Writing Process." *College English* v39, n4 (1977): 449–461.

Flynn, H. C. "A Collaborative Model of Service for LEP Students." Master's thesis, Hamline University, 1992.

Forester, Anne D. and Margaret Reinhard. *The Learners' Way: Brain-Based Learning in Action*, 2nd ed. Winnipeg, MB: Portage & Main Press, 2000.

Fountas, Irene and Gay Su Pinnell. *Guiding Readers and Writers, Grades 3–6: Teaching Comprehension, Genre, and Content Literacy."* Portsmouth, NH: Heinemann, 2001.

_____. *Guided Reading: Good First Teaching for All Children.* Portsmouth, NH: Heinemann, 1996.

Gadda, George, Faye Peitzman, and William Walsh. *Teaching Analytical Writing.* Long Beach: California Academic Partnership Program, 1988.

Galda, Lee, Bernice Cullinan, and Dorothy Strickland. *Language, Literacy and the Child.* 2nd ed. Fort Worth, TX: Harcourt Brace, 1997.

Gándara, Patricia, Julie Maxwell-Jolly, and Anne Driscoll. *Listening to Teachers of English Language Learners: A Survey of California Teachers' Challenges, Experiences, and Professional Development Needs.* Santa Cruz, CA: Center for the Future of Teaching and Learning: 2005.

Gardner, Howard. *Five Minds for the Future.* Boston: Harvard Business School Press, 2007.

Garside, Colleen. *Adventure-Based Learning Across Domains* (paper presented at the annual meeting of the Central States Communication Association, St. Paul, MN, April 18–21, 1996).

Gaskins, Irene. "There's More to Teaching At-Risk and Delayed Readers Than Good Reading Instruction" (Distinguished Educator Series). *The Reading Teacher* v51, n7 (1998): 534–547.

Gee, James. *What Video Games Have to Teach Us About Learning and Literacy.* New York: Palgrave Macmillan, 2007.

Genesee, Fred, ed. *Educating Second Language Children: The Whole Child, the Whole Curriculum, the Whole Community.* New York: Cambridge University Press, 1994.

Genesee, Fred et al. *Educating English Language Learners: A Synthesis of Research Evidence.* New York: Cambridge University Press, 2006.

Goldenberg, Claude. "Teaching English Language Learners What the Research Does—and Does Not—Say." *American Educator:* Summer, 2008 <http://archive.aft.org/pubs-reports/american_educator/issues/summer08> (accessed January 31, 2009).

González, Josué and Linda Darling-Hammond. *New Concepts for New Challenges: Professional Development for Teachers of Immigrant Youth*, Topics in Immigrant Education 2. Washington, DC: Center for Applied Linguistics, 1997.

Goodman, Yetta. "Children Coming to Know Literacy." In *Emergent Literacy: Writing and Reading*, edited by William Teale and Elizabeth Sulzby. Norwood, NJ: Ablex, 1986.

Graham, Carolyn. *Big Chants: I Went Walking.* Fort Worth, TX: Harcourt, 1994.

_____. *Jazz Chants for Children: Rhythms of American English Through Chants, Songs and Poems.* New York: Oxford University Press, 1979.

Graham, Steve, Charles A. MacArthur, and Jill Fitzgerald, eds. *Best Practices in Writing Instruction.* New York: Guilford, 2007.

Graves, Donald. "An Examination of the Writing Processes of Seven-Year-Old Children." *Research in the Teaching of English* v9, n3 (1975): 227–241.

Gudschinsky, Sarah. *A Manual of Literacy for Preliterate Peoples*. Ukarumpa, Papua-New Guinea: Summer Institute of Linguistics, 1973.

Gunderson, Lee. ESL Literacy Instruction: *A Guidebook to Theory and Practice*. Englewood Cliffs, NJ: Prentice Hall, 1991.

_____. "Second Language Reading Instruction in ESL and Mainstream Classrooms." In *Issues in Literacy: A Research Perspective*, Thirty-Fourth Yearbook of the National Reading Conference, edited by Jerome Niles and Rosary Lalik. Chicago, IL: National Reading Conference, 1985.

Hakuta, Kenji, Yuko Goto Butler, and Daria Witt. "How Long Does It Take English Learners to Attain Proficiency?" Stanford, CA: The University of California Linguistic Minority Research Institute Policy Report, 2000.

Hamayan, Else, J.A. Kwiat, and R. Perlman. *The Identification and Assessment of Language Minority Students: A Handbook for Educators*. Arlington Heights, IL: Illinois Resource Center, 1985.

Handscombe, Jean. "A Quality Program for Learners of English as a Second Language." In *When They Don't All Speak English: Integrating the ESL Student into the Regular Classroom*, edited by Pat Rigg and Virginia Allen. Urbana, IL: National Council of Teachers of English, 1989.

Haverson, Wayne and Judith Haynes. *ESL: Literacy for Adult Learners*. Washington, DC: Center for Applied Linguistics, 1982.

Haynes, Judie. "Challenges for ELLs in Content Area Learning." <everythingESL.net> (accessed January 7, 2010).

Heath, S.B. *Ways With Words: Language, Life, and Work in Communities and Classrooms*. Cambridge, MA: Cambridge University Press, 1983.

Hoffman, James. "When Bad Things Happen to Good Ideas in Literacy Education: Professional Dilemmas, Personal Decisions, and Political Traps." *The Reading Teacher* v52, n2 (1998): 102–112.

Hudelson, Sarah. "Janice: Becoming a Writer of English" (paper presented at the Annual Meeting of the Teachers of English to Speakers of Other Languages [17th, Toronto, Ontario, March 16–19, 1983]).

Igoa, Cristina. *The Inner World of the Immigrant Child*. New York: St. Martin's Press, 1995.

International Reading Association. "Making a Difference Means Making it Different: Honoring Children's Rights to Excellent Reading Instruction." Newark, DE: International Reading Association, 2000.

International Society for Technology in Education website, "ISTE National Educational Technology Standards (NETS) and Performance Indicators for Teachers." <www.iste.org/Content/NavigationMenu/NETS/ForTeachers/2000Standards/NETS_for_Teachers_2000.pdf> (accessed August 14, 2009).

Johnson, Jerry and Marty Strange. *Why Rural Matters 2007: The Realities of Rural Education Growth*. Arlington, VA: Rural School and Community Trust Policy Program, 2007.

Judy, Stephen, and Susan Judy. *The English Teacher's Handbook: Ideas and Resources for Teaching English*. Boston: Scott, Foresman and Company, 1983.

Kaye, Hannah. "Meeting the Needs of Young Refugees by Meeting the Needs of Everyone: A Discussion Paper on Refugee Education." London, UK: The Children's Society, 2006 (<www.childrenssociety.org.uk/resources/documents/Policy/Meeting_the_needs_of_ young_refugees_by_meeting_the_needs_of_everyone_A_discussion_paper_on_refugee_ education_2823_full.pdf> [accessed September 23, 2009])

Kingwell, Gail, and Dan Clarke. "English as a Second Language: Senior High Guide to Implementation." Edmonton: Alberta Learning, Learning Resources Centre, 2002.

Kolb, David. *Experiential Learning: Experience as the Source of Learning and Development*. Englewood Cliffs, NJ: Prentice-Hall, 1984.

Krashen, Stephen. *Principles and Practice in Second Language Acquisition*. New York: Pergamon, 1982.

Krogness, Mary. *Just Teach Me, Mrs. K: Talking, Reading, and Writing with Resistant Adolescent Learners*. Portsmouth, NH: Heinemann, 1995.

Kuhlman, N. A. and J. Vidal. "Meeting the Needs of LEP Students Through New Teacher Training: The Case in California." *The Journal of Educational Issues of Language Minority Students* v12 (1993): 97–113.

Lamott, Anne. *Bird by Bird: Some Instructions on Writing and Life*. New York: Anchor, 1995.

Law, Barbara and Mary Eckes. *Assessment and ESL: An Alternative Approach*, 2nd ed. Winnipeg, MB: Portage and Main Press, 2007.

Leki, I. *Understanding ESL Writers: A Guide for Teachers*. Portsmouth, NH: Boynton/Cook, 1992.

Linik, Joyce Riha. "When the Music Stops: The Cost of NCLB's Data Demands." *Northwest Education* v10, n4 (2005).

Literature Circles Resource Center website. "What Are Literature Circles?" <www.litcircles. org> (accessed November 4, 2009).

Lucas, Tamara. *Into, Through, and Beyond Secondary School: Critical Transitions for Immigrant Youths*. Washington, DC: Center for Applied Linguistics, 1997.

_____. "What Have We Learned from Research On Successful Secondary Programs for LEP Students?" (*Proceedings of the Third National Research Symposium on Limited English Proficient Student Issues: Focus on Middle and High School Issues*, v1). Washington, DC: Department of Education, Office of Bilingual Education and Minority Language Affairs, 1993.

Martinez-Roldan, Carmen and Julia Lopez-Robertson. "Initiating Literature Circles in a First-Grade Bilingual Classroom." *The Reading Teacher* v53, n4 (1999–2000): 270-281.

McCracken, Robert and Marlene McCracken. *Reading, Writing, & Language: A Practical Guide for Primary Teachers*, 2nd ed. Winnipeg, MB: Peguis (Portage and Main), 1995.

_____. *Reading Is Only the Tiger's Tail*, 12th ed. Winnipeg, MB: Peguis (Portage and Main), 1987.

McMahon, Susan. "Reading in the Book Club Program." In *The Book Club Connection: Literacy Learning and Classroom Talk*, edited by Susan McMahon et al. New York: Teachers College Press, 1997.

Met, Mimi. "Teaching Content Through A Second Language." In *Educating Second Language Children: The Whole Child, the Whole Curriculum, the Whole Community*, edited by Fred Genessee. New York: Cambridge University Press, 1994.

Michaels, Sarah. "'Sharing Time': Children's Narrative Styles and Differential Access to Literacy." *Language in Society* v10, n3 (1981): 423–442.

Bibliography

Moe, Melissa. "Placing English Language Learners in a Program of Instruction." Wisconsin Department of Public Instruction Info Update 2_06, CESA #11, Fall 2006 (<http://dpi.wi.gov/ell/servingells.html> accessed February 1, 2010).

Moffett, James. *Drama: What is Happening: The Use of Dramatic Activities in the Teaching of English*. Champaign, IL: National Council of Teachers of English, 1967.

Mohan, Bernard. *Language and Content*. Reading, MA: Addison-Wesley, 1986.

Monson, D. "Choosing Books for Literature Circles." In *Literature Circles and Response*, edited by Bonnie Campbell Hill, Nancy J. Johnson, and Katherine L. Schlick Noe. Norwood, MA: Christopher-Gordon 1995.

Moustafa, Margaret. *Beyond Traditional Phonics: Research Discoveries and Reading Instruction*. Portsmouth, NH: Heinemann, 1997.

Newman, Judith. *The Craft of Children's Writing*. Portsmouth, NH: Heinemann, 1984.

Noble, Grant, Paul Egan, and Sandra McDowell. "Changing the Self-Concepts of Seven-Year-Old Deprived Urban Children by Creative Drama or Video-Feedback." *Social Behavior and Personality* v5, n1 (1977): 55–64.

Nord, James. "Listening Fluency Before Speaking: An Alternative Paradigm." East Lansing, MI: Learning and Evaluation Service (Michigan State University), 1977.

Ocean View School District. *Survival Guide for Teachers of NES/LES Students*. Huntington Beach, CA, 1980.

Ontario Ministry of Education. *Supporting English Language Learners: A Practical Guide for Ontario Educators: Grades 1–8*. ON: Queen's Printer for Ontario, 2008.

Peterson, Ralph and Maryann Eeds. *Grand Conversations: Literature Groups in Action*. Toronto, ON: Scholastic, 1990.

Philips, S. "Participant Structures and Communicative Competence: Warm Springs Children in Community and Classroom." In *Functions of Language in the Classroom*, edited by Courtney B. Cazden, Vera P. John, and Dell Hymes. New York: Teachers College Press, 1972.

Proett, Jackie and Kent Gill. *The Writing Process in Action: A Handbook for Teachers*. Urbana, IL: National Council of Teachers of English, 1986.

Raimes, Ann. *Keys for Writers: A Brief Handbook,* 2nd ed. Boston: Houghton Mifflin, 1999.

Rathmell, George. *Bench Marks in Reading*. Hayward, CA: Alemany, 1984.

Read, Donna and Henrietta Smith. "Teaching Visual Literacy Through Wordless Picture Books." *The Reading Teacher* v35, n8 (1982): 928–933.

Reeves, Douglas. *Accountability in Action: A Blueprint for Learning Organizations*. Englewood, CO: Advanced Learning Press, 2005.

Reid, Joy. *Teaching ESL Writing*. Englewood Cliffs, NJ: Prentice Hall, 1993.

Reutzel, D. Ray, and Robert Cooter. *Teaching Children to Read: Putting the Pieces Together,* 4th ed. Upper Saddle River, NJ: Merrill/Prentice Hall, 2004.

Robertson, Kristina. "Math Instruction for English Language Learners." <www.colorincolorado.org/article/30570> (accessed August 2009).

Roessingh, Hetty and Susan Elgie. "Early Language and Literacy Development Among Young English Language Learners: Preliminary Insights from a Longitudinal Study." *TESL Canada Journal* v26, n2 (2009): 24–45.

Rosenshine, B. "Teaching Functions in Successful Teaching Programs" (paper presented at the Centre for the Study of Teacher Education, University of British Columbia, Vancouver, October 1983).

Roser, Nancy, James Hoffman, and Cynthia Farest. "Language, Literature, and At-Risk Children." *The Reading Teacher* v43, n8 (1990): 554–559.

Routman, Regie. *Literacy at the Crossroads: Crucial Talk About Reading, Writing, and Other Teaching Dilemmas*. Portsmouth, NH: Heinemann, 1996.

Samway, Katharine Davies and Denise McKeon. *Myths and Realities: Best Practices for English Language Learners*, 2nd ed. Portsmouth, NH: Heinemann, 2007.

Samway, Katharine Davies and Gail Whang. *Literature Study Circles in a Multicultural Classroom*. York, ME: Stenhouse, 1996.

Sargent, Judy Werder and Ann Smejkal. *Targets for Teachers: A Self-Study Guide for Teachers in the Age of Standards*. Winnipeg, MB: Portage and Main, 2000.

Saville-Troike, Muriel. "What Really Matters in Second Language Learning for Academic Achievement?" *TESOL Quarterly* v18, n2 (1984): 199–219.

Scarcella, Robin. *Academic Language and English Language Learners* (webcast) <www.colorincolorado.org/webcasts/academiclanguaged> (accesses August 11, 2009).

_____. *Academic English: A Conceptual Framework* (Technical Report 2003-1). Santa Barbara, CA: The University of California Linguistic Minority Research Institute, 2003 (available at <www.lmri.ucsb.edu/publications/03_scarcella.pdf>).

Schickedanz, Judith. *More Than the ABCs*. Washington, DC: National Association for the Education of Young Children, 1986.

Schinke-Llano, Linda. "Foreigner Talk in Content Classrooms." In *Classroom Oriented Research in Second Language Acquisition*, edited by Herbert Seliger and Michael Long Rowley, MA: Newbury House, 1983.

Schirmacher, Robert. *Art and Creative Development for Young Children*. Albany, NY: Delmar Publishing, 1997.

Sheorey, Ravi. "Error Perceptions of Native-Speaking and Non-Native Speaking Teachers of ESL." *ELT Journal* v40, n4 (1986): 306–312.

Short, Deborah. "Integrating Language and Content for Effective Sheltered Instruction Programs." In *So Much To Say: Adolescents, Bilingualism, and ESL in the Secondary School*, edited by Christian Fáltis and Paula Wolfe. New York: Teachers College Press, 1999.

Short, Deborah and Shannon Fitzsimmons. "Double the Work: Challenges and Solutions to Acquiring Language and Academic Literacy for Adolescent English Language Learners" (Report to Carnegie Corporation of New York). Washington, DC: Alliance for Excellent Education, 2007.

Short, Deborah, Jodi Crandall, and Donna Christian. *How to Integrate Language and Content Instruction: A Training Manual*. Los Angeles: University of California Center for Language Education and Research, 1989.

Shrum, Judith and Eileen Glisan. *Teacher's Handbook: Contextualized Language Instruction*, 3rd ed. Boston: Heinle, 2005.

Smith, Frank. *Understanding Reading*, 6th edition. Mahwah, NJ: Erlbaum, 2004.

_____. *Reading Without Nonsense*, 3rd ed. New York: Teachers College Press, 1997.

Soven, Margot. *Teaching Writing in Middle and Secondary Schools: Theory, Research and Practice*. Boston: Allyn & Bacon, 1998.

Sowers, Susan. "Six Questions Teachers Ask About Invented Spelling." In *Understanding Writing: Ways of Observing, Learning and Teaching*, 2nd ed, edited by Thomas Newkirk and Nancie Atwell. Portsmouth, NH: Heinemann, 1988.

Spandel, Vicki. *Seeing with New Eyes: A Guidebook on Teaching and Assessing Beginning Writers.* Portland, OR: Northwest Regional Educational Lab, 1997.

Spangenberg-Urbschat, Karen and Robert Pritchard, eds. *Kids Come in All Languages: Reading Instruction for ESL Students.* Newark, DE: International Reading Association, 1994.

Spiegel, Dixie Lee. "Silver Bullets, Babies, and Bath Water: Literature Response Groups in a Balanced Literacy Program." *The Reading Teacher* v52, n2 (1998): 114–124.

Stewig, John Warren and Carol Buege. *Dramatizing Literature in Whole Language Classrooms,* 2nd ed. New York: Teachers College Press, 1994.

Strong American Schools. *"Diploma to Nowhere."* Washington, DC: Strong American Schools, 2008 (available at <www.deltacostproject.org/resources/pdf/DiplomaToNowhere.pdf>) (accessed October 1, 2009).

Sturgeon, Julie. "Is Bill Gates a Good School Leader?" District Administration website, 2006: <www.districtadministration.com/viewarticle.aspx?articleid=975> (accessed October 23, 2008).

Suárez-Orozco, Marcelo and Carola Suárez-Orozco. "Teach in Two Languages," in "The Best Ways to Teach Young Newcomers" (series of articles). Room for Debate website, March 11, 2009, <http://roomfordebate.blogs.nytimes.com/2009/03/11/the-best-ways-to-teach-young-newcomers> (accessed Dec. 30, 2009).

Teachers of English to Speakers of Other Languages (TESOL). *ESL Standards for Pre-K–12 Students.* Alexandria, VA: TESOL, 1997.

Teale, William and Elizabeth Sulzby, eds. *Emergent Literacy: Writing and Reading.* Norwood, NJ: Ablex, 1986.

Thomas, Wayne and Virginia Collier. *A National Study of School Effectiveness for Language Minority Students' Long-Term Achievement.* Washington, DC: Center for Research on Education, Diversity and Excellence (CREDE), 2002.

Tompkins, Gail. *Teaching Writing: Balancing Process and Product,* 3rd edition. Upper Saddle River, NJ: Merrill, 2000.

Trelease, Jim. *The Read-Aloud Handbook.* New York: Penguin, 1985.

Valdez, Guadalupe. "Non-Native English Speakers: Language Bigotry in English Mainstream Classrooms." *ADDL Bulletin* v31, n1 (1999): 43–48.

Ventriglia, Linda. *Conversations of Miguel and Maria: How Children Learn a Second Language.* Reading, MA: Addison-Wesley, 1982.

Waggoner, D. "Who are Secondary Newcomer and Linguistically Different Youth?" In *So Much to Say: Adolescents, Bilingualism, and ESL in the Secondary School,* edited by Christian Fáltis and Paula Wolfe. New York: Teachers College Press, 1999.

Wausau School District, "English Language Learners." <www.wausau.k12.wi.us/curriculum/esl> (accessed March 15, 2009).

Wells, Gordon. *The Meaning Makers: Children Learning Language and Using Language to Learn.* Portsmouth, NH: Heinemann, 1986.

Wiggins, Grant and Jay McTighe. *Understanding by Design.* Alexandria, VA: Association for Supervision and Curriculum Development, 1998.

Wiley, Terrence. *Literacy and Language Diversity in the United States.* Washington, DC: Center for Applied Linguistics, 1996.

Williams, Trish, Kenji Hakuta, Edward Haertel et al. "Similar English Learner Students, Different Results: Why Do Some Schools Do Better?" Mountain View, CA: EdSource, 2007.

Wisconsin Learns (Wisconsin Literacy Education and Reading Network Source). "English Language Learners." <http://wilearns.state.wi.us/apps/default.asp?cid=740> (accessed March 15, 2009).

Wollman-Bonilla, Julie. "Reading Journals: Invitations to Participate in Literature." *The Reading Teacher* v43, n2 (1989): 112–120.

Wong, Harry, and Rosemary Wong. "Effective Teaching: A Well-Oiled Learning Machine." <http://teachers.net/wong/MAR04> (accessed March 1, 2010).

Yoshihara, Karen. Paper presented at California TESOL Conference, 1988.

Zamel, Vivian and Ruth Spack. *Negotiating Academic Literacies: Teaching and Learning Across Languages and Cultures*. Mahwah, NJ: Erlbaum, 1998.

Zemelman, Steven, Harvey Daniels, and Arthur Hyde. *Best Practice: New Standards for Teaching and Learning in America's Schools*, 2nd ed. Portsmouth, NH: Heinemann, 1998.

Zhang, Hong and Nola Kortner Alex. *Oral Language Development Across the Curriculum, K–12*. Bloomington IN: ERIC Clearinghouse on Reading English and Communication, 1995.

Zygouris-Coe, Vicky. "Balanced Reading Instruction in K–3 Classrooms." Orlando, FL: Florida Literacy and Reading Excellence Center, 2001.

Book List

Buss, Fran Leeper. *Journey of the Sparrows*. New York: Lodestar Books, 1991.

Carle, Eric. *The Very Hungry Caterpillar*. New York: Philomel, 1994.

Cisneros, Sandra. *The House on Mango Street*. New York: Vintage Contemporaries, 2009.

Cowley, Joy. *The Ghost*. DeSoto, TX: Wright Group, 1998.

Dahl, Roald. *George's Marvelous Medicine*. New York: Knopf, 2002.

Dr. Seuss. *One Fish, Two Fish, Red Fish, Blue Fish*. New York: Beginner Books, 1987.

Frank, Anne. *The Diary of a Young Girl*. New York: Globe, 1988.

Friedman, Ina. *How My Parents Learned to Eat*. Boston: Houghton Mifflin, 1984.

Hersey, John. *Hiroshima*. New York: Vintage Books, 1989.

Hinton, S. E. *The Outsiders*. New York: Penguin, 2006.

Hutchins, Pat. *Rosie's Walk*. New York: Aladdin, 2005.

Lee, Harper. *To Kill a Mockingbird*. New York: HarperCollins, 1995.

Levine, Ellen. *I Hate English!* New York: Scholastic, 1989.

MacLachlan, Patricia. *Sarah, Plain and Tall*. New York: Harper & Row, 1985.

Martin, Bill Jr. *Brown Bear, Brown Bear, What Do You See?* New York: Henry Holt, 1996.

McCunn, Ruthanne Lum. *Thousand Pieces of Gold: A Biographical Novel*. Boston: Beacon Press, 2004.

Naylor, Phyllis Reynolds. *Shiloh*. New York: Atheneum, 1991.

Nazario, Sonia. *Enrique's Journey*. New York: Random House, 2007.

Paterson, Katherine. *Bridge to Terabithia*. New York: HarperEntertainment, 2007.

Rathmann, Peggy. *Officer Buckle and Gloria*. New York: Putnam, 1995.

Rice, Elizabeth. *Jacki*. Chicago: Children's Press, 1969.

Scieszska, Jon. *The Good, the Bad and the Goofy*. New York: Puffin, 2004.

Selznick, Brian. *The Invention of Hugo Cabret: A Novel in Words and Pictures*. New York: Scholastic, 2007.

Slobodkina, Esphyr. *Caps for Sale: A Tale of a Peddler, Some Monkeys, and Their Monkey Business*. New York: Harper & Row, 1985.

Taylor, Mildred. *Roll of Thunder, Hear My Cry*. New York: Phyllis Fogelman, 2001.

Taylor, Theodore. *The Cay*. Austin, TX: Holt, Rinehart and Winston, 2000.

Tolstoy, Alexei. *The Great Big Enormous Turnip*. New York: F. Watts, 1968.

Tsuchiya, Yukio. *Faithful Elephants: A True Story of Animals, People, and War*. Boston: Houghton Mifflin, 1988.

Wakatsuki, Jeanne Houston and James D. Houston. *Farewell to Manzanar: A True Story of Japanese American Experience During and After the World War II Internment*. Boston: Houghton Mifflin, 2002.

Wilder, Laura Ingalls. *On the Banks of Plum Creek*. New York: HarperTrophy, 2004.

Williams, Sue. *I Went Walking*. Orlando: Harcourt, 2006.

Yashima, Taro. *Crow Boy*. New York: Viking, 1995.

Young, Ed (translator and illustrator). *Lon Po Po: A Red Riding-Hood Story from China*. New York: Philomel Books, 1989.

Websites

<www.cal.org>
The Center of Applied Linguistics is a comprehensive site that provides information on new publications, current news about language education, and professional development events. The topic areas for the site range from adult ELL literacy, to language testing, to refugee concerns.

<www.ef.com>
Education First (EF) is the world's largest language school. It provides programs for high school and adult students as well as for professionals and corporations. Through this site, Education First gives students and teachers the opportunity to discover new places, cultures, and languages through group travel adventures.

<www.eslcafe.com>
Dave's ESL Café is a great site for both teachers and students that makes learning English fun. It includes discussion forums, a help center, a book store, a job center, and helpful links that can provide any surfer with the information and assistance they need.

<languagemagazine.com>
An independent publication for language and literacy professionals and students, *Language Magazine* promotes increased multilingualism, multiculturalism, and international education. Each month and online, *Language Magazine* covers literacy, ESL, world languages, bilingual education, and study abroad, with features and resources on methodology, professional development, funding, policy decisions, curriculum and testing issues, educational travel, and advocacy.

<www.tesol.org/s_tesol/index.asp>
The TESOL (Teachers of English to Speakers of Other Languages) site contains a multitude of services for teachers including an extensive catalog of publications and materials, conventions, ESL standards for pre-K–12, and information on professional development.

Index